MACMILLAN ENGLISH

Tina Thoburn

Macmillan Publishing Company
New York
Collier Macmillan Publishers
London

ACKNOWLEDGMENTS

The publisher gratefully acknowledges permission to reprint the following copyrighted material:

"Jenny" by Sam Savitt. Reprinted by permission of Dodd, Mead, & Compay, Inc. from *Sam Savitt's True Horse Stories* by Sam Savitt. Copyright © 1970 by Sam Savitt.

"A Garden Grows on Spring Street" by Steven Otfinoski © 1982 by Macmillan Publishing Co., Inc.

"The Octopus," "The Panther," "The Rhinoceros," and "The Ostrich" from *You Can't Get There From Here* by Ogden Nash. Copyright 1933, 1942, 1956 by Ogden Nash; Copyright 1940 by The Curtis Publishing Company. "The Panther" first appeared in the *The Saturday Evening Post*. "The Octopus," "The Rhinoceros," and "The Ostrich" first appeared in *The New Yorker.* Reprinted by permission of Little, Brown and Company and Curtis Brown, Ltd.

"The Kite," "River," and "A Better View," three haikus from *Cricket Songs: Japanese Haiku*, translated and © 1964 by Harry Behn. Reprinted by permission of Harcourt Brace Jovanovich, Inc. and Curtis Brown, Ltd.

Haiku, "The falling flower..." from *A Poetry Handbook: A Dictionary of Terms*, 4th edition, by Babette Deutch (Funk & Wagnalls). Copyright © 1957, 1962, 1969, 1974 by Babette Deutsch. Reprinted by permission of Harper & Row, Publishers, Inc.

Illustration Credits:
Michael McNelly, Meredith Nemirov, Meryl Treatner

Photography Credits:
© Lisa Alt, 308
© Terry Bisbee, 371
© James Church/Shostal Associates, 256
© John Claridge/The Image Bank, 268
© CLI Colour Library International, 40, 100, 202
© Lisa DuBois, 374
© Ray Ellis 1983, 24
© Lawrence Frank, 23, 201, 287, 331
© G. Gladstone/The Image Bank, 130
© Kerry Hayes, 68
© Lisl '75/The Image Bank, 116
© Steve Liss, 332
© 1982 Yitzhak Margowsky/Design Conceptions, 352
© Tom McHugh, 284
© David Muench, 2
© NASA photo, 86, 99, 277
© Ray Ng, 186, 290, 364
© Shostal Associates, 228, 240
© Frank Siteman, 363
© Unique, 162

Cover Design:
Josie Yee

Parts of this work were published in earlier editions of Macmillan English.

Macmillan Publishing Company
866 Third Avenue, New York, New York 10022
Collier Macmillan Canada, Inc.

Printed in the United States of America
ISBN 0-02-240080-X
9 8 7 6 5

Table of Contents

LANGUAGE STUDY

Grammar and Usage

Mechanics

LANGUAGE STUDY

- Grammar and Usage
- Mechanics
- Spelling, Vocabulary, and History and Nature of Language

Yosemite Falls, Yosemite National Park

When we try to pick out anything by itself, we find it hitched to everything else in the universe.

JOHN MUIR
Scottish Explorer, Naturalist, and Writer (1838-1914)

1

SENTENCES

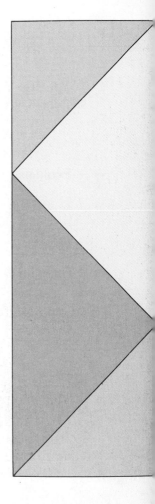

Review: Four Kinds of Sentences

English has four kinds of sentences: declarative sentences, interrogative sentences, exclamatory sentences, and imperative sentences.

> A **sentence** is a group of words that expresses a complete idea. Every sentence begins with a capital letter.

You use different kinds of sentences for different purposes. Some sentences give information. Other sentences ask for information.

> A **declarative sentence** is a sentence that makes a statement. A declarative sentence ends with a period.

Ecologists study relationships in nature.

> An **interrogative sentence** is a sentence that asks a question. An interrogative sentence ends with a question mark.

Do animals and plants depend on each other?

Some sentences express strong feelings.

> An **exclamatory sentence** is a sentence that expresses strong feeling. An exclamatory sentence ends with an exclamation mark.

What important work ecologists do!

Other sentences give commands or make polite requests. In a request or a command, the subject *you* is "understood," even though it is not stated.

> An **imperative sentence** is a sentence that gives a command or makes a request. An imperative sentence ends with a period.

Look at these animals. Please preserve our wildlife.

Imperative sentences that express an immediate need are often followed by an exclamation mark. Some examples are the following commands: Help! Hurry! Stop! In each of these imperative sentences the subject *you* is "understood."

Class Exercises

Read each sentence. Tell if it is a **declarative, interrogative, imperative,** or **exclamatory** sentence. Then tell how to capitalize and punctuate each sentence correctly.

1. ecologists study the world's population
2. they also study the world's food supply
3. do ecologists study air pollution, too
4. they tell us about the effects of air pollution on our lives

Exercises

Write each sentence. Capitalize and punctuate each sentence correctly. Then write if it is a **declarative, interrogative, imperative,** or **exclamatory** sentence.

1. ecologists study the effects of water pollution on our wildlife
2. look to the oceans for food in the future
3. what fine work marine biologists do
4. what other kinds of information do ecologists use
5. they use knowledge from physics and mathematics
6. ecologists explain the importance of protecting our environment
7. do other scientists aid them in their work
8. what a resource team they have
9. study your environment for signs of changes
10. scientists study one area of knowledge at a time
11. do they study the movement of energy
12. what a great source of energy the sun is
13. get these books on energy from the library
14. ecologists study water pollution

Writing Sentences

Suppose that you and a few friends are asked to plant some trees in your neighborhood. Write six sentences about the trees.

1. Write two declarative sentences that describe the trees.
2. Write one interrogative sentence that asks for information.
3. Write two imperative sentences that tell someone what to do.
4. Write one exclamatory sentence that expresses strong feeling.

Sample Answer 1. Ecologists study the effects of water pollution on our wildlife. declarative

Sentences and Sentence Fragments

A group of words that expresses a complete thought is a *sentence*. A group of words that expresses part of a thought is a *sentence fragment*.

- Read each group of words below. Which groups of words are sentences? Which are sentence fragments?

Lush forests.	Forests provide scenic land for recreation.
Inhabits the woodlands.	Wildlife inhabits the woodlands.

Each group of words on the left expresses only part of a thought. These words are sentence fragments. Each group of words on the right expresses a complete thought. These groups of words are complete sentences.

A **sentence** is a group of words that expresses a complete thought.

A **sentence fragment** is a group of words that is only part of a sentence. It does not express a complete thought.

You know that every sentence has two parts. One part is the complete subject, or the subject part. The other part is the complete predicate, or the predicate part. Both parts are necessary to make a complete sentence.

The **complete subject,** or the **subject part,** of a sentence names whom or what the sentence is about. The complete subject part of a sentence may be more than one word.

The **complete predicate,** or the **predicate part,** of a sentence tells what action the subject does. Sometimes it tells what the subject is or is like. The complete predicate may be more than one word.

- Read these sentences.

Foresters	control forest conditions.
Most trees in the forest	are healthy.

In the first sentence the complete subject in the blue box, *Foresters*, names whom the sentence is about. The complete predicate in the red box, *control forest conditions*, tells what the subject does. Both parts together express a complete idea, but each part by itself does not make sense. In the second sentence the complete subject in the blue box, *Most trees in the forest,* names what the sentence is about. The complete predicate in the red box, *are healthy,* tells what the subject is like. Both parts together express a complete idea, but each part by itself does not.

Class Exercises

Tell whether each group of words is a **sentence** or **sentence fragment.**

1. Most nations own their forests.
2. Independent land owners.
3. Followed government's laws.
4. Healthy forest land.
5. Forests provide benefits.
6. Nations protect their lands.

Exercises

Write each group of words that forms a complete sentence. Underline the complete subject once and the complete predicate twice. If the group of words is not a complete sentence, write **fragment.**

1. Acres of forest land support many types of wildlife.
2. Giant redwood trees grow in the Pacific Northwestern region.
3. People throughout the world.
4. Dense forests thrive in tropical climates.
5. Cleared acres of forest land.
6. Special machinery plows the dense area.
7. Farmers used the land to grow crops.
8. Devoted to wildlife protection.
9. Furniture companies.
10. The lumberjacks cut one percent of the woodland section.
11. Timber from southern climates.
12. Builders use large amounts of forest trees.

Writing Sentences

Think about a park or forest that you have been to or seen in a book. Write six sentences using one of the sentence fragments below.

1. the visitors
2. cleaned the area
3. the squirrels
4. many types of wildlife
5. the vast woodlands
6. watched the park ranger

Sample Answer 1. Acres of forest land support many types of wildlife.

Complete and Simple Subjects

Every sentence has a complete subject, or subject part, and a complete predicate, or predicate part. The *complete subject* names whom or what the sentence is about and may be more than one word.

- Read each sentence. Study the complete subjects in the blue boxes. What is the main word in each complete subject?

The capable foresters | study the forests first.

Foresters with knowledge of trees | make plans.

Foresters is the main word in each complete subject. The main word or group of words of a complete subject is called the *simple subject.* The simple subject is usually a noun or a pronoun. A *noun* is a word that names a person, place, thing, or idea. A *pronoun* is a word that takes the place of one or more nouns.

The **simple subject** is the main word or group of words in the complete subject.

In some sentences the simple subject is the complete subject.

Foresters | study the rate of growth.

They | look for healthy, mature plants.

The complete subject in an interrogative sentence often comes after the first word in the sentence.

- Read the interrogative sentences below. Notice that the subject part comes after the first word in each sentence.

Do loggers cut special trees? Are some trees too small?

A good way to find the subject of an interrogative sentence is to reword it as a declarative sentence.

Loggers do cut special trees. Some trees are too small.

In an imperative sentence someone commands or requests that you do something. Consider a logger's shout to a co-worker: "Watch out!" What is the subject part of the sentence? The subject part is the word *you.* The logger actually means: "You watch out!" *You* is the "understood" subject part in an imperative sentence, even though it is not stated.

Class Exercises

Name the complete subject in each sentence. Then name the simple subject. If a sentence is interrogative, reword it as a declarative sentence.

1. Capable loggers cut only special trees.
2. Some simple procedures protect the conditions of the forest.
3. Do expert foresters study the trees in the region?
4. Read this plan for the production of cheap timber.

Exercises

Write each sentence. If a sentence is interrogative, reword it as a declarative sentence. Then underline the complete subject of each sentence. Draw a second line under the simple subject. Write the word **You** if it is the understood subject of an imperative sentence.

1. The production of clean timber takes several years.
2. Lumber companies buy large amounts of timber.
3. Growers of trees divide the forest into several sections.
4. Do skillful loggers work one section each year?
5. The expert workers cut individual trees.
6. Think of the heavy chain saws.
7. Do the loggers leave some trees?
8. Do plants sprout easily in the region?
9. Some small plants fill the gaps in the forest.
10. One special method uses only some of the land.
11. They trim the broadleaf trees.
12. Look at the wildlife in the forest.
13. Tree roots hold the soil in place.

Writing Sentences

Imagine you are a forester. Describe your forest to a group of people. Expand each sentence below. Add one or more words to each simple subject to describe the subject more completely. Write your new sentences.

1. Trees grow.
2. Plants spread.
3. Animals run.
4. People hike.
5. Loggers cut.
6. Foresters watch.

Sample Answer 1. The production of clean timber takes several years.

Complete and Simple Predicates

The complete predicate, or predicate part, of a sentence sometimes tells what action the subject does. At other times it tells what the subject is or is like. The predicate part may be more than one word. It is usually at the end of a declarative sentence.

- Read each sentence. The complete predicates are in red boxes. What is the main word in each complete predicate?

| People | | change their environment. |

| They | | are dependent on animal and plant life. |

Change their environment and *are dependent on animal and plant life* are the complete predicates in these sentences. *Change* and *are* are the main words in the two complete predicates above. The main word or group of words in a complete predicate is called the *simple predicate.* The simple predicate is also called the *verb.*

> The **simple predicate** is the main word or group of words in the complete predicate.

In some sentences the simple predicate is also the complete predicate.

| Some animals in danger of extinction | | survive. |

An interrogative sentence often begins with part of the predicate. The rest of the predicate part is at the end of the sentence after the subject.

- Read the interrogative sentence below. Notice that the subject divides the predicate into two parts.

| Do | | most people | | understand the delicate balance of nature? |

A good way to find the predicate part of an interrogative sentence is to reword it as a declarative sentence.

| Most people | | do understand the deiicate balance of nature. |

Remember that in an imperative sentence someone commands or requests that you do something. The "understood" subject of the sentence is *you.* The predicate part is the command itself, or what the person actually tells you. Suppose your teacher says, "Study your environment." Your teacher really means, "You study your environment." The "understood" subject is the word *You. Study your environment* is the complete predicate and *study* is the simple predicate.

Class Exercises

Read each sentence. Reword each interrogative sentence as a declarative sentence if you need to. Name the complete predicate in each sentence. Then name the simple predicate.

1. Can scientists control changes in the environment?
2. Ecologists counteract the effects of forest fires, erosion, and floods.
3. Can people preserve natural resources?
4. Watch for new plants.

Exercises

Write each sentence. Reword each interrogative sentence as a declarative sentence if you need to. Then underline the complete predicate of each sentence. Draw a second line under the simple predicate.

1. Many kinds of bacteria help the environment.
2. Can human beings change their environment?
3. Green plants need a certain amount of light.
4. Do ecologists study animal populations?
5. Scientists reduce the number of undesirable insects.
6. Can the kinds of plants in a geographical area change?
7. Look at the new plants in this region.
8. Does the climate determine the region's inhabitants?
9. Do flowers grow after a forest fire?
10. Grasses grow after the flowers.
11. Trees are important for stopping erosion.
12. Notice the different kinds of evergreen trees.

Writing Sentences

Expand each sentence. Add one or more words to each simple predicate to make a more interesting sentence. Use words that describe *where, how,* or *when* the action occurs. Write your new sentences.

1. Ecologists learn.
2. Farmers study.
3. Dogs herd.
4. Animals eat.
5. People need.
6. Plants live.

Sample Answer 1. Many kinds of bacteria help the environment.

Subject-Verb Agreement

The subjects of sentences are often nouns. Nouns may be either singular or plural. They can name one or more than one person, place, thing, or idea. The form of the verb, or simple predicate, in each sentence must *agree in number* with the singular or plural subject in the sentence.

- Read the sentences in the box below. Notice the singular and plural noun subjects. Notice the verb forms that go with the singular and plural nouns.

The ranger works in the forest.	The rangers work in the forest.
The tree appears tall.	The trees appear tall.
The branch hangs low.	The branches hang low.
The scientist examines the sample.	The scientists examine the sample.

In each sentence in the left column, the subject is a singular noun. Each verb agrees with the singular subject of the sentence. In each sentence in the right column, the subject is a plural noun. Each verb agrees with the plural subject of the sentence.

- Now study these sentences. The subject of each sentence may seem to be plural, but the meaning is singular. Thus the verb agrees with a singular subject.

Mathematics is my best course. (one subject)
Travels with Towser tells about a dog. (one book)
The United States has a beautiful flag. (one nation)
Five dollars is the price. (one amount)
Nine hours is a good night's sleep. (one time period)
The United Nations has several conferences. (one organization)

When the subject is singular in meaning, even though plural in form, use the form of the verb that agrees with the singular subject.

Class Exercises

Read each sentence. Use the correct form of the verb in parentheses to complete each sentence.

1. Rain ___ pollutants into the ground. (washes/wash)
2. Furnaces ___ pollutants into the air. (releases/release)
3. The mountain ___ a good place for clean air. (is/are)
4. Plant growth ___ in polluted areas. (decreases/decrease)

Exercises

Write each sentence using the correct form of the verb in parentheses to complete it.

1. The air ___ many gases. (contains/contain)
2. Most natural gases ___ no danger to the environment. (presents/present)
3. Air pollution ___ the growth of plants. (affects/affect)
4. All animals ___ on clean air. (depends/depend)
5. Solid particles ___ the amount of sunlight. (reduces/reduce)
6. Scientists ___ the air for dangerous gases. (tests/test)
7. The greenhouse effect ___ the temperature. (raises/raise)
8. Carbon dioxide ___ the sun's heat in the air. (keeps/keep)
9. Carbon monoxide ___ the air, too. (pollutes/pollute)
10. Many scientists ___ for uses for the sun's energy. (searches/search)
11. Stoves ___ fuels such as gasoline, wood, or coal. (burns/burn)
12. The United States ___ many environmental laws. (passes/pass)
13. A machine ___ the amount of smog in the air. (measures/measure)
14. Scientists ___ the effects of air pollution on our wildlife. (examines/examine)

Writing Sentences

Suppose you are writing an article about ecology for the school newspaper. Write six sentences using the subjects below. Make sure that the verb agrees with the subject in each sentence.

1. wildlife
2. inspectors
3. resources
4. gases
5. ecology clubs
6. two months

Sample Answer 1. The air contains many gases.

Compound Subjects and Predicates

Sometimes a sentence may have more than one simple subject, more than one simple predicate, or both. The sentence then contains a *compound* subject or predicate.

> A **compound subject** has two or more simple subjects that have the same predicate. The subjects are joined by *and* or *or.*

- Read these sentences.

Rangers and loggers study the forest.

Both rangers and loggers study the forest.

Notice that when the two simple subjects are joined by *and* or by *both...and,* the compound subject is plural. Use the plural form of the verb to agree with this plural compound subject.

Sometimes compound subjects are not plural. When simple subjects are joined with *or,* the compound subject may be singular or plural.

- Read these sentences.

A ranger or a logger always watches from the observation tower.

A ranger or his assistants always watch from the observation tower.

In these sentences the predicate part must agree with the *nearer* simple subject. *Logger* is the nearer subject in the first sentence, and the verb *watches* agrees with the singular subject. However, in the second sentence, *assistants* is the nearer subject, and the verb *watch* agrees with the plural subject.

A sentence may also have a compound predicate.

> A **compound predicate** has two or more verbs that have the same subject. The verbs are connected by *and* or *or.*

- Study this sentence. Notice the two simple predicates.

Rangers explore and protect the forest.

Explore and *protect* are the simple predicates, or verbs, in the compound predicate. The plural noun *rangers* is the subject of both verbs. Notice that both verbs agree with the plural noun in the subject part.

Some sentences have both compound subjects and compound predicates. When the two subjects are joined by *and,* each verb agrees with the plural subject. When the two parts are joined by *or,* each verb agrees with the simple subject closest to it.

| The <u>rangers</u> and <u>loggers</u> | <u>study</u> and <u>work</u> in the forest. |

Class Exercises

Read each sentence. Tell which form of the verb or verbs in parentheses complete the sentence correctly.

1. Both trees and grass ___ soil in place. (holds/hold)
2. Winds and rain ___ vast amounts of soil. (erodes/erode)
3. Erosion ___ and ___ acres of valuable land. (damages/damage, ruins/ruin)
4. Plants and minerals ___ the soil. (enriches/enrich)

Exercises

Write each sentence using the correct form of the verb or verbs in parentheses to complete each one.

1. Rachel Carson and other biologists ___ people about the dangers of air pollution. (warns/warn)
2. Plants and trees ___ oxygen into the air. (releases/release)
3. Some chemicals ___ and ___ pests. (fights/fight, controls/control)
4. Humans and animals often ___ the same foods. (eats/eat)
5. The chemicals ___ and ___ in the food chain. (travels/travel, mixes/mix)
6. Either smog or acid rain ___ the environment. (injures, injure)
7. Air pollution and water pollution ___ the soil. (affects/affect)
8. Acid rain and loud noise ___ urban areas. (pollutes/pollute)
9. Many fertilizers ___ and ___ the soil. (enriches/enrich, stimulates/stimulate)
10. Fertilizers and chemicals often ___ better crops. (grows/grow)

Writing Sentences

Write six sentences about the seashore. Write about what people have done or what they can do to keep it clean. Make sure the verb agrees with the subject. Write three sentences with compound subjects. Then write three other sentences with compound predicates. Use *and* in one and *both...and* in another.

Sample Answer 1. Rachel Carson and other biologists warn people about the dangers of air pollution.

Compound Sentences

You know that a *sentence* is a group of words that expresses a complete thought. A simple sentence expresses a single idea.

Sometimes you may want to combine two related thoughts into one longer sentence to form a *compound sentence.* In such cases, you may use one of these coordinating conjunctions, or connecting words, to join two simple sentences: *and, or,* or *but.* Use a comma **(,)** before the conjunction to separate the two parts of a compound sentence.

> A **compound sentence** is a sentence that contains two or more simple sentences joined by a coordinating conjunction. It has at least two subjects and two predicates.

- Note the conjunction in each of these compound sentences.

  Ecologists | divide the world into three levels, | and | these levels | include populations and natural communities.

  One ecologist | sees the insects, | but | the insects | fly away.

  Weather | controls insect populations, | or | ecologists | search for other methods.

Each conjunction has a different meaning.

Use *and* to connect related thoughts or ideas. Use *but* to contrast related thoughts. Use *or* to connect alternative ideas.

Some conjunctions work together in pairs. They are called *correlative conjunctions.* Correlative conjunctions, such as *either...or,* or *neither...nor,* connect words or groups of words. They make the relationship between these words clearer than coordinating conjunctions.

- Read these sentences.

  Either students or assistants work with ecologists in the field.

  Neither humans nor animals thrive without a balance in nature.

Sometimes two parts of a compound sentence are not joined by a conjunction. Use a semicolon **(;)** to separate the two parts. When there are already commas within the parts of a compound sentence, use a semicolon **(;)**.

Environmentalists | talk with ecologists in other parts of the world; | they | exchange ideas.

Ecologists | study the relationships of plants, animals, and people; | they | investigate their natural surroundings for more information.

Class Exercises

Some of the sentences below are **compound sentences** and some are **simple sentences** with **compound subjects** or **compound predicates.** Tell what kind of sentence each one is.

1. Ecologists study forests, and their research provides important information for the rangers.
2. Ecologists study and work in modern laboratories.
3. The laboratories develop new instruments of science, but the instruments must work well in the field.
4. Either ecologists or researchers suggest improvements.

Exercises

Write each sentence. Write whether it is a **simple sentence** or a **compound sentence.** If the sentence has a compound subject, draw one line under each subject. If the sentence has a compound predicate, draw two lines under each verb. If it is a compound sentence, draw a line between the two simple sentences.

1. Some problems arise in forest environments; ecologists develop solutions to these problems.
2. Neither the homes nor the food sources of animals escape the effects of the unwise use of resources.
3. Wood products satisfy many human needs, but plastic products save many trees.
4. Small plants grow under tall trees and provide food for the smaller animals of the forest.
5. Either ecologists or rangers report the number of forest fires.
6. Companies replant trees, and they grow new kinds of trees.
7. Ecologists work with the companies; these teams insure many trees for the future.
8. Foresters improve the land with new trees, or ecologists develop other forest areas.
9. Small trees grow and survive with the help of such ecologists.
10. Birds and insects return and fill the forest with life.

Sample Answer 1. Some problems arise in forest environments; | ecologists develop solutions to these problems. compound sentence

Complex Sentences

You know that a *compound sentence* is a sentence that contains two simple sentences joined by the conjunctions *and, or, but,* or by a semicolon.

Nearly 1,700 kinds of plants | grow in the Arctic region, *and* these plants | include about 900 varieties of flowers.

The two simple sentences joined together in the compound sentence above are called *independent clauses.*

An **independent clause** has one subject part and one predicate part. It expresses a complete thought and it can stand alone.

Sometimes sentences have more than one clause, but only one of the clauses is an independent clause.

- Study the sentences below.

Herds of reindeer | huddle together | while the Arctic snowstorms cause cold winds.

After the storms pass, | the reindeer | paw through the deep snow for dried grasses.

In each sentence the independent clause is underlined once. These groups of words express complete thoughts and can stand alone as sentences. Each sentence also has a group of words that is underlined twice. These groups of words are called *subordinate clauses.*

A **subordinate clause** is a group of words that has a subject part and a predicate part, but it cannot stand alone. It does not express a complete thought. It is always combined with an independent clause.

A subordinate clause may be joined to an independent clause by a *subordinating conjunction.* Here is a list of subordinating conjunctions: *after, although, as, because, before, if, since, though, unless, until, when, while.* Use a comma **(,)** after a subordinate clause introduces a sentence.

A sentence with an independent clause and a subordinate clause is called a *complex sentence.*

A **complex sentence** is a sentence that has an independent clause and one or more subordinate clauses.

Class Exercises

Read each complex sentence. Identify the independent clause and the subordinate clause in each. Tell what subordinating conjunction begins each subordinate clause.

1. When lemmings eat large areas of grass, deer go elsewhere for food.
2. Soil forms slowly because the erosion of rocks takes a long time.
3. Although willows grow in the Arctic, they are shorter than shrubs.
4. Before the 20th century arrived, people survived in the Arctic without the help of scientists.

Exercises

Write each sentence. Draw one line under the independent clause and two lines under the subordinate clause. Then write the subordinating conjunction that begins each subordinate clause.

1. Many plants and animals survive in the Arctic though temperatures often fall below 32 degrees Fahrenheit.
2. Because the subarctic region is south of the Arctic, it has warmer summers.
3. Snowy owls and other birds fly north when the lemming population increases.
4. As winter approaches, less sunlight shines on the region.
5. Until March arrives, the sun shines on few regions in the Arctic.
6. The tree line provides an important boundary because it separates the Arctic from the northern forests.
7. The Arctic people eat some kinds of meat although fish is the most popular food.
8. As local groups form, more people plan ways to save rare animals.
9. Arctic animals dig in the snow for food until spring arrives.

Writing Sentences

Write six complex sentences about the animals, plants, or climate in your region. Describe the changes that you see take place throughout the year.

Sample Answer 1. Many plants and animals survive in the Arctic though temperatures often fall below 32 degrees Fahrenheit. /though

Unit Review

SENTENCES

Write each sentence. Capitalize and punctuate each sentence correctly. Then write if it is a **declarative, interrogative, imperative,** or **exclamatory** sentence. *pages 4-5*

1. forest rangers improve the quality of trees
2. do they want more trees with rapid growth rates
3. how tall the giant redwoods grow
4. scientists have increased the resistance of trees
5. how important resistance to pests and diseases is
6. these scientists search the forest for tall, straight trees
7. do they select trees with fast growth rates from each species
8. what an interesting job they have

Write each group of words that forms a complete sentence. Underline the complete subject once and the complete predicate twice. If the group of words is not a complete sentence, write **fragment.** *pages 6-7*

9. Government officials create laws to protect rare animals.
10. The ecology club.
11. Some people preserve natural resources.
12. Each geographic area produces certain kinds of crops.
13. Informed the public about our wildlife.
14. Laws for our natural resources.
15. Ecologists work to save our natural resources.
16. Other scientists make charts of an animal's behavior.
17. Preserved the resources.
18. Local residents cleaned Lake Erie.

Read each sentence. If it is interrogative, reword it as a declarative sentence. Then write the complete subject of each sentence. Draw a line under the simple subject. Write the word **You** if it is the understood subject of an imperative sentence. *pages 8-9*

19. Write your representatives in Congress.
20. A strong wind blows air pollutants out to sea.

21. Environmental laws require antipollution parts on every car.
22. Feel the strong breeze.
23. Do some ecologists study weather conditions?
24. Many factories burn different types of fuel for power.
25. People breathe exhaust fumes and smoke particles.
26. Do all automobiles burn fuel?
27. Concerned citizens plan programs to help clean the air.

Read each sentence. Reword each interrogative sentence as a declarative sentence if you need to. Then write the complete predicate of each sentence. Draw a line under the simple predicate. *pages 10-11*

28. Most forests provide water for rivers and streams.
29. Does the forester measure the level of water in the rivers?
30. Soil with many tree roots collects water from rain and snow.
31. Local ecology groups are busy in many clean-up projects.
32. One water shed stores water for the entire area.
33. Look at the large oak tree.
34. Foresters control the quality of soil.
35. Does she know the total amount of rainfall for this year?
36. Feel the texture of this soil.

Write each letter that is next to the correct form of the verb that completes each sentence. *pages 12-13*

37. Melting snow ___ over the ground as water.
    a. flows   b. flow
38. Small streams ___ mud and other materials with them.
    a. carries   b. carry
39. Ecologists ___ ways to control water waste.
    a. plans   b. plan
40. Most soils ___ made up of sand and clay.
    a. is   b. are
41. A plant's root system ___ water from the soil.
    a. draws   b. draw
42. The United States ___ concerned with water waste.
    a. is   b. are

Unit Review

Read each sentence. Write the correct form of the verb or verbs in parentheses to complete each one. *pages 14-15*

43. Both deer and other large animals ___ low shrubs. (needs/need)
44. Sometimes a forester ___ and ___ sections of the trees. (trims/trim, sprays/spray)
45. Many bushes ___ and ___ in the dry areas. (withers/wither, dies/die)
46. Sometimes an animal ___ and ___ in barren land. (lives/live, roams/roam)
47. Large animals or small creatures ___ the thicker areas of the region. (visits/visit)
48. Food and shelter ___ in variety for the animals. (decreases/decrease)
49. Large mammals and birds ___ the first to leave. (is/are)
50. Overpopulation or drought ___ their food. (destroys/destroy)
51. A scientist ___ and ___ the problems of overpopulation. (studies/study, examines/examine)
52. Animals and businesses ___ on the forest. (depends/depend)

Write each sentence. Write whether it is a **simple sentence** or a **compound sentence.** If the sentence has a compound subject, draw one line under each subject. If the sentence has a compound predicate, draw two lines under each verb. If it is a compound sentence, draw a line between the two simple sentences. *pages 16-17*

53. Some animals feed on bark, buds, and branches; they damage trees.
54. Livestock needs grass and shrubs for food, and small woodland areas provide them with this food.
55. Large herds of animals arrive and endanger the food supply in some areas.
56. Foresters regulate the use of the lands, or the animals roam to other areas for food.
57. Either foresters or rangers preserve the land with seeding and plants.
58. Regulations provide the most important protection for lands, but the laws require enforcement by rangers.
59. Rangers hike or ride over the protected regions.

2

NOUNS

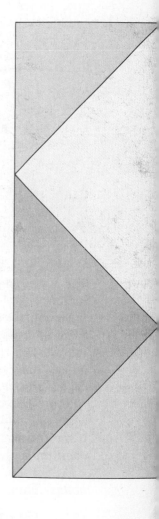

Review: Nouns

The people and things you see every day, the places you visit, and the feelings and thoughts you experience all have names. *Friend, zoo, bicycle,* and *peace* are such names. These names are different, but they all belong to one word group. The words in this group are called *nouns.*

A **noun** is a word that names a person, place, thing, or idea.

• Look at the incomplete sentence in the box below. Which words from the box can complete the sentence?

The inventor created many new ________.

machines	goes	things
across	products	processes

The nouns *machines, products, things,* or *processes* can complete the sentence.

Sometimes you can find nouns in a sentence by looking for adjectives or articles. In the example sentence above, the second noun follows the two adjectives, or descriptive words, *many* and *new.* Nouns may also follow the words *a, an,* or *the. A, an,* and *the* are called *articles.* The noun *inventor* follows the article *the.*

Some nouns name things you can see or touch, such as *snow, raincoat,* or *puddle.* These nouns are called *concrete nouns.* Other nouns name feelings and ideas that cannot be seen or touched, such as *peace, comfort,* and *year.* These nouns are called *abstract nouns.*

All of the nouns you have looked at so far are called *common nouns.* Even the words *person, place,* or *thing* are common nouns.

A **common noun** is a noun that names any person, place, thing, or idea.

Another kind of noun names a specific person, place, thing, or idea. Your name, the name of your town, and the title of a song or book are all *proper nouns.*

A **proper noun** is a noun that names a specific person, place, thing, or idea.

The first word and the other important words in a proper noun are capitalized.

Thomas Alva Edison	Museum of Science and Technology
Naples, Florida	United States Patent Office
Kitty Hawk	The Middle Ages

Class Exercises

Read each sentence. Find the nouns. Tell whether each noun is a **common noun** or a **proper noun.** Then tell whether each noun is a **concrete noun** or an **abstract noun.**

1. Thomas Saint designed an invention in the eighteenth century.
2. The new machine sewed leather with a needle and thread.
3. People in England found his idea impractical.
4. Barthelemy Thimonnier had a different notion forty years later.
5. The inventor sewed uniforms for soldiers on a machine.

Exercises

Write the nouns in each sentence below. Write **common noun** after each common noun and **proper noun** after each proper noun. Then write **concrete noun** after each concrete noun and **abstract noun** after each abstract noun.

1. The government of France thanked the man for his cleverness.
2. Many people lost their jobs in factories unfortunately.
3. Elias Howe invented a new model later.
4. Men and women in the United States liked the new machine.
5. Other inventors designed improvements about the same time.
6. A. B. Wilson of America introduced a special feature.
7. The new part allowed greater variety in the design of the switch.
8. Isaac Singer added a pedal for increased comfort.
9. The Singer Sewing Machine Company introduced the electric motor.
10. Workers in this country and in Europe sew goods faster now.

Sample Answer 1. government, common noun/concrete noun; France, proper noun/concrete noun; man, common noun/concrete noun; cleverness, common noun/abstract noun

Nouns in the Subject and Predicate

The *subject part* of a sentence names whom or what the sentence is about. The *predicate part* sometimes tells what action the subject does. Other times it tells what the subject is or is like. Often you use nouns in both parts of a sentence. Both common and proper nouns appear throughout your writing.

> A **common noun** is a noun that names any person, place, thing, or idea.
>
> A **proper noun** is a noun that names a specific person, place, thing, or idea.

- Find the common and proper nouns in the sentence below. Which nouns are in the subject part? Which nouns are in the predicate part?

Jacques Cousteau of France | developed techniques for the exploration of our oceans.

The subject part of the sentence is in the blue box. The predicate part of the sentence is in the red box. *Jacques Cousteau* and *France* are proper nouns in the subject part. *Techniques, exploration,* and *oceans* are common nouns in the predicate part.

- Look at the sentence below. Find the nouns in the subject part and in the predicate part. Remember that nouns often follow an adjective or an article.

This famous man explored the Mediterranean Sea.

The subject part of the sentence is *This famous man. Man* is a common noun in the subject part. The predicate part of the sentence is *explored the Mediterranean Sea. Mediterranean Sea* is a proper noun in the predicate part.

Class Exercises

Tell which is the subject part and the predicate part. Find each noun. Tell whether it is a **common noun** or a **proper noun.**

1. Jacques Cousteau is a leader among scientists of the sea.
2. This scientist and his crew explored the Red Sea.

3. Cousteau made the first color photographs and films about underwater life.
4. France and America honored Cousteau for his films.
5. The National Geographic Society sponsors much of his new work.

Exercises

Write each sentence. Draw a line between the subject part and the predicate part. Write each noun. Write whether it is a **common noun** or a **proper noun.**

1. Cousteau invented many useful devices during his long career.
2. This inventor developed the aqualung during World War II.
3. The aqualung provides air to divers beneath any body of water.
4. Jacques Cousteau made *The Silent World* after the war.
5. This original film came to the United States.
6. The film developed from a book by Cousteau and Frederic Dumas.
7. Cousteau designed an underwater laboratory for long periods under water.
8. At first two men spent a week below the Mediterranean Sea.
9. Six scientists lived in a larger underwater laboratory three years later.
10. Today, Cousteau travels widely in his own ship.
11. The name of the ship is Calypso.
12. The decks of this ship hold many tons of scientific equipment.
13. The famous Diving Saucer rests on the upper deck.
14. The Diving Saucer is another useful invention.
15. Cousteau works tirelessly on new devices, films, books, and other projects.

Writing Sentences

Think about something that you think needs to be invented. Write six sentences on your topic. Draw a line between the subject part and the predicate part in each sentence. Draw one line under each noun in the subject part and two lines under each noun in the predicate part.

Sample Answer 1. Cousteau | invented many useful devices during his long career. Cousteau, proper noun; devices, common noun; career, common noun.

Plural Nouns and Irregular Plurals

You know that a *noun* names a person, place, thing, or idea.

A **singular noun** names one person, place, thing, or idea.

A **plural noun** names more than one.

You need to know special rules to form the plurals of nouns.

To make most singular nouns plural, add **-s.**

For some singular nouns, add **-es** to form the plural.

The plural form of other nouns is formed in an irregular way, and there are no special rules for making these nouns plural. You have probably used these nouns, such as *children, women,* and *men*.

Sometimes you use the letters of the alphabet as nouns. Numerals, signs (+, −), and words referred to as words may all be used as nouns, too.

- Read the following sentences.

There are three *r*'s in *mirror.* (letter)

The equation has many *3*'s in it. (numeral)

This formula has too many +'s in it. (sign)

There are two *and*'s in this sentence. (word referred to as a word)

To form the plural of letters, numerals, signs, or words referred to as words, add an **apostrophe** and **s**.

When you use letters, numerals, signs, and words by themselves, you underline them. Underlining in manuscript is the same as italics in print.

Class Exercises

Read each sentence using the correct form of the noun in parentheses.

1. Today about 310 million ___ travel on the highways. (car, cars)
2. People can travel to another ___ or city faster now. (town, towns)
3. Both men and ___ drive automobiles. (woman, women)
4. A ___ may enjoy a short trip by car. (child, children)
5. There are two ___ in the license number of our car. (3, 3's)

Exercises

Write each sentence using the correct form of the noun in parentheses.

1. This country produces about 9 million ___ a year. (car, cars)
2. It also produces about 3½ million ___ a year. (bus, buses)
3. About 15 million ___ work in the automobile industry. (person, persons)
4. Today, a ___ usually buys a small car instead of a large model. (consumer, consumers)
5. Now, more ___ drive automobiles than ever before. (woman, women)
6. A lightweight ___ gets better mileage than a large model. (car, cars)
7. Most ___ spend large sums of money on research. (automaker, automakers)
8. A ___ may do research for an automobile company. (chemist, chemists)
9. Often there are three ___ in a chemist's formula. (+, +'s)
10. Researchers may test one ___ of a new design many times. (part, parts)
11. An auto manufacturer tests an ___ on a special track. (automobile, automobiles)
12. Many different ___ in the car register the reactions of different parts. (instrument, instruments)
13. Most ___ bring out new models every year. (automaker, automakers)
14. There are two ___ on the price tag of that car. (5, 5's)
15. How many ___ are in the name of that new model? (r, r's)

Writing Sentences

Imagine that you are at an automobile show. Write six sentences about what you see at the show. Write one sentence for each word below.

window headlights tires horn hood seats

Sample Answer 1. This country produces about 9 million cars a year.

Possessive Nouns

People have or own things. People, animals, and things also have characteristics and qualities.

- Read the sentences below. Notice the underlined nouns.

  Miko owns a book about inventions. The book has a large index.
  Miko's book is about inventions. The book's index is large.

  Miko is a singular proper noun. *Book* is a singular common noun. We call the forms *Miko's* and *book's* singular *possessive nouns.*

  A **possessive noun** is a noun that names who or what has something.

- Read the singular nouns and their possessive forms below. What is added to each singular noun to make it possessive?

  a girl—a girl**'s** coat Martha Coston—Martha Coston**'s** discovery

  Add an **apostrophe** and **s** (**'s**) to form the possessive of most singular nouns.

- Read these plural nouns and their possessive forms. What possessive endings are added?

  girls—girls**'** shoes children—children**'s** toys
  the Wrights—the Wrights**'** plane women—women**'s** organization

  Add an **apostrophe (')** to form the possessive of most plural nouns that end in **s.**

  Add an **apostrophe** and **s** (**'s**) to form the possessive of plural nouns that do not end in **s.**

- Read the singular nouns and their possessive forms below. Notice that you have two choices when writing the possessive form of a singular noun that ends in **s.** You may add an apostrophe or an apostrophe and **s.**

  Joseph Ives—Joseph Ives**'** clock—Joseph Ives**'s** clock
  Nina Masters—Nina Masters**'** book—Nina Masters**'s** book

An apostrophe is also used in a contraction. A *contraction* is a word made by combining two words into one by leaving out one or more letters. The apostrophe shows where the letters are left out.

Elaine's invention is a new bell. Elaine's going to the exhibit.

Notice that in the sentence on the left *Elaine's invention* means the invention of Elaine. In this sentence *Elaine* is a singular possessive noun. In the sentence on the right *Elaine's going* means *Elaine is going.* In this sentence *Elaine's* is a contraction of the words *Elaine is.*

Class Exercises

Tell what each underlined noun below needs to make it possessive.

1. Marie Curie discovery
2. scientists experiments
3. the children plans
4. C.L. Sholes typewriter

Exercises

Write the correct possessive form of each noun below.

1. Tabitha Babbit
2. one company
3. women
4. Emma G. Hirsch
5. men
6. one engineer
7. two principals
8. many animals
9. Mrs. Burns

Write each sentence and add an apostrophe in the right place. Write whether the word with the apostrophe is a **singular possessive noun,** a **plural possessive noun,** or a **contraction.**

10. Ben Franklins invention was the lightning rod.
11. At one time lightning destroyed many citizens homes.
12. Lightning rods saved the inventors home.
13. Today lightning rods protect residents homes from damage.
14. Lightning rods also protect farmers barns.
15. Anitas going to the library for information about the lightning rod.
16. Maria Blass science class is studying electricity.
17. This womens group is reading about famous inventors.
18. Juanita will write about the inventors contributions.

Writing Sentences

Write three sentences for each of these words: *woman, athlete, biker.* In the first sentence use the singular possessive form of the word. Use the plural possessive form of the word in the second sentence. In the third sentence use a contraction of the word and *is* or *has.*

Sample Answers 1. Tabitha Babbit's **10.** Ben Franklin's invention was the lightning rod. singular possessive noun

Distinguishing Plurals and Possessives

Most plural nouns and most possessive nouns end with the letter *s*. They sound alike, but their spellings and meanings are different.

- Read the chart below. Notice the meaning of each underlined word.

Example	Meaning
Plural Noun: The scientists made an important discovery.	more than one scientist
Plural Possessive Noun: The scientists' discovery was important.	the discovery of the scientists
Singular Possessive Noun: This scientist's photograph is in the newspaper.	the photograph of one scientist

- Study the lists below.

Plural Nouns	Plural Possessive Nouns	Singular Possessive Nouns
doctors	doctors'	doctor's
heroes	heroes'	hero's
diaries	diaries'	diary's

No plural nouns have apostrophes. The plural possessive nouns end with an apostrophe. The singular possessive nouns end with an apostrophe and *s*. You can tell these words apart by the way they are used in a sentence. When you write one of these noun forms in a sentence, remember the difference between a plural noun and a possessive noun.

> A **plural noun** is a noun that names more than one.
>
> A **possessive noun** is a noun that names who or what has something.

Class Exercises

Read each sentence. Choose the word in parentheses that correctly completes each sentence. Tell whether it is a **plural noun, singular possessive noun,** or **plural possessive noun.**

1. Modern (rockets/rockets') carry satellites into space.
2. Some of the (satellites/satellites') equipment gets its power from sunlight.

3. Ground (stations/stations') antennas send signals to satellites.
4. These (stations/stations') also receive signals from satellites.
5. In the future each (home's/homes) antenna may receive signals for television programs directly from satellites.
6. (America's/Americas) rockets carry satellites into orbit.

Exercises

Write each sentence. Underline the word in parentheses that correctly completes the sentence. Write whether it is a **plural noun, singular possessive noun,** or **plural possessive noun.**

1. The (satellites/satellites') uses are varied.
2. (Farmers/Farmers') crops need good weather.
3. Satellites in space send weather (reports/reports') back to earth.
4. Some satellites take photographs of distant (galaxies/galaxies').
5. Other (satellites/satellites') relay telephone calls between countries.
6. One satellite has 240 telephone (channels/channels') between two continents.
7. An American can speak to her (friend's/friends) relatives in Asia.
8. My (aunt's/aunts) conversation with her family in England usually lasts three minutes.
9. Her (sisters/sisters') letters travel very slowly.
10. A special satellite watches another (nation's/nations) rivers.
11. This (satellite's/satellites) photographs show pollution.
12. Television (programs/programs') reach many people by satellite.
13. (Teams/Teams') fans all around the world can watch them play.

Writing Sentences

Write three sentences for each of these words: *pilot, inventor.* Use the plural form of the word in the first sentence. Use the singular possessive form of the word in the second sentence. In the third sentence use the plural possessive form of the word.

Sample Answer 1. The satellites' uses are varied. plural possessive noun

Collective Nouns

English has a kind of noun that presents a special agreement problem. This noun is called a *collective noun.*

> A **collective noun** names a group of people or things. The noun has a singular meaning when you speak about a group that acts as a unit. The noun has a plural meaning when you want to show that each member of the group acts separately or individually.

- Read these commonly used collective nouns. Each names a group of people or things. The group may act as a unit or as individuals.

family	herd	audience	team	flock	committee
group	fleet	club	crowd	band	class

- Note the collective nouns in these sentences. Every collective noun can have a singular or plural meaning. If you speak about the group as a unit, the noun has a singular meaning. If you refer to the individual members of the group, the noun has a plural meaning.

  The whole flock enters the meadow through a gate.
  (a unit-singular)

  The flock enter by different gates.
  (individual members-plural)

  The entire audience applauds the performers.
  (a unit-singular)

  The audience applaud their favorite performers.
  (individual members-plural)

When you are thinking of the group as a unit, use a collective noun and the form of the verb that agrees with a singular noun. When you want to refer to the individual members of the group, use the collective noun and the form of the verb that agrees with a plural noun.

To help you determine whether a collective noun in a sentence is singular or plural, substitute the word *it* for the collective noun. If the sentence still makes sense when you substitute *it,* the collective noun is singular. If you can substitute *they,* the collective noun is plural.

The team works on its project. (it, singular)

The team work on their separate projects. (they, plural)

Class Exercises

Name the collective noun in each sentence. Tell whether the meaning of the collective noun is **singular** or **plural.**

1. The group shakes the stadium with its school cheer.
2. The group leave the stadium by different exits.
3. The committee argue with one another over the rules.
4. The committee holds its first meeting tonight.

Exercises

Write each sentence. Underline the collective noun. Write whether the meaning of the collective noun is **singular** or **plural.**

1. The chorus disagree about which song to sing in the concert.
2. The chorus sings its five favorite songs in the show.
3. The baseball team plays its first game tonight.
4. The baseball team individually answer the reporter's questions.
5. The rock group performs its new number downtown.
6. The rock group, one by one, sign their autographs for a fan.

Write each sentence using the correct form of the verb in parentheses that agrees with the subject.

7. The whole class ___ the convention. (attends, attend)
8. The class individually ___ the different exhibits. (visits, visit)
9. One family together ___ to an exhibitor. (listens, listen)
10. The family, one at a time, ___ their thoughts. (expresses, express)
11. The crowd ___ the booth by different exits. (leaves, leave)
12. Another crowd ___ together in front of the same booth. (gathers, gather)

Writing Sentences

Write two sentences for each of these collective nouns: *family, audience, club.* In the first sentence give the collective noun a singular meaning. Give the collective noun a plural meaning in the second sentence.

Sample Answers 1. The chorus disagree about which song to sing in the concert. plural
7. The whole class attends the convention. singular

Unit Review

NOUNS

Write the nouns in each sentence below. Write **common noun** after each common noun. Write **proper noun** after each proper noun. Then write **concrete noun** after each concrete noun and **abstract noun** after each abstract noun. *pages 26-27*

1. Whitcomb L. Judson invented the zipper.
2. Judson wanted an easier way to fasten shoes.
3. The name of the first zipper was C-Curity.
4. The B.F. Goodrich Company gave the zipper its present name.

Write each sentence. Draw a line between the subject part and the predicate part. Find each noun. Write whether it is a **common noun** or a **proper noun.** *pages 28-29*

5. The emperor needed food for his armies.
6. Napoleon offered a prize for the invention of a new process.
7. Nicholas Appert experimented in his kitchen for ten years.
8. This man invented a method for the preservation of food.

Write the letter next to the correct form of the noun that completes each sentence. *pages 30-31*

9. A ___ magnifies extremely small objects.
   a. microscope   b. microscopes
10. A ___ can see small objects easily under a microscope.
   a. person   b. persons
11. Biology students can study many small ___ under the microscope.
   a. plant   b. plants

Write the correct possessive form of each noun below. *pages 32-33*

12. radio
13. broadcasters
14. pilots
15. women
16. object
17. waves

Write each sentence and add an apostrophe in the right place. Write whether the word with the apostrophe is a **singular possessive noun,** a **plural possessive noun,** or a **contraction.** *pages 32-33*

18. Vladamir Zworkins television was the first practical television.
19. Scientists improvements in equipment provide clearer pictures.

20. Today there are many popular childrens programs.
21. One researchers studying the quality of programs for children.

Write the word in parentheses that correctly completes each sentence. Write whether it is a **plural noun,** a **singular possessive noun,** or a **plural possessive noun.** *pages 34-35*

22. A person in Holland invented the first (telescopes/telescopes').
23. We do not know the name of these simple (instruments'/instruments) inventor.
24. Galileo Gallilei pointed his telescope at the (planets/planet's).
25. This (astronomer's/astronomers) discoveries changed science forever.

Write the collective noun from each sentence. Write whether the meaning of the collective noun is **singular** or **plural.** *pages 36-37*

26. The Cali family express their personal opinions about the exhibits.
27. The family gives its contribution to the new science museum.
28. The committee, with their many interests, listen to different speakers.
29. The whole committee applauds enthusiastically.

Write the correct form of the verb in parentheses that agrees with the subject. *pages 36-37*

30. The buffalo herd ___ in different directions. (stampede, stampedes)
31. The scientific team together ___ the herd. (study, studies)
32. Overhead, a flock of geese ___ in formation. (pass, passes)
33. The flock, one by one, ___ down over the lake. (swoop, swoops)

Careers

Copy editors are important members of a newspaper staff. After a news article is written, the story goes to the copy desk, where the editors make sure the facts are correct and well organized. They check spelling and punctuation, too. Copy editors also write headlines for the stories. Today many copy editors on large newspapers edit stories on a video display terminal.

A photo finish in a women's relay race

Winning can be defined as the science of being totally prepared.

GEORGE ALLEN
U.S. Pro football coach
(1922-   )

3

VERBS

Review: Verbs

If a word expresses action and tells what a subject does, it is an *action verb.*

An **action verb** is a word that names an action.
It may contain more than one word.

• Notice the action verbs in the following sentences.

Sports experts write about the football player Jim Thorpe even today. Thorpe blocked like a tank. He tackled like a tornado. In every game Thorpe attacked his opponents with all his might. He received and ran the ball swiftly. Experts still remember and agree on Thorpe's greatness.

Words like *write, blocked,* and *ran* express physical action. Words like *agree* and *remember* are words that express mental activity.

Every sentence has a subject part and a predicate part. In some sentences the predicate part is just an action verb.

The punter	kicks.		The coach	advises.

Usually sentences provide more information. The predicate part often names who or what received the action of the verb.

The punter	kicks the football.		The coach	advises the players.

In the sentences above, *football* and *players* receive the action of the verbs *kicks* and *advises.* They answer the questions *what?* or *whom?* after the action verbs. They are called *direct objects* of verbs.

The **direct object** of a verb receives the action of the verb.
It answers the question **whom?** or **what?** after an action verb.

In some sentences the action verb does not always have a direct object.

The team	played the game.		The team played	well.

In the sentence on the left *game* is the direct object because it answers the question *what*? after the action verb *played.* In the sentence on the right *well* does not answer the question *whom*? or *what*? after the verb *played.* Therefore it is not a *direct object.* Action verbs that have no direct object are called *intransitive verbs.*

A **transitive verb** is a verb that has a direct object. An **intransitive verb** is a verb that does not have a direct object.

Most action verbs like *played* can be either transitive or intransitive. You must examine how an action verb is used in the sentence in order to determine whether it is transitive or intransitive.

Class Exercises

Read each sentence below. Find the action verb. Name the direct object, if there is one. Tell whether the verbs are **transitive** or **intransitive.**

1. Many track athletes copied Jim Thorpe's style.
2. Jim Thorpe ran fast.
3. "Pop" Warner coached other runners at Carlisle College.
4. Again and again Thorpe scored.

Exercises

Read each sentence. Find the action verb. Name the direct object, if there is one. Tell whether the verbs are **transitive** or **intransitive.**

1. Many sports fans remember the great Jim Thorpe.
2. Many people recognized his picture.
3. The athlete ran with great concentration.
4. Thorpe won track events in the 1912 Olympics.
5. The man set world records in the decathlon.
6. Thorpe raced against many runners in the Olympics.
7. Thorpe broke many world records.
8. The talented player participated in many sports.
9. Thorpe wrestled with great strength.
10. This great American Indian also boxed.

Writing Sentences

Suppose that you are a sportswriter. Write six sentences that could describe some of the actions seen at a football game. Use transitive verbs in three of the sentences and intransitive verbs in three other sentences. Choose action verbs from the list below.

scored	tackled	looked	defeated	passed
blocked	kicked	threw	dropped	fell

Sample Answer 1. Many sports fans remember the great Jim Thorpe.
transitive

Linking Verbs

You have already learned that an *action verb* names what action the subject of a sentence does. Some verbs do not tell what the subject does. Instead they tell what the subject is or is like.

- Read these sentences.

John McGraw	was the manager.	Mathewson	is remarkable.

The words *was* and *is* are verbs, but they do not name actions. Instead they connect, or link, the subject to a word in the predicate. The word *manager* tells what the subject John McGraw *is*. The word *remarkable* tells what the subject Mathewson *is like*. Verbs such as *was* and *is* are called linking verbs.

A **linking verb** is a verb that connects the subject part with a noun or adjective in the predicate part. It tells what the subject is or is like.

The word that follows a linking verb may be a noun or an adjective. If the word in the predicate is a noun, it tells what the subject *is*. It names a person, place, thing, or idea. A noun that follows a linking verb is called a *predicate noun*.

A **predicate noun** is a noun that follows a linking verb. It tells what the subject is.

If the word in the predicate is an adjective, it tells what the subject *is like*. It describes a noun or pronoun in the subject. An adjective that follows a linking verb is called a *predicate adjective*.

A **predicate adjective** is an adjective that follows a linking verb. It describes the subject by telling what it is like.

- Read these sentences. Find the linking verbs. Do they connect the subject with a noun or with an adjective?

Many fans seem eager.

The team appears ready.

The first pitch is a strike.

The winners become the champions.

The forms of the verb *be* (*is, am, are, was, were*) and the verbs *seem, appear, taste, feel, smell, grow, sound, look, become,* and *turn* are often used as linking verbs.

Class Exercises

Find each verb. Tell whether it is an **action verb** or a **linking verb.** If it is a linking verb, name the **predicate noun** or **predicate adjective.**

1. Our pitcher appears nervous today.
2. The catcher ran very quickly.
3. The pitcher was a good hitter.
4. The player at third base threw the baseball.

Exercises

Write each sentence. Draw one line under each verb. Then write whether it is an **action verb** or a **linking verb.** If it is a **linking verb,** write whether it is followed by a **predicate noun** or a **predicate adjective.**

1. Fans of the home team seem confident today.
2. The home team was the winner of thc game yesterday.
3. Today's winners become members of the state's Hall of Fame.
4. The players on both teams seem eager at the start of the game.
5. The mayor ran to the field.
6. He is an honorary member of the team.
7. The team's members appear professional in their new uniforms.
8. The pitcher pounded his fist into the glove.
9. The members of both teams seem ready now.
10. The first hit is a homerun.
11. The crowd in the stands becomes wild with excitement.
12. Even the sports announcer seems joyous.
13. The visiting team played very poorly throughout the entire game.
14. The catcher behind the plate appears calm.
15. He becomes coach of the All-Star Team with this victory.

Writing Sentences

Imagine that you are a sports writer at a baseball game. Write six sentences describing what you see. Use a different linking verb in each sentence.

Sample Answer 1. Fans of the home team seem confident today. seem, linking verb; confident, predicate adjective

Verbs with Predicate Nouns or Direct and Indirect Objects

You know that linking verbs connect the subject part of a sentence with nouns or adjectives in the predicate part. If the word in the predicate part is a noun, it is called a predicate noun. A *predicate noun* is a noun that follows a linking verb. It tells what the subject is.

The captain of the home team was the most valuable player last season.

The captain is an inspiration to the other members of the team.

Action verbs, too, are often followed by nouns and pronouns. Nouns or pronouns that answer the question *whom*? or *what*? after an action verb are called *direct objects*.

Jabaar tossed the ball twelve times before the end of the quarter.

Jabaar lead his team to the championship again that year.

Sometimes two kinds of objects follow an action verb. The object that directly receives the action of the verb is called the *direct object*. Sometimes another object called an indirect object follows the verb. An *indirect object* tells *to whom* or *for whom* the action was done.

Jabaar shows his teammates new shots.

The star basketball player gives a fan his autograph.

The direct object in the first sentence is *shots*. The indirect object is *teammates*. The direct object in the second sentence is *autograph*. The indirect object is *fans*.

Two easy clues help you to recognize indirect objects. First, the indirect object always comes before a direct object. Second, you can add the preposition *to* or *for* before the indirect object and change its position. The sentence will still make sense. Compare the following two sentences.

The helper gives the players towels.

The helper gives towels to the players.

You can figure out that in the first sentence *players* is the indirect object. First, it comes before the direct object. Second, its position can be changed to follow the preposition *to*.

Class Exercises

Tell whether each underlined noun in the predicate part is a **predicate noun, direct object,** or **indirect object.**

1. One player gets his team three points in the first quarter.
2. That very tall player is a rookie.
3. The students were players from a local university.
4. The referee asked the players questions two minutes into the game.

Exercises

Write each sentence and draw a line under each verb. Write whether it is a **linking verb** or an **action verb.** Write whether each underlined word in the predicate part is a **predicate noun,** a **direct object,** or an **indirect object.**

1. The teams were rivals in the first basketball game of the season.
2. Thousands of fans eagerly paid the cashiers money for their tickets.
3. The coach gave the players new instructions.
4. The players planned many different shots.
5. The fans were students from different schools.
6. Mr. Eckert was the referee during the game.
7. Our center was a third-year student.
8. The player took many shots.
9. Don scored the most points in the game.
10. Don was the captain of our team.
11. The two coaches gave their teams advice during the second quarter.
12. One coach offered the team a new plan.
13. Our coach gave the players a loud cheer at the end of the game.
14. The final score was a tie.

Writing Sentences

Think about a basketball game you have played or watched. Write six sentences, using action verbs with a direct and an indirect object. In three sentences use a linking verb with a predicate noun.

Sample Answer 1. The teams were rivals in the first basketball game of the season. were, linking verb; rivals, predicate noun

Distinguishing Action and Linking Verbs

Most verbs are *action verbs.* They name what action the subject of a sentence does. Verbs such as *be, seem,* and *appear* are usually *linking verbs.* A *linking verb* tells what the subject *is* or *is like.* It connects the subject of a sentence to a noun or adjective in the predicate part.

- Look at these sentences. Notice how the linking verb connects the subject to a noun or adjective in the predicate.

  The rider is the owner of the horse.

  The horse seems calm in his stable today.

  The rider appears ready for the important show.

Other linking verbs tell how something tastes, feels, smells, grows, or looks. Sometimes they are called "sense verbs."

- Read these sentences. All these verbs tell what the subject is or is like.

  The race course looks difficult to one rider.

  The juice in the thermos tastes good.

  The riders feel eager for the show.

  All the spectators grow impatient.

  The saddle leather smells good to the rider.

These same verbs can also be used to express action. Except for *be* and *seem,* all verbs that are used as linking verbs can also be used as action verbs.

- Study the following sentences.

Linking Verb	**Action Verb**
The oats *tasted* good.	The horses *tasted* the oats.
The victory roses *smelled* sweet.	The rider *smelled* the roses.
The race *looked* hard.	Ann *looked* at the horses.
One horse *grew* lazy.	The colt *grew* very quickly.
The winner *felt* good.	She *felt* the horse's mane.

To check whether a verb in a sentence is a linking verb, substitute *seem, seems,* or *seemed* for the verb. If the sentence still makes sense, the original verb is probably a linking verb.

Class Exercises

Tell whether the underlined verb is being used as a **linking verb** or as an **action verb.**

1. The horse's coat feels dry to his groom.
2. Donna feels the horse's coat before the show.
3. The racetrack looks wet to the spectators.
4. Greg looks at race horses during his free time.
5. Marianne smells the new hay in the fields.
6. The new hay smells wonderful to her.

Exercises

Write each sentence. Draw a line under each verb. Write whether each verb is used as a **linking verb** or as an **action verb.**

1. The horse tasted the hay in the morning.
2. The hay tasted fresh to the horse.
3. The horse appeared at the gate at the start of the show.
4. The course appeared bumpy to the rider.
5. The audience grew restless during one part of the show.
6. White hair grew in the horse's mane.
7. People looked at the different horses through binoculars.
8. The riders looked nervous toward the end of the show.
9. One spectator felt the sleek coat of the horse.
10. Another spectator felt dizzy from the excitement of the show.
11. The horse smelled the victory flowers around its neck.
12. The air smelled sweet that afternoon.

Writing Sentences

Suppose you have been to an animal show. Write six sentences about the show, using three of the following words: *look, feel, smell, taste,* and *grow.* Write two sentences for each word. Use the word as a linking verb in the first sentence. Use the word as an action verb in the second sentence.

Sample Answer 1. The horse tasted the hay in the morning. action verb

Present, Past, and Future Tenses

You know that a verb names an action. A verb also shows the time when the action takes place.

The fans applaud the winner. (right now, in the present)

The fans applauded the winner. (in the past)

The fans will applaud the winner. (in the future)

The form of a verb that shows the time when the action takes place is called the *tense* of the verb. When you name an action that takes place now, in the present, use the *present tense.*

The **present tense** of a verb names an action that happens now.

- Study this chart for the present tense of the verb *race.* Notice the form used with a singular noun or with the pronouns *it, she,* or *he.* Remember, a verb in a sentence must agree with its subject.

PRESENT TENSE	
Singular	**Plural**
I race.	We race.
You race.	You race.
It, she, or he races.	They race.
The dog races.	The cats race.

In the present tense, the verb *race* is used with all subjects except for singular nouns, and for the pronouns *it, she,* or *he.* The present tense for singular nouns, and for *it*, *she*, or *he* is usually formed by adding *-s* to the verb.

When you name an action that happened in the past, use the *past tense.*

The **past tense** of a verb names an action that already happened.

The past tense of many verbs is formed by adding *-ed* to the verb.

The runner trained yesterday. She also exercised this morning.

When you name an action that will happen in the future, use the *future tense.*

The **future tense** of a verb names an action that will take place in the future.

FUTURE TENSE	
Singular	**Plural**
I will (shall) go.	We will (shall) go.
You will go.	You will go.
It, she, or he will go.	They will go.
The coach will go.	The players will go.

In the future tense, the helping verb *will* is used with the verb. Sometimes the helping verb *shall* is used with the verb to form the future tense for the pronouns *I* and *we*.

Class Exercises

Read these sentences. Decide whether to use the **present, past,** or **future** tense of the verb in parentheses.

1. Wilma Rudolph ___ many races in the 1950s. (enter)
2. During her youth Wilma ___ many difficulties. (suffer)
3. Today Wilma Rudolph ___ other young runners. (encourage)
4. In future years people ___ her success on the track. (remember)

Exercises

Write each sentence. Use the correct tense of the verb in parentheses. Then write whether the form of the verb is in the **present, past,** or **future** tense.

1. Today Wilma Rudolph ___ a full life. (live)
2. As a child Wilma carefully ___ her future. (consider)
3. At an early age she ___ the importance of good health. (learn)
4. Wilma ___ over many illnesses. (triumph)
5. The young Wilma ___ an active life. (want)
6. She ___ several different sports. (enjoy)
7. After basketball season she ___ track competitions. (enter)
8. For many years she ___ long and hard. (train)
9. Finally in 1960 Wilma ___ an Olympic medal in track. (obtain)
10. Now this great runner ___ sports events on television. (describe)
11. Even today Wilma ___ many young athletes. (inspire)
12. In the years ahead injured runners ___ her example. (follow)

Sample Answer 1. Today Wilma Rudolph lives a full life. present

Making Subjects and Verbs Agree

A verb must always agree with its subject. Your first step is to decide whether the subject is singular or plural. Your second step is to make sure the verb agrees with the subject.

- Look at the sentences below.

Football *and* baseball are exciting games.

Both baseball *and* football use umpires.

A compound subject joined by *and* or by *both...and* is always plural, and the verb must agree with a plural subject.

- Now read these sentences.

Their outfielders *or* our catcher makes a mistake.

Our catcher *or* their outfielders make a mistake.

Either the umpire *or* the players are wrong.

Neither the players *nor* the umpire is wrong.

When a sentence has a compound subject joined by *or,* by *either...or,* or by *neither...nor,* the verb must agree with the *nearer* subject.

In a sentence beginning with *there* or *here,* the subject follows the verb. Notice the position of the complete subject and complete predicate in the sentences below.

There is a catcher's glove in the locker.

Here in the locker is a catcher's glove.

By rearranging each sentence so that the subject comes first, you can see the subject and verb in their usual position.

A catcher's glove is in the locker. (One glove means–use singular verb *is.*)

- Now study these sentences.

There are many people at the game. (Many people are at the game.)

There is one announcer in the booth. (One announcer is in the booth.)

In the first sentence *people* is a plural noun. Therefore the verb *are* agrees with the plural subject *people.* In the second sentence *announcer* is a singular noun. Therefore the verb *is* agrees with the singular subject *announcer.*

Class Exercises

Read each sentence. Use the correct form of the verb in parentheses that agrees with the subject.

1. Joggers and cyclists ___ warm-up exercises. (do/does)
2. Neither a cyclist nor a runner ___ a lot of equipment. (need/needs)
3. Either muscle damage or other injuries ___ possible. (is/are)
4. Both joggers and cyclists ___ proper shoes. (require/requires)

Exercises

Write each sentence. Use the correct form of the verb in parentheses that agrees with the subject.

1. There ___ many sports shoes in that store. (is/are)
2. Both leather and nylon ___ popular materials. (is/are)
3. Neither Mary nor her sister ___ nylon shoes. (buys/buy)
4. Both proper shoes and socks ___ necessary. (is/are)
5. Blisters and bruises ___ from poor equipment. (result/results)
6. There ___ a new bicycle path in the park. (is/are)
7. A runner and a cyclist ___ strong legs. (need/needs)
8. Both a pulled muscle and a sprain ___ painful. (is/are)
9. Either hills or potholes ___ many injuries. (cause/causes)
10. Neither a bicyclist nor a runner ___ the rain. (like/likes)
11. Both Tom and Andrea ___ five miles each. (run/runs)
12. The park and the stadium ___ places for runners. (provide/provides)
13. A friend and his relatives ___ the runners. (watch/watches)
14. Here ___ the winner around the far turn. (come/comes)

Writing Sentences

Write six sentences about runners in a marathon. In the first two sentences join a compound subject with *and* or with *both...and.* In the next two sentences join a compound subject with *either...or* and *neither...nor.* Start the last two sentences with *there* and *here.*

Sample Answer 1. There are many sports shoes in that store.

Principal Parts, Helping Verbs, and Verb Phrases

Verbs have four principal parts. All tenses of a verb can be formed from these principal parts and helping verbs. These are the four principal parts of the verb *jump.*

Present	Present Participle	Past	Past Participle
jump	jumping	jumped	jumped

Notice that the first principal part of the verb is the verb itself. For most verbs, this part is used to make the present tense. The present participle is formed by adding *-ing* to the verb. The past and past participle are the same for most verbs. They are often formed by adding *-ed* to the verb.

You already know how to use the present and past tenses of verbs. You also know how to combine a verb with the helping verb *will* or *shall* to form the future tense.

Present	The athletes jump rope now.
Past	The athletes jumped rope yesterday.
Future	The athletes will jump rope tomorrow.

Often a principal part of a verb is combined with a helping verb in a verb phrase to form other tenses.

> A **helping verb** helps the main verb to name an action or make a statement.
>
> A **verb phrase** consists of one or more helping verbs followed by a main verb. It names the action or tells what the subject is or is like.

- Look at these examples of a participle with a helping verb.

They are jumping rope now. They have jumped rope before.

In these sentences *are* and *have* are helping verbs. *Jumping* and *jumped* are main verbs.

The most common helping verbs are forms of the verbs *be* and *have.* The present participle is usually used with forms of the helping verb *be.* The past participle is usually used with forms of the helping verb *have.*

Be and the Present Participle		Have and the Past Participle	
I am jumping.	I was jumping.	I have jumped.	I had jumped.
You are jumping.	You were jumping.	You have jumped.	You had jumped.
He is jumping.	He was jumping.	He has jumped.	He had jumped.
She is jumping.	She was jumping.	She has jumped.	She had jumped.
It is jumping.	It was jumping.	It has jumped.	It had jumped.
We are jumping.	We were jumping.	We have jumped.	We had jumped.
You are jumping.	You were jumping.	You have jumped.	You had jumped.
They are jumping.	They were jumping.	They have jumped.	They had jumped.

Class Exercises

Read each sentence. Use the correct form of the helping verb in parentheses to complete the sentences. Name the participle and tell whether it is a **present participle** or a **past participle.**

1. They ___ making archery a more popular sport. (were/had)
2. The equipment ___ changed very little. (are/has)
3. Many people ___ playing in tournaments each year. (are/have)
4. Tournaments ___ increased people's interest in archery. (have/are)

Exercises

Write each sentence. Use the correct form of the helping verb in parentheses to complete the sentence. Draw a line under each participle, and write whether it is a **present participle** or a **past participle.**

1. Archers ___ making archery a more popular sport. (were/had)
2. We ___ learning about archery this year. (are/have)
3. Archers ___ working hard in today's competition. (are/have)
4. That archer ___ earning the most points today. (is/has)
5. She ___ scored several bull's-eyes. (is/has)
6. Sarah's arrow ___ landed away from the target. (is/has)
7. Some archers ___ fished with bows and arrows. (are/have)
8. Many campers ___ learning archery last summer. (were/had)
9. Some campers ___ attempted archery before. (were/had)
10. Most campers ___ enjoying the sport. (were/had)
11. One camper ___ earned a medal. (was/had)
12. One camper ___ working especially hard. (was/had)

Sample Answer 1. Archers were making archery a more popular sport.
present participle

Present and Past Progressive

You have already learned that the form of a verb that shows the time when an action takes place is called the *tense* of a verb. The present participle of the main verb, together with the helping verb *be,* form the present progressive and past progressive *tenses.*

The *present progressive* tense is formed with the present participle of the main verb and the present tense form of the helping verb *be* (*is, am,* and *are*).

- Look at these verb phrases. Notice the use of the present participle and the present tense of the verb *be.*

I am enjoying this baseball game at Candlestick Park.

The outfielders are watching carefully.

The underlined verb phrases are in the present progressive tense. The phrases *am enjoying* and *are watching* suggest that the actions are in progress at this very moment.

> The **present progressive** tense of a verb names an action or condition that is continuous in the present.

The *past progressive* tense consists of the present participle of the main verb and the past tense forms of the helping verb *be* (*was* and *were*).

- Look at these verb phrases. Notice the use of the present participle with the past tense of the verb *be.*

They were winning the game.   The pitcher was becoming tired.

The underlined verb phrases are in the past progressive tense. The phrases *were winning* and *was becoming* indicate that the actions took place over a period of time in the past.

> The **past progressive** tense of a verb names an action or condition that continued for some time in the past.

- Find the verb phrases in each example. Tell whether each is in the present progressive or the past progressive tense.

The fans are buying tickets for the game.

The catcher was carrying his chest protector.

All the batters were wearing protective helmets.

Class Exercises

Read each sentence. Use the present progressive tense of the verb in parentheses to complete the sentence.

1. I ___ a great soccer game on television now. (watch)
2. The players ___ very hard. (try)

Read each sentence. Use the past progressive tense of the verb in parentheses to complete the sentence.

3. The fans ___ the team after the game. (cheer)
4. The team ___ for the bus. (look)

Exercises

Write each sentence. Use the present progressive tense of the verb in parentheses to complete the sentence.

1. The soccer coach ___ a team for the next season. (plan)
2. He ___ players from other teams to the tryouts. (ask)
3. Many old players ___ out also. (try)
4. Some old players ___ for the next season. (train)
5. The goal tender ___ for the game. (prepare)

Write each sentence. Use the past progressive tense of the verb in parentheses to complete the sentence.

6. My friend ___ at the players at the tryouts. (look)
7. The players ___ the ball back and forth. (kick)
8. Some players ___ by the goal post. (stand)
9. The coach ___ the players work out. (watch)
10. The team captain ___ some new plays. (arrange)

Writing Sentences

Imagine that you are the announcer for a sports event. Write six sentences about the actions that are taking place or were taking place. In three sentences use a verb in the present progressive tense. In three other sentences use a verb in the past progressive tense.

Sample Answers 1. The soccer coach is planning a team for the next season.
6. My friend was looking at the players at the tryouts.

Present and Past Perfect

The past participle of the main verb is used with the helping verb *have* to form the present perfect and the past perfect *tenses*.

The *present perfect tense* consists of the past participle of the main verb together with the present tense forms of the verb (*has* and *have*).

- Look at these verb phrases in the present perfect tense.

My family has attended many sports events.

I have watched baseball games for years.

In the first sentence above, the family began to attend sports events at some time in the past and still attends them.

> The **present perfect** tense of a verb names an action that happened at an indefinite time in the past. It also names an action that started in the past and is still happening in the present.

The *past perfect tense* consists of the past participle of the main verb together with the past tense of the verb have (had).

- Now study these verb phrases in the past perfect tense.

Tom had studied before the game.

His friends had waited outside for him.

In the first sentence above, Tom started and finished studying before another event, the game.

> The **past perfect** tense of a verb names an action that happened before another past action.

A complex sentence has two clauses. Sometimes the action in one clause happened before the action in the other clause. Then the verb in one clause may be in the past tense, and the verb in the other clause may be in the past perfect tense.

- Read this complex sentence. Notice the tense of the verb in each clause.

Before the Braves started the game, they had exercised.

In the sentence above, the verb *had exercised* is in the past perfect tense because it happened before the game started. The verb *started* is in the past tense.

Class Exercises

Read each sentence. Use the present perfect tense of the verb in parentheses to complete the sentence.

1. Some players ___ their warmup routines. (start)
2. The practice session ___ for this week. (end)

Read each sentence. Use the past perfect tense of the verb in parentheses to complete the sentence.

3. The players ___ on time for the coach's speech. (arrive)
4. The coach ___ for them in his office. (wait)

Exercises

Write each sentence. Use the present perfect tense of the verb in parentheses to complete the sentence.

1. The coach ___ many plays during her career. (watch)
2. She ___ an early practice this evening. (call)
3. Most players ___ to the new rules. (agree)
4. They ___ at school early for more practice. (arrive)
5. The players ___ a week of hard work. (plan)
6. The team ___ for several hours. (practice)

Write each sentence. Use the past perfect tense of the verb in parentheses to complete the sentence.

7. The skater ___ a medal by the age of six. (won)
8. She ___ a place on her school's skating team. (want)
9. The speed skater ___ twice before.(try)
10. The coach ___ her another tryout. (offer)
11. She ___ the many expert speed skaters. (train)
12. On her third tryout she ___ the team. (make)

Writing Sentences

Write six sentences about a sport. Use three verbs in the present perfect tense. Use three other verbs in the past perfect tense.

Sample Answers 1. The coach has watched many plays during her career.
7. The skater had won a medal by the age of six.

Irregular Verbs

Thousands of verbs in the English language are *regular verbs.* You add *-ed* to a regular verb to form the past and past participle. Other verbs form the past and past participle in different ways. These verbs are *irregular verbs.*

- Study the chart below. It shows you forms for some irregular verbs.

Verb	**Past**	**Past Participle**
become	became	(have, has) become
begin	began	(have, has) begun
come	came	(have, has) come
drink	drank	(have, has) drunk
ring	rang	(have, has) rung
run	ran	(have, has) run
shrink	shrank	(have, has) shrunk
sink	sank	(have, has) sunk
sing	sang	(have, has) sung
spring	sprang	(have, has) sprung
swim	swam	(have, has) swum
bet	bet	(have, has) bet
burst	burst	(have, has) burst
cut	cut	(have, has) cut
put	put	(have, has) put
set	set	(have, has) set
bring	brought	(have, has) brought
buy	bought	(have, has) bought
catch	caught	(have, has) caught
creep	crept	(have, has) crept
fling	flung	(have, has) flung
lay	laid	(have, has) laid
lead	led	(have, has) led
lend	lent	(have, has) lent
lose	lost	(have, has) lost
say	said	(have, has) said
seek	sought	(have, has) sought
sit	sat	(have, has) sat
sting	stung	(have, has) stung
swing	swung	(have, has) swung
teach	taught	(have, has) taught

Class Exercises

Read each sentence. Use the past tense or the past participle of the verb in parentheses to complete each one. Remember to watch for *have* or *has.*

1. Sonja Henie ___ on the skating scene in the 1920s. (come)
2. Experts have ___ that she made figure skating popular. (say)
3. Other figure skaters, too, have ___ high standards. (set)
4. These skaters ___ patterns, or figures, on the ice. (cut)

Exercises

Write each sentence. Use the past tense or the past participle of the verb in parentheses to complete each one. Remember to watch for *have* or *has.*

1. Ballet has ___ many movements to figure skaters. (lend)
2. Figure skaters have ___ themselves into the air like dancers. (fling)
3. The silver skate blades ___ on the ice. (ring)
4. The skater's partner has ___ the woman expertly. (catch)
5. Errors have ___ into some skaters' routines. (creep)
6. The judges ___ their voting after each performance. (begin)
7. The coach has ___ the skaters as well as possible. (teach)
8. That skating team ___ last year's gold medal. (win)
9. Many people have ___ on the same team this year. (bet)
10. One judge has ___ the opinion of another judge. (seek)
11. The crowd ___ up during the announcements. (sit)
12. An unknown team has ___ the competition so far. (lead)

Write the past and the past participle of each of the following verbs.

13. bring	**16.** burst	**19.** buy	**22.** sing	**25.** swim
14. drink	**17.** swing	**20.** put	**23.** lose	**26.** lay
15. become	**18.** sink	**21.** sting	**24.** spring	**27.** run

Sample Answers 1. Ballet has lent many movements to figure skaters.
13. brought, brought

More Irregular Verbs

Some irregular verbs follow a certain pattern to make their past and past participle forms. Other irregular verbs do not follow a pattern. They must be studied carefully and used often.

Verb	Past	Past Participle
bite	bit	(have, has) bitten
blow	blew	(have, has) blown
break	broke	(have, has) broken
choose	chose	(have, has) chosen
do	did	(have, has) done
draw	drew	(have, has) drawn
drive	drove	(have, has) driven
eat	ate	(have, has) eaten
fall	fell	(have, has) fallen
fly	flew	(have, has) flown
freeze	froze	(have, has) frozen
get	got	(have, has) gotten
give	gave	(have, has) given
go	went	(have, has) gone
grow	grew	(have, has) grown
know	knew	(have, has) known
ride	rode	(have, has) ridden
see	saw	(have, has) seen
shake	shook	(have, has) shaken
speak	spoke	(have, has) spoken
steal	stole	(have, has) stolen
swear	swore	(have, has) sworn
take	took	(have, has) taken
tear	tore	(have, has) torn
throw	threw	(have, has) thrown
wear	wore	(have, has) worn
write	wrote	(have, has) written

One special verb that you see and use often is the verb *be*.

Verb	Past	Past Participle
be	was, were	(have, has) been

Here are some examples of tenses using the past participle of *be*.

Present Perfect Handball *has been* popular for years.
Past Perfect A form of handball *had been* popular in Egypt.

Class Exercises

Read each sentence. Use the past tense or the past participle of the verb in parentheses to complete each one. Remember to watch for *have* or *has*.

1. I have ___ a game of handball in the city recently. (see)
2. The champion ___ the old record for high score in a game. (break)
3. She has ___ the game ball to a fan in the crowd. (throw)
4. The court's walls ___ from the cheers. (shake)

Exercises

Write each sentence. Use the past tense or the past participle of the verb in parentheses to complete each one. Remember to watch for *have* or *has*.

1. Gail has ___ with the director of a handball club. (speak)
2. The director has ___ out her membership card. (write)
3. He also ___ Gail a few visitors' passes. (give)
4. The handball ___ across the room. (fly)
5. She ___ the shot against the front wall. (drive)
6. One of the players has ___ her sweatshirt. (tear)
7. A player has ___ during an exciting play. (fall)
8. The director ___ the foul lines across the handball court. (draw)

Write the past and the past participle of each of the following verbs.

9. eat	11. go	13. blow	15. grow
10. ride	12. freeze	14. know	16. bite

Sample Answers 1. Gail has spoken with the director of a handball club.
9. ate, eaten

Unit Review

VERBS

Write each action verb. Then write whether the verb is **transitive** or **intransitive.** If it is transitive, write the direct object. *pages 42-43*

1. About 400 B.C., Eastern monks developed karate.
2. This form of self-defense improved rapidly.
3. Most karate schools taught a different style.
4. The art of karate emphasizes defense of one's person.
5. Kicks and strikes come only later.
6. Only advanced students learn techniques of offense.

Write each verb. Then write whether it is an **action verb** or a **linking verb.** If it is a linking verb, write whether it is followed by a **predicate noun** or a **predicate adjective.** *pages 44-45*

7. Karate is a combination of science, art, and sport.
8. Karate teachers seem intelligent about health improvement.
9. Exercises were vital for every muscle in the body.
10. The exercises are ancient.
11. Students become masters of the art after several years.
12. The techniques are the results of many centuries.

Write each verb. Write whether it is an **action verb** or a **linking verb.** Then write whether each underlined word in the predicate part is a **predicate noun,** a **direct object,** or an **indirect object.** *pages 46-47*

13. A karate school holds <u>classes</u> several times each week.
14. Most schools give <u>students</u> <u>uniforms</u> of light white cotton.
15. A colored belt is a <u>sign</u> of the student's degree of skill.
16. Before class students practice <u>skills</u> on their own.
17. Advanced students are often <u>instructors</u> to the new students.
18. Soon the teachers clap their <u>hands</u> for the start of class.

Write each verb. Write whether each verb is used as a **linking verb** or as an **action verb.** *pages 48-49*

19. A hang-glider appears in the sky above the hills.
20. Its rider appears weightless beneath the colorful sail.
21. This new sport looks interesting and adventurous.

22. Riders feel the breezes high above the earth.
23. They look down with a true "bird's-eye view."
24. The air tastes fresh during the long and silent flight.

Write the correct tense of the verb in parentheses. Then write whether the form of the verb is in the **present, past,** or **future** tense. *pages 50-51*

25. Today gliding ___ more and more fans of free-flight. (attract)
26. Gliders ___ very popular during the 1970s. (become)
27. Future gliders ___ through better technology. (improve)
28. Now builders ___ lighter aircraft. (construct)
29. Early gliders ___ too much for long flights. (weigh)
30. Today West Germany ___ as the industry's leader. (rank)
31. In the years ahead, new designs ___. (appear)

Write the letter that is next to the correct form of the verb that completes each sentence. *pages 52-53*

32. Here at the dock ___ a large modern sailboat.
    a. is **b.** are
33. There ___ many sails on the boat.
    a. is **b.** are
34. Both sails and engines ___ pleasure boats.
    a. drives **b.** drive
35. Neither sails nor an engine ___ in all situations.
    a. works **b.** work
36. Either the captain or the mates ___ orders to the crew.
    a. gives **b.** give

Write the correct form of the helping verb in parentheses and the participle that goes with it. Then write whether the participle is a **present participle** or **past participle.** *pages 54-55*

37. All scuba divers ___ received careful training. (are/have)
38. They ___ learning more about the sea all the time. (are/have)
39. Their equipment, too, ___ improved since the 1940s. (has/have)
40. All new divers ___ studying safety measures. (is/are)
41. The measures ___ increasing the pleasure of each dive. (are/had)
42. Pools and beaches ___ served as their classrooms. (have/were)

Unit Review

Write each sentence. Use the present progressive tense of the verb in parentheses to complete the sentence. *pages 56-57*

43. Now I ___ about my first scuba-dive in the ocean. (think)
44. That day ___ back to me very clearly. (come)
45. My friends and I ___ our equipment on for the dive. (put)
46. We ___ strangely toward the sea in our long flippers. (walk)
47. The sea ___ us out beyond the bathers on the beach. (carry)
48. I ___ the bare, sandy bottom far behind me. (leave)

Write the past progressive tense of the verb in parentheses to complete each sentence. *pages 56-57*

49. Yesterday we ___ above small hills and dense green seaweed. (swim)
50. Little crabs ___ everywhere on the rocky bed of the sea. (move)
51. My friend ___ to a lobster beneath a huge boulder. (point)
52. A school of minnows ___ in the weak sunlight. (shimmer)
53. Bubbles ___ to the surface from our air tanks. (rise)
54. I ___ for another tankful of air already. (wish)

Write the present perfect tense of the verb in parentheses to complete the sentence. *pages 58-59*

55. The canoe ___ transportation for centuries. (provide)
56. People today ___ long journeys into the wild. (make)
57. Canoes ___ explorers up shallow streams. (carry)
58. Even the horse ___ before the versatile canoe. (fail)
59. Canoe races ___ many large audiences. (entertain)
60. The rapids of a river ___ many expert canoe riders. (challenge)

Write the past perfect tense of the verb in parentheses to complete the sentence. *pages 58-59*

61. After lunch Bill ___ his canoe far up a stream. (paddle)
62. He ___ the river's main course several miles back. (leave)
63. Soon he ___ a dense and silent part of the woods. (enter)
64. Bill ___ along his fishing rod and camping gear. (bring)

65. A huge tree ___ across the stream ahead of his canoe. (fall)
66. He ___ about this good fishing place for years. (know)

Write the past tense or the past participle of the verb in parentheses to complete the sentence. Remember to watch for *have* or *has*. *pages 60-61*

67. The sport of ice hockey ___ in Canada during the 1850s. (begin)
68. Since the 1850s this sport has ___ more fast and rough. (become)
69. Special rules and pads have ___ safety into this fast game. (put)
70. The size of a hockey team has ___ since the early games. (shrink)
71. The original rules ___ nine players on each side. (set)
72. The play ___ more swift with six-player teams. (become)

Write the past and the past participle of each of the following verbs. *pages 60-61*

73. spring **74.** catch **75.** swim **76.** say **77.** lose

Write the past tense or the past participle of the verb in parentheses to complete the sentence. Remember to watch for *have* or *has*. *pages 62-63*

78. Amateur hockey teams have ___ on many new players. (take)
79. These teams have ___ young skaters together for years. (draw)
80. Many beginners later ___ into professional stars. (grow)
81. Some amateurs have ___ to special camps for training. (go)
82. Scouts ___ the top players at the camp. (choose)
83. Unknown players ___ many records. (break)

Write the past and the past participle of each of the following verbs. *pages 62-63*

84. eat **85.** speak **86.** write **87.** fly **88.** choose

Exploring Language

Many ordinary words are used in special ways in sports.

What do *diamond*, a *run*, and a *walk* mean in baseball?
What do a *basket*, a *court*, and a *dribble* mean in basketball?
What do *love*, *doubles*, and *service* mean in tennis?

Can you think of some other words that have special meanings in sports?

The Ring of Brogar, an ancient monument in the Orkney Islands, Great Britain

Myths are not believed in, they are conceived and understood.

GEORGE SANTAYANA
Spanish philosopher and author
(1863-1952)

4

PRONOUNS

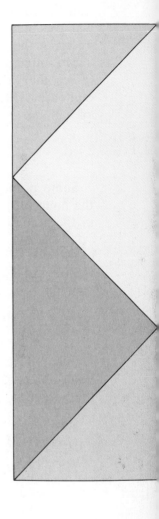

Review: Pronouns

Nouns perform different jobs in sentences. A *noun* is a word that names a person, place, thing, or idea. Nouns can be subjects, and they can be objects of action verbs. Remember, the *subject* of a sentence names whom or what the sentence is about. The *direct object* of a verb receives the action of the verb. It answers the question *whom?* or *what?* after an action verb.

Another group of words can perform these same jobs in a sentence. These words are pronouns. A *pronoun* can be used in place of a noun.

A **pronoun** is a word that can take the place of a noun.

Some pronouns are used as the subjects of sentences. Notice that the noun subjects in the first column are replaced by subject pronouns in the second column.

Rita likes myths.	She especially likes "Atalanta's Race."
Rita and I read Greek myths.	We read the myths aloud.

A **subject pronoun** is used as the subject of a sentence.

Other pronouns are used as the objects of verbs. Notice that the noun objects in the first column are replaced with object pronouns in the second column.

Sara wants *Myths of the Greeks and Romans.*	Mary Renault wrote it.
The librarian sees Sara.	The librarian helps her.

An **object pronoun** is used as the object of a verb or of a preposition.

Here is a chart of subject pronouns and object pronouns.

Subject Pronouns		Object Pronouns	
I	we	me	us
you	you	you	you
it, she, he	they	it, her, him	them

Class Exercises

Read each sentence about the ancient Greek poets. Tell which pronoun you would use in place of the underlined word or words. Tell whether the pronoun you use is a **subject pronoun** or an **object pronoun**.

1. Greek poets developed many myths from old stories.
2. Rita studied the myths for their factual information.
3. Myths about historical events interest Dan.
4. Rita traced the different versions of one myth.

Exercises

Write each sentence about Atalanta. Replace the underlined word or words with a pronoun. Then write whether the pronoun you use is a **subject pronoun** or an **object pronoun**.

1. The myth of Atalanta tells modern readers about a foot race.
2. Atalanta is a beautiful woman and a very fast runner.
3. Many men want Atalanta as their bride.
4. Atalanta refuses the men time after time.
5. Atalanta arranges a race for the fastest runner.
6. Atalanta will marry a man faster than she is.
7. Atalanta passes the runners with graceful ease.
8. Hippomenes especially wants Atalanta as his wife.
9. Hippomenes asks Venus for help in his race against Atalanta.
10. Venus helps Hippomenes with three golden apples and instructions.
11. Hippomenes and Atalanta dash swiftly toward their goal.
12. Hippomenes drops the golden apples along the way.
13. Atalanta wants the golden apples instead of victory in the race.
14. Hippomenes wins the race and takes Atalanta for his bride.

Writing Sentences

Write six sentences about a contest. Each sentence should contain an object of a verb. Then rewrite each sentence replacing the subject with a subject pronoun and the object with an object pronoun.

Sample Answer 1. The myth of Atalanta tells us about a foot race.
object pronoun

Possessive Pronouns

You often use pronouns to replace nouns that are subjects and nouns that are direct objects in sentences. You can use pronouns in place of possessive nouns, too. A *possessive noun* is a noun that names who or what has something.

> A **possessive pronoun** is a pronoun that shows who or what has something. A possessive pronoun may take the place of a possessive noun.

- Read these sentences. Notice the possessive nouns and the possessive pronouns that replace them.

This is Homer's story.	This is his story.
This story is Homer's.	This story is his.

Possessive pronouns have two forms. One form is used before a noun. The other form is used alone. The chart below shows the two forms of possessive pronouns.

Possessive Pronouns

Used Before Nouns		Can Stand Alone	
my	our	mine	ours
your	your	yours	yours
his, hers, its	their	his, hers	theirs

- Read these sentences. Note how the two forms of the possessive pronouns differ in use.

The *Odyssey* is my book.	This book is mine.
The *Odyssey* is your book.	This book is yours.
The *Odyssey* is his book.	This book is his.

Notice that possessive pronouns do not have apostrophes. The pronoun its, for example, shows possession. The word it's, on the other hand, is actually a contraction of it is.

- Read these sentences. Note the meaning of the underlined words.

Its central character is Odysseus. (possession)

It's a poem about the adventures of Odysseus. (contraction of It is)

Class Exercises

Find the possessive noun in each sentence about Odysseus. Tell which possessive pronoun you could use to replace it. Then tell whether the possessive pronoun is **used before a noun** or if it **stands alone.**

1. Odysseus' adventures engage readers of every generation.
2. The poem's title comes from the name Odysseus.
3. Few characters possess a personality like Odysseus'.
4. The Romans renamed him "Ulysses" in the Romans' list of heroes.

Exercises

Write each sentence about the *Odyssey*. Find the possessive noun, and replace it with a possessive pronoun. Then write whether the possessive pronoun is used **before a noun** or if it **stands alone.**

1. The goddess Athena helped the Greeks make the city of Troy the Greeks'.
2. With Athena's help, the Greeks defeated the Trojans.
3. Athena said to Odysseus, "Return to Odysseus' home."
4. The crew told Odysseus, "The crew's ships stand ready."
5. The crew's eagerness for experience was strong.
6. Odysseus saved Odysseus' crew many times.
7. Many exciting adventures were Odysseus'.
8. The Sirens sang to Odysseus from the Sirens' island.
9. The dangerous Sirens sang, "Visit the Sirens' island, Odysseus."
10. Odysseus said to his sailors, "Block your ears but do not block Odysseus'."
11. Odysseus ordered Odysseus' men, "Tie me to the mast of the ship."
12. In this way Odysseus heard the song but escaped the Sirens' trap.

Writing Sentences

Write three pairs of sentences about a character from a book you have read. The first sentence in each pair should have a possessive pronoun used before a noun. The second sentence in each pair should have a possessive pronoun that stands alone.

Sample Answer 1. The goddess Athena helped the Greeks make the city of Troy theirs. stands alone

Pronouns and Antecedents

Pronouns are useful words, but they must be used with care. When using pronouns, be sure you are clear and be sure that your pronouns agree with the nouns they replace.

- Read each of these sentences. Can you tell to whom the word *she* refers?

Arachne competes against Athena. She weaves with great skill.

The sentence is not clear because the word *she* could refer to either Arachne or to Athena. You can't tell who weaves with great skill. A clearer way is to write:

Arachne competes against Athena. Athena weaves with great skill.

Now you know that *she* in the sentence above refers to Athena. Athena weaves with great skill.

The noun or group of words that a pronoun refers to is called its *antecedent*. When using a pronoun, you should be sure that it refers to its antecedent clearly. You should also be sure that it agrees with its antecedent in number (singular or plural) and gender. The *gender* of a noun may be masculine (male), feminine (female), or neuter (referring to things).

- Read each sentence. The pronouns agree with their antecedents.

The myth of Arachne is amusing. I enjoyed it.

The bystanders see Athena. They watch her at the loom.

Arachne and Athena are skillful weavers. They weave beautiful fabrics.

In the first pair of sentences *it* agrees with *The myth of Arachne*. In the second pair of sentences *They* agrees with *The bystanders* and *her* agrees with *Athena*. In the third pair of sentences *They* agrees with *Arachne and Athena*.

Class Exercises

Read each pair of sentences. Tell which pronoun belongs in each blank. Then tell the antecedent for each pronoun.

1. The maiden Arachne lives in Lydia. ___ is a country in Asia.

2. Arachne is a skillful weaver. ___ boasts about her weaving.

3. People watch Arachne. They tell her, "Pallas Athena must have taught ___."
4. Arachne denies the people's comments. She challenges ___ remarks.
5. The listeners are frightened by Arachne's words. ___ caution her against such comments.
6. Suddenly Athena appears. ___ speaks with Arachne.

Exercises

Write the second sentence of each pair, using the correct pronoun for each blank. Then write the antecedent for each pronoun.

1. Athena and Arachne enter into a contest. The people watch ___ .
2. Athena weaves pictures of a story about the god Poseidon. In her story, ___ loses a contest to her.
3. The people watch Athena's pictures. They see ___ take shape on her cloth.
4. Arachne weaves a story about the god Zeus. ___ comes alive and seems to speak.
5. The contest continues for many hours. No one knows which woman will win ___ .
6. At the end of the contest, Athena is the winner. ___ fabric shines like a rainbow.
7. However, Athena admires Arachne's skill. She says to Arachne, "___ must weave forever."
8. Arachne drinks a magical potion. ___ turns her into a spider.
9. Arachne will weave forever. ___ will weave webs in old houses.
10. Arachne's descendents are all spiders. ___ get their scientific name, Arachnids, from Arachne.

Writing Sentences

Think of an old tale or legend you know. Write three pairs of sentences about a character in it. The second sentence in each pair should have a pronoun. Be sure your antecedents are clear.

Sample Answer 1. The people watch them. Athena and Arachne

Pronouns as Objects of Prepositions

Some words in our language work in sentences as relating and connecting words. Prepositions are words of this type.

- Read these sentences.

  The knights bring Prince Arthur to Merlin.
  Merlin takes Arthur from the knights.

In the first sentence the preposition *to* connects *Prince Arthur* with *Merlin* and shows the relationship between them. In the second sentence the preposition *from* connects *Arthur* with *the knights* and shows the relationship between them.

> A **preposition** is a word that relates a noun or pronoun to another word.

- Here are some of the most frequently used prepositions.

about	behind	during	of	to
above	below	for	on	toward
across	beside	from	out	under
after	between	in	outside	until
at	by	inside	over	up
before	down	into	through	with

- Look at the underlined words in the following sentences.

  Arthur goes with him.
  King Uther speaks to them.

Each group of underlined words begins with a preposition and ends with a pronoun. The pronoun is the *object of the preposition*. You use an object pronoun for the object of a preposition.

- Here is a list of object pronouns. Remember to use an object pronoun after a preposition.

Object Pronouns: me you him her it us you them

Class Exercises

Read each pair of sentences. Tell which pronoun in parentheses correctly completes the second sentence.

1. The countryside is vast. Merlin takes Arthur across ___ . (she, it)
2. Arthur meets his foster mother. He goes to ___ . (her, she)
3. Later King Uther becomes ill. Merlin appears before ___ . (him, he)
4. Merlin speaks to the king. He asks, "Shall Arthur rule the land and all that belongs to ___ ?" (it, he)
5. The king replies. He wants Arthur to rule after ___ . (him, he)

Exercises

Write the second sentence in each pair. Use the correct pronoun in parentheses.

1. The king and queen speak to Merlin. They say, "Please protect Arthur for ___ ." (us, we)
2. Merlin agrees. He takes care of Arthur for ___ . (them, they)
3. Merlin calls together the nobles. They meet with ___ . (he, him)
4. Merlin and the nobles ride to a churchyard. They see a large stone with a sword stuck in ___ . (she, it)
5. The nobles look at the stone. However, they cannot remove the sword from ___ . (it, he)
6. One afternoon Arthur's brother, Sir Kay, speaks to Arthur. He asks, "Would you get my sword at home for ___ ?" (I, me)
7. Arthur answers. He says, "I'll bring your sword to ___ ." (you, he)
8. Instead Arthur removes the sword from the large stone. Arthur gives it to ___ . (him, he)
9. Later Sir Kay reports to his father. He says, "Arthur brought this sword to ___ ." (me, I)

Writing Sentences

Write six sentences about a legend. Use a preposition in each sentence. Use an object pronoun as the object of each preposition.

Sample Answer 1. They say, "Please protect Arthur for us."

Indefinite Pronouns

Most pronouns refer to a specific noun or pronoun antecedent. *Indefinite pronouns* do not. They refer to certain people or things but do not name them.

- Read each sentence.

Everyone reads "Icarus and Daedalus." Many like the myth.

The words *everyone* and *many* are indefinite pronouns. They refer to certain individuals without definitely naming who they are.

An **indefinite pronoun** is a pronoun that does not refer to a particular person, place, or thing.

Most indefinite pronouns are singular. When they are the subjects of sentences, the verbs must agree with these singular pronouns.

Singular Indefinite Pronouns

another	either	much	no one	somebody
anybody	everybody	neither	nothing	someone
anyone	everyone	nobody	one	something
each	everything			

Everyone discusses the plot.   Someone dislikes the ending.

Other indefinite pronouns are plural. When they are the subjects of sentences, the verbs must agree with these plural pronouns.

Plural Indefinite Pronouns

both	few	many	several	others

Both talk about King Minos.   Few like this character.

Possessive pronouns also must agree with their antecedents.

He has his own opinion of the story. (masculine, singular)

She has her own opinion of the story. (feminine, singular)

They discuss their opinions with friends. (plural)

However, the singular indefinite pronouns can cause problems. When possible, try to avoid awkward constructions like this one.

Each has his or her own opinion.

One solution is to use a plural indefinite pronoun instead.

Both have their own opinions.

Class Exercises

Read each sentence. Find the indefinite pronoun. Tell which word in parentheses correctly completes the sentence.

1. Many enjoy ___ study of the myth of Daedalus and Icarus. (his, their)
2. Both ___ on the island of Crete. (live, lives)
3. Many ___ Daedalus a symbol of the artist. (calls, call)
4. Few ___ Daedalus' clever inventions. (matches, match)
5. Several model ___ careers in art on Daedalus. (her, their)

Exercises

Write each sentence using the correct word in parentheses.

1. Many devote ___ works of art to Crete's great cities. (his, their)
2. Everything ___ well at first for Daedalus and his son. (go, goes)
3. Everyone ___ Daedalus' ideas for the huge palace. (praises, praise)
4. No one ___ more pleased than King Minos. (are, is)
5. Few know ___ craft as well as Daedalus. (his, their)
6. Many ___ the rest of this story of escape. (knows, know)
7. Nobody ___ Daedalus and Icarus of their plot. (suspects, suspect)
8. Both ___ an escape across the Sea of Crete. (plans, plan)
9. Something ___ shape in Daedalus' skilled hands. (take, takes)
10. Each ___ on a pair of waxy, feathery wings. (puts, put)
11. Several ___ Daedalus and Icarus flying in the sky. (sees, see)
12. Others ___ Icarus' flight toward the sun. (watches, watch)

Writing Sentences

Write six sentences about a creative person you know. Describe the person as if you were beginning a story. Show how this person is creative. In each sentence use an indefinite pronoun from this lesson. You might begin in this way:

"Few know that my friend ___ is a very creative person.

Sample Answer 1. Many devote their works of art to Crete's great cities.

Reflexive and Intensive Pronouns

Some pronouns reflect the action of the verb back to the subject. These pronouns are called *reflexive pronouns.*

- Compare these sentences. Notice how the reflexive pronoun in the second sentence reflects the action of the verb back to the subject and clarifies the meaning.

The girl bought the girl the book.

The girl bought herself the book.

Herself is a *reflexive pronoun.* In the first sentence it is unclear whether there are *two girls* or *one girl.* The meaning is clear in the second sentence.

A **reflexive pronoun** points the action of the verb back to the subject.

- Look at this chart of reflexive pronouns.

Singular	Plural
myself	ourselves
yourself	yourselves
himself, herself, itself	themselves

Sometimes *hisself* is mistakenly used for *himself* and *theirselves* for *themselves.* There are no such words as *hisself* and *theirselves.*

The reflexive pronouns in the chart above may also be used to intensify a statement. When they are used for that purpose, they are called *intensive pronouns.*

An **intensive pronoun** is a pronoun that adds emphasis to a noun or pronoun already named.

George himself bought *Paul Bunyan and His Great Blue Ox.*

He himself paid for the book.

Reflexive and intensive pronouns have special uses. They should never be used where a subject pronoun or an object pronoun belongs.

Correct	Incorrect
Anita and I read the legend.	Anita and myself read the legend.
The legend pleased me more.	The legend pleased myself more.

Class Exercises

Read each sentence. Tell which pronoun you would use to complete the sentence. Give your reasons.

1. I bought ___ a book about Paul Bunyan. (me, myself)
2. The book ___ is a collector's item. (it, itself)
3. Several friends and ___ find the legends amusing. (I, myself)
4. Paul Bunyan ___ has a good sense of humor. (him, himself)
5. The imaginative legends provide ___ with much laughter. (us, ourselves)
6. Perhaps lumberjacks ___ began the tales. (them, themselves)

Exercises

Write each sentence using the correct pronoun in parentheses to complete the sentence.

1. ___ call Paul Bunyan's adventures "tall tales." (We, Ourselves)
2. The students bought ___ a copy of the tales. (them, themselves)
3. In the tales Bunyan forms much of America ___ . (it, itself)
4. ___ digs Washington's Puget Sound for the loggers. (He, Himself)
5. The smaller lumberjacks thank ___ for his help. (him, himself)
6. Now the logs ___ float easily to the mills. (them, themselves)
7. The giant blue ox Babe makes ___ Bunyan's friend. (it, itself)
8. Bunyan gives ___ many gifts during their friendship. (it, itself)
9. The Great Lakes ___ are Babe's own drinking water. (them, themselves)
10. ___ may doubt the incredible weight of Babe's shoes. (You, Yourself)
11. Bunyan makes ___ with the iron from an entire mine. (them, themselves)
12. Such tall tales interest my friends and ___ . (me, myself)

Writing Sentences

Write six sentences about a book or a movie hero or heroine. Use a different reflexive pronoun in each sentence.

Sample Answer 1. We call Paul Bunyan's adventures "tall tales."

Interrogative Pronouns

Pronouns can be used to begin interrogative sentences to ask questions. A pronoun used to introduce an interrogative sentence is called an *interrogative pronoun.*

An **interrogative pronoun** is a pronoun used to introduce an interrogative sentence.

- Read these sentences. Notice the underlined interrogative pronouns.

Who creates beautiful things?

For whom does Hephaestos make the staff?

What is Pandora's curiosity about?

Whom does Zeus call?

Whose son is Hephaestos?

Which gift does Pandora receive?

The interrogative pronouns *who* and *whom* have special uses. Both *who* and *whom* refer to people, but they have different uses in sentences. Use *who* when the interrogative pronoun is the subject of the sentence. Use *whom* when the interrogative pronoun is the object of the verb or of a preposition.

Who gives Pandora her name? (subject)

Whom does Zeus dislike? (object)

To whom does Zeus give Pandora? (object of preposition)

The interrogative pronouns *which*, *what*, and *whose* also have special uses. Use *which* and *what* to refer to things. Use *whose* to indicate possession.

Some gifts are for Pandora. Which are they?

Athena makes Pandora a robe. What does Hephaestos make her?

The jar is in Pandora's house. Whose is it?

Notice *whose* in the sentence above. *Whose* is an interrogative pronoun that shows someone possesses something. When writing, be careful that you do not confuse *whose* with *who's*. Remember, *who's* is the contraction of *who is*. Contractions are used in informal writing.

- Study these examples.

Who's reading the myth? (Contraction of Who is)

Whose is it? (Interrogative pronoun showing possession)

Class Exercises

Tell which word in parentheses correctly completes each sentence.

1. ___ myths tell about a quest for a great treasure? (Who, Which)
2. To ___ do you read those myths? (whom, who)
3. ___ other things may be the object of a quest? (What, Whom)
4. ___ is the hero in the first story? (Who, Which)
5. ___ advice usually helps the person on the quest? (Who's, Whose)

Exercises

Write the second sentence of each pair below using the correct word in parentheses to complete the sentence.

1. Jason is a famous Greek hero. ___ Jason? (Whose, Who's)
2. His quest is for the Golden Fleece. ___ is the Golden Fleece? (What, Whom)
3. Jason's father Aeson is the king until Pelias removes him. ___ does Pelias remove from the throne? (Who, Whom)
4. Aeson sends young Jason to the teacher called Chiron. ___ house is Chiron's? (Which, Who's)
5. When Jason grows up, he wants Pelias' throne. ___ throne does Jason want? (Whom, Whose)
6. Pelias promises Jason the throne if Jason brings him the Golden Fleece. ___ is Pelias' demand? (Whose, What)
7. Jason sails on the *Argo* with a group of brave friends. ___ ship do the Argonauts take? (Who's, Which)
8. Before he obtains the fleece, Jason accomplishes several great tasks. ___ helps Jason accomplish them? (Who, Whom)
9. The princess Medea advises Jason. To ___ does Medea give advice? (who, whom)

Writing Sentences

Write six questions that you would like answered about a legendary or mythological character. Begin each sentence with an interrogative pronoun.

Sample Answer 1. Who's Jason?

Unit Review

PRONOUNS

Read each sentence about the city of Troy. Write a pronoun to replace the underlined word or words. Then write whether the pronoun you use is a **subject pronoun** or an **object pronoun**. *pages 70-71*

1. Heinrich Schliemann discovered <u>the city</u> during the 1870s.
2. <u>The city</u> fascinated Heinrich Schliemann.
3. <u>Heinrich Schliemann</u> received credit for its discovery.
4. The discovery pleased <u>Schliemann</u> very much.

Read each sentence about the Trojans' city. Find the possessive noun, and write a possessive pronoun to replace it. Then write whether the possessive pronoun is used **before a noun** or if it **stands alone**. *pages 72-73*

5. The city of Troy was the Trojans'.
6. Then Greece sent Greece's ships to the city.
7. The Trojans fought well with help from the Trojans' allies.
8. Odysseus helped to defeat Troy with Odysseus' Trojan horse.

Write the correct pronoun for each blank. Then write the antecedent for each pronoun. *pages 74-75*

9. Athens was a naval power. ___ usually controlled the sea.
10. Spartan soldiers were very disciplined. Sparta trained ___ well.
11. Athens and Sparta competed for Greece. ___ fought for years.
12. Alexander the Great came to power. ___ conquered Greece.

Write the correct pronoun in parentheses to complete each sentence with a blank. *pages 76-77*

13. The Amazons support the Trojans. These women fight beside ___ in the Trojan War. (them, they)
14. The Amazons have a queen. Homer writes about ___ . (she, her)
15. My friend bought this book about the Trojan War for ___ . (us, we)
16. She showed the story about the Amazons to ___ . (I, me)

Write the correct word in parentheses to complete each sentence. *pages 78-79*

17. Many ___ something about the hero Hercules. (know, knows)

18. Several have ___ own opinions about Hercules' deeds. (his, their)
19. Others ___ Hercules in poetry and paintings. (portrays, portray)
20. Nobody ___ victories like Hercules. (achieves, achieve)

Write the letter next to the pronoun that correctly completes each sentence. *pages 80-81*

21. I ___ read a legend about John Henry. (a) me (b) myself
22. Henry ___ worked on West Virginia's railroads. (a) him (b) himself
23. He entered ___ into a contest with a machine. (a) him (b) himself
24. The machine gave ___ a workout. (a) himself (b) him

Write the correct word in parentheses to complete each sentence with a blank. *pages 82-83*

25. The Egyptians' legends tell about the Nile and its animals. ___ animal is the most important? (Who's, Which)
26. Thoth is the Egyptians' birdlike patron of writers and of libraries. ___ does Thoth serve? (Whom, Who)
27. The winged god Osiris is the son of a goddess. ___ son is Osiris? (Who's, Whose)
28. The Egyptians expected help from the gods and goddesses. To ___ did they give aid? (who, whom)

Exploring Language

Sometimes you use figures of speech in your writing or in your speech. A *figure of speech* uses words in an unusual way to create specific, vivid images. One kind of figure of speech is a simile. A *simile* is a comparison of two different things using the words *like* or *as*. Read each simile below. Then see if you can think of your own similes.

1. The runner runs as fast as Hermes. (Greek god— messenger for the gods)
2. The teacher is as wise as Athena. (Greek goddess of wisdom)
3. My cousin has a large appetite like Paul Bunyan. (logger in folklore)

Planet Earth, photographed from Skylab

There is a single light of science, and to brighten it anywhere is to brighten it everywhere.

ISAAC ASIMOV
American writer
(1920-)

5

ADJECTIVES

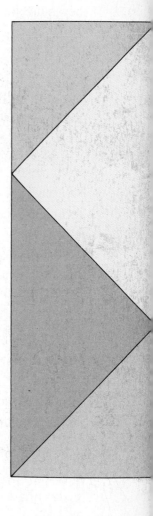

Review: Adjectives

One way to make your writing or speech livelier is to use words that describe nouns or pronouns. These words are called *adjectives*, and they help you tell more about the nouns or pronouns you are using.

An **adjective** is a word that modifies, or describes, a noun or pronoun.

One or more adjectives often appear just before the noun they describe. These adjectives may occur in the subject part or in the predicate part of a sentence.

- Look at the adjectives in the sentences below.

Thorough present-day preparations protect astronauts during their journeys.

Technicians prepare for sudden emergencies.

In the first sentence the adjectives *Thorough* and *present-day* appear before the noun *preparations* in the subject part of the sentence. In the second sentence the adjective *sudden* appears before the noun *emergencies* in the predicate part of the sentence.

Sometimes an adjective follows a linking verb. Although that adjective is in the predicate part of that sentence, it describes the noun or pronoun that is the subject of the sentence. Some linking verbs are *seem, appear,* and *be.*

- Notice the adjectives in the sentences below.

The engineers are diligent.

They seem cautious about the spacecraft.

In the first sentence the adjective *diligent* follows the linking verb *are* and describes the subject noun *engineers* in the subject part. In the second sentence the adjective *cautious* follows the linking verb *seem* and describes the subject pronoun *They* in the subject part.

An adjective in the predicate part of a sentence that describes the subject noun or pronoun is a predicate adjective.

A **predicate adjective** is an adjective that follows a linking verb. It modifies, or describes, the subject by telling what it is like.

Class Exercises

Read each sentence. Find the adjectives in each sentence. Then tell which noun each adjective describes.

1. Serious engineers planned the successful space flights.
2. Numerous scientists played great parts in the program.
3. Huge machines and many plans developed during the 1950s.
4. Ideas were plentiful for the new space program.
5. A seven-stage plan evolved by the early 1960s.

Exercises

Write each sentence. Draw one line under each adjective. Draw two lines under the noun or pronoun each adjective describes. If a linking verb connects the subject and adjective, circle the predicate adjective.

1. The small *Sputnik I* blasted into orbit from Russia on October 4, 1957.
2. The launch began the modern Space Age.
3. Enormous problems challenged imaginative workers.
4. Yuri A. Gagarin of Russia made the first flight into space on April 12, 1961.
5. He seemed heroic to all people.
6. Then Alan Shepard and John Glenn made solo flights into space.
7. Pride was high in the two countries.
8. America and Russia launched twelve capsules in two years.
9. The spacecraft were full of scientific equipment.
10. Astronauts and engineers discussed possible improvements.
11. Two-astronaut flights became frequent in America and Russia.
12. Russia sent brave women into space.

Writing Sentences

Imagine that you are making one of the first walks in space. Write six sentences about what you see, do, and feel. Use one of the words below as an adjective in each sentence.

light   slow   dark   bright   dull   distant   first   great

Sample Answer 1. The small *Sputnik 1* blasted into orbit from Russia on October 4, 1957.

Articles

An adjective is a word that modifies, or describes, a noun or pronoun. *A, an,* and *the* are three very common words that are a special kind of adjective. *A, an,* and *the* are called *articles*.

A and *an* are most often used with a noun that has not been mentioned before. *A* and *an* are called *indefinite articles* because they refer to one of a general group of people, places, things, or ideas. *The* is usually used with a noun that has been mentioned before. *The* is called a *definite article* because it identifies a specific person, place, thing, or idea.

- Look at the words below. Which use *a*, and which use *an*?

  a pilot a new spacecraft an astronaut an unusual outfit

Notice that you use *a* before words beginning with a consonant sound, and these words may be nouns or adjectives. You use *an* before words beginning with a vowel sound, and these words may be nouns or adjectives.

- Now read these words.

  a unit a uniform an hour an honor

Notice that *unit* and *uniform* begin with a vowel letter. However, these nouns take *a* because they begin with a consonant *sound*. Now look again at *hour* and *honor*. These words begin with a consonant letter. However, they take *an* because they begin with a vowel *sound*.

Class Exercises

Tell which **indefinite article** belongs before each word or group of words.

1. hurricane
2. expedition
3. typical day
4. surface
5. unusual time
6. universe
7. honest effort
8. activity

Exercises

Write each word or group of words with the **indefinite article** that belongs before it.

1. satellite
2. electrical storm
3. transmitter
4. vehicle
5. usual night
6. accident
7. unexplored part
8. unknown rock
9. instrument
10. high altitude
11. experiment
12. hourly report

Sample Answer 1. a satellite

Proper Adjectives

An adjective formed from a proper noun is called a *proper adjective.* A proper adjective is capitalized.

- Read the words below. Notice which words are capitalized.

San Francisco climate	French toast	Scottish wool
Italian food	Californian oranges	Maine lobster

Sometimes an adjective formed from a proper noun has the same spelling as the noun, for example, *San Francisco climate*. Sometimes, though, the adjective and the noun are spelled differently, for example, *On my vacation in Italy, I ate only Italian food.*

When you form adjectives from the names of places, be sure to check the spelling in a dictionary. The adjectives and the nouns may be spelled differently.

Class Exercises

Read the following list of words. Tell which words you would capitalize.

1. african sculptures
2. woven threads
3. arizona desert
4. irish lace
5. japanese camera
6. delicate cloth

Exercises

Write the following list of words. Capitalize where necessary.

1. mexican tiles
2. car factory
3. german cars
4. attractive woman
5. kansas wheat
6. new car
7. french perfume
8. american flag
9. english countryside
10. pretty cup
11. chinese silk
12. hawaiian pineapple
13. greek food
14. british writer
15. woman astronaut
16. korean vase
17. indian fabric
18. new england winter

Writing Sentences

Imagine that you are touring the United States. Write six sentences about what you see. Use a proper adjective in each sentence. Remember to use the dictionary for help with spelling.

Sample Answer 1. Mexican tiles

Comparative and Superlative Adjectives

You know that adjectives can *describe* nouns or pronouns. Adjectives can also *compare* two or more nouns or pronouns.

The **comparative form** of an adjective compares two people or things. You often add **-er** to an adjective to form the comparative.

The **superlative form** of an adjective compares more than two people or things. You often add **-est** to an adjective to form the superlative.

- Look at the chart below. Notice the three forms of an adjective.

Adjective	Comparative	Superlative
short	short**er**	short**est**
warm	warm**er**	warm**est**
cold	cold**er**	cold**est**

Adjective: A capsule made long trips. (one thing — a capsule)

Comparative: Apollo made a longer trip than Gemini. (two things– Apollo flight and Gemini flight)

Superlative: A space probe makes the longest trip of all. (more than two things — a space probe and all other spacecraft)

- Notice that some adjectives do not add *-er* or *-est*. These adjectives have special comparative and superlative forms.

Adjective	Comparative	Superlative
good / well	better	best
bad	worse	worst
many / much	more	most

Adjective: The weather is bad for a launch today.

Comparative: Today is worse than yesterday.

Superlative: Tomorrow will be the worst day of all.

Class Exercises

Read each sentence. Tell which form of the adjective in parentheses completes each sentence correctly.

1. The Gemini astronauts practiced ___ skills in orbit than the Mercury astronauts. (many, more, most)
2. Each crew faced ___ challenges than the last one. (great, greater, greatest)
3. They learned the ___ of all ways to live in space. (good, better, best)
4. The ___ problems of all concerned new equipment. (bad, worse, worst)

Exercises

Write each sentence using the correct form of the adjective in parentheses.

1. The Gemini flight was a ___ flight to the moon than the one before it. (close, closer, closest)
2. At first the walk in space seemed the ___ problem of all for the astronauts. (small, smaller, smallest)
3. Astronauts soon made ___ sudden motions in zero gravity than before. (few, fewer, fewest)
4. American and Russian space walks provided the ___ information of all about movement outside a spacecraft. (much, more, most)
5. Perhaps Gemini's ___ task of all was the rendezvous in orbit. (hard, harder, hardest)
6. *Gemini 6* and *Gemini 7* made the ___ meeting of all the space flights. (close, closer, closest)
7. These meetings were practices for ___ missions to the moon. (late, later, latest)
8. Docking activity required the ___ training of all. (good, better, best)
9. Gemini capsules docked with the ___ *Agena* rockets. (small, smaller, smallest)
10. By 1967 Gemini crews had solved even the ___ of all problems. (bad, worse, worst)

Sample Answer 1. The Gemini flight was a closer flight to the moon than the one before it.

More Comparative and Superlative Adjectives

You know that the *comparative form* of an adjective compares two people or things. You often add *-er* to an adjective to form the comparative. You also know that the *superlative form* of an adjective compares more than two people or things. You often add *-est* to form the superlative. Some comparative and superlative forms of adjectives, however, do not have an *-er* or *-est* ending. Use **more** and **most**, or **less** and **least**, to form the comparatives and superlatives of these adjectives.

• Look at the chart below. Notice the three forms of each adjective.

Adjective	**Comparative**	**Superlative**
impressive	more impressive	most impressive
curious	less curious	least curious

Adjective: The early Apollo missions were *impressive* events. (one thing — early Apollo missions)

Comparative: Apollo's orbit of the moon was *more impressive* than Gemini flights. (two things — orbit of the moon and Gemini flights)

Superlative: The moon landing was the *most impressive* event of the decade. (more than two things — moon landing and all other events)

Adjective: The public was *curious* about the moon landing.

Comparative: The public was *less curious* about the orbit around the earth than about the landing on the moon.

Superlative: The public was the *least curious* about the first artificial satellite of all the spacecraft.

Generally a one-syllable adjective uses *-er* or *-est*. An adjective of three or more syllables uses *more* and *most* or *less* and *least*. Adjectives with two syllables vary. Some two-syllable adjectives take the *-er* or *-est* ending; others take the words *more* and *most* or *less* and *least*.

Do not use *more* or *most* and *less* or *least* before adjectives that already have a comparative (*-er*) or superlative (*-est*) ending.

Class Exercises

Tell which word in parentheses correctly completes each sentence.

1. Apollo was the ___ adventurous stage of the whole program. (more, most)
2. Safety was ___ important than the date of the moon landing. (more, most)
3. Tests were sometimes ___ successful than the early ones. (less, least)
4. The ___ unfortunate accident of all occurred in 1967. (more, most)
5. Three of the ___ famous astronauts lost their lives during a fire in the Apollo test capsule. (more, most)

Exercises

Write each sentence. Complete each sentence with the correct word in parentheses.

1. The accident soon made all program workers ___ careful than before. (more, most)
2. The cause of the fire was the ___ vital of all questions. (more, most)
3. Faulty electric wires were ___ responsible for the fire than the ship's environment of pure oxygen. (less, least)
4. Engineers added gases ___ dangerous than pure oxygen to the new ship's air supply. (less, least)
5. The new gases were the ___ important change of all in the program. (more, most)
6. People became ___ confident than before about the improved spacecraft. (more, most)
7. Even the ___ curious people of all wanted news about the Apollo mission's progress. (less, least)
8. The ___ impressive Apollo flight of all began in 1968. (more, most)
9. The second Apollo flight around the moon was the ___ positive of all early tests. (more, most)
10. Everyone grew ___ doubtful than before of a moon landing by 1970. (less, least)

Sample Answer 1. The accident soon made all program workers more careful than before.

Demonstrative Adjectives and Pronouns

The words *this, that, these*, and *those* are *demonstrative words* that "demonstrate," or point out, people, places, or things. *This* and *these* point out people or things near to you, and *that* and *those* point out things or people at a distance from you. *This* and *that* describe singular nouns, and *these* and *those* describe plural nouns.

This, that, these, and *those* are demonstrative adjectives when they describe nouns.

• Read these sentences.

This rock is heavy.
It shines like that rock.
The crew brought back these samples.
Those astronauts knew their work.

The underlined words in the sentences above are demonstrative adjectives. *Demonstrative adjectives* point out something and they describe nouns by answering the questions *Which one*? or *Which ones*?

Do not use *here* or *there* when using a demonstrative adjective.

Correct: This sample is interesting.
Incorrect: This here sample is interesting.

Correct: Who made that voyage?
Incorrect: Who made that there voyage?

Do not use the object pronoun *them* in place of the demonstrative adjective *those*.

Correct: Apollo astronauts wore those space suits.
Incorrect: Apollo astronauts wore them space suits.

Correct: Those first women in space were national heroes.
Incorrect: Them first women in space were national heroes.

The words *this, that, these*, and *those* are demonstrative pronouns when they take the place of nouns.

• Read these sentences.

This is a moon rock.
That is a small meteor.
These are very precious stones.
Those are glass beads in the stones.

The underlined words in the sentences above are demonstrative pronouns. *Demonstrative pronouns* point out something and they take the place of nouns.

Class Exercises

Read each sentence. Use the correct word or word in parentheses to complete each sentence.

1. ___ stage of the space program completes decades of hard work. (This, These)
2. ___ landing was the chief goal of the 1960s. (That, Those)
3. ___ was the great task for Neil Armstrong's crew. (That, Those)
4. The launch of *Apollo 11* symbolized many things to ___ on the ground. (them, those)
5. ___ flight began on the morning of July 16, 1969. (That, Those)

Exercises

Write each sentence using the word or words in parentheses that correctly completes each sentence.

1. ___ astronauts tested every system while in earth orbit. (These here, These)
2. ___ was necessary before the beginning of the trip to the moon. (This, These)
3. *Apollo 11* left the earth orbit with ___ systems in perfect readiness. (them, those)
4. The crew and equipment traveled ___ distance in about two days. (that, those)
5. *Apollo 8* and *Apollo 10* had done ___ already without a landing. (that, those)
6. The July twentieth moon landing completed ___ years of hard work. (that, those)
7. On the moon's surface Neil Armstrong said, " ___ is one small step for a man, one giant leap for mankind." (That, Those)
8. ___ hours on the barren moon were full of activity. (Them, Those)
9. Armstrong and Aldrin collected ___ pounds of samples. (these here, these)
10. ___ samples still undergo new tests today. (Those, Them)

Sample Answer 1. These astronauts tested every system while in earth orbit.

Unit Review

ADJECTIVES

Write each adjective and the noun or pronoun it describes in each sentence below. If a linking verb connects the subject and adjective, circle the predicate adjective. *pages 88-89*

1. *Skylab* began its important work after the last moon mission.
2. Americans launched the large laboratory into space in 1973.
3. Three astronauts spent many days at different projects.
4. The pilots seemed comfortable.
5. *Skylab* was similar to *Salyut* of 1971.

Write each word or group of words with the indefinite article that belongs before it. *page 90*

6. explorer	**8.** honor	**10.** new land	**12.** ancient city
7. continent	**9.** brave woman	**11.** useful tool	**13.** unusual response

Write the following list of words. Capitalize where necessary. *page 91*

14. canadian territory	**18.** portuguese sailors
15. continental breakfast	**19.** italian leather
16. new england chowder	**20.** chinese porcelain
17. florida oranges	**21.** japanese trees

Write the form of the adjective in parentheses that completes each sentence. *pages 92-93*

22. Pictures from telescopes in space are ___ than those taken through telescopes on earth. (clear, clearer, clearest)
23. The ___ pictures of all reveal new stars in deep space. (sharp, sharper, sharpest)
24. Space contains ___ gas than our earth's atmosphere. (little, less, least)
25. Space scientists gather the ___ information of all while in orbit. (much, more, most)

Write the letter next to the word that correctly completes each sentence. *pages 94-95*

26. After decades of effort the ___ interesting work of all remains.
    a. more b. most

27. Life in space seems ___ fantastic now than before.
   a. less   b. least
28. Even the ___ of all the restrictions of gravity disappear in orbit.
   a. less   b. least
29. The ___ enormous structures in history may be assembled in a weightless environment.
   a. more   b. most

Write each sentence using the word or words in parentheses that correctly complete each sentence. *pages 96-97*

30. ___ canals on Mars are larger canyons than any on Earth. (Them, Those)
31. Tomorrow's explorers will not find much shelter on ___ worlds. (this, these)
32. ___ are simply too near or too far from the sun. (That, Those)
33. World technology has not yet reached ___ stage of development. (that, those)
34. ___ awaits today's inventors as an important task. (This, These)

Careers

Hundreds of kinds of jobs contribute to each advance in space exploration today. Careers as astronauts may be few, but many other careers are available. Many kinds of scientists, such as biologists, geologists, and chemists, are at work in space exploration. Engineers of all kinds work in the space programs also. Physical and mechanical engineers design, develop, and launch new ships. Other engineers improve ground systems. Technicians in space exploration build, maintain, and repair the tools needed for space flight.

Business people also find a rewarding place in today's space age.

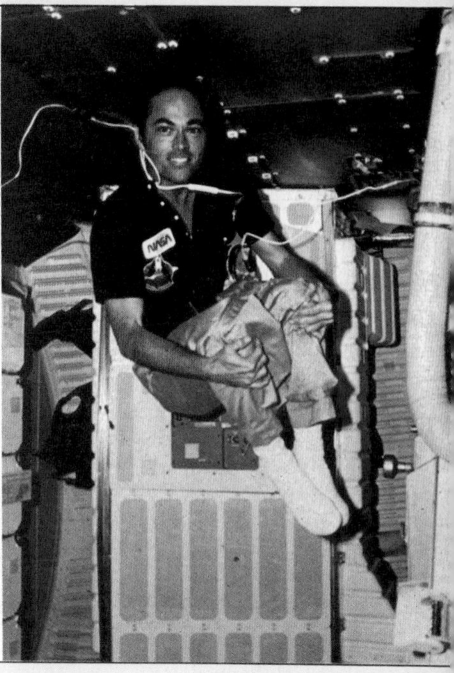

San Francisco's Bay Bridge

We shape our buildings, thereafter they shape us.

SIR WINSTON CHURCHILL
British statesman,
former Prime Minister (1874-1965)

6

ADVERBS

Review: Adverbs

You know that a word that describes a noun or a pronoun is called an adjective. An *adverb* is another kind of word that describes. It often describes an action verb. Remember, an *action verb* names an action.

The Incan Indians worked carefully on their buildings.

In this sentence the adverb *carefully* describes the verb *worked.* Sometimes an adverb describes another adverb or an adjective.

The Incas left their ancient cities quite suddenly.

Machu Picchu is a very large Incan city in the Andes Mountains.

In the first sentence the adverb *suddenly* describes the verb *left* and the adverb *quite* describes the adverb *suddenly.* In the second sentence the adverb *very* describes the adjective *large.*

An **adverb** is a word that modifies, or describes, a verb, an adjective, or another adverb.

An adverb may describe *how* or *in what manner* the action is done. It may describe *when* or *how often* the action is done. Also, it may describe *where* or *in what direction* the action is done.

Machu Picchu sits mysteriously in the Andes Mountains. (How?)

Many scientists now explore this city. (When?)

Scientists dig there for facts about the ancient Incans. (Where?)

Common Adverbs

How? (In what manner?)		**When?** (How often?)		**Where?** (In what direction?)	
completely	fast	afterward	once	away	close
carefully	hard	frequently	daily	there	backward
patiently	alike	sometimes	next	here	together
slowly	loudly	finally	later	far	everywhere

When an adverb describes another adverb or an adjective, it generally appears just before the word it describes.

The Incans built their great temples very carefully.

The air in their cities is too thin for many people.

When an adverb describes a verb, it may appear in a variety of positions.

Scientists patiently study the buildings for information.
Scientists study the buildings patiently for information.
Patiently, scientists study the buildings for information.

Class Exercises

Find each adverb. Name the word it describes. Then tell whether the word described is an **action verb**, an **adverb**, or an **adjective**. Some sentences have more than one adverb.

1. Hiram Bingham searched diligently for the lost Incan cities.
2. Bingham and his aides looked everywhere in western South America.
3. They traveled through extremely thick jungles.
4. They studied the legends very carefully for clues.

Exercises

Write each adverb. Then write the word it describes. Write whether the word described is an **action verb**, an **adverb**, or an **adjective**.

1. Bingham and his searchers climbed up the extremely steep mountainsides.
2. The Urubamba River snaked below.
3. The lost city of Machu Picchu lay above.
4. Once many people came to the Incan city.
5. Now the Peruvian jungle growth covered Machu Picchu.
6. Bingham's group worked hard at their task of discovery.
7. The city's emptiness seemed very strange to them.
8. Its irrigation system carried water quite efficiently.
9. The Incans had placed their houses close together by the temples.
10. The explorers spent much time there in Peru.

Writing Sentences

Think of a great building you have visited or read about. Write six sentences using the following adverbs: *down, very, yesterday, completely, never, carefully.*

Sample Answer 1. extremely, steep, adjective

Comparative and Superlative Adverbs

Adverbs may help to describe a single action. They may also be used to compare two or more actions. Like adjectives, some adverbs have comparative and superlative forms.

Use the **comparative form** of the adverb to compare two actions.

The people of Crete built cities earlier than the Greeks.

Use the **superlative form** of the adverb to compare more than two actions.

The Cretans built cities earliest of all Europeans.

To form the comparative of adverbs of one syllable and of some adverbs of more than one syllable, simply add *-er*. Add *-est* to these adverbs to form the superlative. When the adverb ends in **y**, change the *y* to *i* before adding *-er* or *-est*.

early + -er → earlier (comparative)

early + -est → earliest (superlative)

Use the words *more* and *most* before most long adverbs ending in *-ly* to form the comparative and the superlative.

The Cretans lived more peacefully than the Greeks. (comparative)

They lived most peacefully of all early Aegean peoples. (superlative)

Use the words *less* and *least* before both short and long adverbs to form the comparative and the superlative.

The Cretans built their buildings less high than Egyptian buildings. (comparative)

Perhaps the Cretans built the palace of Zakro least high of all. (superlative)

Do not use *more* or *most* or *less* or *least* before adverbs that already have *-er* or *-est* added to them.

Correct: Cretan ships sailed farthest of all early traders.

Incorrect: Cretan ships sailed most farthest of all early traders.

A few adverbs have irregular comparatives and superlatives. Study the chart of irregular adverbs on the next page.

Adverb	Comparative	Superlative
badly	worse	worst
well	better	best
far (distance)	farther	farthest
far (degree)	further	furthest
little (amount or degree)	less	least

Class Exercises

Read each sentence. Use either the comparative or superlative form in parentheses to complete the sentence. Spell the answer.

1. The Egyptians came to Crete ___ of all the peoples. (earlier, earliest)
2. Cretans arrived in Greece ___ than the Greeks. (earlier, earliest)
3. Some people think the Cretans built the palace of Knossos ___ of all their buildings. (better, best)
4. Its hundreds of rooms sheltered people ___ than other palaces. (more comfortably, most comfortably)
5. The Cretans went the ___ in making a palace a real home. (further, furthest)

Exercises

Write each sentence. Use either the comparative or superlative form in parentheses to complete the sentence.

1. Cretan ships sailed ___ of all early vessels. (swifter, swiftest)
2. Knossos was powerful and needed protection ___ than other cities. (less frequently, least frequently)
3. This civilization developed trade ___ than the arts of war. (further, furthest)
4. Cretans practiced their arts ___ of all in their palaces. (more enthusiastically, most enthusiastically)
5. Perhaps they painted scenes of sports the ___ . (better, best)
6. Lively scenes decorated their palace rooms ___ than pictures of grave subjects. (more often, most often)
7. We understand Cretan writings the ___ of all early languages. (less well, least well)

Sample Answer 1. Cretan ships sailed swiftest of all early vessels.

Intensifiers

You have seen that very often an adverb describes a verb. An adverb may give information about *when*, *where*, and *how* the action of a sentence takes place. An adverb may also describe adjectives and other adverbs. In this role, an adverb emphasizes or intensifies the adjective or adverb.

An adverb that emphasizes or intensifies an adjective or adverb is called an **intensifier**.

- Read these sentences.

The people of Easter Island built large statues.

The people of Easter Island built <u>extremely</u> large statues.

In the first sentence you learn that the people built large statues. The adjective *large* describes the noun *statues*. In the second sentence you learn that the statues were extremely large. The intensifier *extremely* describes the adjective *large*.

- Read these sentences.

Scientists examined the old statues carefully.

Scientists examined the old statues <u>very</u> carefully.

In the first sentence you learn that the scientists carefully examined the statues. The adverb *carefully* describes the action *examined*. In the second sentence you learn how carefully they examined them. The intensifier *very* describes the adverb *carefully*.

Here is a list of some intensifiers often used to describe adjectives and other adverbs. Perhaps you can think of others.

very	quite	just	enormously
too	really	somewhat	so
rather	extremely	nearly	almost

- Read these sentences. Notice the word each underlined adverb describes.

People looked at the <u>really</u> impressive statues. (adjective *impressive*)

People looked at the statues <u>thoughtfully</u>. (verb *looked*)

People looked at the statues <u>rather</u> thoughtfully. (adverb *thoughtfully*)

Class Exercises

Find the intensifier in each sentence. Tell whether it describes an **adjective** or another **adverb**.

1. The Easter Island statues are somewhat mysterious.
2. According to some, visitors from space almost surely helped make them.
3. Scientists have tried extremely hard to explain their origin.
4. The statues were made almost exclusively of volcanic rock.
5. We have learned just recently about their beginnings.
6. Some really clever scientists built a modern copy of one of them.

Exercises

Write each sentence. Underline each intensifier once and the word it describes twice. Write whether the word described is an **adjective** or an **adverb**.

1. Quite convincingly the new statue disproved some old ideas.
2. No one had been too happy with the idea of help from space travelers.
3. Scientists worked rather laboriously on the new statue.
4. The old statues had been cut so magnificently from solid rock.
5. The scientists' tools were exactly similar to the ancient ones.
6. The really difficult work took many months of steady labor.
7. Very slowly a sixty-foot copy of an old statue took shape.
8. The ancient builders must have been enormously happy with their work.
9. The new statue disproved some old ideas almost immediately.
10. Assistance from outer space was very unlikely.

Writing Sentences

Imagine you have discovered some ancient ruins. Write six sentences about your discovery. In each sentence use one of these adverbs to describe another adverb or adjective.

too almost so very quite nearly somewhat

Sample Answer 1. Quite convincingly the new statue disproved some old ideas. adverb

Adverbs and Adjectives

Some words can be used as either adjectives or adverbs. You can tell the difference between a word used as an adjective and a word used as an adverb by the way it is used in a sentence. Look at the way the word *tall* is used in these sentences:

Ancient Egyptian civilization built tall pyramids.

These magnificent pyramids stand tall in the open desert.

In the first sentence *tall* describes the noun *pyramids*. Thus *tall* is an adjective. Remember, an *adjective* is a word that modifies, or describes, a noun or a pronoun. In the second sentence *tall* is an adverb that describes how the pyramid stands. Remember, an *adverb* is a word that modifies, or describes, a verb, another adverb, or an adjective.

- Note how the words in the chart can be used as adjectives or adverbs.

Word Used as Adjective	Word Used as Adverb
a deep hole	The road ran deep into the desert.
the next worker	The workers painted next.
the right idea	They did it right.
a straight line	They stood straight.
a long time	One person worked too long.
a hard task	Workers pushed hard.
a fast worker	They worked fast.
the first person	She finished first.
a late start	The tour began late.
the last pyramid	The tour stops at the pyramids last.

Many adverbs are formed by adding *-ly* to adjectives, for example, *rapidly*, *sadly*, *cautiously*, and *loudly*.

Words with *-ly* endings usually are adverbs. Sometimes, though, a word with an *-ly* ending is used as an adjective.

People have traveled to the pyramids since early times.

Tourists of the twentieth century also make daily tours.

Lovely works of art decorate the pyramids' inner walls.

Much of the art shows ancient Egyptians in friendly situations.

In each sentence the underlined word is an adjective because it describes a noun. The *-ly* ending is not always a sign that a word is an adverb.

Class Exercises

Read each sentence. Tell whether the underlined word is an **adjective** or an **adverb**.

1. The kindly goddess Isis can be seen in Egyptian paintings.
2. Isis kindly received the worship of many Egyptian people.
3. The artists must have worked on the paintings daily.
4. We learn much about daily life in Egypt from these artworks.

Exercises

Write each sentence. Then write whether the underlined word is an **adjective** or an **adverb**. Write the word it describes.

1. The first pyramid was built 4,500 years ago.
2. Many Egyptian laborers worked hard to build the pyramids.
3. They built the pyramids with blocks of hard limestone.
4. Laborers needed level ground for their construction site first.
5. They dug a deep trench around the outside of the pyramid site.
6. Next they filled the trench with water.
7. They used the water level as a guideline for a flat surface.
8. In the next step they smoothed out the sand to the level of the water.
9. Then they set a layer of blocks flat against the level ground.
10. Gangs of laborers pushed each block straight up a ramp into place.
11. Some pyramids were built in a series of deep steps.
12. Other pyramids had straight sides that sloped down to a wide base.

Writing Sentences

Imagine a new building is being built in your city or town. Write six sentences about the work being done on this building. Write two sentences for each word below. In the first sentence use the word as an adjective. In the second sentence use the word as an adverb.

straight fast right

Sample Answer 1. The first pyramid was built 4,500 years ago.
adjective, pyramid

Using Adverbs and Adjectives

Adverbs and adjectives are often confused. They are especially difficult to distinguish after verbs. A **predicate adjective** follows a linking verb. *Be*, *seem*, *appear*, and *become* are all linking verbs.

- Look at these sentences.

The work at Stonehenge was hard for a people without machinery.

Their accomplishment still seems brilliant to modern visitors.

In the first sentence the predicate adjective *hard* modifies, or describes, the subject, *work*. In the second sentence the predicate adjective *brilliant* modifies, or describes, the subject, *accomplishment*. In both sentences the predicate adjective follows a linking verb.

- Look at these sentences.

Bronze Age people worked hard at the construction of Stonehenge.

The sun shines brilliantly between two special stones each year.

In both sentences the underlined word describes an action verb. *Hard* describes *worked*, and *brilliantly* describes *shines*. The verbs are action verbs, so the words that modify them are **adverbs**.

> Use a **predicate adjective** after a linking verb, such as *be*, *seem*, *appear*, or *become*. Use an **adverb** to describe an action verb.

Four words that people often confuse are *good, bad, well,* and *badly.*

- Look at these sentences.

The builders of Stonehenge were good at the study of the heavens.

An earthquake was bad for the careful positions of the stones.

Stonehenge still works well as a kind of ancient calendar.

Cloudy weather can badly affect the usefulness of Stonehenge.

Good and *bad* are usually adjectives. Use them after linking verbs. *Well* and *badly* are usually adverbs. Use them after action verbs. You may also use *well* as an adjective when you are describing someone's health.

Tanya felt well at Stonehenge.

Class Exercises

Read each sentence. Name the word that correctly completes each sentence. Tell whether it is an **adverb** or an **adjective**.

1. The work on Stonehenge must have seemed ___ . (impossible, impossibly)
2. Each stone at Stonehenge is ___ . (enormous, enormously)
3. Several groups worked on Stonehenge ___ . (separate, separately)
4. Ditches and mounds surround the area ___ . (complete, completely)

Exercises

Write the word in parentheses that correctly completes each sentence. Write whether it is an **adverb** or an **adjective**.

1. The inhabitants of the Salisbury Plain were ___ . (energetic, energetically)
2. Their project at Stonehenge was ___ . (incredible, incredibly)
3. They worked ___ on a large, circular ditch. (diligent, diligently)
4. Then they searched ___ for huge stones. (careful, carefully)
5. They worked ___ on a stone wall inside the ditch. (patient, patiently)
6. The opening in the circle of stones is ___ . (intentional, intentionally)
7. The position of the stone at the opening is ___ . (different, differently)
8. The name Heel Stone seems ___ . (appropriate, appropriately)
9. The people marked the path to Stonehenge ___ . (clear, clearly)
10. The work on Stonehenge progressed ___ . (slow, slowly)
11. Later, people added stones to Stonehenge ___ . (independent, independently)
12. The area inside the stone wall became ___ . (sacred, sacredly)

Writing Sentences

Write six sentences about some old settlement or village you have seen. Use the adjectives and adverbs below in your sentences.

easy bad badly vigorously good well

Sample Answer 1. energetic, adjective

Avoiding Double Negatives

One small word in the English language has the power to change the entire meaning of a sentence. That word, *not*, changes a positive statement to a negative one.

Early American buildings were modeled on European styles.

Early American buildings were not modeled on European styles.

Not often appears in a shortened form as part of a contraction.

A **contraction** is a word made up of two words combined into one by leaving out one or more letters.

Use an **apostrophe (')** in a contraction to show that one or more letters are missing.

- Study the words and their contracted forms below.

is not = isn't	cannot = can't	have not = haven't
was not = wasn't	could not = couldn't	had not = hadn't
were not = weren't	do not = don't	would not = wouldn't
will not = won't	did not = didn't	should not = shouldn't

In all but two of these words, the apostrophe replaces the *o* in *not*. In *can't* both an *n* and the *o* are omitted. *Will not* becomes *won't*.

Two negative words near one another can cause problems for your listeners or readers. Therefore, you should not use a double negative (two negative words) in a simple sentence.

- Read these negative words. Do not use more than one of them at a time.

no	no one	scarcely	but (when used as a negative)
not	nothing	hardly	only (when used as a negative)
none	nobody	barely	never

Incorrect: Americans weren't hardly ready to create new styles.

Correct: Americans were hardly ready to create new styles.

Correct: Americans weren't ready to create new styles.

Notice that the incorrect sentence above uses a contracted form of *not*. If you use *not* or its shortened form, do not use any other negative word near it. Use just one negative word at a time.

Incorrect: Scarcely no new styles were found till the 1800s.

Correct: Scarcely any new styles were found till the 1800s.

Class Exercises

Spell the contraction of each of the following words.

1. cannot
2. would not
3. must not
4. is not
5. will not
6. were not
7. did not
8. was not
9. are not
10. has not

Read each sentence. Tell how to complete each sentence so that there is only one negative word in the sentence.

11. Houses with flat roofs ___ hardly useful in the North. (were, weren't)
12. Thick snow ___ never fall off the house that way. (couldn't, could)
13. Snow wasn't ___ problem for builders in the South. (any, no)
14. No one in the West ___ better homes than Pueblos. (had, hadn't)

Exercises

Use *not* to change each positive sentence to a negative one. Write each sentence using a contraction.

1. The Industrial Revolution did create a need for new architecture.
2. Railroad stations, offices, and factories would be needed.
3. A great time of experiments in building could begin now.

Write each sentence using the correct word in parentheses.

4. Before 1851 the world ___ never seen a building like the Crystal Palace. (had, hadn't)
5. Scarcely ___ missed visiting it in London in 1851. (no one, anyone)
6. The Crystal Palace was built of hardly ___ except iron and glass. (nothing, anything)
7. The architect didn't have ___ earlier models for the Crystal Palace. (any, no)
8. None ___ believe the size of the Crystal Palace. (could, couldn't)
9. No one ___ miss seeing Paxton's style in today's skyscrapers. (can, can't)

Sample Answers 1. The Industrial Revolution didn't create a need for new architecture. **4.** Before 1851 the world had never seen a building like the Crystal Palace.

Unit Review

ADVERBS

Write each adverb. Then write the word it describes. Write whether the word described is an **action verb**, an **adverb**, or an **adjective**. *pages 102-103*

1. Architects work carefully on their plans for buildings.
2. Groups of architects very often create a single new plan.
3. They work together toward a satisfactory building design.
4. A good building meets the needs of its owner completely.
5. Good architects are completely honest with their clients.

Write the comparative or superlative form of the adverb in parentheses to complete each sentence. *pages 104-105*

6. Frank Lloyd Wright is the ___ American architect to many. (better, best)
7. Wright designed the interiors of homes ___ than before. (more spaciously, most spaciously)
8. Wright also used concrete ___ than others. (earlier, earliest)
9. Wright worked ___ of all with designs for public buildings. (more impressively, most impressively)

Write each sentence. Underline each intensifier once and the word it describes twice. Write whether the word described is an **adjective** or an **adverb**. *pages 106-107*

10. In one way the 1871 Chicago Fire was a rather helpful event.
11. The fire very effectively created a need for new ideas.
12. Quite soon the first metal-frame skyscraper was built.
13. A really new style of building developed in Chicago.
14. The steel frame became almost universal in architecture.
15. The "Chicago School" very proudly led the way to modern cities.

For each sentence, write whether the underlined word is an **adjective** or an **adverb**. Write the word it describes. *pages 108-109*

16. Work on the Empire State Building <u>first</u> occurred in 1930.
17. The building rises 1,472 feet <u>straight</u> into the air.
18. It contains miles of <u>deep</u> shafts for its elevators.
19. About 25,000 people enter the building <u>daily</u>.
20. This building was the tallest in the world for a <u>long</u> time.

Unit Review

Write the word in parentheses that correctly completes each sentence. Write whether it is an **adverb** or an **adjective**. *pages 110-111*

21. Energy problems affect ___ the style of new buildings. (great, greatly)
22. Glass is ___ material for energy-minded builders. (good, well)
23. Some walls are built ___ of glass for solar heat. (entirely, entire)
24. New homes may have ___ solar panels on the roof. (special, specially)

Match the contraction with the words it represents. Write the letter of each contraction. *pages 112-113*

25. should not	**a.** couldn't
26. was not	**b.** won't
27. will not	**c.** shouldn't
28. could not	**d.** wasn't
29. had not	**e.** hadn't

Write each sentence using the correct word in parentheses. *pages 112-113*

30. Barely ___ country has more cathedrals than France. (any, no)
31. The world hadn't ___ seen such majestic architecture. (never, ever)
32. Scarcely ___ misses a visit to at least one church in Paris. (no one, anyone)
33. There isn't ___ part of these churches without decoration. (no, any)
34. Tourists ___ hardly believe the size of these churches. (can, can't)

Exploring Language

In the 1920s people used to read adventure stories about a boy named Tom Swift. The writer of these stories used a lot of adverbs. People created jokes called "Tom Swifties."

Read these Tom Swifties and then make up your own.

"Steam escapes from the chimney," Tom said freely.
"A solar home collects energy from the sun," Tom said lively.
"I don't like dull buildings," Tom said plainly.
"I really like the glass walls," Tom said clearly.

This *stabile* sculpture graces a park in St. Paul, France.

The aim of every artist is to arrest motion, which is life, by artificial means, and hold it fixed so that a hundred years later, when a stranger looks at it, it moves again, since it is life.

WILLIAM FAULKNER
American novelist
(1897-1962)

7

PREPOSITIONS, PREPOSITIONAL PHRASES, CONJUNCTIONS, AND INTERJECTIONS

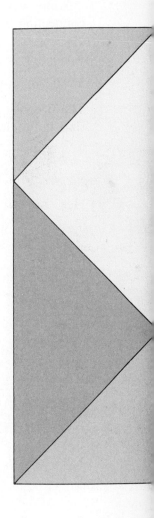

Review: Prepositions and Prepositional Phrases

Some words in our language work in sentences as relating and connecting words. Prepositions are words of this type.

- Read this sentence.

  The paint on the canvas will dry very slowly.

The preposition *on* connects *canvas* with *paint* and shows the relationship between them.

> A **preposition** is a word that relates a noun or pronoun to another word.

- Here are some of the most frequently used prepositions:

aboard	before	during	off	toward
about	behind	except	on	under
above	below	for	out	underneath
across	beneath	from	outside	until
after	beside	in	over	up
against	between	inside	past	upon
along	beyond	into	since	with
among	by	like	through	within
around	concerning	near	throughout	without
at	down	of	to	

A number of prepositions consist of more than one word.

according to	aside from	in front of	instead of
across from	because of	in place of	on account of
along with	by means of	in spite of	out of

- Look at the underlined words in the sentences below.

  Michelangelo was born <u>in a small town</u>.

  He enrolled as an apprentice <u>at a famous artist's studio</u>.

  His accomplishments are astonishing <u>to me</u>.

Each group of underlined words is called a *prepositional phrase.* Notice that each prepositional phrase begins with a preposition and ends with a noun or pronoun. The noun or pronoun is the *object* of the preposition. When the phrase ends with a pronoun, use the object pronouns, *me, you, him, her, it, us,* or *them,* as objects.

> A **prepositional phrase** is a group of words that begins with a preposition and ends with a noun or pronoun as its object.

- Notice that the object of a preposition can be *compound,* or *more than one word.*

inside museums and churches   in marble or oil

Class Exercises

For each sentence name the preposition and the object of the preposition. Then tell whether the object is compound.

1. Some artists study Michelangelo's work for inspiration.
2. His work had a great influence on many other artists.
3. Many artists see perfection in his paintings and sculpture.
4. According to experts the Pieta is Michelangelo's only signed sculpture.

Exercises

Write each sentence. Draw a line under each prepositional phrase. Draw two lines under the object.

1. A great many Renaissance artists were influenced by Michelangelo.
2. He painted the Sistine Chapel ceiling as he lay on a scaffold.
3. He completed the chapel work in three years.
4. He was hailed as an artist after this great work.
5. He painted some frescoes at a Pope's request.
6. He produced some outstanding frescoes during his productive life.
7. His paintings hang in museums or private collections.
8. Wealthy people from many countries desired his sculpture.
9. Michelangelo once worked with the great Leonardo Da Vinci.
10. After thirty years Michelangelo again painted the Sistine Chapel.

Sample Answer 1. A great many Renaissance artists were influenced by Michelangelo.

Prepositional Phrases as Adjectives and Adverbs

You have learned that a prepositional phrase is a group of words that begins with a preposition and ends with a noun or pronoun as its object. The role of a prepositional phrase is to describe a word or group of words that appears in the same sentence. When a prepositional phrase is used to describe a noun, the phrase functions as an adjective.

The priceless fabrics were quite beautiful.

The fabrics from the Orient were quite beautiful.

In the first sentence the adjective *priceless* describes the noun *fabrics.* In the second sentence the prepositional phrase *from the Orient* describes *fabrics.* The phrase *from the Orient* works as an adjective.

> An **adjective phrase** is a prepositional phrase that modifies, or describes, a noun or pronoun.

Sometimes an adjective phrase describes a noun in the subject part of a sentence. Other times it may describe a noun in the predicate part.

These tapestries from other lands are ancient.

These ancient hangings are tapestries from other lands.

In the first sentence the adjective phrase *from other lands* describes the noun *tapestries.* The phrase appears in the subject part of the sentence. In the second sentence the adjective phrase *from other lands* also describes *tapestries.* However, the phrase appears in the predicate part of the sentence.

A prepositional phrase can also work as an adverb by describing a verb. Adverb phrases tell *when, where,* or *how* an action takes place.

> An **adverb phrase** is a prepositional phrase that may modify, or describe, a verb.

- Notice what each phrase below tells about the action of the verb.

Weavers work during the day. (When?) They work with care. (How?) They work in shops. (Where?)

Sometimes the very same prepositional phrase may work as an adjective in one sentence and as an adverb in another sentence.

Adjective Phrase: The fabric on the loom was very colorful.

Adverb Phrase: The fabric fit on the loom.

In the first sentence *on the loom* describes the noun *fabric*. In the second sentence *on the loom* describes the verb *fit*.

Class Exercises

Tell which word each underlined phrase describes. Tell whether the prepositional phrase is an **adjective phrase** or an **adverb phrase.**

1. Weavers of different objects discovered the art ages ago.
2. The earliest weavers worked with long grass strands.
3. The weavers in primitive civilizations discovered new materials.
4. People first wove fabrics during the sixth century B.C.

Exercises

Write each sentence. Draw one line under each prepositional phrase. Draw two lines under the word each phrase describes. Write **adjective phrase** or **adverb phrase** for each prepositional phrase.

1. Many people today make a hobby of this art.
2. They often work on small efficient looms.
3. The young weaver usually begins with an old, simple pattern.
4. Patterns from all over the world teach the necessary skills.
5. A homemade quilt from one person may become valuable.
6. Tapestries with complex patterns fill modern museums.
7. These tapestries often illustrate stories about great people.
8. Medieval weavers worked for kings and queens.
9. The tapestries hung along a castle's high cold walls.
10. Modern weavers still decorate their homes with personal patterns.

Writing Sentences

Write six sentences about a hobby you have or would like to take up. Use each of the following prepositional phrases as an adjective phrase first, and then as an adverb phrase.

on the wall   from Spain   of many different colors

Sample Answer 1. Many people today make a hobby of this art. adjective phrase

Agreement in Sentences with Prepositional Phrases

You know that a verb must agree in number with its subject. Agreement is easy when the subject and verb appear side by side. Sometimes, however, a prepositional phrase comes between the subject and the verb. Then you must make sure the verb agrees with the subject of the sentence and not with the noun in the prepositional phrase.

• Read the sentences below. Note the subjects and the verbs.

The students in the school learn the craft quickly.

This hobby, except for some small expenses, is easily affordable.

In the first sentence *in the school* is a prepositional phrase. The verb *learn* agrees with the subject *students,* not with the noun *school* which is in the prepositional phrase. In the second sentence *except for some small expenses* is a prepositional phrase. The verb *is* agrees with the subject *hobby,* not with the noun *expenses* which is in the prepositional phrase.

A prepositional phrase often contains a noun. Do not mistake the noun in the prepositional phrase for the simple subject. You can avoid confusion by remembering that the simple subject can never be within a prepositional phrase and by asking *who?* or *what?* before the verb. When you are looking for the simple subject, eliminate all prepositional phrases first. Then ask *who?* or *what?* Make sure the verb agrees with the simple subject.

• Read these sentences. Eliminate the prepositional phrases and then tell what the simple subject is.

People with talent create some beautiful custom jewelry.

Custom-designed jewelry in most stores is very expensive.

Class Exercises

Tell which verb in parentheses agrees with the subject of each sentence.

1. That book, of all the manuals, ___ the best information about making jewelry. (give, gives)

2. Silver, among the more popular metals, ___ available in many hobby shops. (is, are)

3. A jewelry hobbyist, like all hobbyists, usually ___ about the subject first. (read, reads)
4. An amateur, within a few weeks, ___ a lovely piece. (makes, make)
5. A wax model from drawings ___ one of the first steps. (are, is)

Exercises

Write each sentence using the correct form of the verb.

1. Most supplies, except for silver, ___ inexpensive. (is, are)
2. Even common stones, of any type, ___ something interesting to bracelets. (adds, add)
3. Handmade rings in all styles ___ becoming popular. (is, are)
4. A gift of earrings ___ a good present for a friend. (makes, make)
5. Handmade bracelets with an old design ___ popular at craft fairs and shows. (is, are)
6. A pin with unusual features ___ very well. (sells, sell)
7. Makers of jewelry ___ for materials by selling their products. (pays, pay)
8. A ring with original designs ___ more interesting than machine-made pieces. (looks, look)
9. Craft books about gem setting ___ available in hobby stores. (is, are)
10. Equipment of all sorts ___ available in these stores, too. (is, are)
11. Ready-made catches and clasps of every type ___ time. (saves, save)
12. A museum display of gold and silver objects ___ a good place to study jewelry design. (is, are)

Writing Sentences

Suppose that you make jewelry. Write six sentences about your jewelry using the subjects below to begin your sentences.

Bracelets of twisted rope	The design on the bracelets
A necklace with colored beads	A pin with peacock feathers
Puzzle rings of silver	Earrings with a matching pin

Sample Answer 1. Most supplies, except for silver, are inexpensive.

Identifying Conjunctions

You know that a conjunction is a word that joins other words or groups of words. One type of conjunction is the *coordinating conjunction. And, but, or, for,* and *nor* are used as coordinating conjunctions.

A **coordinating conjunction** is a single word used to connect parts of a sentence such as words, phrases, or clauses.

Grandma Moses and Georgia O'Keeffe are famous artists.

Georgia O'Keeffe studied art formally and taught it for years.

Grandma Moses never went to art school, but her work is quite professional.

Notice that a coordinating conjunction may join two subjects (as in the first sentence), two predicates (as in the second sentence), or two independent clauses (as in the third sentence).

Sometimes you may wish to make a relationship between words or groups of words you are connecting stronger and clearer than you can with a coordinating conjunction. You can do this by using a *correlative conjunction.*

Correlative conjunctions are pairs of words used to connect parts of sentences such as words, phrases, or clauses.

Common Correlative Conjunctions		
both...and	neither...nor	either...or
not only...but also	whether...or	just as...so

The first part of the correlative conjunction is used before the first word or group of words to be connected, and the second part before the related clause or group of words.

- Read this sentence. Notice how the correlative conjunctions are used.

Both Grandma Moses and Georgia O'Keeffe painted landscapes.

A conjunction may also join a subordinate clause to a main clause in a sentence. A conjunction used to show the relationship between a subordinate clause and a main clause is called a *subordinating conjunction,* or *subordinator.*

A **subordinating conjunction** is a word or group of words that joins a subordinate clause to a main clause in a sentence.

Common Subordinating Conjunctions			
after	before	though	whenever
although	if	unless	where
as	since	until	whereas
because	than	when	while

Notice that some of these words can be used as other parts of speech. For example, *after, before, since,* and *until* can be prepositions.

Georgia O'Keeffe was an art student before she became an artist. (subordinator)

Grandma Moses did not paint before the age of seventy-six. (preposition)

Class Exercises

Read each sentence. Tell whether the underlined conjunction in each is a **coordinating conjunction,** a **correlative conjunction,** or a **subordinator.**

1. The artist mixed the paint because she wanted vivid colors.
2. The painter and the sculptor shared a large studio.
3. Both a painter and a sculptor need a well-lighted work area.
4. The painter took many lessons, but students now learn from her.

Exercises

Write each sentence. Underline each conjunction and write whether it is a **coordinating conjunction**, a **correlative conjunction**, or a **subordinating conjunction**. Draw two lines under any prepositions.

1. Both the sketch and the painting were done from memory.
2. The artist spread the paint with a knife or applied it with a brush.
3. The artist didn't paint because the light was wrong.
4. The sky was cloudy, and the shadows made her stop painting.
5. Whenever artists stop work, they clean their brushes.
6. Neither the canvas nor the frame had been made properly.
7. Although the canvas had been stretched, it was not tight enough.
8. Painters use not only canvas but also other materials.
9. Many artists choose water colors or oils for their work.
10. Some painters sign their work, but other artists only initial theirs.

Sample Answer 1. Both the sketch and the painting were done from memory. correlative conjunction

Interjections

We express our thoughts, ideas, and feelings in units of complete thought called sentences. One type of sentence is the exclamatory sentence. An exclamatory sentence expresses strong feeling. Sometimes people express very strong feelings in a short exclamation which may not be a complete sentence. These exclamations are called *interjections*.

- Look at these examples.

Aha!	Yippee!	Zowie!
Oops!	My goodness!	Hey!

> An **interjection** is a word or group of words that express strong feeling. An interjection has no grammatical connection to any other words.

- Study the examples below to see how interjections may be used.

<u>Wow!</u> The colors in that painting are so bright that they hurt my eyes.

<u>Gee</u>, I wish we could stay longer at the museum.

We are going to the Metropolitan Museum next week. <u>Yippee!</u>

<u>Ouch!</u>

It's time to leave, <u>alas</u>.

Notice that interjections may appear at the beginning or end of a sentence. They may even stand alone. When an interjection is a part of the sentence, it is separated from the rest of the sentence by a comma (as in the second and fifth example above). When it stands alone, it is followed by an exclamation mark. Interjections should be used sparingly. If you overuse them, you will lessen their effectiveness.

Class Exercises

Read the sentences below. Tell what the interjection in each is.

1. Oh no, I am going to be late for my painting class.
2. My! I have never seen anyone who could sketch that fast.
3. Phew! It certainly is hard work to stretch this canvas tight.
4. We may be able to interview a famous artist for the school paper. Hooray!
5. Golly, I hope she will autograph one of her prints for me.

Exercises

Write each sentence. Underline the interjection in each and place the proper punctuation mark after each.

1. Phew Molding this stiff clay is certainly tiring work for me.
2. Tut-tut You always exaggerate about the work you have to do.
3. Fiddlesticks this clay is drying out too quickly.
4. Oh I didn't realize that you had so much artistic talent.
5. Goodness I didn't think it would take this long to make a statue.
6. Ugh these two colors simply do not go well together.
7. Hooray I finally captured the expression of surprise on the subject's face.
8. What an exciting day this has been for me. Whee
9. Oh my I am surprised that you know so much about painting.
10. Ouch I accidentally stuck myself with the end of the paintbrush.
11. Hey that blue you are using is just what I need to finish this painting.
12. Our art teacher is showing us some slides tomorrow. Yippee
13. Hooray My painting just won first prize in the art contest.
14. Boy You are becoming a famous local artist.
15. What a fantastic day this has been for me. Whee
16. Psst have you been taking lessons from a professional?
17. Hey that is a fantastic idea you just gave me.
18. Alas I would take lessons also, but they're too expensive for me.

Writing Sentences

Imagine that your class is taking a trip to an art exhibit. Write six sentences describing some of the art you might see. Use an interjection in or with each sentence.

Sample Answer 1. Phew! Molding this stiff clay is certainly tiring work for me.

Unit Review

PREPOSITIONS, PREPOSITIONAL PHRASES, CONJUNCTIONS, AND INTERJECTIONS

Write the prepositional phrase in each sentence. Draw one line under the preposition and two lines under the object. *pages 118-119*

1. Georgia O'Keeffe was born in Wisconsin.
2. She started painting at an early age.
3. She often did paintings of local scenery.
4. Later she did some paintings of an abstract type.
5. However, she is best known for her wild flowers and bleached animal bones.

Write the prepositional phrase in each sentence. Then write the word each phrase describes. Write **adverb phrase** or **adjective phrase** for each prepositional phrase. *pages 120-121*

6. The history of art is an interesting study.
7. Prehistoric artists carved pictures on cave walls.
8. Some painted the walls with natural dyes.
9. Many Greek and Roman artists worked with stone.
10. During the Renaissance oil painting flourished.
11. There was also a renewed interest in sculpture.
12. Artists perfected the art of fresco painting.
13. Since then artists have become more and more experimental.
14. Today we see interesting creations made from automobile fenders.
15. Innovation is an essential ingredient of art.

Write the simple subject of each sentence. Then write the verb in parentheses that correctly completes the sentence. *pages 122-123*

16. Books on art ___ now quite plentiful. (is, are)
17. In many of these books the works of a single artist ___ reproduced. (is, are)
18. Reproductions of a work of art ___ not always have the impact of the original. (do, does)
19. Sometimes the reproduction of the works ___ an injustice to the original. (do, does)
20. New techniques of reproduction ___ being developed at a phenomenal rate. (is, are)

Decide whether the underlined part of each sentence is a **coordinating conjunction**, a **correlative conjunction**, a **subordinating conjunction**, or a **preposition**. Write the letter of the correct choice. *pages 124-125*

21. Although most artists gravitate to a specific medium, some are extremely versatile.
   a. coordinating **b.** correlative **c.** subordinating **d.** preposition
22. Some artists are comfortable with both painting and sculpture.
   a. coordinating **b.** correlative **c.** subordinating **d.** preposition
23. Others work best in charcoal or pastels.
   a. coordinating **b.** correlative **c.** subordinating **d.** preposition
24. Many artists prepare sketches before they begin a major work.
   a. coordinating **b.** correlative **c.** subordinating **d.** preposition
25. Artists sometimes refurbish a work before a show.
   a. coordinating **b.** correlative **c.** subordinating **d.** preposition

Write each sentence. Underline the interjection in each and place the proper punctuation mark after each interjection. *pages 126-127*

26. Boy I didn't realize how well you paint.
27. Gosh You really use color well.
28. Alas your painting seems better than mine.
29. Psst is that really an original idea?
30. Hooray Your painting won first prize.

Exploring Language

Archaeology comes from a Greek word. It means "the science of ancient things." Archaeologists are people who study civilizations, sometimes those that ended many years ago. *Civilization* is from Latin. It means "a collection of citizens who have developed a high level of culture." In order to find out about a culture or civilization, archaeologists often *excavate*. *Excavate*, from a Latin word, means "to make hollow." Archaeologists, who excavate, dig in ruins or places where they believe evidence of a civilization may lie buried. They may examine pottery, jewelry, written material, parts of buildings, skeletons, furniture, clothes,and other articles that give them insight into that particular civilization.

Trainees at the Air Traffic Control Training Center, Islip, Long Island, New York

Flying in a plane from San Francisco to New York is nothing more than a horizontal elevator ride.

HOWARD GOSSAGE

8

PHRASES, CLAUSES, AND SENTENCES

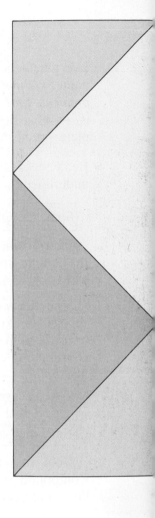

Review: Clauses and Sentences

You know that a *sentence* is a group of words that expresses a complete thought. Some sentences make a single statement.

> A **simple sentence** is a sentence that has one subject part and one predicate part.

Every sentence has two parts. The *complete subject,* or *subject part,* names whom or what the sentence is about. The *complete predicate,* or *predicate part,* tells what action the subject performs, what the subject is, or what the subject is like. Both the complete subject and the complete predicate may be more than one word.

- Read these sentences. The simple subjects and simple predicates are underlined.

Some people	travel.	Good transportation	is necessary.

Every complete subject has a main word, or group of words, called the *simple subject.* Similarly, every complete predicate has a main word, or group of words, called the *simple predicate.*

Sometimes the complete subject of a simple sentence is a *compound subject.* A compound subject has two or more simple subjects that have the same complete predicate. The simple subjects are joined by coordinating conjunctions like *and* or *or,* or by correlative conjunctions like *both ... and* or *neither ... nor.*

Cars and motorcycles	travel fast.	Trains or a jet	travels quickly.
Both men and women	drive.	Neither cars nor jets	are entirely safe.

Note that compound subjects joined by *and* are usually plural. Compound subjects joined by *or* or *nor* may be singular or plural depending on the form of the simple subject *nearer* to the verb.

A simple sentence may also have a *compound predicate.* A compound predicate has two or more verbs that share the same subject.

People at home	walk and drive.	Travelers	fly or sail overseas.

Some simple sentences have both compound subjects and compound predicates.

Trains and buses	carry passengers and transport luggage.

Some sentences express two or more thoughts. When two simple sentences are combined into one, they form a *compound sentence.*

> A **compound sentence** is a sentence that contains two or more simple sentences joined by *and, or,* or *but.* It has two or more subjects and two or more predicates.

Put a comma (,) before the conjunctions *and, or,* or *but* when you form a compound sentence. Use a semicolon (;) between the parts of a compound sentence if they are not joined by *and, or,* or *but.* Also, use a semicolon to separate the parts of a compound sentence if there are commas within one or both parts.

Millions of people	live in cities,	but	many others	reside in suburbs.
Most people	travel to work;	many	go to shopping centers, too.	
Commuters	take trains, buses, or cars;	but	shoppers	use them, too.

Class Exercises

Read each sentence. Tell whether it is a **simple sentence** or a **compound sentence.** Identify each compound subject and predicate.

1. The growth of railroads expanded and connected many cities.
2. People moved out of crowded cities, and commuters used trains.
3. Family members moved to different areas; trains reunited them.
4. Tourists, commuters, and merchants used trains; and railroads prospered.

Exercises

Write each sentence using the correct punctuation. Write whether it is a **simple sentence** or a **compound sentence.** Then draw one line under each complete subject. Draw two lines under each complete predicate.

1. Weather, accidents, and road conditions can cause traffic jams.
2. Helicopter pilots observe traffic patterns and report to the police.
3. A computer selects new traffic routes but police redirect traffic.
4. Bad weather causes a traffic jam or accidents slow the traffic.
5. Commuters observe and concentrate on traffic conditions.
6. Train commuters and passengers appreciate the scenery outside.
7. Passengers can read, sleep, or talk but drivers must pay attention.
8. Too many people drive in the city and narrow streets slow traffic.

Sample Answer 1. Weather, accidents, and road conditions can cause traffic jams. simple sentence

Complex Sentences

A *simple sentence* is a group of words that has one complete subject and one complete predicate. It is independent and expresses a complete thought.

A *compound sentence* is a sentence that contains two simple sentences joined by the coordinating conjunctions *and, or,* or *but,* or by a semicolon.

Colorful caravans of camels	traveled slowly across the desert, and
the journey	lasted several days.

The two simple sentences joined together in the compound sentence above are called *independent clauses.* Each clause in the sentence expresses a complete thought and can stand alone as a sentence.

> An **independent clause** has one subject part and one predicate part. It expresses a complete thought, and it can stand alone.

Sometimes sentences have more than one clause, but only one of the clauses is an independent clause.

- Study the sentences below.

> Colorful caravans of camels traveled slowly as the sands sparkled with sunlight.
>
> When the sun set in the western sky, the caravans stopped for the night.

One part of each sentence above is underlined twice. This group of words is called a *subordinate clause.* A subordinate clause has a subject part and a predicate part, but it cannot stand alone as a sentence. It must be combined with an independent clause to make a complete statement.

> A **subordinate clause** is a group of words that has a subject part and a predicate part. It cannot stand alone because it does not express a complete thought. It is always combined with an independent clause.

A sentence with an independent clause and a subordinate clause is a *complex sentence.*

> A **complex sentence** is a sentence that has an independent clause and one or more subordinate clauses.

A subordinate clause is introduced by a *subordinating conjunction*. The subordinating conjunction signals that the clause is a subordinate clause and cannot stand alone. Here is a list of some common subordinating conjunctions: *after, although, as, because, before, if, since, though, unless, until, when, where, while.*

Class Exercises

Read each complex sentence. Identify the independent clause and the subordinate clause in each. Tell what the subordinating conjunction is.

1. Merchants load their wares on camels when they go to the market.
2. Camels are useful to merchants because they cross the desert easily.
3. If food is hard to find, the camel's hump helps it survive.
4. The hump stores extra fat until the camel uses the fat for energy.

Exercises

Write each sentence. Underline the subordinate clause. Draw two lines under the subordinating conjunction.

1. Because camels are strong, people in Africa depend on them.
2. While camels provide transportation, they also do other things.
3. Although they are stubborn workers, camels will pull plows.
4. A camel will spit or kick if it is annoyed.
5. These animals never really learn to obey though they work hard.
6. Since they can live with little water, camels survive desert life.
7. They withstand sandstorms because they have long, thick lashes.
8. Until the desert sun sets, the camel maintains a 105° temperature.
9. The camel's temperature drops to 93° as the desert cools at night.
10. Although trucks get stuck, camels walk easily on desert sand.
11. A camel will walk for miles after it gets started.
12. When food is hard to find, the fat in the hump provides energy.

Writing Sentences

Suppose you are riding in a caravan on a camel named Dromedary. Write six complex sentences about your experience with the camel.

Sample Answer 1. Because camels are strong, people in Africa depend on them.

Adverb Clauses

Both the independent clause and the subordinate clause in a complex sentence give information. The independent clause expresses a complete thought and can stand alone as a sentence. The subordinate clause does not express a complete thought and cannot stand alone.

A subordinate clause that adds information about a verb, an adjective, or an adverb in the independent clause is called an *adverb clause.*

> An **adverb clause** is a subordinate clause that tells more about a verb, an adjective, or an adverb in the independent clause.

Adverb clauses are introduced by subordinating conjunctions like *after, as, as if, as though, before, since, than, until, when, whenever, where, wherever,* and *while.* Like adverbs, adverb clauses tell *how, when,* or *where* the action takes place.

Jack rode his bicycle quickly.

Jack rode his bicycle as if his life depended on it.

In the sentences above, the adverb *quickly* and the adverb clause *as if his life depended on it* modify the verb *rode.* They tell *how* Jack rode.

Mary rides her bicycle daily.

Mary rides her bicycle whenever she can ride it.

In these two sentences the adverb *daily* and the adverb clause *whenever she can ride it* modify the verb *rides.* They tell *when* Mary rides.

The twins ride their bicycles everywhere.

The twins ride their bicycles wherever they go.

In these sentences the adverb *everywhere* and the adverb clause *wherever they go* modify the verb *ride.* They tell *where* the twins ride.

The subordinating conjunction *than* is often used to introduce an adverb clause that modifies, or describes, an adjective or an adverb.

Peter rides his bicycle faster than Susan rides hers.

Bea is smarter than Jack is.

In the first sentence the adverb clause *than Susan rides hers* describes the adverb *faster.* In the second sentence the adverb clause *than Jack is* describes the adjective *smarter.*

Class Exercises

Read each sentence. Identify the adverb clause and its subordinating conjunction. Then tell what word the clause modifies. Identify that word as a **verb,** an **adjective,** or an **adverb.**

1. When gasoline prices rose, many people reverted to bicycles.
2. In city traffic bicycles sometimes move faster than cars maneuver.
3. Some city bicyclists move through traffic as if they were the only vehicles on the streets.
4. Wherever you go, you must avoid them.
5. To pedestrians, moving vans sometimes seem safer than bicycles do.

Exercises

Write each sentence. Underline the adverb clause once and the subordinating conjunction twice. Write the word the clause modifies. Then write whether that word is a **verb,** an **adjective,** or an **adverb.**

1. Before automobiles were available, many people used bicycles for transportation.
2. They could travel faster on bicycles than they could on foot.
3. After motoring became popular, some people still rode bicycles for pleasure and sport.
4. Since the first recorded bicycle race took place in 1868, bicycle racing has grown in popularity.
5. Today thousands of people participate in the sport whenever officials announce a competition.
6. Professional riders practice wherever they can find a good area.
7. Some amateur riders are better than some professionals are.
8. These amateurs ride as if they were racing professionally.
9. Today most bicyclists ride when they need exercise.
10. When gasoline became scarce, more and more people turned to bicycles for transportation again.
11. Now business executives pedal as if they were going to a fire.
12. Many messenger services use cyclists when they make short-distance deliveries.

Sample Answer 1. Before automobiles were available, many people used bicycles for transportation. used; verb

Appositives

You know that you can use an adjective or a prepositional phrase to modify or describe a noun in a sentence.

The enormous balloon rose quickly.

The passengers with radiant smiles enjoyed the ride.

In the first sentence the adjective *enormous* describes the noun *balloon.* In the second sentence the prepositional phrase *with radiant smiles* tells more about the noun *passengers.*

- Now read these sentences.

Joseph and Jacques Montgolfier, the first balloonists, were brothers.

In 1783 they took their first flight, a successful event.

In the first sentence the phrase *the first balloonists* modifies or describes the compound subject *Joseph and Jacques Montgolfier.* In the second sentence the phrase *a successful event* tells more about the noun *flight.* These phrases that identify or tell more about nouns are called *appositives.*

> An **appositive** is a noun or a pronoun that is placed next to another noun or pronoun to identify it or to give additional information about it. An appositive often includes modifiers.

Notice the commas in the sentences with appositives. An appositive is always set off from the rest of the sentence by commas. When it is in the middle of a sentence, two commas set it apart from the rest of the sentence. When it is at the end of a sentence, only one comma is used.

The balloon, a large colorful sphere, floated to the heavens.

The observers watched the balloon, a large colorful sphere.

Two men hung from the balloon, a large colorful sphere.

In each sentence the appositive *a large colorful sphere* identifies or gives additional information about the noun *balloon.* In the first sentence the noun is the subject of the sentence. In the second sentence the noun is the direct object of the verb *watched.* In the third sentence the noun is the object of the preposition *from.* In each sentence, however, the phrase *a large colorful sphere* is an appositive and tells more about the noun *balloon.*

Class Exercises

Read each sentence. Identify the appositive word or phrase in each. Tell where commas are needed. Then name the noun or pronoun that the appositive identifies.

1. Amelia Earhart a famous American aviator was born in 1898.
2. As a child she attended Ogontz School a school for girls in Pennsylvania.
3. During World War I she was a nurse in Canada our neighbor to the north.
4. She later moved to California the Golden State where she learned to fly.

Exercises

Write each sentence. Draw one line under the appositive phrase in each sentence. Put commas where they are needed. Draw two lines under the noun or pronoun the appositive phrase identifies.

1. In 1931 Ms. Earhart set an altitude record in an autogyro a kin to the modern helicopter.
2. Her solo Atlantic flight an historic event occurred in May of 1932.
3. In 1935 her solo Pacific flight a daring undertaking made headlines.
4. Ms. Earhart a true pioneer was the first woman to make such flights.
5. Her last endeavor a solo flight around the world resulted in tragedy.
6. She was lost at sea in July, 1937, somewhere near Howland Island a small island in the Pacific.
7. Ms. Earhart a legend in her own time lived an exciting and productive life.
8. She would have gloried in the achievements of Valentina Tereshkova-Nikolayev the first woman cosmonaut.
9. Ms. Tereshkova-Nikolayev a junior lieutenant at the time attained an altitude of 143.5 miles on her historic mission.
10. On that mission Ms. Tereshkova-Nikolayev reached a speed of 17,470 m.p.h. a record speed for a woman.

Sample Answer 1. In 1931 Ms. Earhart set an altitude record in an autogyro, a kin to the modern helicopter.

Participles in Verb Phrases and as Adjectives

The *present participle* of a verb is formed by adding *-ing* to the verb. The *past participle* of regular verbs is formed by adding *-ed* to the verb. Sometimes a participle functions as a main verb in a *verb phrase*.

> A **verb phrase** is one or more helping verbs followed by a main verb. It names the action or tells what the subject is or is like.

The pilot may be landing here.
The pilot must have landed here before.

In these sentences *may be* and *must have* are helping verbs. *Landing* is a present participle, and *landed* is a past participle. Both are main verbs. The complete group of underlined words is a *verb phrase*.
In a verb phrase the present participle is usually used with a form of the helping verb *be*, and the past participle is usually used with a form of the helping verb *have*.

FORMS OF THE HELPING VERB BE

am, is, are, was, were	can (may) be	could (should, would) be
might be	will (shall) be	could (should, would) have been
must be	may have been	might have been
must have been	will (shall) have been	have (has, had) been

FORMS OF THE HELPING VERB HAVE

have, has, had	can (may) have	could (should, would) have
might have	must have	will (shall) have

Present and past participles may perform more than one job in a sentence. Sometimes a participle functions as the main verb in a verb phrase. At other times a participle functions as an *adjective* when it modifies or describes a noun or pronoun.

> A **participle** can be used as an adjective to modify or describe a noun or a pronoun.

The train raced along the curving track.
The curved edges of the engine decreased the air resistance.

In the first sentence the present participle *curving* is used as an adjective to describe the noun *track*. In the second sentence the past participle *curved* is used as an adjective to describe the noun *edges*.

Compare the functions of the participles in these sentences.

Participles Used in Verb Phrases	**Participles Used as Adjectives**
The plane is speeding aloft.	The speeding train arrived early.
The attendants had informed the passengers.	The informed passengers departed.

Class Exercises

Find the verb phrase in each sentence. Name the helping verb.

1. Otto Lilienthal had designed an aircraft long before anyone else.
2. He was conducting test flights in different gliders of his own design.

Find the participle in each sentence. Tell if it is used as **part of a verb phrase** or as an **adjective**.

3. People mistakenly credit the flying Wright brothers as the first pilots.
4. They were flying early in the twentieth century.

Exercises

Write each sentence. Draw one line under the verb phrase in each sentence. Draw a second line under the helping verb or verbs.

1. The Wright brothers have found a place in aviation history.
2. The public has considered them pioneers since the early 1900s.
3. Before that the brothers had published a newspaper.
4. Later they were writing about aeronautics.
5. Pilots have been flying aircraft since their historic flight.

Write each sentence. Underline the participle in each sentence. Write whether it is used as **part of a verb phrase** or as an **adjective.**

6. They had experimented with wing control and balance in gliders.
7. Then the two experienced glider pilots were ready for an airplane.
8. They took their first daring flight at Kitty Hawk, North Carolina.
9. They were attempting this flight in a plane of their own design.
10. The tested plane was the first aircraft with a gasoline engine.

Sample Answers 1. The Wright brothers have found a place in aviation history.
6. experimented, part of a verb phrase

Gerunds and Gerund Phrases

Some verb forms express action, but they do not function as verbs. You know that a present participle is a verb form that may be used as an adjective to describe a noun or pronoun. A verb form ending in *-ing* may also function as a noun. When a verb form ending in *-ing* is used as a noun, it is called a *gerund*. Remember, a *noun* names a person, place, thing, or idea.

A **gerund** is a verb form ending in **-ing** that is used as a noun.

Sometimes a gerund functions as the subject of a sentence. It names what the sentence is about.

Moving involves a lot of work. Traveling is important to people.

At other times, a gerund functions as the direct object of a verb. Remember, a *direct object* of a verb receives the action of the verb. It answers the question *what?* after an action verb.

People enjoy traveling. We like flying.

The three kinds of verb forms that end in *-ing* all have different jobs in a sentence. You can tell them apart by distinguishing their *functions* in a sentence. A verb form ending in *-ing* may be the *main verb in a verb phrase*. A verb form ending in *-ing* may be used as an *adjective* to describe a noun or pronoun. A verb form ending in *-ing* may also function as a *noun*. Then it is called a *gerund*.

main verb in a verb phrase	The family have been packing all week.
participle as adjective	They will take an exciting trip.
gerund	Traveling will be fast.

In some sentences a gerund is part of a *gerund phrase*.

A **gerund phrase** is a group of words that includes a gerund and other words that describe the gerund.

Inventors have developed a variety of vehicles for long-distance traveling.

Naming the types of transportation illustrates our interest in travel.

Class Exercises

Tell whether each underlined word below is the **main verb** in a verb phrase, a participle used as an **adjective**, or a **gerund**. Tell whether each gerund is the **subject** of the sentence or the **direct object** of the verb.

1. Many people enjoy traveling.
2. People had been transporting objects long before the wheel.
3. Traveling must have presented problems for people with packages.

Read each sentence. Identify the gerund phrase in each.

4. In ancient times people used litters for carrying heavy packages.
5. Transporting large objects was necessary for most activities.
6. People must have preferred hauling their packages on these litters.

Exercises

Write each sentence. Write whether the underlined word is the **main verb** in a verb phrase, a participle used as an **adjective**, or a **gerund.** Write whether the gerund is the **subject** of the sentence or the **direct object** of the verb.

1. People had been using logs as rollers for litters with heavy loads.
2. Eventually people started floating crude rafts of logs.
3. They transported various goods on these sailing rafts.
4. Sailing on these rafts was difficult.

Write each sentence. Underline the gerund phrase in each.

5. Eventually raft builders tried experimenting with the design.
6. Adding a wall of logs along each edge of the raft formed a boat.
7. Then the builders used hides or bark for covering the framework.
8. The shipping of goods was much easier in these improved vessels.

Writing Sentences

Write eight sentences that describe what it is like to ride in a car or a bus. Use a gerund or gerund phrase in each sentence. Make certain that words ending in *-ing* do not function as the main verb in a verb phrase or as an adjective.

Sample Answers 1. main verb **5.** Eventually raft builders tried experimenting with the design.

Infinitives and Infinitive Phrases

Verb forms express action and perform different functions in sentences. A *participle* can be used as an adjective to describe a noun. A *gerund* acts as a noun. A third kind of verb form is called an *infinitive*.

> An **infinitive** is formed from the word **to** together with the basic form of a verb. It is often used as a noun in a sentence.

When the word *to* is used immediately before a verb, the word *to* is not a preposition. Remember a *preposition* is a word that relates a noun or a pronoun to another word in the sentence. A *prepositional phrase* is a group of words that begins with a preposition and ends with a noun or pronoun as its object.

- Read these sentences.

Once only children liked to skate.
Now some adults skate to their jobs.

In the first sentence the underlined words are an infinitive. In the second sentence the underlined words are a prepositional phrase.

Sometimes an infinitive functions as the simple subject of a sentence. The simple subject is the most important word or group of words in the complete subject. It names *whom* or *what* the sentence is about. Other times the infinitive may function as the direct object in a sentence. The direct object of a verb receives the action of the verb. It answers the question *whom?* or *what?* after an action verb.

- Read these sentences. Tell whether the infinitive is the simple subject of the sentence or the direct object of the verb.

S To race must be thrilling. Beginning skaters need D to practice.

Sometimes an infinitive is part of an *infinitive phrase*.

> **An infinitive phrase** is a group of words that includes an infinitive and other words that describe the infinitive.

An infinitive phrase can be short or long, depending on how the infinitive is expanded.

To skate well demands practice.
Racers need to develop speed and control.

The underlined parts of the sentences illustrate infinitive phrases.

Class Exercises

Look at the underlined words in each sentence. Tell whether the words are an **infinitive** or a **prepositional phrase**. Then tell whether each infinitive is the **simple subject** of the sentence or the **direct object** of the verb.

1. To skate is often the best choice of transportation in a city.
2. City dwellers with skates speed across town to their destinations.
3. City traffic is usually too slow for people who need to hurry.

Read each sentence. Identify the infinitive phrase in each sentence.

4. To sit in a car amid the traffic is a waste of time.
5. People on skates need to follow traffic rules.
6. Skaters with experience learn to move through crowds easily.

Exercises

Write whether the underlined words in each sentence are an **infinitive** or a **prepositional phrase**. Then write whether each infinitive is the **simple subject** of the sentence or the **direct object** of the verb.

1. To skate requires some practice for most people.
2. People still crowd to the 4,000 skating rinks in this country.
3. Some skaters like to speed.
4. Instructors teach technique to beginning skaters.

Write each sentence. Underline the infinitive phrase.

5. People began to roller-skate in the early part of this century.
6. Today many skaters choose to enjoy their sport out-of-doors.
7. These athletes on wheels like to demonstrate their skill.
8. Advanced skaters prefer to participate in figure skating.

Writing Sentences

Imagine that you are a roller skater. Write five sentences about what you do on roller skates. Include an infinitive or an infinitive phrase in each sentence.

Sample Answers 1. To skate requires some practice for most people. infinitive, simple subject

5. People began to roller-skate in the early part of this century.

Parts of Speech in Sentences

Each word in a sentence performs a particular job. Each word can be put into a category called a *part of speech*. The part of speech depends on the job that the word performs in the sentence. You have learned about all eight parts of speech.

Noun	A **noun** names a person, place, thing, or idea.
Verb	An **action verb** names an action. It may contain more than one word. It may contain a helping verb. A **linking verb** tells what a subject is or is like.
Pronoun	A **pronoun** takes the place of one or more nouns.
Adjective	An **adjective** describes a noun or pronoun.
Adverb	An **adverb** describes a verb, an adjective, or another adverb.
Preposition	A **preposition** relates a noun or pronoun to another word.
Interjection	An **interjection** expresses strong feeling or surprise.
Conjunction	A **conjunction** connects words or groups of words.

- Read these sentences.

  Airplanes fly over Chicago often. Wow! They are huge and powerful.

- Study the chart. It tells the part of speech of each word and explains the reason.

Word	Part of Speech	Reason
Airplanes	noun	names a thing
fly	action verb	names an action
over	preposition	relates Chicago to fly
Chicago	noun	names a place
often	adverb	describes the verb fly
Wow	interjection	expresses strong feeling
They	pronoun	takes the place of Airplanes
are	linking verb	tells what They are like
huge, powerful	adjectives	describe the pronoun They
and	conjunction	connects the two adjectives

• Read the sentence below. Note that the same word can serve as two or more parts of speech.

Airplanes fly to Chicago. A fly landed on the seat.

The word *fly* is a different part of speech in each sentence. In the first sentence *fly* is an action verb. In the second sentence *fly* is a noun.

Class Exercises

Read each sentence. Tell the part of speech of each underlined word.

1. Powerful airplanes land at the airport throughout the day.
2. The control tower gives pilots permission to land.
3. They land and taxi slowly toward the hangar.
4. The pilot is responsible for the safety of his passengers.

Exercises

Read each sentence. Write each underlined word and its part of speech.

1. Computers help control flight patterns in most large airports.
2. Radar detects all planes within several hundred miles.
3. It scans the sky for airplanes continually.
4. One operator carefully checks the radar screen for problems.
5. Another operator in the control tower contacts the pilot on the radio.
6. She reports bad weather conditions and air traffic.
7. The airplane is in a holding pattern.
8. The cautious operator approves the landing of the airplane.
9. The pilot adjusts the position of the plane.
10. She skillfully lands the airplane at the airport.

Writing Sentences

Imagine that you are an operator in a control tower. Write six sentences to describe your day. Use all the parts of speech defined on the opposite page to write your sentences. Draw a line under one example of each part of speech. Write the part of speech of each word you underline.

Sample Answer 1. Computers, noun; patterns, noun; large, adjective

Unit Review

PHRASES, CLAUSES, AND SENTENCES

Write each sentence using the correct punctuation. Write whether it is a **simple sentence** or a **compound sentence**. Then draw one line under each complete subject. Draw two lines under each complete predicate. *pages 132-133*

1. Ancient hunters and food-gatherers dragged their loads on crude sleds called *litters*.
2. Workers in Babylonia attached the litters to teams of oxen.
3. Either the people dragged their loads themselves or the oxen pulled the litters.
4. Some loads were manageable but heavy loads proved more difficult.
5. Inventive workers used large logs as rollers under the litters.
6. Eventually, the concept of the wheel emerged and wheels were used.
7. Originally, only two wheels were attached to litters and carts.
8. The wheels were permanently attached to a pole or axle and a wagon with four wheels could not turn easily.
9. These awkward vehicles were not really useful for most work.
10. Inventors later designed a more flexible attachment for the wheel and vehicles with four wheels became more useful.

Write each subordinate clause. Draw a line under the subordinating conjunction that begins each subordinate clause. *pages 134-135*

11. Since canals link oceans, ships sail quickly from ocean to ocean.
12. Some ships are pulled by a tugboat because they are so large.
13. Large ships sail quickly when a canal has a lock system.
14. As the canal lock opens, water from the ocean rushes into the channel.
15. When the water level is high, the ship enters the canal.
16. The canal lock behind the ship closes after the ship is in the channel.
17. The ship waits until the canal lock in front opens.
18. While the water flows out into the ocean, the ship leaves the canal.
19. When the ship has passed safely beyond the canal, the lock closes.
20. Trade between countries is spreading because ships use the canals.

Write each adverb clause. Draw two lines under the subordinating conjunction. Then write the word the clause modifies. Write whether that word is a **verb**, an **adjective**, or an **adverb**. *pages 136-137*

21. During the 1800s people used various vehicles when they traveled.
22. Whenever they went on short journeys, they usually used a lightweight gig.
23. The family brake also served whenever the trip was fairly short.
24. These carts were inconvenient when the journey was long.
25. Wealthy families rode in chauffeured coaches wherever they traveled.
26. When people rode through the park, they used the victoria.
27. The phaeton traveled more quickly than most other vehicles did.

Write each sentence. Draw one line under the appositive phrase in each sentence. Put commas where they are needed. Draw two lines under the word the appositive phrase identifies. *pages 138-139*

28. The automobile a popular means of transportation today developed through a series of inventions.
29. Its history began in the eighteenth century with the invention of the first motor vehicle a steam-driven wagon.
30. The engine a steam-operated motor rested on a single wheel.
31. The inventor designed the vehicle a tractorlike machine especially for hauling weapons.
32. The inventor made the creation a strange-looking machine in 1769.
33. The inventor took the vehicle out for a demonstration a ride through the streets of Paris.
34. This first automobile a self-propelled vehicle cruised through Paris at three miles per hour.

Write the verb phrase in each sentence. Draw two lines under the helping verb or verbs. *pages 140-141*

35. Since the development of self-propelled vehicles, people have been depending more and more on fuels.
36. For early models wood and coal had served satisfactorily.
37. Today plants can process up to 600,000 barrels of crude oil a day.
38. The use of natural gas is increasing.

Unit Review

Write the participle in each sentence. Then write whether it is used as **part of a verb phrase** or as an **adjective**. *pages 140-141*

39. Exciting stories of pioneer days are still popular.
40. People were traveling across the continent in Conestoga wagons.
41. They often had constructed rafts to carry the wagons across rivers.
42. The Conestoga wagon, or covered wagon, was a home on wheels.
43. Often pioneers had lived in the wagons for more than a year.
44. Many pioneers had thrilling tales to tell.

Read each sentence. Write whether the underlined word is the **main verb** in a verb phrase, a participle used as an **adjective**, or a **gerund**. Write whether the gerund is the **subject** of the sentence or the **direct object** of the verb. *pages 142-143*

45. The first public transportation system tried carrying passengers in horse-drawn streetcars.
46. Using streetcars was an effective method of public transportation.
47. Rolling streetcars followed their routes smoothly.
48. In some cities people were getting around in the horse-drawn bus.

Write the gerund phrase for each sentence. *pages 142-143*

49. Pulling busloads of people was difficult for the horses.
50. New York City began installing a system for streetcars in 1837.
51. Operating streetcars for transportation did not occur in Britain until 1860.
52. People in San Francisco tried moving the cars by a cable beneath the surface of the street.
53. Riding in cable cars is a favorite activity for tourists in San Francisco today.
54. Even the natives of the city enjoy using these vehicles.

Write whether the underlined words in each sentence are **infinitives** or **prepositional phrases**. Then write whether each **infinitive** is the **simple subject** of the sentence or the **direct object** of the verb. *pages 144-145*

55. To arrive at their destinations quickly is important to passengers.
56. For them, the jet aircraft promised to provide a faster ride.
57. Aircraft designers added improvements to their building plans.

58. Travelers now go to distant places in a very short period of time.
59. To fly means total relaxation and comfort during the journey.

Write the infinitive phrase for each sentence. *pages 144-145*

60. The noise and pollution of early jets started to offend the public.
61. To improve the product became a goal of manufacturers.
62. Aircraft designers have continued to alter weak details.
63. The larger, more luxurious carriers are a comfort to experience.

Read the paragraph below. Write each underlined word and its part of speech as it is used in the paragraph. *pages 146-147*

During the 1800s a mode of transportation flourished on the Mississippi River. This was the steamboat. Steamboats transported goods and passengers between cities and towns along the river shore. Famous races took place between competitive captains. Often shows were provided for the passengers' entertainment. The industry flourished for over a century, but by 1935 it was almost nonexistent. Alas, the romantic days of the Mississippi steamboat are no more.

ENTER BY THE NEAREST ADIT
(or, Where Have All the Adits gone?)

One of the common terms used in both transportation and commerce is the word *exit*, of Latin origin, meaning "a going out," or "a way out." The counterpart of exit is *adit*, which means an approach or access, an entrance. The word entrance seems to have taken the place of the word *adit* in modern times.

We see the word *exit* frequently on highway signs. People give directions, such as "Get on the turnpike at Exit 9." The driver is entering, not leaving, the turnpike. If we had kept the old word, the directions would be: "Get on the turnpike at Adit 9." Think of another sentence using the word adit.

Exploring Language

Diagraming Simple Sentences

A *sentence diagram* shows you how words, phrases, and clauses work together within a sentence. With a sentence diagram you can see just how the parts of a sentence combine to express a complete thought. All sentences have a subject and a predicate. As you add parts to a sentence, the sentence tells more, and its diagram grows larger.

All sentence diagrams begin with a horizontal line. You divide the line into a subject part and a predicate part. Then you build your diagram around that first horizontal line.

Diagram 1: Subject and Action Verb

Place the subject on the left and the predicate on the right of the dividing line. Be sure the dividing line extends above *and* below the horizontal line. This separates the sentence's two main parts.

Sentence: Insects build.

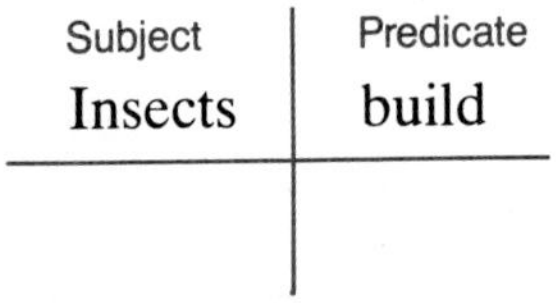

Diagram 2: Subject, Action Verb, and Direct Object

A direct object is part of the predicate. Place it to the right of the action verb. Separate the direct object from the verb with a vertical line. Do *not* extend this dividing line below the horizontal line.

Sentence: Insects build nests.

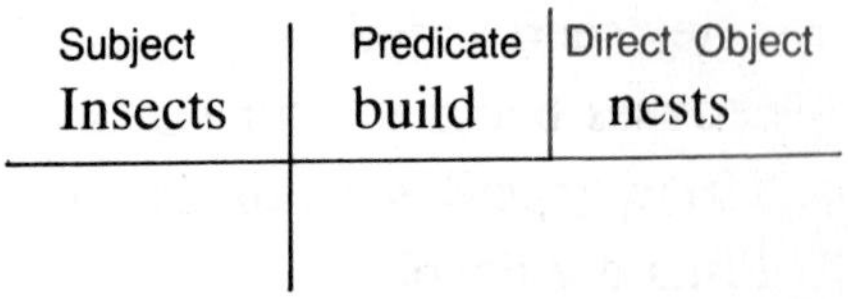

Diagram 3: Subject, Linking Verb, and Predicate Adjective

Place a predicate adjective to the right of the linking verb. Separate it from the verb with a *slanted* vertical line.

Sentence: Insects are industrious.

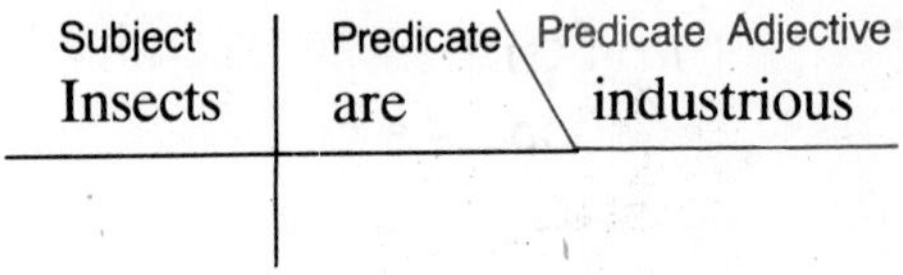

Diagram 4: Subject, Linking Verb, and Predicate Noun

Place a predicate noun to the right of the linking verb. A predicate noun is also separated from the verb by a *slanted* vertical line.

Sentence: Insects are workers.

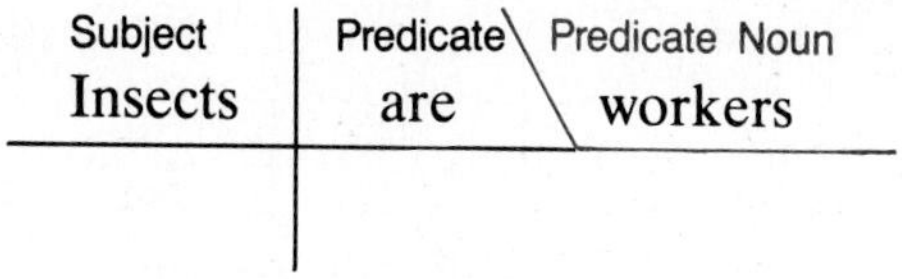

Diagram 5: Subject and Action Verb with Adjective and Adverb

Place a modifying word such as an adjective or adverb on a *slanted* line *below* the word it modifies.

Sentence: Small termites build quickly.

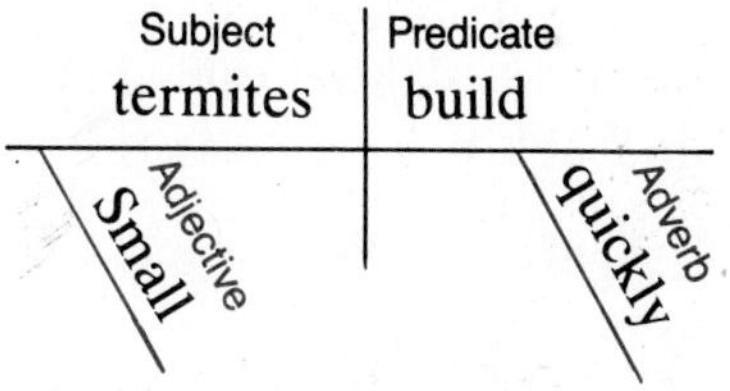

Exercises

Diagram the following sentences.

1. Insects work constantly.
2. Their homes vary widely.
3. Many insects eat wood.
4. They seem insatiable.
5. Houses become their homes.
6. Their appetites do the work.
7. Ants dig deeply.
8. The colonies are complex.
9. Some ants remain workers.
10. They burrow new passages.
11. Larger ants are guards.
12. These ants look fierce.
13. African termites make nests.
14. They cooperate amazingly.
15. The nests appear tall.
16. Termites build upward.
17. Mud is their material.
18. The sun bakes the mud.
19. It becomes hard.
20. These nests endure storms.
21. Workers dig small chambers.
22. Cool air flows.
23. Moisture seems precious.
24. Hives are different homes.
25. A hive is fragile.
26. Bees produce new hives fast.
27. Honeycombs are storehouses.
28. A honeycomb has six sides.
29. Workers hatch.
30. Young workers become busy.

Diagraming Simple, Compound, and Complex Sentences

The examples below will show you how to diagram more complicated sentences. Each diagram will help you to see how the parts of a sentence combine to express a complete thought.

Even the most complicated sentences follow simple rules. All sentences have a subject and a predicate. Therefore each diagram begins with those two parts. They sit on one divided horizontal line.

Diagram 6: Simple Sentence with Prepositional Phrase

Place the subject, predicate, and other predicate parts on the horizontal line. Now draw a *slanted* line beneath the word modified by the prepositional phrase. Write the preposition on that line. Then write the object of the preposition on a *horizontal* line that extends from the slanted one. Place words that modify the object on a *slanted* line below it.

Sentence: Westerners of today enjoy the events in annual rodeos.

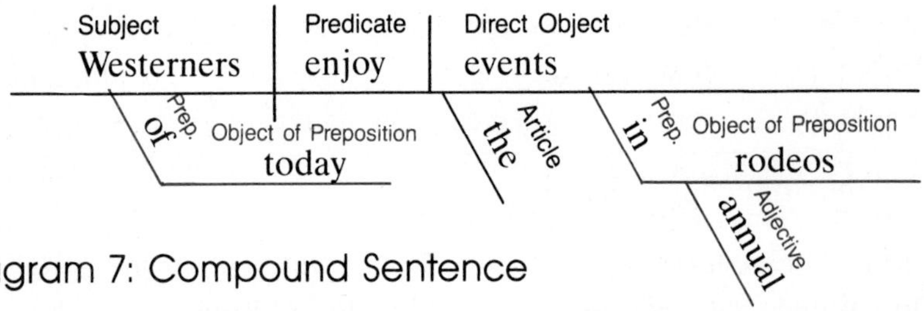

Diagram 7: Compound Sentence

Place the subject, predicate, and other predicate parts of each main clause on a horizontal line. Diagram the first main clause above the second. If a semicolon connects the main clauses, draw a *dotted* line to connect the two predicates. If a conjunction connects the main clauses, write the conjunction on a *solid* line.

Sentence: Cowboys ride wild horses, and cowgirls join the competition.

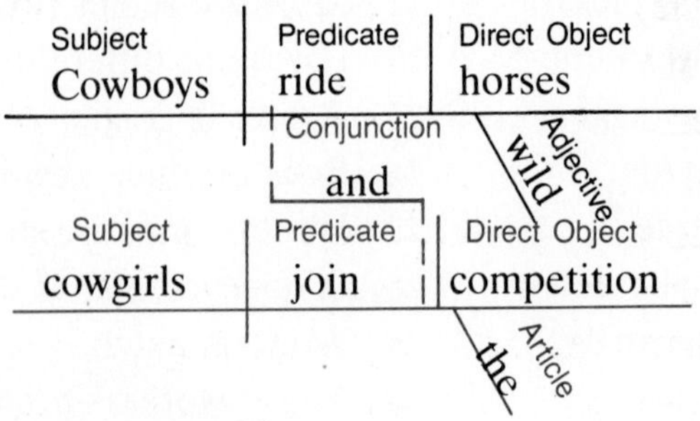

Diagram 8: Complex Sentence

Diagram the subject, predicate, and other predicate parts of each clause. Place the independent clause above the subordinate clause. Connect the two *predicates* with a *slanted dotted* line. Write the subordinating conjunction on that line.

Sentence: Clowns distract the bulls while contestants leave the ring.

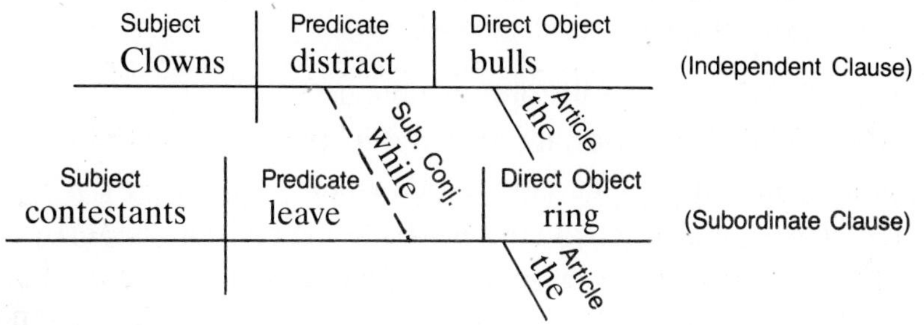

Exercises

Diagram the following sentences.

1. The many parts of a rodeo form a pageant of high excitement.
2. After a parade reaches the fairgrounds, the true rodeo begins.
3. Crowds in the stands shout loudly, and the animals hear them.
4. The animals enter small pens while announcers name contestants.
5. A bronco behind the gate kicks eagerly.
6. The first rider feels nervous, but the bronco nudges the gate.
7. The rider on its back grips the single rope tightly.
8. The bronco bucks powerfully as the first moments of the ride pass.
9. Friends around the ring cheer the rider in the saddle.
10. The bronco is victorious and the rider falls down.
11. A clown with bright clothing emerges when the rider falls.
12. The movements of the clown capture the attention of the bronco.
13. The clown calms the bronco, or he draws the bronco away.
14. The next contestant for the prize is a cowgirl.
15. She rides a different horse, but her horse looks powerful.
16. As the gate before her opens, the announcer shouts her name.
17. She sets a new record for the event, and she takes the prize.
18. Animals in the rodeo are valuable, and they receive good care.
19. Events with prize cattle follow after the riders finish.
20. Children of the contestants often take a part in the events.

Section Review

GRAMMAR AND USAGE

Write **sentence fragment** for each sentence fragment. Write each complete sentence correctly. Then write whether each sentence is **declarative, interrogative, imperative,** or **exclamatory.** Finally, rearrange each complete sentence if necessary, and draw a line between the complete subject and the complete predicate. *pages 4-11*

1. list a few facts about the history of submarines
2. did people many centuries ago invent designs for submarines
3. Alexander the Great and Leonardo da Vinci
4. the Dutch doctor Cornelius Drebbel built a submarine in 1620
5. how adventurous Doctor Drebbel must have been

Write the form of the verb in parentheses that completes each sentence correctly. Then write whether the subject is **singular** or **plural.** *pages 12-15*

6. Diving bells and the snorkel ___ old inventions. (is, are)
7. Six minutes ___ once the longest known dive. (was, were)
8. Underwater pressure ___ a very important factor. (seem, seems)
9. Electronics and navigation ___ to underwater travel. (add, adds)

Write whether each sentence is a **simple sentence,** a **compound sentence,** or a **complex sentence.** *pages 16-19*

10. Doctor Drebbel guided the first submarine beneath the River Thames while he propelled the craft with wooden oars.
11. His oars extended through a watertight frame of wood and leather.
12. Thirty-two years passed before Le Son built a submarine.
13. A paddlewheel drove Le Son's craft, but it traveled too slowly.

Write each sentence. Draw a line between the subject part and the predicate part. Then underline each noun. Label each one as a **common noun** or as a **proper noun**. Write whether each noun is **concrete** or **abstract.** *pages 26-29*

14. The small *Turtle* made naval history in the American Revolution.
15. The operator of the craft cranked its propeller by hand.
16. David Bushnell of Yale built the submarine.
17. The attack was a military failure but a scientific success.

Section Review

Write the form of the word in parentheses that correctly completes each sentence. *pages 30-37*

18. ___ a famous name in naval history. (*Nautilus, Nautilus*'s)
19. ___ Robert Fulton built the first Nautilus. (America's, Americas)
20. Copper ___ gave his submarine a strong hull. (plates', plates)
21. Today a team individually ___ on a submarine. (works, work)
22. The submarine crew together ___ the submarine. (guides, guide)

Write the verb in each sentence. Write whether it is an **action verb** or a **linking verb**. Write whether the action verb is **transitive** or **intransitive.** Then write whether each underlined word is a **predicate noun,** a **predicate adjective,** a **direct object**, or an **indirect object.** *pages 42-49*

23. Wilhelm Bauer was the next <u>experimenter</u> with submarines.
24. In 1850 Bauer gave the <u>submarine</u> more safety <u>devices</u>.
25. This inventor became <u>confident</u> enough for several dives himself.
26. Successful submarines looked <u>probable</u> for a short time.

Write each sentence. Use the **present, past,** or **future** tense of the verb in parentheses to complete each. *pages 50-51*

27. Bauer's bravery in those years ___ his fame. (ensure)
28. Today his name ___ in many modern history books. (appear)
29. Yet his lost submarines ___ on the sea bottom forever. (remain)

Write the form of the verb that agrees with each subject. *pages 52-53*

30. Neither Fulton nor Bauer ___ truly successful to us. (seem, seems)
31. Either a submarine or the early designs ___ faulty. (is, are)
32. Both wartime and peacetime ___ more efficient submarines. (require, requires)
33. Here in the next part ___ a story of an early success. (is, are)

Write the form of the helping verb that correctly completes each sentence. Write the participle. Label it as a **present participle** or as a **past participle.** *pages 54-55*

34. All early submarines ___ lacked an efficient motor system. (were, had)
35. By 1880 people ___ installing steam engines in submarines. (were, had)

Section Review

36. This period ___ formed a major part of submarine history. (had, is)
37. Today we ___ seeing the true submarine's development. (is, are)

Write the verb phrase in each sentence. Then write whether the tense is **present progressive, past progressive, present perfect,** or **past perfect.** *pages 56-59*

38. A Britisher was developing steam-submarines in 1885.
39. They had perfected this system after much experimentation.
40. Now Isaac Peral is experimenting with electric batteries.
41. Peral, a Spaniard, has received credit most often for the work.

Write the past tense or the past participle of the verb in parentheses to correctly complete each sentence. Watch for *have* or *has*. *pages 60-63*

42. A new era of naval history had ___ with these batteries. (begin)
43. The submarine ___ beneath the surface for long periods. (run)
44. Batteries had ___ all submarines until the Nuclear Age. (drive)
45. France ___ all submarine developers until about 1900. (lead)

Replace the underlined word or words in the first sentence with a pronoun. Write whether the pronoun is a **subject pronoun,** an **object pronoun,** or a **possessive pronoun.** Then write the antecedent for the underlined pronoun in the second sentence of each pair. *pages 70-77*

46. Jim takes <u>Jim's</u> dog to the doctor. <u>It</u> needs an examination.
47. Jim carries <u>the dog</u>. <u>It</u> has an injured paw.
48. The doctors check the <u>dog's</u> foot. Jim looks at <u>it</u>, too.
49. <u>The doctors'</u> aides bring bandages. Then <u>they</u> watch the doctors.

Complete each sentence by writing the correct word in parentheses. *pages 78-79*

50. Everyone ___ forward to the winter weekend. (look, looks)
51. Many ___ a skiing trip or an ice hockey game. (plan, plans)
52. Others ___ for work with their snow shovels. (hope, hopes)
53. Nobody ___ too much trouble from the storm. (expect, expects)

Write the letter next to the pronoun that correctly completes each sentence. *pages 80-83*

54. Tim shovels snow ___ . a. he b. himself

55. The snow ___ is light and powdery. a. itself b. it
56. ___ dog runs past Tim? a. Who's b. Whose
57. To ___ does the dog run? a. who b. whom

Write each sentence. Underline each adjective once. Underline twice the noun or pronoun each adjective describes. Circle each article and write whether it is **definite** or **indefinite.** Finally, if a linking verb connects the subject and adjective, write **predicate adjective** above the adjective. *pages 88-91*

58. Many species of the buffalo roam wild areas of the world.
59. The famous American buffalo appears safe from extinction today.
60. A member of the species in Asia often does heavy work.
61. Gigantic waterwheels seem light to a buffalo.

Complete each sentence by writing the correct word in parentheses. Then write whether the form used is **comparative, superlative,** or **demonstrative.** *pages 92-97*

62. Cats seem the ___ pets of all in an apartment. (good, better, best)
63. They are usually ___ than dogs. (quiet, quieter, quietest)
64. They are the ___ troublesome for owners. (little, less, least)
65. ___ cats beside me are very playful. (This, These)
66. ___ kitten over there is only three weeks old. (That there, That)

Write each sentence. Underline the adverb. Then write the word the adverb describes. Write whether the word described is an **action verb,** an **adverb,** or an **adjective.** *pages 102-103*

67. Wanda Landowsky played the harpsichord beautifully.
68. Her music was known for its uniquely dramatic vitality.
69. She studied the piano early in her career.
70. However, she performed so successfully on the harpsichord.

Write the word in parentheses that correctly completes each sentence. Write whether the word is an **adverb** or an **adjective.** *pages 110-111*

71. The discovery of the Rosetta Stone was ___ . (incredible, incredibly)
72. The French unearthed the stone ___ . (accidental, accidentally)
73. Almost ___ they recognized its worth. (immediate, immediately)
74. Its value to scholars was ___ . (enormous, enormously)

Section Review

Write each sentence. Draw one line under each prepositional phrase and two lines under the object of the preposition. Write the word each phrase describes. Write **adjective phrase** or **adverb phrase** for each prepositional phrase. *pages 118-121*

75. Margo Fonteyn is one of the greatest modern ballerinas.
76. One of her most famous partners is Rudolf Nureyev.
77. Nureyev was a member of the Leningrad Kirov Ballet.
78. He defected to the West in 1961 and created a legend.

Write the correct form of the verb in parentheses to complete each sentence. Then write each conjunction and write whether it is a **coordinating conjunction,** a **correlative conjunction,** or a **subordinating conjunction.** Draw two lines under any prepositions. *pages 122-125*

79. Both the Washington Monument and the Lincoln Memorial ___ magnificent structures. (is, are)
80. They are impressive tributes to two great Presidents, and tourists from all parts of the country ___ each monument. (visits, visit)
81. Anita ___ to Washington often because there are so many museums there. (goes, go)

Write each sentence using the correct punctuation. Write whether it is a **simple sentence** or a **compound sentence**. Draw one line under each complete subject. Draw two lines under each complete predicate. *pages 132-133*

82. The aardvark is the only anteater with teeth.
83. It is no relation to a pig but its name means earth pig.
84. It has the ears of a donkey.
85. The aardvark lives in small family groups and the female bears a single young once a year.

Copy each sentence. Draw one line under the adverb clause and two lines under the subordinating conjunction. Write the word the clause modifies. Then write whether that word is a **verb,** an **adjective,** or an **adverb.** *pages 136-137*

86. After motorcycles were invented, many people bought them for transportation.
87. After some time had passed, the motorcycle became a vehicle for sport.
88. Drivers are happy with motorcycles because they are convenient.
89. They travel fast on certain terrain unless the weather is bad.

Section Review

Write each sentence. Draw one line under the appositive phrase in each sentence. Put commas where they are needed. Draw two lines under the noun or pronoun the appositive phrase identifies. *pages 138-139*

90. The Grand Canyon National Park a spectacular natural wonder is located in Arizona.

91. This park a showplace of erosion hosts many visitors each year.

92. The canyon the park's main feature resulted from the action of the Colorado River.

93. Mules sure-footed beasts carry visitors from the top of the canyon to its base.

Write the participle or participles in each sentence. Then write whether each is used as **part of a verb phrase** or as an **adjective.** *pages 140-141*

94. During the seventh century B.C. the leaders were introducing a coinage system.

95. At that time an alphabetic written language was spreading throughout the area.

96. In the following century a great building period occurred.

97. By 480 B.C. the Persians had destroyed most of the sixth century B.C. structures.

Write each sentence. Draw one line under each gerund phrase and two lines under each infinitive phrase. *pages 142-145*

98. Swimming for health and recreation is becoming very popular in the United States.

99. Many people enjoy recreational swimming.

100. Many people like to swim in Barbados.

101. To visit the country can be a pleasurable experience.

Read the paragraph. Write each underlined word and its part of speech. *pages 146-147*

Chicago, the largest city (**102.**) in the midwest, has a rough (**103.**) climate. Summers (**104.**) are extremely hot, (**105.**) and winters can be (**106.**) bitterly cold. Nevertheless, the city supports one of the (**107.**) finest symphonies in the nation. (**108.**) It also (**109.**) possesses one of the (**110.**) greatest museums. (**111.**) Gee, I would like to live there if I could do it in (**112.**) spring or fall.

The moon rises above China's Great Wall.

You can see the Great Wall from the moon. Or see the moon from the Great Wall.

SALÉN LINDBLAD
CRUISING COMPANY

9

CAPITALIZATION, PUNCTUATION, ABBREVIATIONS, AND CONTRACTIONS

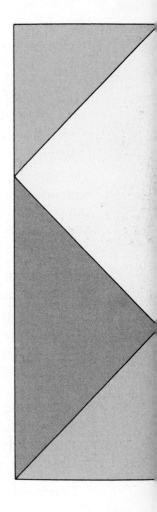

Review: Beginning and Ending Your Sentences

Some sentences give information. Other sentences ask for information. All sentences begin with a capital letter.

> A **declarative sentence** is a sentence that makes a statement. Use a period (**.**) at the end of a declarative sentence.
>
> An **interrogative sentence** is a sentence that asks a question. Use a question mark (**?**) at the end of an interrogative sentence.

My friends and I have traveled widely by railroad.
When did the first public railroad open for business?

The first sentence is declarative. It makes a statement. The second sentence is interrogative. It asks a question. Note that the pronoun *I* can only be the *subject* of a sentence. In sentences with *I* and one or more other simple subjects, the pronoun *I* always comes last.

Some sentences give commands or make requests. In a request or a command, the subject *you* is understood. Other sentences express strong feelings.

> An **imperative sentence** is a sentence that gives a command or makes a request. Use a period (**.**) at the end of an imperative sentence.
>
> An **exclamatory sentence** is a sentence that expresses strong feeling. Use an exclamation mark (**!**) at the end of an exclamatory sentence.

Sit by the window on the train. (This sentence gives a command.)
Please sit by the window. (This sentence makes a request.)
I saw such scenery! (This sentence expresses strong feeling.)

Commands that express an immediate need like *Help!*, *Stop!*, or *Hurry!* are often followed by an exclamation mark.

Some exclamations are not complete sentences. These incomplete sentences are usually used in conversation and are called *interjections*.

> An **interjection** is a word or group of words that expresses strong feeling. Use an exclamation mark (**!**) after an interjection when it stands alone. Use a comma (**,**) to separate an interjection from the rest of a sentence when it is a part of the sentence.

Oh!   Great!   By all means!   Alas, I cannot go to Maine with you.

Class Exercises

Tell how to capitalize and punctuate each group of words correctly.

1. what fuel did the first railroad engines use
2. how crowded a commuter train can be in the morning
3. the first public railroads opened during the 1820s
4. look up the number of miles of American railroad track
5. what a busy station we have
6. how is a monorail different from a railroad

Exercises

Write each sentence or group of words. Capitalize and punctuate each one correctly. Then write **declarative, interrogative, imperative, exclamatory,** or **interjection** for each one.

1. travelers can ride commuter trains or intercity trains
2. oh
3. do commuter trains stop at each town outside a city
4. take a brief train ride from Long Island to New York City
5. please purchase an extra commuter ticket for me
6. an intercity train offers many more services to people
7. great
8. between what cities do these trains carry passengers
9. plan on a trip of several days to cross the country
10. the conductor and i talked about routes to the West

Writing Sentences

Imagine you and your friends will be going on a trip. Write six sentences. Check your sentences for correct punctuation and capitalization.

1. Write two declarative sentences about how you will travel.
2. Write an interrogative sentence about the place or places you will visit.
3. Write two imperative sentences about what you will take with you.
4. Write an exclamatory sentence and an interjection about your topic.

Sample Answer 1. Travelers can ride commuter trains or intercity trains. declarative

Capitalizing Proper Nouns and Proper Adjectives

You know that a common noun names any person, place, thing, or idea. You also know that a proper noun names a specific person, place, thing, or idea. Your name, the name of the street you live on, and the name of your school are examples of proper nouns. Remember, only the important words in a proper noun are capitalized.

- Read the chart below. Notice which nouns are capitalized.

People:	Japanese, Ann Dorsey, Queen Mary, Professor Smith, Aunt Nancy, but *my aunt*
Languages:	English, Swahili, Spanish, Arabic
Countries, Continents, Planets:	United States of America, Asia, Mars
Cities, States, Counties:	San Francisco, North Carolina, Dade County
Areas, Regions:	New England, Wild West, North Pole, the East (Capitalize a compass direction when it refers to a region. Do not capitalize it when it just refers to a direction: *east.*)
Streets, Roads:	Monroe Street, Pennsylvania Avenue, Route 66
Geographical Features:	Pacific Ocean, Yellowstone Park, Niagara Falls
Buildings, Monuments:	White House, Statue of Liberty
Companies, Institutions:	Home of the Raisin Restaurant, Natural Foods Company, Federal Bureau of Investigation, Benjamin Franklin High School
Calendar Items, Seasons:	Friday, June, Fourth of July (Do not capitalize the names of the seasons: *summer.*)
Events:	Rose Bowl Game, Columbus Day Parade
School Subjects:	Algebra I, Biology II, but *two mathematics courses*
Periods of Time:	Stone Age, Middle Ages, Space Age
Titles of Works:	*Encyclopaedia Britannica*, *You're a Good Man, Charlie Brown*

An adjective formed from a proper noun is called a *proper adjective*. A proper adjective is capitalized.

- Read the words below. Notice which words are capitalized.

San Francisco skyline African art Japanese car English tea

San Francisco, African, Japanese, and *English* come from the proper nouns *San Francisco, Africa, Japan,* and *England*. Therefore, they are capitalized.

When you form adjectives from the names of places, be sure to check the spelling in a dictionary. The adjectives and the nouns may be spelled differently.

Class Exercises

Read each item below. Tell where capital letters are needed.

1. rudolph diesel
2. irish lace
3. ann arbor, michigan
4. nevada desert
5. geology teacher
6. wabash river
7. department of labor
8. lost city of atlantis
9. general eisenhower

Exercises

Write each sentence. Use capital letters where they are needed.

1. The state of texas, on the gulf of mexico, has huge cities.
2. Travelers in the south may visit corpus christi or houston.
3. The lyndon B. johnson space center is in houston.
4. It is the headquarters for american space flight.
5. The space center is named after president johnson.
6. It supervised the *apollo, skylab*, and space shuttle missions.
7. Corporations and universities carry on research in houston.
8. The space center has helped the texan economy to grow.
9. The national aeronautics and space administration created jobs for texans.
10. Travel to mars may be controlled from the space center.

Writing Sentences

Imagine you are traveling by train through the United States. Write six sentences about places and things you visit or see. Use a proper noun or proper adjective in each sentence. Use the dictionary if necessary.

Sample Answer 1. The state of Texas, on the Gulf of Mexico, has huge cities.

Commas I

Commas signal a pause or separation between parts of a sentence. When used properly, commas make sentences easier to understand.

> Use a **comma** (,) to separate each noun, verb, or adjective in a series of three or more nouns, verbs, or adjectives.

Sailors, passengers, cargo, and mail cross the Atlantic. (nouns)

Passengers swim, dine, dance, and rest aboard ship. (verbs)

Slow, pleasant, restful cruises make good vacations. (adjectives)

> Use **commas** (,) to separate the different items in addresses and dates. Use a **comma** after the last part of the address or date when it appears in the middle of a sentence.

Tickets are sold at 9 Harbor Place, New York, each day.

On April 11, 1983, ten cruise reservations were made.

Commas are also used to set off words and expressions that interrupt a sentence. These words and expressions interrupt the flow of thought in a sentence to introduce new information, or to add emphasis.

> Use a comma (,) to set off words such as *well, yes,* and *no* when they begin a sentence.

Yes, the ships are large. No, they do not have sails.

> Use **commas** (,) to set off expressions such as *by the way, of course*, and *however* when they interrupt a sentence.

The sailors on cruise ships, of course, are experts.

The ship's captain, however, knows every part of the liner.

> Use **commas** (,) to set off appositives when they interrupt a sentence with more information.

The airplane, a quick means of travel, offers little adventure.

Robert took the "Cruise to Nowhere," a trip without a destination.

Another kind of interruption in a sentence occurs when you speak to a person by name.

> Use **commas** (,) to set off a person's name when you address the person directly.

Mr. Roberts, please come immediately. Will you meet me, Ann?

When you leave, Sarah, use the gangplank.

Commas are also used in friendly letters.

Use a **comma** (,) after the salutation of an informal letter and after the closing of all letters.

Dear June, Dear Aunt Sally, Yours truly, Love,

Class Exercises

Tell where a comma or commas belong in each sentence below. Give the reason.

1. Travel by ship a luxury nowadays still pleases most passengers.
2. Much time of course is needed for a cruise.
3. Leaving Boston on June 1 1982 you may reach France by June 5.
4. Even huge ships rock toss sway and lose speed in those waters.

Exercises

Write each sentence using commas where necessary. Give a reason by writing **series, address, date, interrupting word** or **expression, appositive,** or **person's name.**

1. Mrs. Marshall do you know much about the *Queen Elizabeth 2*?
2. It is a huge luxurious famous passenger ship.
3. Yes the *QE2* was added to Britain's fleet in 1967.
4. The *Queen Mary* a museum now was smaller than the *QE2*.
5. The *QE2*'s average cruising speed by the way is 28-1/2 knots.
6. I have a post card dated May 23 1978 from its gift shop.
7. The return address is 99 Dockside Avenue Hamilton Puerto Rico.
8. The letter began "Dear Marie Enjoy your cruise."
9. Packets by the way were sailing ships of the early 1800s.
10. Passengers ate slept and traveled in comfort.
11. The steamship however was quickly being developed for travel.
12. Steamships were faster safer more comfortable and more punctual.
13. The British leaders of such services competed with the French.

Writing Sentences

Write six sentences about a cruise or other trip you have taken or would like to take. Include a series, address, date, interrupting word or expression, appositive, or person's name in each sentence.

Sample Answer 1. Mrs. Marshall, do you know much about the *Queen Elizabeth 2*? person's name

Commas II

You know that commas are used to separate words in a series, different items in addresses and dates, words and expressions that interrupt sentences, and the name of a person addressed. They are also used to separate parts of compound and complex sentences.

A *compound sentence* has two or more simple sentences joined by the conjunction *and, or,* or *but.* The simple sentences are called independent clauses. Each *independent clause* has a subject part and a predicate part. Each expresses a complete thought and could stand alone.

> Use a **comma** (,) before *and, or,* or *but* when they join simple sentences.

Camels can travel for days, and people call them ships of the desert.

Camels work hard, but they are often quite stubborn.

A *subordinate clause* has a subject part and a predicate part, but it cannot stand alone as a complete sentence. When one or more subordinate clauses are joined together with an independent clause, the new sentence is a *complex sentence.* Adverb clauses begin with subordinating conjunctions, such as *after, as, as if, as though, before, since, than, until, when, whenever, where, wherever*, and *while.* Like adverbs, adverb clauses may tell *how, when,* or *where* the action takes place.

> Use a **comma** (,) after an adverb clause that introduces a sentence.

When camels travel through the desert, they often go for days without water.

Notice that a comma follows the introductory adverb clause. The comma separates the two clauses within the complex sentence. You do not usually use a comma with an adverb clause that comes at the end of a sentence.

Travelers appreciate the shade when caravans arrive at oases.

Class Exercises

Tell where a comma belongs in each sentence. Give the reason.

1. Horses are swift runners but camels are better for desert travel.

2. When camels pass through sandstorms their noses shut tightly.
3. Wherever the nomads traveled they used camels for transportation.
4. Days in the desert are extremely hot and the travelers traveled mostly at night.
5. When you visit the Pyramids you may travel to them on a camel's back.

Exercises

Write each sentence and underline the subordinate clause. Use commas where necessary. Give the reason.

1. When my group and I mounted our camels the camels began to whine and kick.
2. Other camels carried goods and they lined up behind us.
3. The camels complained loudly until they began to move.
4. The ride was not too smooth but it was certainly a different experience.
5. Camels are stubborn but they work fairly hard.
6. Cars can travel through the desert but they often get stuck in the sand.
7. When cars do get stuck camels help to get them free.
8. The riders sang and the camels made noises with them.
9. When our camels passed an overheated car they broke into a quick trot.
10. We stopped at a small oasis when the temperature reached 110 degrees Fahrenheit.
11. After we rested we started out again.
12. We rode steadily over the desert until we reached an ancient oasis.

Writing Sentences

Write six sentences about your favorite means of travel. Use three compound sentences and three complex sentences containing adverb clauses. Use commas where necessary.

Sample Answer 1. When my group and I mounted our camels, the camels began to whine and kick. introductory adverb clause

Semicolons and Colons

The semicolon and the colon are punctuation marks that may be used to separate parts of a sentence.

A compound sentence has two or more simple sentences joined by a comma and one of the conjunctions *and, or,* or *but*. When there are already commas within one or both of the parts of the compound sentence, use a *semicolon* to separate the parts of the sentence.

Use a **semicolon** (;) to separate the parts of a compound sentence if there are commas within one or both of the parts.

Automobiles are used for travel, business, and pleasure; and they have changed greatly in appearance over the years.

Sometimes the conjunctions are omitted when two simple sentences are joined to form a compound sentence. When the conjunctions are not used, separate the parts of the compound sentence with a semicolon.

Use a **semicolon** (;) to separate the parts of a compound sentence if they are not joined by *and, or*, or *but*.

Steam, electricity, and gasoline have powered automobiles; gasoline has become the most successful method.

Another punctuation mark that shows separation is the *colon*.

Use a **colon** (:) between the hour and minute when writing the time.

The plane for Chicago will leave at 1:46 P.M.

Use a **colon** (:) after the greeting in a business letter.

Dear Sir: Dear Madam: Dear Ms. Cartney:
Dear Macmillan Publishing Co.:

Use a **colon** (:) to show that a list of items will follow in a sentence.

Cars have these uses: travel, business, and pleasure.

Class Exercises

Tell where the punctuation should be placed in each sentence. Tell whether the punctuation should be a **semicolon** or a **colon**.

1. Early motorists had three problems road conditions, long distances, and gas prices.
2. Roads were not paved at that time the heavy cars sank in the mud.
3. These first cars, of course, couldn't travel far and gasoline was very expensive.
4. Then people asked for these changes smoother roads, better cars, and more available oil.

Exercises

Write the sentences below. Punctuate them correctly using semicolons and colons.

1. The American Automobile Association aids travelers it was founded in 1902.
2. I wrote to the AAA for information I eagerly waited for a reply.
3. I received a letter at 330 P.M. it was from the AAA.
4. They sent me three things a trip route, a guide book, and a useful pamphlet.
5. I planned, at first, to cross the country and I intended to return by another route.
6. The AAA information was up-to-date it was also accurate.
7. As they wrote, I reached Kansas by 900 A.M. and I was tired.
8. I ate, rested, and checked my things my map, my money, and my car.
9. The map even showed a closed bridge when I reached it, it was closed.
10. The AAA also offers emergency services luckily I didn't need them.

Writing Sentences

Imagine you are traveling in a car along a seashore road. Write six sentences about what you see. Use semicolons and colons in your sentences.

Sample Answer 1. The American Automobile Association aids travelers; it was founded in 1902.

Quotation Marks and Italics

Quotation marks are used to set apart a speaker's exact words in a sentence. A direct quotation is a restatement of the speaker's exact words. Notice the use of quotation marks in the sentences below.

"Have you ever traveled on an airplane?" Jimmy asked.

"I flew once," replied Kathy, "in a huge jet."

Quotation marks are used to set apart technical terms or unusual expressions in a sentence. Quotation marks are also used around the title of a short story, poem, or song.

Pilots call the early morning flight the "red-eye special."

Jay likes a song called "Leavin' on a Jet Plane."

In sentences with direct quotations, a comma separates the exact words from words such as *he said* and *she replied*. Commas and periods at the end of direct quotations are always placed inside the closing quotation marks. Question marks and exclamation marks are placed inside the closing quotation marks if the quotation is a question or an exclamation. Otherwise those punctuation marks are placed outside. A new paragraph is also started for each new speaker in a dialogue.

Notice the use of quotation marks and punctuation marks in the sentences below.

Karen asked, "Do you remember your first plane trip?"

Jack said, "What an exciting experience that was!"

Had Jack flown on one of the new "jumbo jets"?

The verb often used with quotations is *said*. Here are some verbs you might use instead of *said*.

remarked	shouted	announced	asked	stated
explained	replied	suggested	laughed	answered

An indirect quotation tells what a person said without quoting the words exactly. Quotation marks are not used in an indirect quotation.

Kathy said, "I was not nervous on my first flight." (direct quotation)

Kathy said that she was not nervous on her first flight. (indirect quotation)

The first sentence is a direct quotation. The second sentence is an indirect quotation. The second sentence tells what Kathy said. It does not quote her exact words. The word *that* after the verb *said* signals an indirect quotation.

Italics are a special slanted kind of print. (*This is printed in italics.*) Use italics to set apart special names of things and titles of artworks.

When you write these special words, you underline them in your writing to show that they are italicized.

"I began reading a novel, Giant, during the flight," said Kathy.

Here is a list of names and titles that are italicized. Underline them when you write them.

The Hobbit (book)
Pieta (sculpture)
Moonlight Sonata (long musical work)
Autumn Rhythm (painting)
Raiders of the Lost Ark (film)
H.M.S. *Bounty* (ship)
As You Like It (play)
Patterson (long poem)
the *Boston Globe* (newspaper)
Cosmos (television series)
Apollo 11 (spacecraft)
the *Red Ball Express* (train)

Class Exercises

Tell where quotation marks, punctuation marks, and italics are needed in the sentences below.

1. I'll be nervous on such a big plane Jimmy said.
2. Do you know said Kathy that flying is safer than driving
3. I think I belong on the ground Jimmy shrugged.
4. Maybe Carol said, "you could travel on the U.S.S. United States.
5. Kathy remarked, You might see the film Star Wars on your flight.

Exercises

Write the sentences below correctly. Use quotation marks, punctuation marks, and italics correctly.

1. I once did some traveling in a small airplane said Leo.
2. Leo added that the airplane Western Angel belonged to his uncle.
3. Where did you travel to asked Ellen.
4. We flew from Colorado to Wyoming Leo answered.
5. Was it more fun asked Ellen than flying in a jet
6. I thought so Leo remarked. He showed me the kinds of turns an airplane can make
7. Your uncle must be a good pilot Ellen said.
8. Is he as good at flying as the man on that old television show, Sky King asked Ellen.
9. Did Leo remember if his uncle could do a loop-the-loop
10. I really couldn't say Leo laughed.

Sample Answer 1. "I once did some traveling in a small airplane," said Leo.

Other Punctuation Marks

You will find these additional punctuation marks useful in your writing. Each one helps in a different way to make your writing clear.

The hyphen (-) has several uses. Notice its use in these examples.

ex-football player	Robert Goddard (1882-1945)	mid-August
ex-president	thirty-seven	mother-in-law

Always use a hyphen after the prefix *ex-*. A hyphen is also used when a prefix comes before a capital letter: *mid-August* or *pro-British*.

The hyphen provides a quick way of saying that a person or thing existed between two dates: *(1882-1945)*. Or, if an airplane (for example) flies between Boston and New York, it is the *Boston-New York* flight.

Some words require hyphens as an essential part of their spelling, for example, compound numbers such as *thirty-seven* and some compound words such as *mother-in-law, singer-composer, Irish-American, Mexican-American, man-of-war, small-scale, warm-hearted, knee-high, panic-stricken,* and *tried-and-true*. When you use compound words, be sure to check the spelling in the dictionary.

The dash (—) is used in sentences. The dash shows an abrupt change, or an interruption, in the main thought of a sentence.

I'm going to be an astronaut—I love flying—when I finish school.

Tommy went running off toward his home—he'd forgotten his books.

What did Maria say—I forgot—that I should read?

Joli was surprised—it was her birthday—to get such nice gifts.

Joe planned ahead—he's so wise—for his vacation.

Emily—she's my mother's friend—visited yesterday.

Parentheses ( ) are used to set off extra information within a sentence. Parentheses are always used in pairs.

Robert Goddard (1882-1945) was a pioneer in rocketry sciences.

His first launching (quite successful) was in the winter of 1926.

Goddard's hard work (and a bit of genius) brought him fame.

Class Exercises

Tell what kind of punctuation mark or marks are needed for each item.

1. Michelangelo 1475 1564 painted the Sistine Chapel.
2. pre January
3. My wallet thank goodness was found.
4. forty six
5. ex governor
6. The film it was good was made in France.
7. post Picasso
8. The trip quite difficult was worthwhile.

Exercises

Write each sentence. Use a hyphen, dash, or parentheses where necessary.

1. The space shuttle first launching, April 1981 began a new era in travel.
2. Many other ex spacecrafts found homes in museums after their flights.
3. The shuttle it can be used over again promises something new.
4. When space stations are built, the shuttle will make earth station trips.
5. Every station in orbit will not be for scientific industrial use only.
6. Ordinary people not only astronauts may travel there.
7. By then it seems hard to imagine we might not think too much of such trips.
8. After all, the lunar landings 1969 1972 once seemed impossible.
9. A person does not need an ex astronaut's abilities to fly coast to coast.
10. What would the usual vacation two weeks in orbit be like?

Writing Sentences

Imagine that you are spending a week on a space station in earth orbit. Write six sentences about how life is different in such a place. Use a hyphen, dash, and parentheses in your sentences.

Sample Answer 1. The space shuttle (first launching, April 1981) began a new era in travel.

Abbreviations

The important words in proper nouns are capitalized. The abbreviations and initials that are sometimes used in place of proper nouns are also capitalized.

- Read the names below. Notice the use of periods.

Mary Smith Baldwin—M. S. Baldwin   Jon Rob Duffy—J. R. Duffy

Some common nouns become proper nouns when used with names. These words include *mister, doctor, reverend, junior*, and *senior.* When they are used with names, they are capitalized and abbreviated.

Mr. James L. Twadell, Jr.	Rev. Ramón Díaz, Sr.	Dr. Marie S. Hoyt
Miss Catherine Williams	Ms. Amy Corsten	Mrs. Angelo Berera

- Note the use of *Mrs., Miss,* and *Ms.* in the names above. *Mrs.* identifies a married woman. It was originally the abbreviation of the British term *mistress. Miss* refers to an unmarried woman and is never abbreviated. *Ms.* can identify either a married or unmarried woman.

Professional and academic degrees are abbreviated and used after a person's name. Note the use of commas and periods.

Doctor of Medicine—Janet Barkley, M.D.

Doctor of Philosophy—J. Fuentes, Ph.D.

Some abbreviations are used in charts and lists, but not in sentences. *May, June,* and *July* are not abbreviated.

Days:	Sun.	Mon.	Tues.	Wed.	Thurs.	Fri.	Sat.
Months:	Jan.	Feb.	Mar.	Apr.	May	June	
	July	Aug.	Sept.	Oct.	Nov.	Dec.	

- Note the use of commas and periods with days and dates.

Thursday, January 3 or Thurs., Jan. 3

Proper names of streets are often abbreviated in addresses.

Street—St.	Court—Ct.	Avenue—Ave.	Road—Rd.
Place—Pl.	Square—Sq.	Drive—Dr.	Boulevard—Blvd.

The post office prefers that you use its abbreviations of state names when you write addresses. Note the use of commas. Periods are not used.

Houston, Texas or Houston TX

States:

Alabama	AL	Idaho	ID	Missouri	MO	Pennsylvania	PA
Alaska	AK	Illinois	IL	Montana	MT	Rhode Island	RI
Arizona	AZ	Indiana	IN	Nebraska	NB	South Carolina	SC
Arkansas	AR	Iowa	IA	Nevada	NV	South Dakota	SD
California	CA	Kansas	KS	New Hampshire	NH	Tennessee	TN
Colorado	CO	Kentucky	KY	New Jersey	NJ	Texas	TX
Connecticut	CT	Louisiana	LA	New Mexico	NM	Utah	UT
Delaware	DE	Maine	ME	New York	NY	Vermont	VT
		Maryland	MD	North Carolina	NC	Virginia	VA
District of Columbia	DC	Massachusetts	MA	North Dakota	ND	Washington	WA
Florida	FL	Michigan	MI	Ohio	OH	West Virginia	WV
Georgia	GA	Minnesota	MN	Oklahoma	OK	Wisconsin	WI
Hawaii	HI	Mississippi	MS	Oregon	OR	Wyoming	WY

Class Exercises

Shorten each address correctly. Tell where you would use capital letters and punctuation marks. Use initials for first and middle names. Use the post office abbreviation for each state.

1. doctor amos wilson Brundy, junior
   23 Rosehaven boulevard
   Jackson, mississippi 39209
2. nan evans Larr, doctor of medicine
   1 Robson court
   San Antonio, texas 78201

Exercises

Change each word group, using capital letters and punctuation marks. Abbreviate each word underlined. Write the new phrase.

1. doctor Carol Bard
2. the reverend Carl Garcia
3. friday, november 13
4. Des Moines, iowa
5. Mrs. jane Kurtin
6. Mister Bill Jackson
7. tuesday, June 12
8. Joseph Turner, senior
9. 345 Jones avenue
10. Lucia Sierra, doctor of philosophy
11. Salt Lake City, utah
12. 62 Marley court

Sample Answer 1. Dr. Carol Bard

Contractions

Our language is full of shortcuts. Words like *plane, phone,* and *dorm* are all short forms of longer words. Another common shortcut in our language is the *contraction*.

> A **contraction** is a word made up of two words combined into one by omitting one or more letters. Use an **apostrophe** (') in a contraction to show where letters are missing.

Pronouns are often joined to certain verbs to form contractions. Note how pronouns are joined with the forms of the verb *be* in these sentences.

I'm a pretty fast traveler on a racing bicycle. (I am)
You're going to meet me at the end of my trip. (You are)
He's putting a new pair of tires on my bicycle. (He is)
She's planning a bicycle trip along the same route. (She is)
It's one of the best routes for bicycle travel. (It is)
They're going to build a special lane for bicycles. (They are)
We're hoping that the lane will be open for us. (We are)
Who's carrying the maps that show the path of the lane? (Who is)

Several contractions are easily confused with possessive pronouns because they sound the same. Remember the two parts of the contraction when you are spelling it. Then you will not have trouble remembering which is the contraction and which is the possessive pronoun.

Contractions	Possessive Pronouns
Who's (Who is) the rider?	Whose map is this?
It's (It is) a fine bike.	Its owner is Lee.
You're (You are) lucky.	Your map is here.
There's (There is) my bike.	That map is theirs.
They're (They are) ready.	Their bikes are new.

The apostrophe also has another use. It shows that a noun or proper noun is possessive.

a rocket's noise.	Ross' bicycle or Ross's bicycle
two dogs' collars	the women's group

Class Exercises

Read each sentence. Tell which word correctly completes each sentence.

1. ___ a growing interest in travel by bicycle today. (There's, Theirs)
2. The bicycle, with ___ lack of a need for fuel, is very practical. (it's, its)
3. Many city dwellers travel to and from ___ jobs by bicycle. (they're, their)
4. ___ interested in becoming a serious cyclist? (Who's, Whose)
5. Besides exercise, traveling on ___ bicycle gives you a sense of freedom. (you're, your)

Exercises

Write each sentence. Use an apostrophe where necessary.

1. The friends bicycles are ready for the long trip.
2. Ellen, whos going to lead the way, makes sure shes ready.
3. "Im anxious to start; its a long ride to the state forest," Ellen says.
4. "Were ready when youre ready," say Jess and Kim.
5. "Its a beautiful day for bicycling," says Don.
6. Ellen says that shes riding too fast, and Jess says that hes too slow.
7. "Youre both missing the great view Im enjoying," says Kim.
8. "This roads view is really scenic," remarks Ellen.
9. "I think theres another scenic route on Jess map," says Kim.
10. The friends pull over and watch a childrens baseball game.
11. "Theyre good," says Ellen.
12. "Youre good at bike travel, Ellen," says Kim.

Writing Sentences

Imagine that you are bicycling across your state. Write six sentences about your trip. Use three contractions and three possessive pronouns from this lesson in your sentences.

Sample Answer 1. The friends' bicycles are ready for the long trip.

Unit Review

CAPITALIZATION, PUNCTUATION, ABBREVIATIONS, AND CONTRACTIONS

Write each sentence or group of words. Capitalize and punctuate each one correctly. Then write **declarative, interrogative, imperative, exclamatory,** or **interjection** for each one. *pages 164-165*

1. many kinds of trains operate in the United States
2. does every American train carry travelers between cities
3. list a few facts about the many kinds of trains in America
4. by all means
5. my brother and i have a large model railroad in our home
6. it looks just like a small town
7. read this survey about commuter services after school

Write each sentence. Use capital letters where they are needed. *pages 166-167*

8. Americans and europeans have plans to build a space station.
9. The station will be called *spacelab* and will orbit earth for years.
10. Vehicles like the united states' space shuttle will carry people there.
11. When *spacelab*'s early work is done, ordinary people may travel in it.
12. The department of transportation in washington, D.C., may be involved.
13. Everyone, from presidents to physics I teachers, will want to go.
14. A space age *guide to travel* might list *spacelab* as one destination.
15. In a few minutes, one would cross the atlantic from new england to england.
16. Traveling west in orbit, one might catch up with yesterday.
17. Rounding the asian coastline, californian shores would appear.

Write each sentence. Insert commas where necessary. Then write the reason for commas in each sentence by writing **series, address, date, interrupting word** or **expression, appositive,** or **person's name.** *pages 168-169*

18. Toni do you know that ships were once the only travelers over seas?
19. The airplane a fairly recent invention hasn't such a long history.
20. No but it has undergone many changes.
21. Tell me by the way how you first traveled across an ocean.

22. I flew from California to Hawaii on August 19 1981 with my family.
23. Think of how quick easy and convenient that seems beside ship travel!
24. A trip from Boston Massachusetts to Los Angeles California took months.

Write each sentence and underline the subordinate clause. Use commas where necessary. Give the reason. *pages 170-171*

25. The llama does not have a hump but it is a relative of the camel.
26. When llamas climb mountain trails they are extremely sure-footed.
27. Llamas grow about four feet tall and they have coats of many colors.
28. Llamas are bad-tempered animals and in that respect they are quite like camels.
29. When a llama wants to rest it will stubbornly lie down.
30. South American Indians use llamas almost exclusively when they need transportation.
31. When a load is less than one hundred pounds the llama will cope with it cheerfully.

Write the sentences below. Punctuate them correctly using semicolons and colons. *pages 172-173*

32. Electric autos are not new they existed decades ago in the 1890s.
33. Electric autos offer three things quiet, easy care, and no fumes.
34. These autos, though popular, had problems and they lost their popularity.
35. Their top speeds in miles per hour are the following 18, 20, and 24.
36. Their batteries, too, needed recharging a driver couldn't travel too far.
37. The gasoline car took over but, of course, it has its drawbacks.
38. Interest in electric autos has returned however, making them is not easy.
39. I received a letter yesterday at 1200 P.M.

Unit Review

Write the sentences below correctly. Use quotation marks, punctuation marks, and italics correctly. *pages 174-175*

40. There are ways to help travelers from the ground Ira explained.
41. Do you mean working in the control tower asked Ben.
42. Yes, it's a job that requires much training Ira said, and the responsibility is great
43. The tower Ira added, is the center of the whole airport
44. Ira continued It's so busy I could write a play called Grand Central Station in the Sky
45. Maybe you could have worked on Apollo or something Ben replied.

Write each sentence. Use a hyphen, dash, or parentheses where necessary. *pages 176-177*

46. William the Conqueror's knights sat on horses in mid Channel.
47. Ex warhorses lived out their days in honor on their masters' estates.
48. North American horses descendants of Spanish ones were numerous by 1600.
49. American Indians particularly on the Plains couldn't be better riders.
50. Today, people who travel by horse, like my sister in law, travel mainly for pleasure.
51. The U.S. Army gave up its cavalry during World War II 1939 1945.

Change each word group, using capital letters and punctuation marks. Abbreviate each underlined word. Write the new phrase. *pages 178-179*

52. <u>professor</u> irwin corey
53. clare king, <u>doctor of medicine</u>
54. <u>wednesday</u>, <u>march</u> 9
55. <u>the reverend</u> <u>william</u> <u>thomas</u> burke
45 broadway
stoneham, <u>massachusetts</u> 02180
56. <u>ralph</u> <u>michael</u> burns
57. philip donne, <u>senior</u>
58. <u>february</u> 29
59. mary kay taylor
1090 harper <u>place</u>
bangor, <u>maine</u> 01034

Unit Review

Write the correct word for each sentence. *pages 180-181*

60. People used ___ feet before any other means of travel was found.
a. they're b. their

61. The "walking tour" has not lost ___ popularity yet.
a. it's b. its

62. ___ no better way to see the countryside than by traveling.
a. There's b. Theirs

63. Scientists, with ___ inventiveness, have even created *pedometers*.
a. they're b. their

64. A pedometer lets the person ___ carrying it measure distances.
a. who's b. whose

65. If ___ traveling by foot, allow yourself plenty of time.
a. you're b. your

Write each sentence. Use an apostrophe where necessary. *pages 180-181*

66. Im reading a book about walking tours.
67. Aristotle, whos a famous writer, is mentioned in the book.
68. Hes known mainly as a thinker, but theres more to know about him.
69. In my class were still reading Aristotle's journals.
70. John Keats, whos a famous poet, was a great walker.
71. Keats walked great distances in Englands cities and on its farms.
72. Its helpful to know about Keats travels when Im reading his works.

Exploring Language

Some common nouns that we use are taken from proper nouns that name people or places. Many of us have forgotten the connections. The words are treated as common nouns and not capitalized. Here are some of them.

sandwich cantaloupe gauze limousine cologne

Match the common nouns above with the proper nouns below. Think of the common noun that belongs in each blank space.

1. A large car was used in Limousin, France. It is a ___.
2. A thin cloth was invented in Gaza, Palestine. It is ___.
3. The Earl of Sandwich invented a snack. It is a ___.
4. A melon was grown first in Cantalupo, Italy. It is a ___.
5. A perfume was made in Cologne, Germany. It is called ___.

Students match their word power in a game of Scrabble.

Words should be an intense pleasure just as leather is to a shoemaker.

EVELYN WAUGH
British novelist
(1903-1966)

10

SPELLING

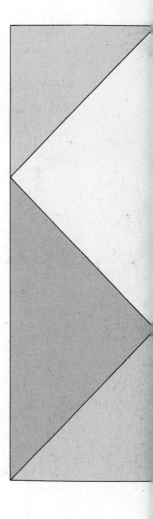

Using the Table of English Spellings

Sometimes you want to look up a word in a dictionary, but you don't know how to spell the word. Most dictionaries have a Table of English Spellings. This table shows the different ways that the sounds in words are spelled in written English. The spellings for each sound are listed in the order in which they most frequently occur. You can use the table to help you find words that you know how to pronounce but do not know how to spell.

- Look at the Table of English Spellings below.

TABLE OF ENGLISH SPELLINGS

Sound	Spelling
/a/	hand, have, laugh, plaid
/ā/	paper, rate, rain, pay, eight, steak, veil, obey, ballet, straight, gauge
/ä/	father
/är/	car, heart, sergeant
/ãr/	dare, hair, where, pear, their, prayer
/b/	bit, rabbit
/ch/	chin, nature, batch, question, cello
/d/	dive, ladder, would, failed
/e/	met, bread, many, said, friend, leopard, aesthetic, says, heifer
/ē/	he, city, bee, beach, athlete, machine, field, receive, key, Caesar, amoeba, people
/ėr/	fern, turn, thirst, worst, earth, courage, amateur, myrtle
/f/	fine, phone, off, half, laugh
/g/	go, stagger, vague, guard, ghost
/h/	he, whom
/hw/	wheel
/i/	bit, myth, give, damage, build, been, pretty, carriage, busy, women
/ī/	fine, tiger, try, high, tie, dye, eye, stein, height, buy, aisle
/ir/	clear, cheer, here, cashier, souvenir, weird
/j/	magic, jump, ledger, graduate, adjust, exaggerate, soldier
/k/	cat, key, tack, chord, account, mosquito, Iraq, walk
/kw/	quit
/l/	line, hall, isle
/m/	mine, hammer, climb, salmon, hymn
/n/	nice, gnome, knee, funny, pneumonia
/ng/	sing, link, tongue
/o/	lock, watch
/ō/	so, bone, boat, know, soul, foe, beau, oh, mauve, sew
/ô/	off, fall, author, jaw, bought, caught, broad
/oi/	foil, toy
/ôr/	fork, war, ore, oar, four, door
/ou/	out, now, bough
/p/	pill, happy
/r/	ray, parrot, wrong, rhyme
/s/	song, city, mess, scene, listen, psychology, waltz, sword
/sh/	nation, shin, special, mission, expansion, machine, sugar, tissue, conscience, ocean
/t/	ten, bitter, topped, doubt, two, ptomaine, yacht, thyme
/th/	thin
/u/	sun, son, touch, come, flood, does
/u̇/	full, look, should, wolf
/ü/	tool, luminous, who, flute, soup, jewel, true, lose, fruit, maneuver, canoe
/ū/	music, use, few, feud, cue, view, beautiful, adieu
/v/	vine, halve, of
/w/	we, queen
/y/	onion, yes
/z/	has, zoo, xylophone, fuzz, scissor, czar, tsar
/zh/	division, treasure, garage, azure, equation
/ə/	summon, alone, April, moment, furious, circus, oxygen, ancient, bargain, surgeon
/ər/	better, color, dollar, augur, picture, giraffe

Suppose you want to look up the meaning of the word *species* in the dictionary. However, you are not sure how to spell the */sh/* sound in the middle of the word. When you look at the Table of English Spellings, you find that */sh/* may be spelled *ti, sh, ci, ssi, si, ch, s, ss, sci,* or *ce.* Start looking for the word in the dictionary using each of the possible spellings until you find the word: speties, speshies, species.

Class Exercises

1. How many sounds are listed in the Table of English Spellings?
2. What does the symbol /a/ represent?
3. How many spellings represent the /ō/ sound?
4. What spellings represent the /ī/ sound?
5. What words are used to illustrate the /r/ sound?

Exercises

Read each sentence. Use the dictionary and the Table of English Spellings to correct the spellings of the underlined word in each sentence. Then write each sentence correctly.

1. Old legends and fables describe many apocriphal animals.
2. The unikorn was a magical horse with one spiraled horn on its head.
3. Its horn was said to bestow the gift of immoretality.
4. Another legendary horselike animal is the centore.
5. Its upper annatomy was human, while its body and legs were horselike.
6. In Western legends dragons are usually antaganistic animals.
7. Dragons of Eastern fables are more often benificent creatures.
8. The Sphynx had the head of a woman and the body of a lion.
9. This mithological creature was extremely frightening to passersby.
10. Anyone who could not answer its eniggmatic riddles was killed.
11. In Greek mythology the Minotaur was a monstur, half bull and half man.
12. The Minotaur was cunfined in an underground maze by King Minos.
13. During the Middle Ages salors spoke about mermaids.
14. The mermaid had the head and body of a beautiful woman and the tail of a fish insted of legs.

Sample Answer 1. Old legends and fables describe many apocryphal animals.

Spelling Rules I

You can improve your spelling skills by learning a number of rules.

> Write **i** before **e** except after *c* or when sounded like *a* as in *neighbor* and *weigh*.

grief frontier piece niece relieve

- Notice some exceptions to this rule in the words that follow.
  either weird height their

A prefix is a letter or group of letters added to the beginning of a word.

> Do not change the spelling of a word when you add a prefix to it.

re + enter → reenter dis + satisfied → dissatisfied

mis + spell → misspell un + noticed → unnoticed

A suffix is a letter or group of letters added to the end of a word.

> When a word ends in **e**, generally keep the **e** when adding a suffix that begins with a consonant.

hope + ful → hopeful care + less → careless

place + ment → placement late + ly → lately

- Notice some exceptions to this rule in the words that follow.

judge + ment → judgment argue + ment → argument true + ly → truly

> When a word ends in **e**, generally drop the **e** when adding **-y** or a suffix that begins with a vowel.

ice + y → icy refuse + ing → refusing arrive + al → arrival

remove + able → removable desire + ed → desired

This rule has two exceptions.

> When a word ends in **ce** or **ge**, keep the final **e** before adding a suffix that begins with **a** or **o**.

notice + able → noticeable advantage + ous → advantageous

> When a one-syllable word ends in **ie**, change the **ie** to **y** before adding **-ing**.

die + ing → dying tie + ing → tying lie + ing → lying

When a word ends in a consonant and **le**, drop the **le** and add **-ly**.

horrible + ly → horri<u>bly</u>   gentle + ly → gen<u>tly</u>   able + ly → a<u>bly</u>

Class Exercises

Determine which rule to use before adding the prefix or suffix to each word. Tell how to spell the new word.

1. mis + state
2. sensible + ly
3. tie + ing
4. exchange + able
5. rose + y
6. grace + ful
7. revive + al
8. remove + ed
9. arrange + ing
10. co + operate

Exercises

Read each pair of words. Write the correctly spelled word in each pair. Check your answers against the spelling rules in this lesson.

1. cuddley, cuddly
2. relief, releif
3. dying, dieing
4. managable, manageable
5. removeing, removing
6. managment, management
7. unatural, unnatural
8. brief, breif
9. bubbly, bubbley
10. advantagous, advantageous
11. refuseal, refusal
12. shiney, shiny
13. useless, usless
14. reducate, reeducate
15. cheif, chief
16. desireable, desirable
17. eraseing, erasing
18. largely, largly
19. tastful, tasteful
20. desirous, desireous

Add the prefix or the suffix to each word. Then write the word. Check your answers against the spelling rules in the lesson.

21. double + ly
22. vie + ing
23. trace + able
24. spice + y
25. survive + al
26. excite + ment
27. re + evaluate
28. enforce + ing
29. outrage + ous
30. un + numbered

Sample Answers 1. cuddly **21.** doubly

Spelling Rules II

The rules that follow will help you spell correctly when you add a suffix to a word.

When a word ends in a consonant and **y**, change **y** to **i** before adding a suffix.

sleepy + ly → sleepily
pity + ful → pitiful
hungry + ness → hungriness
silly + est → silliest
tally + ed → tallied
dairy + es → dairies

However, when you add a suffix to certain one-syllable words or when the suffix begins with **i**, do not change the **y** to **i**.

shy + ly → shyly   dry + ness → dryness   copy + ing → copying

When a word ends in a vowel and **y**, generally keep the **y** when adding a suffix.

annoy + ing → annoying
joy + ous → joyous
valley + s → valleys
play + ed → played

Double the final consonant before a suffix beginning with a vowel (1) if the word ends in one vowel and one consonant and (2) if the word is only one syllable or is accented on the final syllable.

plan + ed → planned
regret + able → regrettable
swim + er → swimmer
begin + er → beginner

Do not double the final consonant if the stress does not fall on the last syllable.

differ + ing → differing
open + er → opener
cover + ed → covered

Do not double a final consonant before a suffix beginning with a consonant.

equip + ment → equipment
win + less → winless
forget + ful → forgetful

The plural of most nouns is formed in a regular way.

To form the plural of most nouns, add **-s**.

tiger + s → tigers   eye + s → eyes   snare + s → snares

To form the plural of nouns ending is **s**, **ss**, **sh**, **ch**, **x**, and **z**, add **-es**.

guess + es → guesses	gas + es → gases	tax + es → taxes
bush + es → bushes	match + es → matches	buzz + es → buzzes

Class Exercises

Determine which rule to use before adding the suffix to each word. Tell how to spell the new word.

1. watch + es
2. commit + ment
3. rub + er
4. journey + s
5. rally + ing
6. rinse + s
7. offer + ing
8. transmit + al
9. joy + ful
10. tally + es

Exercises

Read each pair of words. Use a rule to determine which spelling is correct. Write the correct spelling.

1. waltzs, waltzes
2. joyes, joys
3. regrettful, regretful
4. openning, opening
5. dropped, droped
6. controllable, controlable
7. emplois, employs
8. shyness, shiness
9. lobbys, lobbies
10. happyest, happiest
11. diaries, diarys
12. hurryed, hurried
13. quizzes, quizes
14. lazyly, lazily
15. dutiful, dutyful
16. volleyed, volleied
17. gladen, gladden
18. hoverring, hovering
19. spiner, spinner
20. drippless, dripless

Add a suffix to each word. Then write the word.

21. silly + ness
22. spry + ly
23. delay + ing
24. submit + able
25. thin + er
26. exhibit + ing
27. glad + ly
28. gadget + s
29. circus + es
30. angry + est

Sample Answers 1. waltzes **21.** silliness

Irregular Plural Nouns

You have already learned several rules for spelling the plural forms of nouns. To form the plural of most nouns, you add *-s*. To form the plural of nouns ending in *s, ss, x, z, sh,* and *ch,* you add *-es*. To form the plural of nouns ending in a consonant and *y,* you change the *y* to *i* before adding *-es*. These nouns are regular nouns because the formation of their plurals follows a rule. There are two smaller groups of nouns that change in a regular way when you write their plurals. These groups include nouns that end with *o* and nouns that end with *f* or *ff.*

To form the plural of most nouns ending in a vowel and **o,** add **-s.**

ratio + s → ratios   radio + s → radios   studio + s → studios

To form the plural of most nouns ending in a consonant and **o,** generally add **-s,** but sometimes add **-es.**

solo + s → solos   cello + s → cellos   hero + es → heroes
photo + s → photos   echo + es → echoes   veto + es → vetoes

Some words that end with a consonant and *o* can be made plural by adding either *-s* or *-es.*

volcano + s or es → volcanos, volcanoes
mango + s or es → mangos, mangoes
lasso + s or es → lassos, lassoes
zero + s or es → zeros, zeroes

To form the plural of most nouns ending in **f** and all nouns ending in **ff,** add **-s.**

belief + s → beliefs   gulf + s → gulfs   roof + s → roofs
staff + s → staffs   cliff + s → cliffs   puff + s → puffs

To form the plural of some nouns ending in **f** or **fe,** and many nouns ending in **lf,** change **f** to **v** and add **-s** or **-es.**

shelf + es → shelves   wife + s → wives   life + s → lives
leaf + es → leaves   calf + es → calves   sheaf + es → sheaves

Some nouns have irregular plural forms. They do not follow a spelling rule. You must learn their spellings. Until you know the correct spelling of these words, you should check the spelling in a dictionary.

child → children	woman → women	man → men
ox → oxen	mouse → mice	tooth → teeth
foot → feet	goose → geese	

Some nouns have the same form in both the singular and plural.

sheep → sheep	moose → moose	trout → trout
deer → deer	series → series	species → species

Class Exercises

Determine which rule to use before making each word plural. Then tell how to spell the plural form.

1. cameo	**3.** tomato	**5.** chief	**7.** gentleman	**9.** half
2. halo	**4.** tornado	**6.** cuff	**8.** moose	**10.** sheaf

Exercises

Use a rule to form the plural of each word. Then write the correct plural form or forms of each word.

1. species	**6.** stereo	**11.** child	**16.** knife
2. elf	**7.** wolf	**12.** lasso	**17.** clef
3. gaff	**8.** piano	**13.** mango	**18.** potato
4. ox	**9.** woman	**14.** loaf	**19.** veto
5. patio	**10.** hero	**15.** motto	**20.** series

Use a rule to form the plural of each word. Write the correct phrase.

21. pictures of rare (specieses, species)
22. customs and (beliefs, believes)
23. percentages and (ratioes, ratios)
24. duets and (soloes, solos)
25. husbands and (wives, wifes)
26. sheep and (calves, calfs)
27. televisions and (radios, radioes)
28. peaks and (clives, cliffs)
29. oceans and (gulves, gulfs)
30. bass, sea robins, and (trouts, trout)

Sample Answers 1. species **21.** pictures of rare species

Words Often Confused I

Some words sound alike. However, they have different meanings and are spelled differently. Unless you see the words written or hear the words used in sentences, you cannot be sure what they mean.

Below is a chart of words, their definitions, and examples. Note the meaning of each word as you learn its spelling.

WORD	MEANING	EXAMPLE
aisle (noun)	a passageway	The man walked down the center *aisle.*
isle (noun)	land surrounded by water, a small island	We visited a Pacific *isle.*
council (noun)	a group of advisers	The city *council* meets today.
counsel (verb)	to give advice	Our advisers will *counsel* us.
holy (adjective)	sacred	They celebrated a *holy* day.
wholly (adverb)	completely, entirely	The answer was not *wholly* accurate.
rain (noun)	condensed water vapor, falling from the sky	The Weather Service predicts *rain.*
reign (verb)	to rule, control	How long did the king *reign*?
serf (noun)	a kind of slave	The *serf* worked for the landlord.
surf (noun)	seawaves on the shore	The *surf* rose high during the storm.
wares (noun)	goods for sale	The merchant sold his *wares.*
wears (verb)	has on the body	Gail *wears* boots when she rides.

The possessive pronoun *its* takes the place of a noun in a sentence. The contraction *it's* is a short form of *it is.* Sometimes the two words are confused. Notice that possessive pronouns do not need an apostrophe. Read the examples that follow.

The dog is wagging its tail. It's happy to see the children.

Possessive nouns and contractions with nouns are often confused. Notice that both possessive nouns and contractions with nouns use an apostrophe. Read the examples that follow.

Mary's dog is in the yard. (possessive noun, *the dog belonging to Mary*)

Mary's with the dog in the yard. (contraction, *Mary is*)

Her dog's bark is quite loud. (possessive noun, *bark of the dog*)

The dog's barking at the squirrel. (contraction, *dog is*)

Class Exercises

Read each sentence. Tell which of the two word in parentheses you should use to complete the sentence. Give reasons for your answers.

1. Greg walked up the ___ to give his report to the class. (isle, aisle)
2. He spoke about the coyote and ___ habits. (it's, its)
3. Coyotes survive well in a land with little ___. (rain, reign)
4. A ___ howls help it communicate with others in the desert. (coyotes, coyote's)
5. ___ report concluded with a map. (Gregs, Greg's)
6. The class had seemed ___ interested in his report. (wholly, holy)

Exercises

Write each sentence using the correct word in the blank.

1. John lived on a small ___ off the coast of Maine. (aisle, isle)
2. The ___ became extremely rough during the hurricane. (serf, surf)
3. A fisher sometimes ___ waterproof clothing. (wears, wares)
4. The present monarch will ___ for as long as he lives. (reign, rain)
5. Some societies consider animals to be ___ and to possess magical qualities. (wholly, holy)
6. The attorney will ___ his client to plead guilty. (council, counsel)
7. The principal decided that ___ a matter to take seriously. (its, it's)
8. The teacher said that it was ___ turn to present her report. (Saras, Sara's)
9. The peddler carried his ___ in a horse-drawn cart. (wares, wears)
10. The animal hurt ___ paw when it jumped the fence. (its, it's)
11. A ___ may be established to deal with the problem. (counsel, council)

Writing Sentences

Write eight sentences. Use as many words from this lesson as you can. Include the use of its and it's, contractions, and possessive nouns.

Sample Answer 1. John lived on a small isle off the coast of Maine.

Words Often Confused II

People frequently misspell words because they confuse them with other words that have similar sounds or similar spellings. As you study the words in the chart below, note the meaning of each one as you learn its spelling.

WORD	MEANING	EXAMPLE
presents (noun)	gifts	Jan received many *presents.*
presence (noun)	state of being in a place at a given time	Her *presence* at the meeting was upsetting.
straight (adjective)	proceeding in same direction without curving or bending	He made a *straight* line across the page.
strait (noun)	narrow waterway connecting two larger bodies of water	We steered the boat through the *strait.*
loose (adjective)	not firmly fixed	The bolt is *loose.*
lose (verb)	misplace, be deprived of	Don't *lose* the bolt.
quiet (adjective)	silent	It was a *quiet* night.
quite (adverb)	to a large extent	It was *quite* a dark night.
weather (noun)	atmospheric conditions	The *weather* has been cold.
whether (conjunction)	if	I don't know *whether* to go.
lead (verb)	(lēd) show the way (present tense)	The dogs *lead* the way.
lead (noun)	(led) a heavy metal	That *lead* pipe is in the way.
led (verb)	(led) showed the way (past tense)	Who *led* the way yesterday?
choose (verb)	select or pick out (present tense)	Please *choose* two cards.
chose (verb)	selected or picked out (past tense)	You *chose* two cards.
than (conjunction)	compared with	My bike cost less *than* yours.
then (adverb)	at that time	He *then* left the room.
wear (verb)	to have on	She will *wear* a suit.
where (adverb)	at what place	*Where* shall we meet?
were (verb)	plural past form of *be*	*Were* you meeting them?

Class Exercises

Read each sentence. Tell which of the two words in parentheses you should use to complete the sentence. Give reasons for your answers.

1. It is ___ beautiful here. (quiet, quite)
2. He doesn't know ___ he should leave yet. (weather, whether)
3. What will you ___ to the concert? (wear, where)
4. They requested our ___ at the meeting. (presents, presence)
5. The boat has come ___ from its anchor. (lose, loose)
6. The safe was constructed of ___ . (lead, led)

Exercises

Write each sentence using the correct word in the blank.

1. ___ your partner for the next dance. (Choose, Chose)
2. What ___ they saying? (where, wear, were)
3. Abbie decides ___ she should stay late. (weather, whether)
4. Did Joan ___ a button at the dance? (loose, lose)
5. Ralph ___ Eartha to the dance floor. (lead, led)
6. Esther dances better ___ I do. (then, than)
7. Ira ___ the same partner for every dance. (choose, chose)
8. The legs on the refreshment table were ___ and fell off. (loose, lose)
9. The dancing stopped, and the room was ___ . (quite, quiet)
10. Did you send any ___ to your family? (presents, presence)
11. The path from the house to the store is almost ___ . (straight, strait)

Writing Sentences

Look at the list of words below. Look up each word in a dictionary. Write six sentences, using a different word from this list in each sentence.

cloths/clothes	dessert/desert	counselor/councilor
formally/formerly	advice/advise	affect/effect
counsel/council	proceed/precede	capital/capitol

Sample Answer 1. Choose your partner for the next dance.

Unit Review

SPELLING

Read each sentence. Use the Dictionary and the Table of English Spellings to correct the spelling of the underlined word in each sentence. Then write each word correctly. *pages 188-189*

1. Dogs were first trained to be hunters and retreavers for early humans.
2. They were probably the first animals to be taimed as pets.
3. Ancient Egyptians used the heyena as a hunting animal.
4. The first wild birds to be trained by humans were the pidgeons.
5. While many animals can be trained, they sometimes revirt to wildness.

Write the correctly spelled word in each pair. *pages 190-193*

6. rentry, reentry
7. lateness, latness
8. reviveal, revival
9. lacey, lacy
10. replaceable, replacable
11. tieing, tying
12. terribly, terribley
13. review, reveiw

Add the prefix or the suffix to each word. Then write the word. *pages 190-193*

14. ir + regular
15. incredible + ly
16. courage + ous
17. pure + ly
18. nurse + ing
19. desire + ous
20. cruise + er
21. state + ment

Write the correctly spelled word in each pair. *pages 190-193*

22. tastyest, tastiest
23. prying, priing
24. delaied, delayed
25. runner, runer
26. forbiden, forbidden
27. gardenner, gardener
28. hittless, hitless
29. bunches, bunchs

Add the suffix to each word. Then write the word. *pages 190-193*

30. flurry + es
31. fancy + ful
32. fry + ing
33. turkey + s
34. drum + ed
35. control + able
36. profit + ing
37. allot + ment

Write the correct plural form or forms of each word. *pages 194-195*

38. series
39. trout
40. gentleman
41. child
42. self
43. life
44. huff
45. handkerchief
46. lasso
47. tomato
48. halo
49. rodeo

Unit Review

Choose the correct plural form from the parentheses to complete each phrase. Write the letter of your answer. *pages 194-195*

50. carts pulled by (a. oxes b. oxen)
51. horses, antelopes, and (a. deers b. deer)
52. chimneys on all the (a. roofs b. rooves)
53. paintings and (a. photoes b. photos)
54. recorders and (a. stereoes b. stereos)

Write the word in parentheses that completes the sentence. *pages 196-197*

55. What kind of ___ does the peddler sell? (wears, wares)
56. Does the mayor preside at the ___ meetings? (counsel, council)
57. Which South Sea ___ did your family visit? (aisle, isle)
58. Now ___ time to attend to the problem. (its, it's)
59. ___ population is greater than the United States. (Indias, India's)

Write the word in the parentheses that completes the sentence. *pages 198-199*

60. The driver's ___ was requested in court. (presents, presence)
61. The judge wonders ___ he should fine the driver. (weather, whether)
62. The driver would rather pay a fine ___ lose his license. (than, then)
63. ___ did the violation take place? (Wear, Where, Were)

Writers write to express themselves clearly to their readers. Some writers work on the staff of a newspaper, magazine, or book publisher. Other writers work for themselves. These writers sell their books and articles to a newspaper, magazine, or book publisher. Writers must write each day and spend a lot of time revising their work. Editors sometimes help writers in editing their work. People interested in writing as a career must practice writing everyday.

Careers

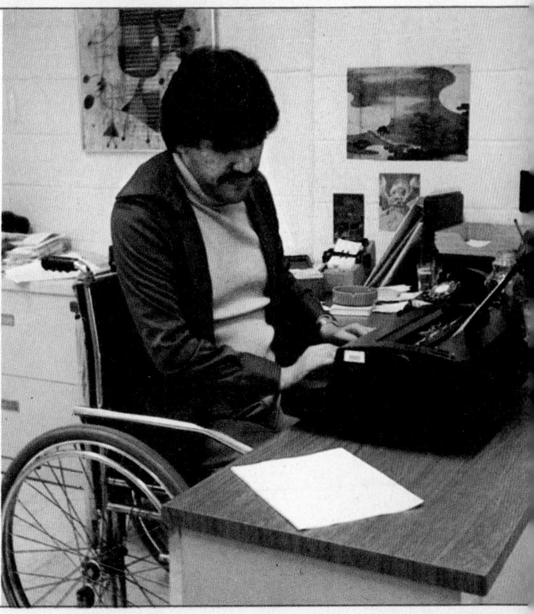

Independence Hall, Philadelphia

Language is the main instrument of man's refusal to accept the world as it is.

GEORGE STEINER
British academic
(1929-   )

11

VOCABULARY

Words in Context

When you find an unfamiliar word in your reading, you may use the dictionary to learn the word's meaning. You can also guess at a word's meaning by looking at the sentence context. *Sentence context* refers to the other words in the sentence. Sentence context often gives you a clue to the meaning of a new word.

- Read the following sentence.

Tony is an amateur, but he hopes to be a professional actor soon.

Suppose you did not know the meaning of *amateur.* The second part of the sentence tells you that Tony *hopes* to be a professional actor. In other words, he is not a professional actor now. An amateur, then, must be someone who is not a professional. The meaning of amateur in this sentence is *nonprofessional.*

Sometimes the meaning of a word may not be clear from the context of a single sentence. You may have to look at the sentence or sentences that come before and after. These sentences can often be helpful in understanding a new word.

- Read the following group of sentences.

The actors and actresses have been learning a new play for weeks. Now the director wants them to work on their parts onstage. They have only a few weeks to rehearse before the first performance.

How can you figure out what *rehearse* means? The first sentence tells you that actors and actresses are working on a new play. The second sentence tells that the director wants them to *practice* onstage. They have only a few weeks to work on or practice for the play. You can see that the word *rehearse* means *practice.*

When a word has more than one possible meaning, it is particularly important to pay attention to the context in which it appears.

- Read these sentences.

Young children closely watch TV commercials.

Tina runs a commercial airline that delivers packages overnight.

In the first sentence, *commercial* refers to TV advertising messages. In the second sentence, *commercial* refers to business or trade.

Class Exercises

Read each sentence carefully. Tell what you think the underlined word means. Give a reason for your answer.

1. The band concert began precisely at 8 P.M. I had not expected it to begin exactly on time.
2. The huge hall was filled to capacity. There was not an empty seat.
3. I had expected many people, but I had not anticipated so great a crowd.
4. At last the sound of music began to fill the hall. Before long the entire building resounded with music.

Exercises

Read each sentence carefully. Write what you think the underlined word means.

1. Ms. Rollins is a well-known dramatist. She has just written a new play.
2. The play has funny dialogue. The opening conversation between the two main characters especially delighted me.
3. As the curtain rises, the audience hears the blatt of a bicycle horn offstage.
4. A collision soon occurs as the two main characters crash their bicycles into each other.
5. A distinguished looking gentleman gropes along the ground on his hands and knees, looking for his glasses.
6. Nearby a sturdy looking lady peeks mischievously from behind her bike. She watches the gentleman with an amused smile and a playful twinkle in her eye.
7. In spite of this unfortunate meeting, the two characters form a lucky partnership.

Writing Sentences

Write six sentences using one of the underlined words from the exercises above in each of your sentences.

Sample Answer 1. a person who writes plays

Words with Multiple Meanings

Some English words have both familiar and specialized meanings. The special meanings of some of these words are frequently associated with certain subject areas. Some of the familiar and specialized meanings of several words are given below. Study the meanings carefully.

meter	**1.** basic rhythmic pattern of beats in music **2.** fundamental unit in the metric system equal to 3.28 feet **3.** instrument for measuring gas, water, or electricity
critic	**1.** one who judges and reviews the arts and reports professionally for publication or broadcast **2.** a person who finds fault
epic	**1.** a long narrative poem about the adventures of a hero **2.** very long or large in scope
hero	**1.** leading male character in a play, story, or poem **2.** brave or noble man
baffle	**1.** a wall or screen set up to control the flow of fluids or sound waves **2.** to bewilder or puzzle
concert	**1.** public performance of vocal or instrumental music **2.** agreement as on a plan or action
scale	**1.** series of musical tones ascending or descending in pitch **2.** device for determining weight. **3.** to climb
compose	**1.** to create a musical or literary work **2.** to make up; constitute
temper	**1.** to adjust the pitch of an instrument; to tune **2.** tendency to give way to anger or irritation
treble	**1.** relating to the highest musical or instrumental voice; soprano **2.** three times; triple

Class Exercises

Read each sentence. Tell which meaning of the underlined word is being used. Look again at the definitions on the facing page.

1. Lara always begins piano practice by playing scales.
2. The sailor made the epic journey around the world in a sailboat.
3. The children clapped hands to count out the song's meter.
4. Paul is a patient boy who seldom loses his temper.

Exercises

Read each sentence. Write each underlined word. Then write the number of the correct meaning from the definitions on the facing page.

1. The critics praised the orchestra's performance of the symphony.
2. In the epic the *Odyssey,* Odysseus overcomes many difficulties.
3. The adventurers scaled the mountain in midwinter.
4. The musicians set up a baffle to get a truer sound from the instruments.
5. We check the gas and electric meters once a month.
6. Aaron Copland has composed music with early American folk themes.
7. The strange case baffled even the cleverest detectives.
8. Nick plays the hero in the class play.
9. Maria must temper the piano so that it will play in tune.
10. Louise sings treble while I sing in a lower register.
11. My whole family will attend the band concert tomorrow night.
12. Max is his own worst critic. He is never satisfied with himself.
13. Superman is a hero to many young and old people.
14. The new room is approximately 4 meters long.
15. Today many supermarkets use computerized scales.

Writing Sentences

Choose three of the words defined in this lesson. Write sentences using all of the meanings of each word.

Sample Answer 1. critics, 1

Prefixes

Many word parts have come into the English language from Greek and Latin. Some of these word parts are called *prefixes* and have special meanings. When you add a prefix to a word, you form a new word.

A **prefix** is a letter or group of letters added to the beginning of a word.

You often use words that contain prefixes. Sometimes you will want to add a prefix to a familiar word to make a new word.

- Look at the prefixes in the boxes below. When you add one of these prefixes to the beginning of a word, you change the meaning of the word. The first four prefixes add a number meaning. The second group of prefixes gives words a negative meaning. They change the meaning of the word completely. The third group gives new meaning to words, too.

Prefix	Meaning	Example
uni-	one	unicycle (one wheel)
mono-	one, single	monotone (a single tone)
bi-	two, twice	bicycle (two wheels)
tri-	three	triangle (three angles)
un-	not; the opposite of	uncomfortable (not comfortable)
im-	not; the opposite of	impossible (not possible)
in-	not; the opposite of	inaccurate (not accurate)
non-	not; the opposite of	nonproductive (not productive)
inter-	between, among	international (among nations)
semi-	half of, partly	semiprivate (partly private) semicircle (half of a circle)
auto-	self	autobiography (a biography of oneself)
super-	extra, beyond better than others of its kind	superhuman (better than other humans)

Class Exercises

Find the prefix in each word below. Tell the meaning of each word.

1. monotone	**3.** bicolor	**5.** superstar	**7.** unparalleled
2. tricycle	**4.** semicircle	**6.** international	**8.** impatient

Exercises

Each word below contains a number prefix. Write the number meaning of each prefix.

1. bimonthly ___ months
2. tricolor ___ colors
3. unicycle ___ wheel
4. monosyllable ___ syllable
5. tripod ___ legs
6. biplane ___ wings

Write each word and underline the prefix. Write the meaning of the word.

7. intermission	**9.** semiclassical	**11.** autograph
8. supernatural	**10.** interject	**12.** semiprivate

The underlined words in each sentence below are the definition of another word. Choose a word with a prefix that can replace the underlined words. Write each sentence using the word you choose.

13. A partly skilled mime performed in front of the museum.
14. It was not possible to see her face behind the makeup.
15. She made us laugh with movements that were not believable.
16. I see her perform here for lunchtime crowds two times weekly.
17. Her act is interesting, but it is still not perfect.
18. She makes the audience act with her quite well.
19. Right now she is miming a person in a chair that is not comfortable.

Writing Sentences

Write six sentences about what kind of performer you would like to be. Use words that begin with these prefixes in your sentences: *mono-*, *bi-*, *un-*, *im-*, *semi-*, *super-*, *auto-*, or *inter-*.

Sample Answers **1.** two **7.** inter mission; between acts
13. A semiskilled mime performed in front of the museum.

More Prefixes

Many new words in our language are formed by adding to other words. When you add to a word, you form a word that has a new meaning. You know that a letter or group of letters that is added to the beginning of a word is called a *prefix*. Here is a chart of common prefixes.

Prefix	Meaning
under-	below, lower in place, lesser in degree
pre-	before
re-	again
over-	extra, beyond, above, over, more
com-	with, together
post-	after, in time or order

- Look at these examples to see how learning prefixes can help enlarge your vocabulary.

underestimate	There were not enough seats. Jerry underestimated the number of seats needed.
overact	Louise sometimes overacts. She moves around too wildly in the last scene of the play.
preperformance	The director held a preperformance meeting to wish the cast luck.
rewrite	The author had to rewrite the play several times before it was ready to be performed.
compress	When packing, Monica compresses things to save space.
postdate	Hal postdated the letter he will mail tomorrow.

Class Exercises

Read each of the following sentences. Substitute a word with a prefix for the underlined words.

1. A director must see over many aspects of a play's performance.
2. Actors and actresses must press together many hours of work into a day.

3. Some actors and actresses work extra during certain times in their careers.
4. Very often they must create again a scene in different ways.
5. A clear understanding of the play must lie below its performance.

Exercises

Write each sentence below. Use a word with a prefix to replace the underlined words.

1. Glenn has joined again an amateur acting company.
2. He had always estimated below his own acting ability.
3. Then a reporter viewed before a play in which Glenn was appearing.
4. When the reporter viewed again the play, she praised Glenn's acting.
5. On opening night the stage was ablaze with above the head lights.
6. Glenn tried not to be extra anxious.
7. Some actors and actresses were extra excited before the beginning of the play.
8. So many weeks of work were pressed together into this night.
9. The director discussed a list of suggestions he had piled together.
10. The audience had paid before for their tickets to the opening performance.
11. The audience acted again warmly to the play's performance.
12. The cast enjoyed a after performance party at Glenn's house.
13. Glenn's mother had cooked before several things early in the day.
14. She left other things slightly cooked to a lesser degree.
15. Everyone was too excited at the party to feel extra tired.
16. Tomorrow at rehearsal they would turn back to their work.
17. The writer might have to write again those scenes that did not run smoothly in the opening performance.

Writing Sentences

Use each of the following words in a sentence that shows its meaning.

undersell preview compile postgraduate replay overextend

Sample Answer 1. Glenn has rejoined an amateur acting company.

Noun Suffixes

A *suffix* is a letter or group of letters added to the end of a word. Adding a suffix sometimes changes the meaning of a word.

- Study each suffix and its meaning in the box below.

Suffix	Meaning	Example
-er	one who	dancer, one who dances
-or	one who	director, one who directs
-ist	one who is expert in	musicologist, one who is expert in music
-ness	state of being	brightness, state of being bright
-ment	result	improvement, result of being improved
-ion	action or state	collection, state of being collected
-ance	the act of	performance, the act of performing
-ence	the act of	dependence, the act of depending

- Read each pair of sentences below. Notice how a noun, verb, or adjective in the first sentence of each pair is changed to a new noun in the second sentence.

Joe *directs* a professional dance company. Joe is a *director.*

Mary *composes* music. Mary is a *composer*.

She *depends* on good musicians. Dancers share this *dependence.*

We watch the dancers *perform*. Their *performance* is superb.

Mary is *happy*. Her eyes show her *happiness*.

Mary is an expert in *music*. Mary is a *musicologist*.

Hao *collects* ballet slippers. His *collection* is immense.

Pat *improves* her dancing every day. You can see the *improvement*.

- Notice the spelling changes that sometimes take place when suffixes are added to a noun, a verb, or an adjective.

happy — happiness	create — creation	drug — druggist
economy — economist	endure — endurance	merry — merriment

There is no rule to tell you when to choose *-ance* and when to choose *-ence.* If you do not know the spelling, check your dictionary.

Class Exercises

Read these sentences. Add a suffix to the word in parentheses. Use **-er, -or, -ness, -ment, -ion, -ist, -ance,** or **-ence.** Complete the sentence. You may wish to check your dictionary.

1. Suzanne is studying to be a professional ballet ___. (dance)
2. She goes to a special school for performing ___. (art)
3. Suzanne practices under the ___ of a ballet master. (supervise)
4. Teachers give special ___ to students in this school. (treat)
5. Practice and study must continue without ___. (interfere)
6. Now Suzanne is preparing for a solo ___. (perform)
7. Her coach gives her much help and ___. (encourage)
8. Students must have talent, determination, and ___. (tough)

Exercises

Add the suffix in parentheses to each word below. Write the word. Check the spelling in your dictionary.

1. connect + (ion)
2. emerge + (ence)
3. endure + (ance)
4. accompany + (ist)
5. interfere + (ence)
6. collect + (or)
7. grieve + (ance)
8. judge + (ment)
9. reform + (er)
10. happy + (ness)
11. special + (ist)
12. annoy + (ance)
13. insure + (ance)
14. botany + (ist)
15. depend + (ence)

Write each sentence. Add **-ist, -ence,** or **-ance** to the word in parentheses. Check your dictionary for spelling changes.

16. Marc Charo has been a ___ for six years. (violin)
17. His mother is a ___ with a symphony orchestra. (piano)
18. Mr. Charo is a classical ___ with a dance company. (guitar)
19. Marc often listens offstage to his parents' ___. (perform)
20. He believes his love for music is part of his ___. (inherit)
21. Marc hopes that he has the ___ to be successful. (persevere)
22. His parents encourage him with ___ and understanding. (patient)

Sample Answers 1. connection **16.** Marc Charo has been a violinist for six years.

Adjective Suffixes

You can change the meaning of a word by adding a suffix. You know that a *suffix* is a letter or group of letters added to the end of a word. A suffix added to a noun or verb can change it to an adjective.

- Read the list of suffixes and their meanings. Note how the addition of a suffix can change a noun or verb to an adjective.

Suffix	Meaning	Adjective
-ful	full of, marked by	harmful meaningful
-less	lacking, without	careless spotless
-ish	like, suggesting	childish stylish
-ous	marked by, given to	humorous dangerous
-ent	doing, showing, tending	different excellent
-ant	doing, showing, tending	pleasant triumphant
-ary	relating to	imaginary
-y	showing, suggesting	bumpy sleepy
-ive	tending to	expensive instructive
-able	able to, capable of being	agreeable enjoyable
-ible	able to, capable of being	convertible flexible
-some	showing, apt to	troublesome quarrelsome

Notice that some words change their spelling when a suffix is added to make an adjective. Check the spelling rules for suffixes on pages 192, 194, and 214.

Class Exercises

Read each sentence pair below. Add the suffix in parentheses to the underlined word to form an adjective. Read the second sentence in each pair using the new adjective.

1. Ron used care with the camera.
Ron was ___ . (-ful)

2. TV cameras are an expense.
TV cameras are ___ . (-ive)

3. Ron excels in his work.
His camera work is ___ . (-ent)

4. Ron instructs others.
He gives ___ information. (-ive)

Exercises

Read each sentence pair below. Add the suffix in parentheses to the underlined word to form an adjective. Write the second sentence in each pair using the new adjective.

1. Aida wants to sleep longer.
She is ___ . (-y)

2. Her alarm will wake her at 5 A.M.
She is often ___ by 4:30 A.M. (-ful)

3. Newscasters must try to please.
Aida always appears ___ . (-ant)

4. People enjoy her humor.
Aida is ___ . (-ous)

5. Aida's reports impress us.
She is ___ . (-ive)

6. Good sense is Aida's guide.
Aida is a ___ newswoman. (-ible)

Read each sentence. Look at the underlined adjective. Write the meaning of the adjective.

7. Paul designed an imaginative set for a children's TV show.

8. The background was a colorful country setting.

9. Bright greens and yellows created a sunny atmosphere.

10. Mischievous looking animals peeked from behind trees.

11. The need to change sets quickly is troublesome for Paul.

12. Paul solved this problem with convertible sets.

Sample Answers 1. She is sleepy. **7.** tending toward the imagination

Roots

You have learned how to add prefixes and suffixes to words to form new words. The original, or base, word to which you add a prefix or suffix is called a *root.* Many English roots come from Latin and Greek. Most of these roots are not independent words in English, but they do have meaning. If you know the meaning of a root, you can add a prefix or a suffix to create a new word.

- Look at these examples.

Root	Meaning	New Word
graph	write	autograph
scrib, scrip	write	scribble, script
sign	sign, mark	signal
port	carry	report, portable
cap, cep	take, receive	captive, reception
pel, puls	drive, push	compel, impulse
pend, pens	hang	impending, suspense
duc	lead	deduct
pos, pon	place, put	deposit
voc, vok	call, voice	vocal, revoke
spec	see, watch	spectator
vid, vis	see	visual
grad, gred, gress	step, walk	progress, gradual
cede, ceed, cess	go, surrender	recede
ped, pod	foot	pedestrian

Use the roots to try to figure out the meaning of the new words. Check your definitions in a dictionary.

Class Exercises

In each sentence below, find the words that contain these roots: *vok, pel, spec, cap.* Tell the meaning of each word.

1. The *Firebird* is a spectacular Russian ballet.
2. A prince, Ivan, captures the magical Firebird.
3. When the Firebird invokes Ivan's mercy, Ivan frees it.
4. Later, the Firebird helps Ivan to repel the evil magician, Kastchei.

Exercises

Write each word below. Write the meaning of the root and then the meaning of the word. Use your dictionary if necessary.

1. podiatrist	**5.** describe	**9.** graduate	**13.** video
2. graphic	**6.** import	**10.** suspend	**14.** recession
3. impel	**7.** pulse	**11.** induct	**15.** vision
4. design	**8.** vocation	**12.** insignia	**16.** pedal

Write the words in the sentences that contain the following roots: *sign, vis, duc, cap, pos, cep, pend, scrib.* Then write the meaning of each word. Use your dictionary if necessary.

17. Ms. Rose composes music for a dance company.
18. She works closely with the conductor and the dancing master.
19. Audiences have been quite receptive to Ms. Rose's music.
20. They are often captivated by its unusual rhythms.
21. The dancers depend on the dancing master to learn new dances.
22. They try to visualize the new dance patterns.
23. In one dance they must inscribe one pattern within another.

Writing Sentences

Choose three roots from this lesson. Write three words from each root. Use six of your new words in six sentences.

Sample Answers **1.** podiatrist, an expert in foot diseases and injuries
17. composes, puts together; makes up

Synonyms

There are thousands of words in the English language. When you speak or write, then, you have many nouns, verbs, adjectives, and adverbs to choose from. You will often find several different words that are similar in meaning. A word that is similar in meaning to another word is called a *synonym.* A knowledge of synonyms can help you communicate your ideas in a clear, colorful, and concrete way. By choosing synonyms with exact meanings, you can avoid vague or unclear expressions of your thoughts.

• Read each pair of sentences below. Notice the underlined words. The first sentence in each pair uses a vague or general word. The second sentence uses a more exact synonym. The second sentence presents an image that is easier to picture.

Mel skates <u>nicely</u>.
Mel skates <u>gracefully</u>.

He <u>moves</u> around the rink.
He <u>glides</u> around the rink.

The ice ballet is <u>pretty</u>.
The ice ballet is <u>dazzling</u>.

<u>People</u> wear splendid costumes.
The <u>performers</u> wear splendid costumes.

It is important to remember that synonyms are similar in meaning but they are not exactly the same in meaning. Synonyms have some shade of difference in their meanings. If you are aware of these slight differences, you can use synonyms to convey your ideas effectively.

• Read the sentences below. Notice the slight difference in meaning each synonym gives to the sentence in which it appears.

Mel <u>skates</u> around the rink.

Mel <u>darts</u> around the rink.

Mel <u>sails</u> around the rink.

Mel <u>plods</u> around the rink.

Mel <u>races</u> around the rink.

Class Exercises

Read the pairs of synonyms. Which of the synonyms in each pair has the more exact meaning?

1. go—trudge
2. drudgery—work
3. loud—blasting
4. nicely—exquisitely

5. soaked—wet
6. fatigue—exhaustion
7. eat—dine
8. fracture—break
9. muddy—dirty
10. smell—fragrance
11. bellow—call
12. very—remarkably
13. deliberately—slowly
14. sweet—sugary
15. roast—cook

Exercises

Write each sentence. Use the word in parentheses that better completes the sentence. Think about which word gives the clearer meaning.

1. Tina was ___ after ice ballet practice. (tired, exhausted)
2. She plays the ___ wolf in *Peter and the Wolf*. (wily, smart)
3. Ruis skates the part of the hero, Peter, ___ well. (very, extremely)
4. Peter's appearance is accompanied by ___ string music. (happy, lilting)
5. Les ___ around as Peter's grave grandfather. (skates, tramps)
6. The ___ bassoon announces the grandfather. (loud, resonant)

Match each word in Column 1 with its synonym in Column 2. Write the words and their synonyms.

Column 1	**Column 2**
7. quiet	**a.** spectator, observer, inspector
8. fall	**b.** inquire, question, interrogate
9. watcher	**c.** peaceful, hushed, calm
10. near	**d.** tiny, minute, elfin
11. ask	**e.** adjoining, neighboring, adjacent
12. small	**f.** plunge, tumble, dive

Writing Sentences

Read the list of words below. Think of a synonym for each word. Then write a sentence using the synonym.

sleep   big   traveler   hot   sad   run   far

Sample Answers: 1. Tina was exhausted after ice ballet practice.
7. quiet—peaceful, hushed, calm

Antonyms

You know that synonyms are words with similar meanings. Some words are opposite in meaning. Words that are opposite in meaning are called *antonyms*.

- Read the pairs of sentences. Look at the underlined words in each pair. These underlined words are antonyms.

  Michael practices a <u>sophisticated</u> melody.
  Jack prefers a <u>simple</u> tune.

  Marta <u>enjoys</u> early morning practice sessions.
  Tovah <u>dislikes</u> early morning practices.

When you select a synonym, you must keep in mind the different shades of meaning words may have. When you choose an antonym, you must also keep in mind the slight differences in meaning among words. This awareness will help you to make the best choice of words.

- Look at the chart. Notice the range of meaning among the groups of antonyms.

hot, fiery, sultry	cold, frigid, chilly
sharp, keen, pointed	dull, boring, blunt
slow, sluggish, leisurely	fast, nimble, rapid
happy, cheerful, jaunty	sad, dreary, mournful

A knowledge of antonyms is particularly helpful when you want to contrast one idea or image with another. When you select antonyms for contrast, it is important to choose ones that are precise. By choosing precise antonyms, you will present a contrast that is sharp and clear.

- Read these sentences. Notice the underlined pairs of words. These are contrasting antonyms.

  Rodney's violin <u>screeched</u> while Tony's <u>hummed</u> sweetly.

  A <u>cool</u> breeze swept through the <u>parched</u> valley.

  The excited <u>chatter</u> of the campers broke the morning <u>stillness</u>.

Class Exercises

Read each group of words. Choose the word in parentheses that is an antonym for the word to the left of the parentheses.

1. kindness (cruelty, tenderness)
2. work (labor, relaxation)
3. rough (smooth, rugged)
4. doze (sleep, awaken)

Choose an antonym for the underlined word in each sentence.

5. Tina practices <u>often</u>, but Sid practices only ___ . (frequently, rarely)
6. The ___ of trumpets pierced the <u>silence</u>. (blare, quietness)

Exercises

From the words in parentheses, choose an antonym for the word to the left of the parentheses. Write the word and its antonym.

1. gloomy (dismal, bright)
2. plod (trudge, saunter)
3. honor (shame, glory)
4. friendly (neighborly, hostile)
5. hero (coward, champion)
6. late (tardy, early)
7. simple (complicated, plain)
8. unhappy (mournful, delighted)

Choose an antonym for the underlined word in each sentence. Write the sentence with the antonym.

9. A <u>fiery</u> sun slowly warms the ___ mountain air. (sultry, chilly)
10. Barrie <u>jogs</u> before music class, while Sue prefers to ___ .(rest, run)
11. At first music theory was <u>difficult</u>, but now it is ___ . (troublesome, easy)
12. I met some <u>famous</u> and some ___ musicians at camp. (unknown, well-known)
13. I play the flute <u>confidently</u> rather than ___ . (nervously, poorly)

Writing Sentences

Think of a camp or a class you have attended in which someone has helped you to improve a skill. Write three sentences using antonyms to contrast how you felt or performed before the help with how you felt or performed afterward.

Sample Answers 1. gloomy, bright
9. A fiery sun slowly warms the chilly mountain air.

Verbs Often Confused

Some verbs are often confused. Study the definitions and examples below. They will help you choose the verb you should use. In the example sentences, the present tense is used first and the past tense second.

lie: to rest or recline An actor lies on a couch. An actor lay down yesterday.	**lay:** to place or put A painter lays a brush down. A painter laid a brush down.
teach: to show how, to instruct The director teaches a child. The director taught a child.	**learn:** to acquire knowledge The children learn their lines. The children learned their lines.
sit: to rest in an upright position The actors sit on the stage. The actors sat on the stage.	**set:** to put or place The director sets the script down. The director set the script down.
leave: to go away Two actors leave the stage. Another actor left earlier.	**let:** to allow or permit Let the children rest now. We let them rest earlier.
rise: to go upward, to get up The director rises from the chair. The director rose from the chair.	**raise:** to move something upward The stage manager raises a set. The stage manager raised a set.
bring: to carry something to A friend brings lunch to us. A friend brought lunch to us.	**take:** to carry something away from Jake takes his script home. Lena took hers home too.

Class Exercises

Read each sentence. Tell the word in parentheses that correctly completes the sentence.

1. Rosanna ___ children to act at the theater workshop. (teaches, learns)

2. Several professional actors ___ to act from Rosanna. (taught, learned)
3. Last year the workshop needed to ___ money. (rise, raise)
4. The management ___ the staff hold a flea market. (left, let)
5. Everyone ___ something to sell at the flea market. (brought, took)

Exercises

Write each sentence using the word in parentheses that correctly completes the sentence.

1. The children ___ down to rest after rehearsal. (lay, laid)
2. Rosanna insists that they ___ down for an hour. (lie, lay)
3. Someone often ___ and reads to them while they rest. (sits, sets)
4. Rosanna ___ the older students during this time. (teaches, learns)
5. Peter must ___ gracefully in an awkward costume. (rise, raise)
6. He has ___ to do this without falling forward. (taught, learned)
7. Rosanna has ___ high standards for her students. (sat, set)
8. She ___ her hand to signal the young actors onstage. (rises, raises)
9. They ___ their scripts down when they see her signal. (lie, lay)
10. After the actors ___ down, Rosanna speaks to them. (sit, set)
11. " ___ your costumes home with you," Rosanna says. (Bring, Take)
12. "Jake ___ his home last night," Max volunteered. (brought, took)
13. " ___ yourselves get used to the costumes," Rosanna said. (Let, Leave)
14. " ___ the costumes back here on hangers," she warned. (Bring, Take)
15. Everyone ___ for home after the meeting. (let, left)
16. When Peter arrived home, he ___ his costume down on a chair. (lay, laid)
17. Then he ___ down to study his lines. (sat, set)

Writing Sentences

Imagine that you are in charge of an acting school or workshop. Use three of the pairs of words below to write six sentences about training actors.

rise/rose   teach/learn   sit/set   leave/let   bring/take

Sample Answer 1. The children lay down to rest after rehearsal.

Words Often Confused

Many English words share similar sounds but have different spellings and meanings. Study the following list:

Word	Meaning	Example
accept (verb):	to take what is offered	They accept your thanks.
except (prep.):	outside of; apart from	I saw no one except you.
beside (prep.):	nearby; at the side of	Please sit beside Joe.
besides (prep.):	in addition to	Besides math, I take history.
capital (noun):	a city which is the official place of government for a country or state	What is the capital of that state?
capitol (noun):	the building in which legislatures meet	The capitol is open to visitors.
coarse (adj.):	not of fine texture	The sand is very coarse.
course (noun):	the direction taken; a series of lessons; a path	That course of action is wrong. The cooking course is fun. The course was hard to run.
passed (verb):	to have gone by (past tense of *pass*)	The Queen passed the cheering people.
past (noun):	time gone by; ended	The old man spoke of the past.
plain (adj.):	easy to see or hear; simple	The stars were in plain view. I'd like a plain meal.
(noun):	open land	Animals live on the plain.
plane (noun):	airplane; a woodworking tool	The plane took off. The carpenter lost his plane.
principal (adj.):	first in importance	The principal reason is clear.
(noun):	head of a school	The principal calls an assembly.
principle (noun):	a basic fact or rule	The principle of honesty is best.

to (prep.):	toward; in the direction of	The dog ran to me.
too (adv.):	also; in addition	The other dog ran, too.
two (adj.):	one more than one	Two dogs ran.

Class Exercises

Read each question. Tell whether a or b is the correct answer.

1. Which sentence names a building?
  a. The senators meet in the capital.
  b. The senators meet in the capitol.

2. Which sentence describes a person?
  a. The principle is interesting.
  b. The principal is interesting.

3. Which sentence is about flat land?
  a. The plain shimmered in the sun.
  b. The plane shimmered in the sun.

4. Which sentence tells where people sat?
  a. Other people sat beside me.
  b. Other people sat, besides me.

Exercises

Write each sentence using the correct word in parentheses.

1. ___ constructing a theater, we are building sets. (Beside, Besides)
2. The fabric for the new stage curtain is ___ . (coarse, course)
3. The ___ set designers will meet with the contractor. (to, two, too)
4. Everyone attended the meeting ___ for Todd. (accept, except)
5. The theater manager has very strong ___ . (principals, principles)
6. He taught my ___ in theater design. (coarse, course)
7. Our new theater is located outside the state ___ . (capital, capitol)
8. In fact, I ___ the Statehouse on my way today. (past, passed)
9. The building itself is a ___ wooden structure. (plane, plain)
10. If you ___ a ride from me, be ready by 7 A.M. (accept, except)
11. Our construction problems are in the ___ now. (past, passed)
12. The theater's ___ season will be during the summer. (principal, principle)
13. We will all go ___ the opening in May. (two, to, too)
14. Our ___ of action has been the correct one. (coarse, course)

Sample Answer 1. Besides constructing a theater, we are building sets.

Unit Review

VOCABULARY

Read each sentence carefully. Use the sentence context to determine the meaning of the underlined word. Choose the best definition. Write the letter of each correct answer on your paper. *pages 204-205*

1. The audience shows its approval of the play with loud applause.
a. silence **b.** clapping **c.** stamping **d.** shouting

2. One actor gratefully acknowledges the cheers with a shy smile.
a. learns **b.** knows **c.** wins **d.** shows thanks for

3. The more experienced actors bow deeply to the audience.
a. curve **b.** bend forward **c.** rod **d.** looped knot

4. The actress's diction was so clear we could understand every word.
a. writing **b.** orders **c.** directing **d.** speech

Read the definitions of *meter*. Then read each sentence. Write each underlined word. Then write the number of the correct meaning for the word. *pages 206-207*

meter **1.** basic rhythmic pattern of beats in music. **2.** fundamental unit in the metric system equal to 3.28 feet. **3.** instrument for measuring gas, water, or electricity

5. The new dining room table is about two meters long.
6. The utility company sent someone to check our gas meter.
7. I cannot seem to play this musical piece in the proper meter.

Write each word and underline the prefix or suffix. Write the meaning of the word. *pages 208-209, 210-211, 212-213*

8. monotone	**13.** semiprecious	**18.** calculation
9. bicentennial	**14.** recall	**19.** fairness
10. triennial	**15.** nonprofessional	**20.** journalist
11. monochrome	**16.** unconcerned	**21.** collector
12. superpower	**17.** embarrassment	**22.** replacement

Add the suffix in parentheses to the underlined word to form an adjective. Write the second sentence using the new adjective. *pages 214-215*

23. You will enjoy this opera. It is quite ___ . (able)
24. The music will delight you. The singing is especially ___ . (ful)
25. The opera also has a lot of humor. We find it ___ . (ous)
26. At first the hero seems to have no heart. He appears ___ . (less)

Write the words in the sentences that contain the following roots:
duc *gress* *cep* *ped* *scrip* *pages 216-217*

27. Joy is a scriptwriter for a TV comedy series.
28. She pedals three miles to work every day on her bicycle.
29. The office receptionist often bicycles to work with Joy.
30. Joy claims that the exercise helps her progress through her work.

Read each item. Choose the answer that completes the item correctly. Write the letter of each answer on your paper. *pages 218-219, 220-221*

31. The most precise synonym for somber is
    a. happy **b.** sad **c.** sleepy **d.** mournful
32. An antonym for weary is
    a. energetic **b.** tired **c.** worn **d.** old
33. An antonym for dismal is
    a. dark **b.** dismiss **c.** cheery **d.** bad
34. The most precise synonym for immense is
    a. huge **b.** large **c.** many **d.** small

Write each sentence using the correct word in parentheses. *pages 222-223, 224-225*

35. Joyce has ___ from her teacher. (taught, learned)
36. Her teacher has ___ for many years. (taught, learned)
37. Her teacher ___ Joyce borrow a costume. (lets, leaves)
38. After class Joyce will ___ the costume home. (take, bring)
39. The costume designer wants some ___ fabric. (coarse, course)
40. She will use all types of material ___ burlap. (accept, except)
41. She finds some ___ cotton and linen. (plane, plain)
42. A bolt of satin lies ___ some silk and velvet. (beside, besides)

Exploring Language

The usual way of forming a new word from an already existing word is to add affixes. The word *print,* then, can become *printer, reprint, printable,* or *prints.* Some new words are formed in a backward sort of way. *Burgle* comes from *burglar* rather than the expected *burglar* from *burgle.* Words like *burgle* are called *back formations.*

Here are some modern back formations. What words do you think they came from?

typewrite baby-sit housekeep housebreak

A meeting of the United Nations Security Council at its headquarters in New York

Perhaps of all the creations of man, language is the most astonishing.

LYTTON STRACHEY
English writer
(1880-1932)

12

THE HISTORY AND NATURE OF LANGUAGE

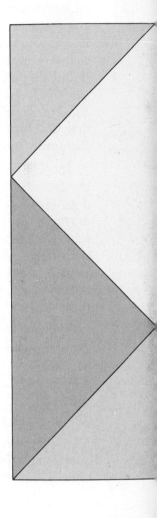

History of the Language

Language experts believe that between 5000 and 3000 B.C. a group of farming people lived in northern or central Europe. These people all spoke one language which today we call *Indo-European*. In time, groups of Indo-Europeans moved to India and other parts of Europe. In response to new experiences and ideas, their language slowly changed in its vocabulary, pronunciation, and structure. Gradually, Indo-European was replaced by a number of separate but related languages. Eventually, such languages as English, Russian, French, and Sanskrit developed from these early languages. All of the languages that developed from Indo-European are said to belong to the *Indo-European* family of languages.

The English you speak today developed from a larger member of the Indo-European family called *Germanic*. Probably around 500 B.C. a group of people called Celts came to what they called Britain from northern or central Europe. They spoke a non-Germanic language related to modern day Welsh. About 1000 years later, three Germanic tribes, the Angles, the Saxons, and the Jutes invaded and conquered Britain. Celtic language and customs all but disappeared, and Britain became England, the "land of the Angles." The Germanic language of these three tribes, what we now call *Old English*, became the dominant language.

Old English was spoken from about A.D. 500 to 1100. During this period Viking invaders conquered parts of England. The Vikings spoke a Germanic language called *Old Norse*. They brought some new words and the *sk* sound to Old English, but they did not drastically change the language or culture of England.

In 1066 French-speaking Normans conquered England. This conquest marked the beginning of the *Middle English* period,which lasted until about 1500. French became the official language of England. During this time the grammar and pronunciation of English changed greatly, but the greatest change took place in the vocabulary. Yet, despite the many changes made by the French, English did not become French, and by the middle of the fourteenth century, English was again the official language of England.

By 1500 the period of *Modern English* had begun. Modern English began with what is known as the *Great Vowel Shift*. For some unknown reason, between 1500 and 1800, English vowel sounds changed. For example, before the shift, the Middle English pronunciation of *see* would have been (sā); after the shift it became (sē), just as it is today. The same thing happened to other vowels. The pronunciation key below will help you with these pronunciations.

> **a**t; **ā**pe; c**ä**r; **e**nd; m**ē**; **i**t; **ī**ce; h**o**t; **ō**ld; f**ô**rk; w**oo**d; f**o͞o**l; **oi**l; **ou**t; **u**p; t**u**rn; si**ng**; **th**in; **th**is; **hw** in **wh**ite; **zh** in trea**s**ure. The symbol ə stands for the sound of **a** in **a**bout, **e** in tak**e**n, **i** in penc**i**l, **o** in lem**o**n, and **u** in circ**u**s.

English has continued to change. Since the Great Vowel Shift, the greatest changes in English have occurred in vocabulary.

Class Exercises

The languages in the chart belong to the Germanic branch of the Indo-European family of languages. Look at the similarities among the words. Then complete the chart with the correct English word.

Dutch	Swedish	German	English
1. moeder	moder	Mutter	
2. vader	fader	Vater	
3. zuster	syster	Schwester	
4. broeder	broder	Bruder	

Match the Old English words from Column 1 with the Modern English words from Column 2.

Column 1		Column 2	
5. leoht	**10.** ofer	**a.** over	**f.** light
6. maniġ	**11.** mihtiġ	**b.** gate	**g.** many
7. weġ	**12.** ġeat	**c.** mighty	**h.** way
8. gylt	**13.** weax	**d.** better	**i.** roof
9. hrōf	**14.** betre	**e.** wax	**j.** guilt

Spell these Middle English words as they would be spelled in Modern English.

15. bytweene	**18.** neer	**21.** sikly	**24.** tresorye	**27.** delit
16. litel	**19.** reyn	**22.** cercle	**25.** sprynge	**28.** gyngebreed
17. ston	**20.** dedly	**23.** straunge	**26.** pitee	**29.** childhede

Say these Middle English words as they would have been pronounced after the Great Vowel Shift.

30. mete (māt′ə) **31.** roote (rōt′ə) **32.** name (năm′ə)

Borrowed Words

One of the most changeable aspects of language is its vocabulary, or word stock, and one of the richest sources of new words is the words of other languages. English has been *borrowing*, or adopting, foreign words from its very beginning. Old English, for example, borrowed words from the Celts, the Romans, and the Vikings.

Borrowing can affect a language in different ways. In some instances, a word is borrowed to name something previously unknown. The Germanic inhabitants of Europe borrowed the word *wine* from Roman merchants and the word *butter* from Roman farmers who settled in Germanic lands. Later, English settlers in America borrowed such words as *squash* and *raccoon* from the American Indians. Squash and raccoons were native to America and so new to the settlers.

Sometimes borrowed words replace the native words of a language. The Old English word blēd was replaced during the Middle English period by the French word *fruit.* The Viking word *sister* eventually replaced the Old English word *sweoster* and in modern times the word *eyeglasses* in most cases has replaced the more old-fashioned *spectacles.*

Most frequently, though, both the borrowed words and the native words remain in the language. Sometimes the borrowed and native words become synonyms like the native Old English *sea* and the borrowed Latin *ocean.* At other times, the native and borrowed words develop specific differences in meaning. One example of such a difference comes from the Middle English period. When the French took over England, the native Old English words *cow, sheep, pig,* and *calf* remained to name the animals, but the French words *beef, mutton, pork,* and *veal* were borrowed to name the same animals when they were served as food.

As you have seen, words are borrowed in a number of ways. Warfare provides one opportunity for borrowing; trade and exploration provide other opportunities. Sometimes a particular country makes important advances in a field such as music, science, art, or law. Other countries adopt the ideas, and, when they do, they borrow the words to express the ideas. Italy, for example, has made important contributions in the field of music. As you might expect, many musical terms like *opera, violin, alto, soprano,* and *allegro* come from Italian.

English has always borrowed extensively from foreign languages. In fact, it often borrows words for the same thing from several different languages. You will also find that English has borrowed from the same language during several different periods in history. The presence of so many different foreign words in English explains why English has so many synonyms, and why it often has many different spellings for the same sound.

Class Exercises

Here are some foreign words which English has borrowed to name previously unknown things. Use a dictionary to tell what each word means and where it comes from.

1. curry
2. polka
3. porgy
4. tomato
5. moccasin
6. shah
7. pecan
8. lasagne

Read the words listed below. Each word is a synonym for *request.* Use a dictionary to find out what language each word comes from. Which synonyms are borrowed? Which ones come from Old English?

9. beg
10. entreat
11. beseech
12. implore
13. importune
14. ask
15. crave
16. plead

Read the words listed below. Each word names a watery lowland region. Use a dictionary to find out which language each word comes from. Which words are borrowed? Which ones come from Old English?

17. marsh
18. bog
19. fen
20. morass
21. swamp
22. sump
23. slough
24. slush

Look at the list of borrowed words. Find out which country each word is borrowed from. Then group the words according to their subject matter. What three subjects do you find? Which language or languages seem to have influenced each subject the most?

25. suede
26. embroidery
27. index
28. appliqué
29. velvet
30. school
31. crochet
32. tragedy
33. episode
34. corduroy
35. scene
36. sequin
37. library
38. drama
39. instructor
40. comedy

Changing Words

You know that the spelling, pronunciation, and structure of words can change. The movement from the Middle English *swete* (swāt′ə) to the modern *sweet* (swēt) is one example of such a change. The meaning of words can also change. Changes in meaning occur in all languages, and although the changes may be difficult to predict, they do tend to follow specific patterns. One of these patterns is known as *generalization.*

When generalization takes place, the meaning of a word is broadened or widened. The new meaning includes more than the original meaning. The word *mill*, for example, originally meant a *place where meal is made by the process of grinding*. Today the meaning of mill has been expanded to mean *a place for making things*. You can refer to a *steel mill*, a *paper mill*, or a *woolen mill* even though nothing is ground in these mills.

The opposite of generalization is *specialization*. In specialization the meaning of a word is narrowed or reduced in scope. In Old English the word *meat* meant *food*. Today, the meaning of *meat* has been narrowed to mean one kind of food, the flesh of animals. The word *sash*, in its original Arabic, meant a kind of cloth called muslin. In modern English usage, a *sash* is a band of cloth or ribbon worn around the waist or across the shoulders.

Sometimes the meaning of a word changes for the better. This process is called *amelioration* (the act of getting better). At one time the word *fickle* had the decidedly negative meaning of *treacherous* or *deceitful*. Today it has the more favorable meaning of *impulsive*, *changeable*, or *unpredictable*.

The meaning of a word can also change for the worse. This process is called *pejoration* (the act of getting worse). Pejoration takes place when a word with a neutral or positive meaning takes on a more negative or unfavorable meaning. The word *beldam* is a rather startling example of extreme pejoration. In its original Old French form *beldam (belle dame)* had the positive meaning of *a respected or beautiful woman.* When English borrowed *beldam* during the Middle English period, the word took on a more neutral meaning, *grandmother*. However, in modern English, *beldam* is defined as *an ugly or loathsome old woman*.

Sometimes a word acquires a new meaning without losing its earlier meaning. Under these circumstances, a single word can have a variety of possible meanings. The word *hall*, for example, can mean a large spacious room, in one case, or a narrow corridor or passageway between rooms, in another case. When a word has such multiple meanings, you must depend on the word's context to determine which of its meanings apply.

Class Exercises

1. Look up the word *circus*. Read the definition and the etymology, or word history, with the definition. Has the meaning of *circus* broadened or narrowed with the passage of time?

Look up the words listed below. Read the definitions and the etymologies. Have the meanings of these words broadened or narrowed with the passage of time?

2. acre
3. roundabout
4. doll
5. sauce
6. contest
7. cringe
8. fraction
9. banquet
10. husband
11. farmer
12. principal
13. grin

14. Look up the word *silly*. Read the definition. Then read the etymology. Has the meaning of *silly* become more favorable or less favorable with the passage of time?

Look up the words listed below. Read the definitions and then read the etymologies. Have the meanings of the words become more favorable or less favorable with the passage of time?

15. clown
16. argue
17. homely
18. fame
19. smug
20. polite
21. guile
22. handsome
23. snob
24. tattle
25. wiseacre
26. weak

Look up the following words. Find at least two very different definitions for each word.

27. mess
28. capital
29. tap
30. harrow
31. principal
32. hedge
33. brilliant
34. top
35. well

Section Review

MECHANICS, SPELLING, AND VOCABULARY

Write each sentence or group of words. Capitalize, punctuate, and write **declarative, interrogative, imperative, exclamatory,** or **interjection.** *pages 164-167*

1. antarctica has become a unique kind of science laboratory
2. wow
3. is antarctica bigger than the united states and mexico combined
4. name the nations that conduct scientific research there
5. that must be the coldest and most barren place on earth
6. do americans africans and others live there in winter
7. technology of the space age usually works well at the south pole

Write each sentence. Use commas, semicolons, and colons where necessary. *pages 168-173*

8. These people live in Antarctica scientists technicians and doctors.
9. Yes they study earth sciences there some scientists and doctors study the animals.
10. Although its motion is slow the entire continent is shifting.
11. Glaciers peaks and plains cover the land but few creatures live there.
12. Scientists by the way have revived some old frozen organisms.
13. They conducted this study during April one of Antarctica's few summer months.
14. While few creatures live on the land the nearby seas hold much life.
15. On May 9 1984 I will write more about this land to you Susan.

Write each sentence. Punctuate each using quotation marks, italics, hyphens, dashes, apostrophes, or parentheses. *pages 174-177*

16. What projects I mean science or exploration took place in Antarctica Stella asked Dean
17. Well Stella began author explorer Jacques Cousteau was there
18. Does Cousteaus film The Silent World show Antarctica Stella
19. The international geophysical year 1957 1958 began a new era of Antarctic exploration
20. Cousteau an independent explorer studied whales habits there.

Section Review

Use a spelling rule to determine the correctly spelled word in each pair. Write the correctly spelled word. *pages 190-193*

21. terribley, terribly
22. confusing, confuseing
23. reenter, renter
24. tieing, tying
25. derivation, deriveation
26. shuter, shutter
27. adzes, adzs
28. abuting, abutting
29. haziness, hazyness
30. buffeting, buffetting
31. latchs, latches
32. pitiful, pityful

Write the letter next to the correctly spelled word. *pages 194-195*

33. a. vetos b. vetoes
34. a. series b. serieses
35. a. chiefs b. chieves
36. a. knifes b. knives
37. a. oxen b. oxes
38. a. mangoees b. mangos
39. a. trout b. trouts
40. a. radioes b. radios
41. a. potatoes b. potatos

Write the word in parentheses that correctly completes each blank. *pages 196-199*

42. The ___ hoped ___ would water the farm. (surf, serf/ rain, reign)
43. The ___ met on a Pacific ___ . (council, counsel/ aisle, isle)
44. My ___ following other ___ tracks. (horse's, horses/ horses, horses')
45. The great designer ___ her ___ . (wares, wears/ wares, wears)
46. I'd rather travel now ___ later. (then, than)
47. The cruiser passed ___ up the ___ . (strait, straight/ strait, straight)
48. Diane ___ just what and ___ we ___ to eat. (choose, chose/ wear, were, where/ were, wear, where)
49. Dark clouds, the color of ___ , passed overhead. (led, lead)
50. Tony hammered the last ___ into the ground while Ada cut ___ for dinner. (steak, stake/ stakes, steaks)

Read each sentence. Write what you think the underlined word means. *pages 204-207*

51. The chef <u>grated</u> the carrots into small pieces.
52. Sara looked <u>ecstatic</u> when the contest judges proclaimed her the winner.
53. Sheila will <u>run</u> in next year's Boston Marathon.
54. Kenny feels proud that he can <u>run</u> the store by himself now.

Section Review

Write a word with a prefix that can replace each underlined phrase. *pages 208-209*

55. Many large mammals remain <u>not active</u> during winter months.
56. The <u>not violent</u> demonstration brought about good changes.
57. For a while each morning I speak in <u>single syllables</u>.
58. Kay rushed home for the message, but it was <u>not important</u>.
59. The <u>two-winged plane</u> towed a colorful banner over the stadium.

Add the given suffix to each word below. Write the new word. Then write whether the new word is a **noun** or an **adjective**. Use the dictionary to check your spelling. *pages 212-215*

60. whole + ness
61. direct + or
62. meddle + some
63. control + er
64. vary + ant
65. scare + y
66. evaluate + ion
67. fool + ish
68. dally + ance
69. guile + less

Write each word and its meaning. Underline the root. Use your dictionary if necessary. *pages 216-217*

70. invoke
71. deception
72. description
73. regress
74. biped
75. pending
76. pulsate
77. insignia
78. visor

Make three columns on your paper. Label them **Word**, **Synonym**, and **Antonym**. Write each word on the left below under *Word*. Then find and write each word's *best* synonym and antonym from the right column below. *pages 218-221*

79. excellent	sloppy, careful, thorough, pleasant
80. courage	depth, valor, breadth, timidity
81. saunter	hurry, meander, travel, cross
82. clever	ponderous, watchful, sly, unimaginative
83. famous	unknown, infamous, celebrated, skilled

Write the word or words in parentheses that complete each sentence correctly. *pages 222-225*

84. Tom ____ a book back ____ school. (took, brought/ too, to, two)
85. The moon ____ over the desert ____. (rose, raised/ plane, plain)
86. Ida ____ to ____ the loss of her ring. (taught, learned/ accept, except)
87. I'll ____ you ____ me at the station. (leave, let/ let, leave)
88. A dog ____ sleeping on the golf ____. (lay, lie/ coarse, course)
89. Dawn ____ down some words about the ____. (set, sat/ passed, past)

COMPOSITION

- Study and Reference Skills
- Sentence Study
- The Writing Process

The planet Saturn, photographed by the *Voyager* spacecraft

The only way to discover the limits of the possible is to go beyond them, to the impossible.

ARTHUR C. CLARKE
British science writer (1917-   )

13

STUDY AND TEST-TAKING SKILLS

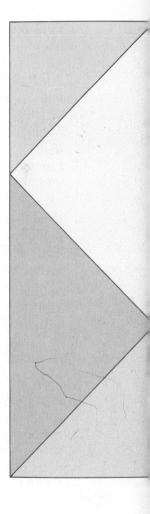

Mechanics of Note-Taking

The ability to write accurate, well-organized notes is a valuable study skill. It is also the key to writing a report based on careful research. Here are some guidelines to help you take effective notes.

1. Find the main ideas in each source. Identify the supporting details about each main idea.
2. Write your notes on notecards. Number each card as you write it. At the top of each notecard, write the name of the book or article and the author's name. If your source is a magazine or newspaper article, include the date it was published and the issue or volume number. If your source is a book, you want to include the copyright date.
3. Use phrases to write the main ideas and headings. Write notes about only one main idea and its supporting details on each notecard. You might indent the supporting details under each main idea. After each note, write the page number on which the information was found so that you can easily find the information again.
4. You may want to use an exact, or direct, quotation from the source. Put quotation marks at the beginning and end of the quotation.

Read the following paragraphs from a book by James Fawcett and some notecards written about them.

from *Land Down Under*

Australia has many strange native animals. Most are marsupials, such as the kangaroo and the koala bear, which carry their young in pouches. The platypus lays eggs and has a furry body, webbed feet, and a bill like a duck. Birds include the kookaburra, which sounds like a donkey braying, and the cassowary, which cannot fly but can run up to 40 miles (64 kilometers) per hour. It can jump six feet (1.8 meters) or higher in the air.

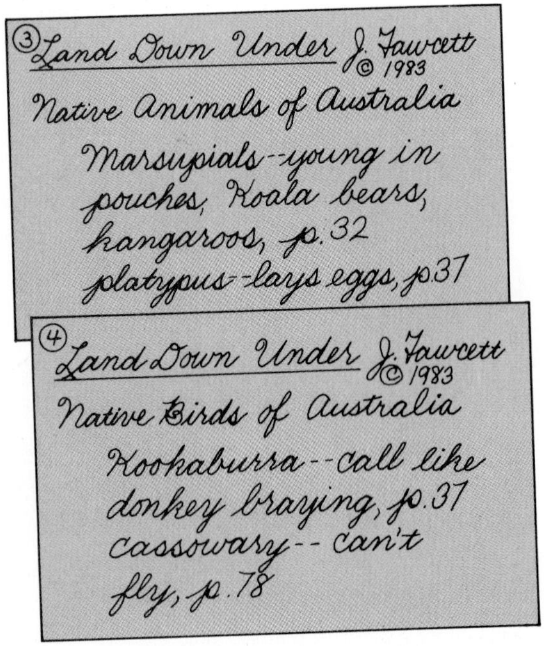
③ Land Down Under J. Fawcett
© 1983
Native Animals of Australia
Marsupials--young in pouches, Koala bears, kangaroos, p. 32
platypus--lays eggs, p.37
④ Land Down Under J. Fawcett
© 1983
Native Birds of Australia
Kookaburra--call like donkey braying, p.37
cassowary-- can't fly, p.78

Among the native plants are wildflowers called bottlebrushes and others called kangaroo paws. Some native trees include the eucalyptus, whose leaves are the only food koala bears will eat, and the bottle tree, with its trunk shaped like a bottle. Another strange plant is the wattle, which may grow more than 80 feet (24 meters) high. It has yellow blossoms. The saltbush, which grows in the dry regions, has leaves that are covered with a grayish, salty substance.

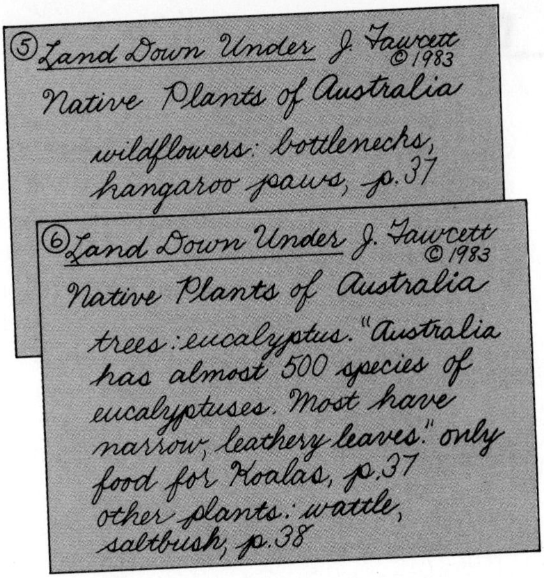
⑤ Land Down Under J. Fawcett
©1983
Native Plants of Australia
wildflowers: bottlenecks,
kangaroo paws, p.37
⑥ Land Down Under J. Fawcett
©1983
Native Plants of Australia
trees: eucalyptus. "Australia
has almost 500 species of
eucalyptuses. Most have
narrow, leathery leaves." only
food for Koalas, p.37
other plants: wattle,
saltbush, p.38

Class Exercises

1. What is the main idea on the first notecard?
2. What supporting detail is written on the card?
3. How do the notes on the cards differ from the paragraph?
4. What are the main ideas and the supporting details on the other notecards?

Exercises

The following paragraph about the early history of France was written by J. Fine in 1980. Read it and take notes about it on notecards. Follow the guidelines for taking notes on the preceding page.

from *France*

In ancient times France was part of a large area called Gaul. The Roman general Julius Caesar conquered Gaul and added it to the Roman Empire. After many years, the empire fell apart. The German tribes came down from the north. One tribe, called the Franks, settled in what is now France. Later came the Normans, who settled in northern France. In those early times Paris was a little town on an island in the Seine River. By 1843, France had grown to be a nation, and Paris was its capital.

Writing an Outline

An outline is a list of words, phrases, or even short sentences that summarize the main ideas in a speech or written composition. In a formal outline, each entry is labeled with a Roman numeral or a capital letter to indicate its relationship to the other entries in the outline.

Outlining is a valuable study aid. Writing an outline of the information you learn as you read or listen helps you remember it. Writing an outline is also a valuable prewriting step when you are organizing the information you want to present in a composition.

• Read the outline one student made from the notes on pages 242-243.

Native Animals and Plants of Australia

Main Topic *I. Native animals of Australia*
Subtopics *A. Marsupials*
B. Platypus
C. Birds

Main Topic *II. Native plants of Australia*
Subtopics *A. Trees*
B. Other plants
C. Wildflowers

• Look at the outline again. Notice the following things:

1. The main subject of the outline is a combination of the two main topics.
2. The main topics of the outline are identified by Roman numerals followed by a period. In your paragraph you will develop the main topic into the topic sentence. Roman numeral *I* could be written like this:

   Visitors to Australia will see many strange native animals.

3. Subtopics of the outline are identified by capital letters followed by a period. In your paragraph you will develop the subtopics into detail sentences. For example under Roman numeral *I*, topic A could be written like this:

   Many of these native animals are marsupials.
   Marsupials carry their young in a pouch.

Notice that the main topics of the outline are written in the same style. The subtopics also follow a pattern. This is called *parallel structure.* The structure of all main topics must be parallel, and the structure of each group of subtopics must also be parallel.

Notice also how the main topics relate to each other. Main topic *I* is a general statement about native animals in Australia. Main topic *II* makes the same kind of general statement about native plants in Australia. The student also put the subtopics into a clear order. The largest group of native animals, marsupials, comes first, and then the most unusual animal. The third subtopic covers birds.

Class Exercises

1. Look back at the notecards on pages 242-243. What main idea or main heading was not used as a main topic in the outline? Why?
2. What is the main subject of the outline? How did you know?
3. What is the first main topic? How are the subtopics related to the main topic?
4. What is the second main topic? How are the subtopics related to it?
5. Can you think of any other main topics or subtopics you might add in a longer report on this subject?

Exercises

Read the list of topics and subtopics on the development of Roman roads. Decide which topics are main topics. Then choose the subtopics that go with each main topic. Write the outline.

1. Description of Roman roads
2. Importance of Roman roads
3. Materials used in Roman roads
4. Aided commerce
5. Thickness of Roman roads
6. Unified the empire
7. Length of Roman roads
8. Made Rome center of empire

Thinking About Fact and Opinion

As a writer or speaker, you give information of two kinds: fact and opinion. A *fact* is something that has actually happened or that people know to be true. An *opinion* is a statement that expresses someone's personal feelings.

• Read these two sentences.

Crown Milk is on sale this week at Golden Foods.

Crown Milk is a delicious drink.

The first sentence states a fact. Anyone can check with Golden Foods to see if the statement is true. The second sentence states an opinion. The truth of the statement can be neither proven nor disproven.

As you read, you will notice that some paragraphs contain facts. The topic sentence of a factual paragraph states the main idea. The detail sentences tell more about the main idea. Each statement can be proven by research or personal observation. Paragraphs of fact are often used in news articles, reports, and business letters.

You will also find that other paragraphs contain opinions. The topic sentence of a paragraph of opinion states the writer's personal feeling. The detail sentences give the writer's reasons for having that opinion. Opinion paragraphs are often found in reviews, editorials, and advertisements.

• Read the two paragraphs below.

Paragraph of Facts

Ty Cobb was a baseball player. He played for a major-league team when he was eighteen. During his career, he played in 3,003 games. In the 1915 season, Cobb stole 96 bases. He is a member of the Baseball Hall of Fame.

Paragraph of Opinions

The greatest baseball player of all time is Ty Cobb. His style of batting and throwing was remarkable. He was an exciting athlete. Cobb did a lot to make baseball America's favorite sport.

In the paragraph of facts each statement about Ty Cobb can be proven. The paragraph of opinion gives the writer's judgment of Ty Cobb. The statements are personal feelings.

Being aware of the difference between a statement of fact and a statement of opinion will make you a better reader and listener. You may find that a writer has given an opinion in a detail sentence that should support a topic sentence of fact. By noting that the detail sentence contains an opinion rather than a fact, you will be able to evaluate the information presented.

Class Exercises

Tell whether each of the sentences is a **statement of fact** or a **statement of opinion.** If it is a statement of fact, tell how you would prove or disprove it.

1. The most important early discoveries were probably accidental.
2. Egyptians invented the spoked wheel around 1800 B.C.
3. A wheel with spokes is lighter than a solid wheel.
4. No invention can rival the wheel for usefulness.

Exercises

Write whether each of the sentences is a **statement of fact** or a **statement of opinion.**

1. Agriculture made all other important inventions possible.
2. Early hunters depended largely on the pursuit of animals.
3. Their lives were too busy for much thought about inventions.
4. The New Stone Age began about 6000 B.C.
5. Crops and herds of cattle fed the first agricultural towns.
6. This period of history was one of the most inventive of all.
7. The art of weaving improved beyond anyone's expectations.
8. Grass, flax, and wool provided the materials of weaving.
9. People of these early towns had plenty of time for thought.
10. By 1000 B.C. several new inventions were in use.

Writing Sentences

Write two paragraphs about an invention. In the first paragraph, use statements of fact to tell about the invention. In the second paragraph, use statements of opinion to show why the invention was or was not important in history. Then read your paragraph aloud. Have classmates tell which paragraph contains facts, and which contains opinions.

Sample Answer 1. statement of opinion

Reading Graphs, Tables, and Maps

Some of the information you find in textbooks and reference works is given in the form of graphs, tables, and maps.

A *graph* is a diagram that shows how one thing changes in relation to another. A graph shows the relationship by the use of bars, lines, or dots.

- Look at the graph below. It shows how the population of Newtown changed over a period of 40 years. The numbers on the left side of the graph report the size of the town's population. The dates along the bottom name the years for which the population of Newtown is given.

Population of Newtown 1940-1980

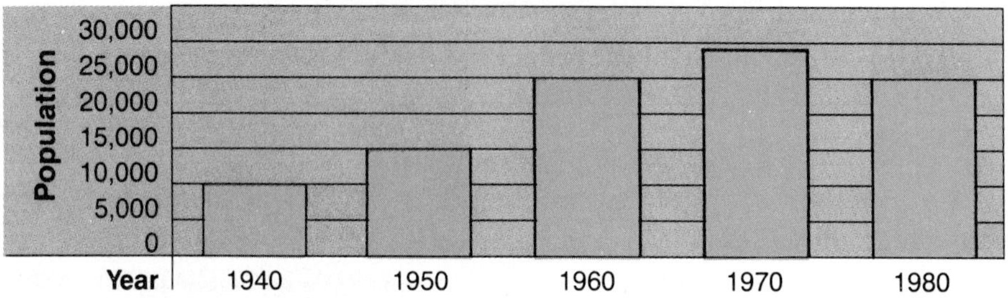

Books and reports of many kinds often present facts and statistics in tables. A *table* is an orderly arrangement of facts and figures.

- Read the table below. The Martin family made this table to compare their living expenses for two different years. The table lists the items of expense and the amount the Martins spent on each for the two years.

Table of Expenses

Basic Expense	1979 Cost	1980 Cost	1980 Increase
Housing	3660	5500	+1840
Transportation	850	300	−550
Food	3600	4160	+560
Clothing	950	1040	+90
Medical	0	1500	+1500
Taxes	1170	1380	+210
TOTAL	10,230	13,880	+3650

A *map* is a representation of a geographical area. A map may use symbols that tell different facts about the area. A *legend* explains the symbols that appear on the map.

• Look at the legend below. It is from a farming and resource map. Suppose *Fe* appears on a green portion of the map. The legend explains that *Fe* means iron ore is found in a forest.

Map Legend

LAND USE		MINERALS	
FORESTS	GREEN	C	COAL
COTTON	RED	Cu	COPPER
GRAIN	YELLOW	Fe	IRON ORE
DAIRY	ORANGE	G	NATURAL GAS
FRUIT	PURPLE	Sn	TIN

Class Exercises

Use the graph, table, or map legend on these pages to answer the questions.

1. What was the population of Newtown in 1940?

2. How much did the Martin family spend on food in 1979?

3. What would *G* on a yellow portion of the map mean?

Exercises

Use the graph, table, or map legend on these pages to write the answer to each question.

1. What did the Martin family spend on housing in 1980?

2. When was the population of Newtown the highest?

3. What item cost less in 1980 than in 1979 for the Martin family?

4. What would *C* on an orange portion of the map mean?

5. What item increased the most in 1980 for the Martin family?

6. When did Newtown have its lowest population?

Sample Answer 1. $5,500

Using Test-Taking Skills

You have probably taken many different kinds of tests in school. To be successful it is important to develop a strategy for each type of test. Two basic kinds of tests are the objective test and the essay test.

Objective tests may include multiple choice, true-or-false, matching, and fill-in-the-blank questions. Each of these kinds of questions tests your knowledge of specific facts.

A *multiple choice question* usually has four or five choices. You should read the question and all the choices carefully. If you are not sure of the answer, eliminate the choices that you know are incorrect. As you eliminate these choices, you increase your chance of choosing the correct answer from the remaining choices.

A *true-or-false question* requires you to decide whether the statement is completely true. If any part of the statement is false, then the entire statement is false. Therefore you must read and think about each statement carefully.

A *matching question* has two lists of items. You must match each item in the first list with an item in the second list. Be sure to read *all* the items in the second list before you begin matching any items.

Fill-in-the-blank questions do not offer answers from which to choose. Even if you are not completely sure of an answer, you should fill in the blank with an answer that seems to make the most sense. On most tests of this kind, a wrong answer does not count against you any more heavily than an empty blank.

Reading comprehension and vocabulary are two skills that are often tested by objective tests. Reading comprehension tests usually give you a short selection to read that is followed by questions about its content. Vocabulary tests usually test your knowledge of synonyms and antonyms or your ability to complete sentences correctly with the most appropriate word from a list of words that is given to you.

An **essay test** generally tests your knowledge of a broad topic. You must write your answer to an essay question in correct paragraph form. First read the question carefully. Jot down ideas that you might use for your answer. Begin your paragraph by answering the question asked. Then include details that give reasons foı your answer.

Class Exercises

Read each question below and choose the best answer.

1. Maria worked much more smoothly at the clothing store after her ___ week at the cottage by the sea.
   a. expensive   b. hurried   c. restful
2. Alaska lies farther north than any other American state.
   a. true   b. false
3. The word *tumult* means ___
   a. a quiet moment   b. an uproar   c. a meeting
4. If *rock* in Column A matched *solid* in Column B, which word below would you match with nitrogen?
   a. vapor   b. matter   c. liquid

Exercises

Read the paragraph below. Choose the best answer for each question based on the paragraph. Write the letter of your answer.

> Alaska is the largest of all American states. It is also a land of sharply contrasting features. While much of Alaska remains wild and uninhabited, its many cities have become homes for millions of immigrants and industries. Glaciers still move down its deep mountain valleys, and volcanoes rumble along its seacoast. Clear cold streams run through its dense pine forests, while hot springs dot its barren plains. Both adventurers and developers find one of their greatest challenges in this vast and valuable land.

1. The Alaskan landscape is ___ .
   a. uniform   b. varied   c. desolate
2. Glaciers and volcanoes ensure Alaska's unchanging appearance.
   a. true   b. false
3. The word ___ tells that many Alaskans come from other places.
   a. industries   b. uninhabited   c. immigrants
4. Cold streams contrast with ___ .
   a. hot springs   b. dense forests   c. huge cities
5. For many adventurers and developers Alaska is a land of ___ .
   a. extremes   b. challenge   c. wilderness

Understanding Verbal Analogies

One kind of question that you will often encounter on a standardized test is the analogy question. Analogy questions test your ability to understand relationships between words and ideas.

- Look at this example.

snake : reptile : : corn :

a. fruit **b.** vegetable **c.** plant

When stated in the form of a sentence, this analogy is really asking, "Snake is to reptile as corn is to which of the following words?" In order to choose the correct answer, you must carefully consider the relationship between the words in the first word pair. Since a snake is one of a number of reptiles, the correct answer must involve the object *corn* as part of a larger group. The choice that best fits this description is *b. vegetable.*

Several types of relationships between words commonly appear on analogy tests. Look at these examples.

Word : Synonym	strong : powerful : : coarse : rough
Word : Antonym	soft : hard : : weak : strong
Whole : Part	window : pane : : chair : cushion
Object : Use	hammer : strike : : shovel : dig
Product : Producer	milk : cow : : honey : bee

You must be careful to choose an answer that expresses a relationship similar to the one expressed in the sample. For example, if the sample expresses a whole : part relationship, an answer that expresses a part : whole relationship would be incorrect. The correct response would have the whole stated before the part. Study the example below.

CORRECT	book : pages : : table : legs
INCORRECT	book : pages : : legs : table

Since the relationship of the sample is that of a whole (the book) to a part (the pages), the correct answer is table (the whole) : legs (the part).

Class Exercises

Read each group of words and the choices that follow. Choose the word that completes each analogy.

1. like : unlike : : careful :

a. careless **b.** dislike **c.** unlike

2. brush : bristle : : belt :

a. dress **b.** buckle **c.** pocket

3. strange : different : : true :

a. correct **b.** lie **c.** fib

4. milk : beverage : : meat :

a. cow **b.** butter **c.** food

Exercises

Read each group of words below. Then write the letter for the word that completes each analogy.

1. daffodils : plants : : dogs :

a. cats **b.** puppies **c.** animals

2. diamond : mineral : : apple :

a. vegetable **b.** fruit **c.** orange

3. elevator : lift : : wheelbarrow :

a. stairs **b.** carry **c.** chair

4. repair : break : : sorrow :

a. glee **b.** pity **c.** sadness

5. ordinary : commonplace : : abandon :

a. find **b.** leave **c.** encounter

6. piano : keys : : ladder :

a. rungs **b.** climb **c.** painter

7. chicken : eggs : : oyster :

a. clams **b.** pearls **c.** crabs

8. gorgeous : beautiful : : wonderful :

a. nice **b.** pretty **c.** marvelous

9. milk : goat : : wool :

a. sheep **b.** fur **c.** silk

10. same : different : : positive :

a. clear **b.** negative **c.** certain

Unit Review

STUDY AND TEST TAKING SKILLS

Read the list of topics and subtopics on the United Nations. Decide which topics are main topics. Then choose the subtopics that belong with each main topic. Write the outline. *pages 244-245*

1. Human Dignity
2. General Assembly Building
3. The Security Council
4. The General Assembly
5. Secretariat Building
6. Goals of the UN
7. Conference Building
8. Dag Hammarskjöld Library
9. Peace
10. Major Branches of the UN
11. The Secretariat
12. Headquarters of the UN

Read each statement below. Write **F** if the sentence states a fact. Write **O** if the sentence states an opinion. *pages 246-247*

13. Milk is a very nutritious substance that most babies drink.
14. Artificially sweetened bubble gum is better tasting than naturally sweetened bubble gum.
15. Everyone should drink at least eight glasses of water every day.
16. Rye bread is better for you than whole wheat bread.
17. Video games are more fun than playing board games.
18. Cow's milk has more nutrients than goat's milk.
19. Most cereals contain sugar.

Study the graph. Write the answers for the questions that follow. *pages 248-249*

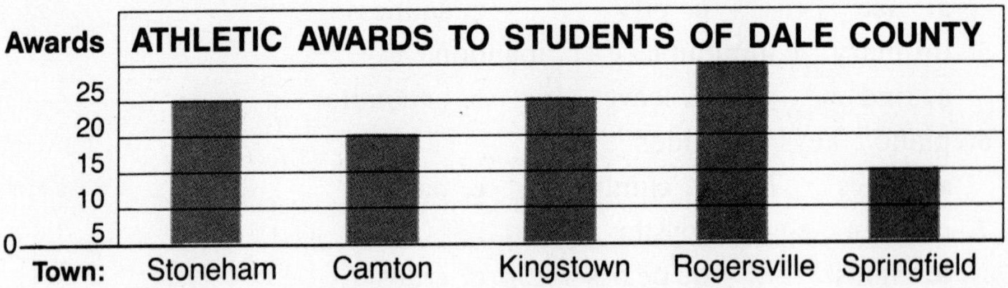

20. Which towns received the same number of awards?
21. How many more awards did Rogersville receive than Camton?
22. Is the difference between Stoneham and Camton greater than the difference between Kingstown and Rogersville?
23. What is the difference between the number of awards to Springfield and the number of awards to the highest-scoring town?

Read the paragraph that follows. Then write the letter of the best answer for each question. *pages 250-251*

> Actors learn to control their faces, voices, and bodies. Many schools can provide some training, but experience onstage is most valuable. The face and body express emotions without a word. The voice, however, must be perfectly adjusted to the role.

24. The best training for an actor is ___ .
a. schools **b.** control **c.** performance

25. No written lines are needed for an actor to express emotion by ___ .
a. memory **b.** face or body **c.** voice

26. The voice is *attuned* to the role when it is ___ to the role.
a. mismatched **b.** well-rehearsed **c.** adjusted

Read each group of words and the choices that follow. Write the letter for the word that completes each analogy. *pages 252-253*

27. bright : shining : : sharp
a. cutting **b.** cut **c.** swift

28. moon : planet : : Earth
a. travel **b.** sun **c.** star

29. cave : building : : cliff
a. basement **b.** tower **c.** cellar

30. sweep : clean : : communicate
a. silence **b.** speak **c.** speaking

Exploring Language

What do the names of animals mean? Some names come from old Greek or Latin words that tell about the animals.

The name for a hippopotamus comes from two words meaning *horse* and *river.* Is *river horse* a good name for a big animal that likes to spend most of its time in the water?

The rhinoceros gets its name from the horns on its snout. The name comes from words meaning *nose* and *horn.*

The name for a porcupine comes from two words meaning *pig* and *thorn.* Do you think a porcupine looks like a pig with thorns?

Design plans are adjusted before the concrete flows into forms.

A people's speech is the skin of its culture.

MAX LERNER
American writer and educator
(1902-)

14

LISTENING AND SPEAKING SKILLS

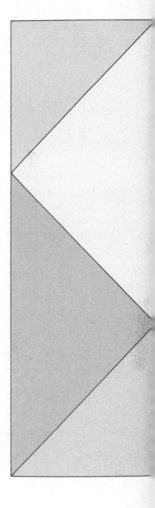

Listening

When you hear a person talking, a singer performing, or a dog barking outside your window, are you really listening? Listening is more than just hearing. When you listen, you are concentrating on and understanding what you hear. It is a skill that you must learn and practice. The guidelines that follow can help you become a good listener.

GUIDES TO EFFECTIVE LISTENING

1. Be sure that you stand or sit in a place that will enable you to clearly hear the speaker. Give the speaker your full attention and courtesy. Do not talk to others while you are listening.
2. Show interest. Look directly at the speaker.
3. Pay detailed attention to what the speaker is saying. Note the main ideas and supporting details as they are presented. Watch the speaker's gestures and facial expressions. Listen for changes in tone of voice and volume. These serve as clues as to when important points are being made. Also notice the speaker's use of logical connecting words such as *first, next, then,* and *finally.* These will help in evaluating the presentation.
4. Take brief notes as you are listening. Write down key words or phrases of the important ideas and details of the speech. After the speaker has finished, review your notes and add to them wherever necessary.
5. Use the question period to clarify statements that you did not remember or did not understand. Raise your hand and wait to be called upon.

Review what you hear. Try to summarize the speaker's words. Then compare your notes with what you remember. Your listening skills will improve with continued practice. Use the listening guidelines as frequently as possible in as many listening situations as you can.

Class Exercises

Imagine that a parachute jumper is speaking on television about the requirements of this sport. You must report back to your class. Answer the following questions using the guidelines on the opposite page.

1. What clues would help you determine the main ideas?
2. How would you ask the speaker a question?
3. What actions would show your interest in the topic?
4. What things would help you evaluate information?

Exercises

1. Listen as your teacher reads the following selection. Take notes on the main idea and several important details. Compare your results.

Alexander G. Bell, Inventor

The telephone may be Alexander Graham Bell's most important invention. This great achievement in communications was the goal of Bell's early life. However, this inventor also contributed to medical science and to education.

Alexander Bell's main interest was communications. As a boy, he helped his father develop new ways to teach speech to the deaf. In Scotland and Canada during the 1870s, Bell and his father became known for their successful teaching methods. Alexander soon became a professor at Boston University. It was there that Bell began work on what would later be called the telephone.

In March of 1876, Bell and Thomas Watson, were successful in sending voices over an electrified wire. Bell spent five more years improving telephones and then began other work.

Bell helped young inventors and scientists. He founded *Science* magazine in 1883, built laboratories, and encouraged research.

2. Choose one of the topic sentences below, or use one of your own. Add detail sentences and a concluding statement. Read your paragraph aloud. Have volunteers restate the main idea and details.

a. A leash law for dogs is (or is not) needed in our community.
b. Students' suggestions for new courses might improve education.
c. A student employment office would help us meet employers.

Speaking

When you communicate your thoughts, you want to be understood. Just as you practice writing skills to express yourself, you must practice your speaking skills as well. Your speaking style may be informal, as when you discuss ideas with friends, or formal, as when you address an audience. To be effective in both situations, you should know your audience and your purpose as well as techniques of delivery.

Audience
- Who is your audience? What do they already know about your subject? What is their point of view?
- Where and when are you speaking? What is the occasion? Be sure that your speech is suited for the audience, the place, and the time.

Purpose
- Why are you speaking? Decide if you are planning to convince, to inform, or to entertain your audience. Then prepare your speech accordingly.
- What is your main idea and what are your supporting details? Will your speech be based upon personal experiences or information you have researched?
- Follow the same procedure that you would use for planning a written report. Be sure your speech flows logically from the introduction to its conclusion.
- Prepare audiovisual materials if appropriate.

Delivery
- Face your listeners. Establish eye contact.
- Know your speech. Glance at your notes without pausing to read them.
- Consider the size of the room and adjust your tone of voice and volume accordingly. Speak clearly and not too quickly. Avoid the frequent use of "uh" or "and."
- Use connecting words such as *first, next, then, finally,* and *and so forth* to clarify thoughts, ideas, and sequences.
- Be poised and relaxed. If you make a speaking error, pause, and then continue.
- Use gestures and facial expressions that are appropriate.
- Be courteous.

Speaking before an audience requires practice. Rehearse with a friend or use a tape recorder. The more you practice, the easier it will be for you.

Class Exercises

Imagine that you are the director of the Class Activities Committee. You have just visited a neighboring school. Its students share the work of restoring historic sites in the area. Now you must convince your school officials of the value and usefulness of the work.

1. What kinds of information will help you persuade your audience?
2. What would you try to learn about your audience?
3. What audiovisual aids would improve your presentation?
4. What tone of voice would be most appropriate?

Exercises

1. Think of an organized sport, cultural activity, or program you enjoy sharing or watching. Prepare a short speech supporting the activity.
2. Practice your speech aloud. Then take turns with classmates in evaluating speaking skills. Use the checklist that follows.

Speaking Checklist

S = Satisfactory ✓ = Needs Improvement

1. Was the speech suited for the audience, the place and the time?
2. Was the purpose clear?
3. a. Did you face your listeners?
   b. Did you maintain eye contact?
   c. Did you know your speech?
   d. Did you adjust your tone of voice and volume?
   e. Did you speak clearly and not too quickly?
   f. Did you pause for clarity and emphasis?
   g. Were your ideas clear and in sequence?
   h. Were you poised?
   i. Did you use gestures and expressions?
   j. Were you courteous?
4. Total Effectiveness
5. Additional comments: ______________________________

____

Interviewing

When you are unable to obtain necessary information for a report or research paper through the library, an interview can be a good source of current information. As an interviewer you will use your listening, speaking, and writing skills. You must organize and prepare before the interview.

You may ask for an interview either by telephone or by letter. State the purpose of the interview and suggest a time and location. Be sure to include the amount of time that will be needed for the interview.

You should have enough knowledge about the topic so that your questions are sensible and meaningful. Prepare your questions in advance. You may want to give a list of the questions to the person before the interview. This will give the person time to consider responses to your questions.

The guidelines that follow can help you do an interview.

GUIDE TO A SKILLFUL INTERVIEW

1. Introduce yourself and state the purpose of the interview.
2. Plan your questions carefully so that you can focus on the topic.
3. Be attentive. Ask politely for more details when necessary.
4. Make notes of the key phrases and ideas mentioned. If you want to use a tape recorder, ask permission to use it from the person being interviewed.
5. Be courteous.
6. Be aware that you must tactfully bring the interview to an end when the allotted time has been reached.
7. Thank the person for the interview and the information.

When you have completed the interview, review your notes. Select and arrange the information that you will need the most. Do not change the meaning of what the person said. If you write a report of the interview, be sure to use quotation marks around the exact words of the person.

Class Exercises

Imagine that you are working on the class yearbook. A very popular teacher will retire this year. It is your job to interview her.

1. How would you arrange for the interview? What would you say?
2. Would the interview improve if you spoke first with some of the teacher's former students? Why?
3. How would you report exactly what the teacher said to you?
4. If you wanted to use a tape recorder during the interview, what would you say to the teacher?
5. What would you say in order to obtain more detailed information?
6. How would you end the interview?

Exercises

1. Have volunteers "role-play" the yearbook writer and the teacher from the Class Exercise above. As they act out the situations that follow, evaluate each situation and the writer's response to it. Use the Guide to a Skillful Interview as you evaluate.

   Situation A. You are meeting the teacher after school to arrange the interview. Decide upon a time and place.

   Situation B. You have been unable to meet with the teacher to arrange the interview. "Role-play" your telephone call to the teacher, introduce yourself, and try to arrange the interview.

2. Prepare a list of ten questions for the teacher. Be sure that they are meaningful. Then have two volunteers from the class act out the interview. Take notes on the teacher's answers to questions.
3. As volunteers act out the interview, notice those moments where more information might be useful. Form questions to ask for more facts.
4. After several pairs of volunteers act out the interview, compare the notes taken by everyone. Which notes show the teacher's ideas and opinions most clearly? Give reasons to support your answer.
5. Write a brief report about the interview. Use quotation marks when writing exact words and responses.

Group Discussions

Clubs, committees, and classes often hold a *group discussion.* The members speak and listen to each other about a particular topic of mutual concern. During the group discussion each member of the group has the opportunity to present information and ideas.

A chairperson presides over the discussion. He or she should be familiar with the topic and know how to direct the discussion.

GUIDELINES FOR LEADING A GROUP DISCUSSION

1. Bring the meeting to order.
2. State the problem or subject and the final goal. Be prepared to summarize the results of previous discussions and to suggest points of view or possible solutions for consideration.
3. Keep the discussion on the topic and moving toward the goal.
4. Recognize different group members to allow them to present their views. Permit one person to speak at a time. Give every person an opportunity to participate. Prevent arguments.
5. Take notes. You will be required to summarize the discussion and results. Avoid taking sides. State facts, not opinions.
6. Adjourn the meeting.

Members who participate in the discussion must also meet certain responsibilities.

GUIDELINES FOR PARTICIPATING IN A GROUP DISCUSSION

1. Prepare yourself to participate in the discussion. Learn as much as you can about the topic prior to the discussion.
2. Listen carefully to what is said. Take notes if necessary. Build your statements on what has already been stated. Consider other points of view as you evaluate what you hear.
3. Raise your hand or stand to be recognized by the chairperson. Never interrupt. When you are recognized, speak clearly, properly, and loudly enough to be heard by everyone. If you disagree with another, do so courteously. Be prepared to support your statements with accurate facts and examples.

Class Exercises

Read the observations made about several students who participated in a recent group discussion. Tell how each student could have improved his or her performance.

1. Michael had an appointment, so he left before the adjournment.
2. Clair was the chairperson. She gave her opinion of the situation.
3. The chairperson allowed Luisa and Thomas to continue arguing.
4. Read and evaluate the following discussion using the guidelines. Tell how each person could have improved.

Chairperson: The discussion group will now come to order.
Juan (without raising his hand)**:** Well, what's this meeting about?
Chairperson: Thank you, Juan. Our group's task is to plan ways to increase attendance at this year's play. More money is needed to cover expenses. One idea is to simply raise ticket prices. Another is to advertise in school and around town—
Mei (interrupting)**:** But advertising will cost us plenty, I think.
Chairperson: Very well, the chair recognizes Mei. Please explain.
Mei: I don't know. Who'll pay for posters or for radio time? And the prices of tickets seemed high to me already, last year.
Lisa (after being recognized)**:** What do you suggest then, Mei?
Mei: I never said that I had any great ideas on the topic.
Juan: Let someone talk who has thought about it, will you?
Chairperson: Order, order, please. Remember that last year we had students make posters at home.
Frank (after being recognized)**:** I think we should ask the theater group to simply perform a play which costs less.
Lisa: You're not listening, Frank. It's too late for that now.
Chairperson: The costumes and scenery are beautiful this year.

Form several discussion groups. Each group will choose a chairperson and discuss one of the following topics.

5. The need for a student art gallery in your school
6. The need for a survey to learn what kinds of new courses or workshops students want in your school
7. The need for guest speakers from various career areas to discuss their professions with interested students

Oral Reports

An oral report combines many listening and speaking skills as well as research and writing skills. An effective oral report must be planned and organized. The steps used to give an oral report are similar to the steps used to write a report. Study the guides that follow.

Prewriting

1. Find a topic that is appropriate to your audience and the occasion.
2. Use your library skills to gather information about your topic. Decide what audiovisual materials or interviews you might use.
3. Read carefully and take notes.
4. Decide upon a purpose. Are you going to inform, entertain, or convince your audience?
5. Organize your materials keeping your purpose in mind. Consider questions that your audience might ask.

Writing

6. Write a draft of your report.

Editing

7. Edit your draft.
8. Make an edited copy as notes or in an outline format.

Practice

9. Practice your report with a friend or on a tape recorder.
10. Begin each part of your report with a topic sentence as you follow your outline or notes. Remember to use connecting words to clarify the sequence of thoughts and ideas.
11. Time your report. Decide if it is too long or too short.
12. Practice your speed, tone of voice and volume, expressions and gestures, and eye contact.

Delivery

13. Face your listeners. Be familiar enough with your report so that you only need to glance at your notes. Look frequently at your listeners.
14. Vary your speed, tone of voice, volume, facial expressions, and gestures.
15. Relax. If you make an error, pause a moment and then continue.
16. Have your audience wait until the end of your report to ask questions or offer comments.
17. Be courteous. Thank your listeners at the conclusion of your report.

At the end of your presentation, evaluate yourself. For your next oral report, focus on improving areas of weakness.

Class Exercises

Read a seventh grade class's observations on some oral reports. Give a general rule for improving each student's performance.

1. Jean spoke from an unedited report which caused confusion.
2. Alan's report seemed to want to convince us of something.
3. Gail needed ten extra minutes to finish her report.
4. Dan's report subject seemed intended for a lower grade level.
5. Read the following report. Tell how it could be improved.

> **Beavers**
>
> I have a short series of slides here to show you how exactly the beaver builds its home, called a lodge. Other kinds of beavers, of course, don't build lodges. They live along river banks. But this report is about the beavers that build lodges. First I'll describe the animal themselves, and then we'll see the slides.
>
> Should I begin with how they look, or with how they live? Well, the beaver, North America's largest rodent, can grow up to four feet. In length, including its 16-inch tail. It has a heavy coat of reddish fur, webbed hind feet for swimming about two miles per hour, and teeth that grow all of its life. It has special muscles in its nose and ears that keep out water as it swims. That map shows where they live in North America. And of course those teeth can cut down a small tree in about fifteen minutes.
>
> See, beavers eat high branches of certain trees. But they can't climb, so they cut the trees down, and dive into the water as it falls. Then they come back, eat, and use the rest for their lodge.
>
> This slide shows the mud and rocks at the bottom of a lodge. This one shows the piled-up trees and branches. They live and have young inside here. It has two entrances. Builders also build canals through the forest so they can carry logs easily.

Exercises

Choose one of the topics below or a topic of your own. Use the guidelines to prepare and deliver an oral report on your topic.

1. An Interesting Animal
2. An Historical Event
3. An Unusual Career
4. A Recent Scientific Discovery

Sunset at the Pyramids of Giza, Egypt

Somewhere, something incredible is waiting to be known.

CARL SAGAN
American astronomer, biologist
(1934–)

15

USING LIBRARY RESOURCES

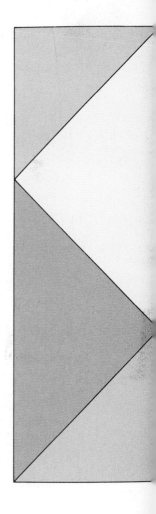

Using the Library: Card Catalog

One way to locate books in a library is by using the card catalog. The *card catalog* is an index to all the books in the library.

Most library books are listed on three separate cards in the card catalog. You can look up a book by its author, title, or subject. Sometimes fiction is listed only by the author and title. The cards are arranged alphabetically.

- Look at these sample card catalog cards.

Subject Card

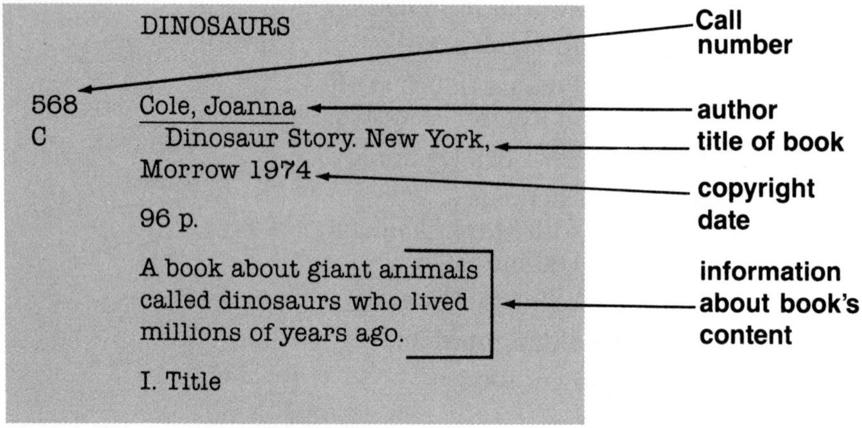

Author Card **Title Card** **Cross-Reference Card**

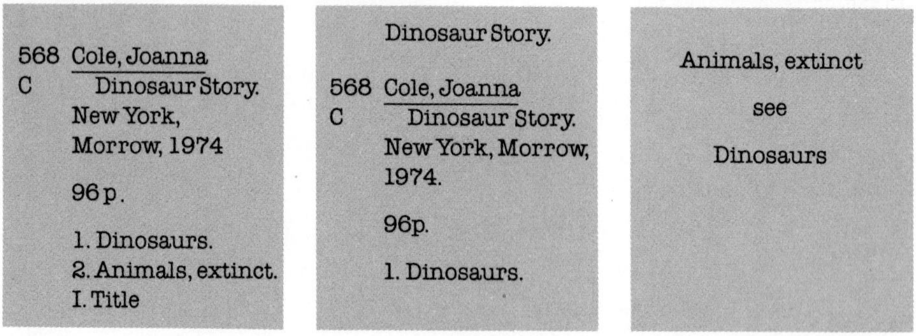

Each card has a Dewey decimal system call number in the upper left corner. This tells you where to find the book on the library shelf. All three cards tell the book's author, title, number of pages, publisher, and date of publication. There is also a brief description of the book's content. The bottom of the card shows the subject headings under which the book is cataloged. The three types of cards allow you to locate a book whether you know its title, its author, or only its general subject.

The card catalog also contains cross-reference cards called *see* or *see also* cards. A *see* card directs you to the subject under which your topic is indexed. A *see also* card tells you to look under another subject to find more information about your topic.

American libraries use one of two systems for classifying nonfiction books. The Dewey decimal system is one method. In this method every book is assigned a number between 000 and 999. The other method is the Library of Congress system. This method uses letters and numbers to group books under twenty-one major subject headings.

Class Exercises

Look again at the card that uses the Dewey decimal system.

1. What is the call number of the book?
2. Under what subject headings could you find the book?
3. When was the book published?
4. Who is the publisher?

Look again at the card that uses the Library of Congress system.

5. Who is the author of the book?
6. What is the title of the book?
7. What is the book about?

Exercises

Write the answers to these questions about the card catalog.

1. How would you find the subject of a book entitled *Puddles and Ponds*?
2. Under what subjects might you look for books about ecology?
3. How would you find a book about jogging and good health?
4. How would you find a book entitled *The Dragons of Eden* if you did not know the author's name or the subject of the book?
5. If you were looking for a book by an author whose last name was Herriot and you knew the book was about a veterinarian, how would you find the book?
6. How would you find a book entitled *Digging Up the Past* if you did not know the author's name?
7. How could you find a book about mythology by a woman named Edith Hamilton?

Sample Answer 1. Look up the title card and then read the subject headings at the bottom of the card.

Using the Library: Periodical Indexes

Newspapers and magazines are called *periodicals* because they are published at regular time periods. The articles that appear in periodicals are not listed in the card catalog. Instead they are listed in *periodical indexes*.

A *periodical index* is a book that catalogs magazine and newspaper articles. One of the most commonly used periodical indexes is *The Readers' Guide to Periodical Literature*. This set of books names the magazines in which particular articles can be found. The articles are listed alphabetically by subject and author. Articles are not usually indexed by title because the titles of magazine articles are often misleading or unimportant. The *Readers' Guide* also gives *see* and *see also* references. A *see* reference tells you to look under another subject heading for the information you want. A *see also* reference directs you to other subject headings that might also contain information on the subject in which you are interested.

Suppose you are looking for a recent magazine article on bears. You could look in the *Readers' Guide* and find the following entry:

BEARS
Grizzly's rage to live. D. Chadwich il Sports Illus
47: 64-91 Jl 18 '77

- Look again at the sample entry. Notice the information that it contains.

1. The title of the article
2. The author's name
3. The name of the magazine in which the article appears
4. The volume number and page number of the magazine
5. The date of the magazine
6. The abbreviation il, which means the article is illustrated.

The above entry is listed by subject. You can find the same entry in the *Readers' Guide* by looking under the name of the author.

The *Readers' Guide* usually abbreviates the name of the magazine and the month of its publication. A key at the beginning of the guide explains all abbreviations.

Class Exercises

Use the sample entry from the *Readers' Guide* to answer the questions.

1. What is the subject of the article?
2. What is the title of the article?
3. What is the author's name?
4. What is the name and date of the magazine?
5. On what page of the magazine does the article begin?
6. What is the volume number?

Exercises

Read these sample entries from the *Readers' Guide*.

FISHER, Jonathan
Birds and airplanes don't mix. il Int Wildlife
8: 17–19 Mr '78

FISHERIES
Fishing the seven seas. S. Solomon
il Forbes 121: Ap 3 '78

Use the first entry to write the answers to these questions.

1. Is this entry listed by subject, title, or author?
2. Who wrote the article?
3. When was it published?
4. In what volume did it appear?
5. What is the title of the article?

Use the second entry to write the answers to these questions.

6. Is this entry listed by subject, title, or author?
7. In what magazine did the article appear?
8. When was it published?
9. Is the article illustrated?
10. What is the title of the article?

Sample Answer 1. author

Reference Works

Many libraries have a separate section reserved for reference works. *Reference works* are special books that contain important information on many different subjects. The most frequently used reference works are encyclopedias, almanacs, atlases, and collections of biographical information.

A *general encyclopedia* is a set of reference books that contain articles on a great variety of topics. The articles within each book, or volume, are arranged in alphabetical order. General encyclopedias have several guides to help you find information: volume numbers, outside guide letters, inside guide words, subject headings, and division and subdivision headings for general subjects. Often there is a separate alphabetical or subject index. In order to keep their information current, many encyclopedias print yearbooks that contain articles on events of the past year. Most encyclopedias also provide bibliographies, or lists of books and articles that were used in the preparation of the articles.

An *almanac* is a single book that contains current or general information on a variety of topics. It also lists facts and figures on records and events. The almanac is particularly valuable when you want to compare current facts and figures with historical information on the same topic.

An *atlas* is a book of maps. The most complete type of atlas is a world atlas. It contains political, historical, economic, and land-surface maps. All the maps in an atlas use special symbols indicating features such as distance, state capitals, and boundaries. A legend usually appears on each map to explain the meaning of the symbols.

A *gazeteer* is a geographical dictionary that lists places such as countries, mountains, seas, and deserts in alphabetical order. A gazeteer is often found within an atlas.

When you need biographical information but do not require a full biography or autobiography, there are several reference works that can help you. You will find biographical information about many famous people in a general encyclopedia, but sometimes the information you find will not be enough. The *Dictionary of American Biography* contains condensed biographies of many famous or important people. Another good source of information is *Webster's Biographical Dictionary*. If you need biographical information about people who are in the news now, you should consult *Current Biography*.

Two other useful reference works found in most libraries are *Bartlett's Familiar Quotations* and *The Oxford Dictionary of*

Quotations. These books list famous quotations arranged by subject or key words.

Class Exercises

Tell which reference work you would use to find the information below.

1. Where would you find information about the Civil War?
2. Where could you find a map of the 19th century United States?
3. Where would you find a general discussion of art?
4. Where could you find a list of last year's Nobel Prize winners?
5. Where would you find a map showing state capitals?
6. Where would you find biographical information about someone you read about in a recent newspaper article?
7. Where would you find some biographical facts about Thomas Jefferson?

Exercises

Which reference work would you use to find the following information? Write the name of the reference work or works.

1. Where would you find information about atoms?
2. Where would you find a map showing the countries of Europe?
3. Where would you find information about polar bears?
4. Where would you find information about past and present Olympic champions?
5. Where would you find information about the world's highest mountain peaks?
6. Where would you use a legend to interpret symbols?
7. What reference book contains articles on events of the past year?
8. What reference work would have a biography of a recently elected senator?
9. What reference work would have a short biography of Benjamin Franklin?
10. What reference work would contain famous quotes on the subject of love?

Sample Answer 1. encyclopedia

Finding Information in Reference Works

Reference books differ from books with stories and plays. All books, however, share a common feature. Books are always organized so that the information in them can be easily found. If you understand how they are organized, you can learn about their contents quickly.

The first part of any reference book you should look at is the title page. The *title page* is the first page of a book. It lists the title of the book, and it usually includes the name of the author and publisher. The copyright date, which is usually printed on the back of the title page, gives the date of publication. This will help you decide whether the book is recent enough to have useful information.

If the book is recent enough, you can begin looking for the information you need by examining the table of contents. A *table of contents* describes the contents of a book. It is found at the beginning of the book, and it lists the units or chapters in a book. It indicates the page on which each unit or chapter begins. The table of contents will give you a general idea of the type of information a book contains.

The next step for information should be the index. The *index*, which is often the last section in a book, is an alphabetical list of the subjects. Page references tell where the subjects can be found. Many indexes contain *see* or *see also* references that direct you to additional information. Some reference works contain more than one type of index. There might be an author index and a title index as well as a subject index.

Another section found in many reference books is the bibliography. A *bibliography* is a list of books, pamphlets, magazines, and other sources of information that the author used while writing the book or article. Bibliographies may be found at the end of each chapter, each section, or at the end of the book. A bibliography provides you with additional sources of information on a particular topic. Sometimes bibliographies are annotated. An annotated bibliography gives a brief summary of the contents of each book listed.

Table of Contents from *Climate and Weather*

Table of Contents

Sample from Index

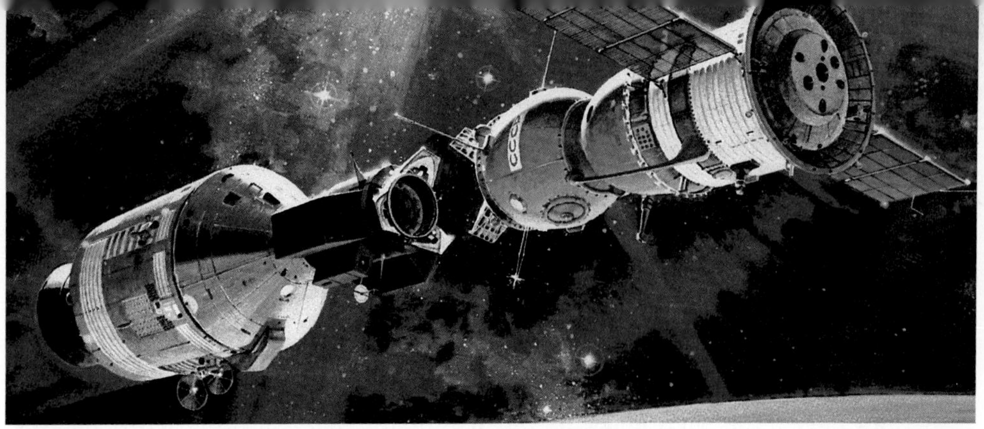

NASA

Class Exercises

Use this textbook to answer the questions below.

1. What information is on the title page?
2. What is the copyright date?
3. How many units are there in this book?
   Where did you find this information?
4. On what page does the index begin?
5. On what page does the handbook begin?
6. On what pages can you read about prepositional phrases?

Exercises

Examine volumes from two different encyclopedias and write answers to these questions.

1. What kind of index does each encyclopedia have?
2. Which encyclopedia provides bibliographies?
3. What is the copyright date of each encyclopedia?
4. Does either encyclopedia have a table of contents?

Use the sample parts of the book on page 276 to write the answers to these questions.

5. How many chapters are in the book?
6. Does the book deal with weather forecasts?
7. What is the title of Chapter 3?
8. On what pages could you read about temperature?
9. On what page can you read about radios?
10. On what pages can you read about solar winds?

Sample Answer 5. 3

Parts of a Dictionary

A dictionary contains an alphabetical list of words and their meanings. *Unabridged dictionaries* give the most complete information available about words in the English language. *Abridged dictionaries* are shortened. They contain a selection of the most common words. In both kinds of dictionaries, each word listed is called an *entry word.* Entry words may be divided by dots or spaces into syllables. When you write, you may need to divide a word at the end of a line. You can check the dictionary to see where to divide it. If a word has no dots or spaces, it has only one syllable and cannot be divided.

- Look at this sample entry word from the dictionary.

> **hu·mor** (hyo͞o′ mər) *n.* **1.** the quality of something that makes it amusing or funny. **2.** the ability to appreciate or express what is amusing or funny: *George has a good sense of humor.* **3.** a speech, writing, or action that is amusing or funny. **4.** a temporary state of mind; mood: *The thought of a vacation put Ruth in a good humor.* [Old French *umor, humor* the fluid that determined a person's health and temperament. In former times, the body was thought to be made up of four liquids.]

1. The pronunciation is shown in parentheses after the entry word. *Pronunciation* is the way the word is spoken. Look at the pronunciation for *humor*.

   hyo͞o′ mər

   Special symbols are used to show the pronunciation. A *pronunciation key* explains these symbols. Using the key, you would find that the vowels in *humor* are pronounced: *o͞o* as in fool; ə as the *u* in circus.

- Look again at the pronunciation for *humor*. A slanted line (′) follows the first syllable, *hyo͞o*. This line is called the *accent mark*. The mark tells you to stress the first syllable, *hu*, when you say this word.

2. The part of speech is given for the entry word. The *part of speech* indicates how the word is used in a sentence. Notice the part of speech given for *humor* is *n*. This abbreviation, *n.,* stands for *noun*. The dictionary tells you that humor is used as a *noun*. For example, He has a weird sense of *humor*. Here are some other abbreviations you would find in a dictionary for parts of speech.

adj. adjective *v.* verb *adv.* adverb *pron.* pronoun

3. The definition follows the part of speech. The *definition* is the *meaning* of the word. When a word has two or more definitions, the dictionary lists them by number. Notice the four definitions for *humor*. A sample sentence or sample phrase may follow the definition. The sample helps to explain the meaning. What sample sentences are given for *humor?*

4. Sometimes the dictionary gives the derivation, or history, of the word in brackets. Look at the derivation of *humor*.

[Old French *umor, humor* the fluid that determined a person's health and temperament. In former times, the body was thought to be made up of four liquids.]

Class Exercises

Answer these questions about the parts of a dictionary.

1. What can you use to learn how to pronounce a word?
2. What does the abbreviation *pron.* stand for?
3. What does the number **1** in front of a definition indicate?
4. What is the purpose of a sample sentence or sample phrase?
5. What is meant by the derivation of a word?

Exercises

Use the dictionary entry on the right to answer the questions on the left. Write each answer.

chap·ter (chap′ter) *n.* **1.** a main division, as of a book. **2.** a part or episode: *a chapter of one's life.* **3.** the branch of a club: *Our chapter will meet now.* [From Latin *caput,* head.]

1. Which syllable is stressed when you say *chapter*?
2. What part of speech is *chapter*?
3. How many definitions does *chapter* have?
4. What is the second definition?
5. What is the derivation of *chapter*?
6. What sample phrase is given for *chapter*?

Sample Answer 1. chap

Dictionary: Words with More Than One Definition

When you find an unfamiliar word in your reading, you may use the dictionary to learn the word's meaning. However, some words have more than one meaning. You must determine which definition applies to the word you have read.

In order to choose the correct definition of an unfamiliar word, you need to consider the sentence context. *Sentence context* refers to the other words in the sentence. Reading the other words in the sentence may help to make the meaning of an unfamiliar word clear. When you know the other words in the sentence, you can decide which meaning of the unfamiliar word will make sense.

- Read each of these definitions for the word *bank*.

bank (bank). *n.* **1.** a place for receiving or depositing money. [From Italian *banca,* a moneylender's table.] **2.** a bench for rowers on a ship. **3.** a steep slope, as of a hill. [From Old English *benc,* bench.] **4.** a row of keys on an organ or piano.

- Now read the following sentence.

He ran up the *bank* to look from the hilltop.

Although the word *bank* has four meanings, only one meaning makes sense in the sentence context. The meaning is number 3. Look at the following sentences. Which of the definitions of *bank* applies to each sentence?

The bandits robbed the *bank* of all its money.
We cannot play our piano because the *bank* is broken.
The men on the *bank* drowned when the ship sank in the storm.
The *bank* of that mountain is dangerous to climb.
I can get more cash from the *bank*.
Sit on that *bank* and start rowing.
You spilled glue on the *bank* of our organ.
Jody just deposited all her money in the *bank*.

Class Exercises

Read the following definitions for the word *shock*. Then tell which definition applies to each sentence below.

> **shock** (shok). *n.* **1.** a sudden or strong upsetting of the mind or feelings. [From Middle Dutch *schokken*, to collide.] **2.** the effect of an electrical current passed through the body. **3.** a number of sheaves of grain stacked together on end. **4.** a thick, bushy, or tangled mass, as of hair.

1. The barber cut a *shock* of the boy's hair.
2. I just received a *shock* from that loose wire over there.
3. It was quite a *shock* to learn my house had burned down.
4. I was struck by lightning and received a large *shock*.
5. The corn was tied in a *shock* and left in the field to dry.
6. Hand me that brush so I may straighten that *shock* of hair.

Exercises

Read the following definitions for the word *deal*. Then write the number of the definition that applies to each sentence below.

> **deal** (dēl) *n.* **1.** a bargain or agreement, especially when secret. **2.** a large amount [From Old English *dael*, a part.] **3.** the act of dealing playing cards. **4.** fir or pine wood. [From Middle Dutch *dele.*]

1. I will make a *deal* with you, but do not tell anyone.
2. Since you lost the last game, it is your *deal*.
3. The price of *deal* went up at the lumberyard.
4. I have a good *deal* of work to complete today.
5. Carmen is in a great *deal* of trouble with her neighbors.

Sample Answer 1. 1.

Using a Thesaurus

You know that you can look in a dictionary to find the definition of a particular word. However, there are often times when you need a synonym or antonym for a word rather than its definition. Remember, a synonym is a word that has nearly the same meaning as another word. An antonym is a word that means the opposite of another word. A *thesaurus* is a reference work that contains synonyms and antonyms.

A thesaurus does not give definitions of words. It lists several synonyms and antonyms for each word. You must select from the list the best synonym or antonym for the word in your sentence. Sometimes you may have to consult a dictionary to see if you have chosen the best word.

Some thesauruses list words in alphabetical order exactly like dictionaries, but many libraries have a thesaurus called *Roget's Thesaurus*. In this widely used thesaurus words are organized into groups that are listed by number. Guide numbers rather than guide words help you to locate entries. An index of words in alphabetical order is located at the back of the book.

Suppose you want to use a synonym for the word *carve*. There are three steps to follow when you use *Roget's Thesaurus*. First find the word *carve* in the index. Next look at the group of words listed under *carve*. The list would look like the one at the right. Notice the number after each word.

Sample from Index

carve cut 44
make 161
form 240
sculpture 557
apportion 786

Finally choose from this list the general word that best fits your need and look up the number of that word in the body of the book. If you wanted to use *carve* in the sense of sculpture, for example, you would look up number 557. Under *sculpture* you would find a list of words like that at the right from which to choose the exact word you need.

Sample Thesaurus Entry

557. Sculpture
1. carve, sculpt, chisel, cut, mold, model

Keep in mind that a thesaurus gives you a wide range of synonyms and antonyms for each word listed. No definitions or explanations of words are given. While meanings may be *nearly* the same, not all synonyms will fit every sentence. If necessary check a dictionary.

- Read this sentence. Choose a more exact synonym from the thesaurus for the underlined word. Check the meaning in the dictionary.

  We chugged up the first high rise of the roller coaster, and I was afraid.

Class Exercises

Use the preceding information to answer the following questions.

1. What is the difference between a dictionary and a thesaurus?
2. What are the two ways a thesaurus can be arranged?
3. What are the three steps used to look up a synonym in *Roget's Thesaurus*?

Exercises

Read each sentence. Use the list of words taken from the thesaurus at the right. Choose a more exact synonym for *give* as it is used in each sentence. Check the dictionary for meanings if necessary.

accede
crumbled
present
yield
part with
surrender
weakened
abandoned

1. The farmer refused to *give* up the land.
2. The old bridge *gave* under the heavy traffic.
3. The article *gave* me some good ideas.
4. I always *give* in to your arguments.

Replace the underlined word in each sentence with a synonym. Use a thesaurus. Write the synonym.

5. The criminals received their right punishment.
6. We all have basic human rights.
7. I believe that what you say is right.

Sample Answer 1. yield

Nonprint Media

Many libraries have collections of films, filmstrips, records, tape cassettes, microfilm, and microfiche. These materials are called *nonprint media*. In some libraries nonprint media are listed in the main card catalog. In other libraries each kind of media has a separate card catalog. Nonprint materials are valuable research tools.

Films are particularly valuable for showing visual images or processes. For example, you may watch animals live in their natural surroundings or see plants grow from seeds to flowers in just a few seconds. It is often difficult to take notes while watching a film. Therefore it is a good idea to follow up a film by reading related information in a book or magazine.

Filmstrips do not move automatically as a film does. You need to move each frame or picture by hand. Note taking is easier because you can control the speed of the filmstrip.

Records and *cassette tapes* allow you to hear something dramatized or explained. They can be used with filmstrips or by themselves.

Microforms are photographs of printed material reduced to a very small size. The two most common microforms are microfilm and microfiche.

Micro means "very small," so *microfilm* is a reel of film with small pictures on it. A *microfiche* is a plastic card measuring about four by six inches with many small pictures on it. Each microfiche holds between sixty and ninety-eight pages of printed material. To read materials on microforms, you need to use a special machine called a reader. The librarian will help you learn how to operate these readers.

Some material a library has on microforms may also be available in book form. Other material, such as back issues of newspapers or magazines, may be available only on microforms. Microforms are often used to protect rare, valuable, or easily damaged material from being ruined through careless handling. Because microforms are so small, they can be stored easily in file drawers or cabinets. Libraries no longer need large spaces to hold all their books and periodicals.

Class Exercises

Read each question. Tell which of the nonprint media would be a helpful source for each piece of information.

1. Where could you hear Robert Frost reading his own poems?
2. Where could you get an introduction to atoms?
3. How could you read a 1954 news report?
4. How could you read a 1892 periodical?
5. Where could you see the development of a hurricane?

Exercises

Read each question. Write the answer.

1. Where could you watch animals adapting to their surroundings?
2. How could you read a 1960 news report?
3. Where could you find an introduction to nutrition?
4. How could you listen to a review of fractions?
5. How could you read a 1903 periodical?
6. Where could you watch the hatching of an egg?
7. How could you listen to a play or story?
8. Why is it easier to take notes on a filmstrip than on a film?
9. What is a reader?
10. How are microfilm and microfiche helpful to libraries?
11. How could you read a rare and valuable book?
12. How could you read a newspaper account of President Kennedy's inauguration?

Sample Answer 1. film

Unit Review

USING LIBRARY RESOURCES

Write the answers to these questions about the card catalog. *pages 270-271*

1. Does the card catalog list every book in the library?
2. On what three cards is a library book listed in the card catalog?
3. What is the purpose of using three cards for each book?
4. What type of card would you use to look up a book if the author's name is Rutherford Johnson?

Write the answers to these questions about periodical indexes. *pages 272-273*

5. Why are newspapers and magazines called periodicals?
6. How are articles indexed in the *Readers' Guide to Periodical Literature*?
7. What is the difference between a *see* and a *see also* reference?
8. Where is the key that explains abbreviations in the *Readers' Guide*?

Write the answers to these questions about reference works. *pages 274-275*

9. Where would you find a city's record cold temperature?
10. Where would you find biographical information on the United States' current Secretary of State?
11. What book would you use to find information on various subjects?
12. Where would you find more biographical information if you were writing a report on Mark Twain?
13. What is the name of a geographical dictionary found in an atlas?
14. Where would you find quotations on the subject of freedom?

Write the answers to these questions about finding information. *pages 276-277*

15. What are the three steps you should follow when deciding whether a book is a good reference work to use?
16. What is the difference between the table of contents of a book and its bibliography?
17. Where is the index of a book generally found?
18. Name two of the possible indexes you may find in a book.
19. What is an annotated bibliography?

Write the answers to these questions about the parts of a dictionary. *pages 278-279*

20. Why are entry words divided into syllables in a dictionary?

21. What does it mean if an entry word has no dots or spaces?

22. What part of the dictionary should you refer to if you do not understand the pronunciation symbols?

Write the word from the sample entries on pages 280 and 281 that completes each sentence. Then write the number of the definition. *pages 280-281*

23. We had a ___, but he changed his mind.

24. I was ___ to hear about his accident.

25. Get up that ___ and go to the road.

26. We sat down at the table, and he began to ___ the cards.

Using a thesaurus, find a specific synonym for each underlined word in the following sentences. Write the synonym. *pages 282-283*

27. The <u>subtle</u> movement caught my eye.

28. We are <u>exhausted</u> after our climb.

29. The grasshopper <u>springs</u> from branch to branch.

Write the answers to these questions about using nonprint media. *pages 284-285*

30. How could you listen to a recording by the Boston Symphony?

31. What are the two most common microforms?

32. Are microforms also available in book form?

Careers

Librarians classify, select, and catalog books and other materials. Medical librarians maintain patient records. Law librarians catalog legal cases and opinions. Librarians who preserve ancient or fragile manuscripts and books are called archivists.

Section Review

STUDY AND REFERENCE SKILLS

1. Choose the three subtopics that go with each main topic on the Trojan hero Aeneas. Write each group. *pages 244-245*

fall of Troy	life in Troy	wanders to Carthage
Aeneas, Trojan prince	Rome's Virgil	trip to Italy
founding of Rome	writes the story	leaves Carthage
His wanderings	battles in Italy	escape from Troy

Read each sentence. Write **fact** if the sentence states a fact. Write **opinion** if the sentence states an opinion. *pages 246-247*

2. The heart is the most important organ in the human body.
3. Arteries, veins, and capillaries carry blood from the heart.
4. Two large chambers make up the two halves of the human heart.
5. Vigorous exercise is the best way to keep the heart healthy.

Read the paragraph below. Write the best answer for each question based on what is stated in the paragraph. *pages 250-251*

In 19th century realism, artists limited the use of form and color to depict nature as it really was. Abstract art departed greatly from this format. Abstract painters changed real appearances to communicate their inner visions. Form and color found a new freedom in abstract art.

6. Realistic painters usually changed the appearance of nature.
a. true **b.** false

7. While realists painted the world, abstract painters ___ .
a. copied them **b.** turned inward **c.** used old forms

8. Abstract art changes natural appearances to communicate ___ .
a. inner emotions **b.** dislike of nature **c.** realism

Write the word that correctly completes each analogy. *pages 252-253*

9. swallow: sky:: trout: ___
a. stream **b.** fish **c.** fins

10. vacation: pleasure:: journey: ___
a. seashore **b.** follow **c.** work

11. scribe: printer:: guide: ___
a. travel agent **b.** book **c.** doctor

Section Review

Write the answers to these questions about finding information in the library. *pages 270-273*

12. How would you find a book written by a person named Hillary and dealing with Mt. Everest?

13. You are looking for a book about bird migrations. You find one subject card, and that card says *see migration* and *see also seabirds, migratory.* Which *see* reference would you check first?

14. Where would you find an article called "Army Ants of Africa"?

15. Under what subjects would you look for books about boomerangs?

Write the answers to these questions about finding information in reference works. *pages 276-277*

16. Where would you look for a *short* biography of Emily Bronte?

17. Describe the contents of a *gazeteer.*

18. What reference would you use to find facts on college costs?

Write an answer for each question about the dictionary. *pages 278-279*

19. What facts are often found in brackets after an entry word?

20. Why would you not find accent marks for one-syllable words?

Write the word from the sample entries on pages 280-281 that completes each sentence. Then write the number of the definition. *pages 280-281*

21. Please comb that unruly ___ back over your forehead.

22. Eileen put a coat of varnish on the new ___ furniture.

23. The Roman galley's ___ was full of hardworking oarsmen.

24. A great ___ of language comes from imitation of natural sound.

Using a thesaurus, find a specific synonym for each underlined word in the following sentences. Write the synonym. *pages 282-283*

25. The house, with its fancy gardens, seemed ostentatious.

26. The bright whorls in the seashell fascinated Stella.

27. A horse makes many people think of symmetry, grace, and power.

Write answers to the questions about nonprint media. *pages 284-285*

28. Where could you watch the changing styles of sculpture?

29. Where would you find a newspaper from Thomas Jefferson's day?

30. How could you hear a dramatic reading of the *Odyssey*?

A gathering of "friends" around the writer's key position

The wastepaper basket is a writer's best friend.

I. B. SINGER
American writer (1904-   )

16

WRITING AND EDITING SENTENCES

Expanding Simple Sentences with Adjectives and Adverbs

Thinking About Expanding Simple Sentences

A *simple sentence* is a sentence that has one subject part and one predicate part.

Families drove wagons.

A sentence must have a subject and a verb. However, your readers would soon become bored if they had to read writing that consisted of short three-word sentences. You can capture and hold your readers' interest by using different kinds of sentences. In this unit you will learn to make your writing lively and interesting. You can express your ideas more clearly and write better, more descriptive sentences by adding words that tell more about the nouns and verbs in simple sentences.

You can add adjectives to a simple sentence to describe the nouns in the subject and predicate parts of a sentence.

<u>Pioneer</u> families drove wagons. Families drove <u>covered</u> wagons.

You can also add adverbs to a simple sentence to describe verbs. Adverbs may tell *when, where,* or *how* something happened.

<u>Long ago</u> families drove wagons. (when)
Families drove wagons <u>westward</u>. (where)
Families <u>bravely</u> drove wagons. (how)

Talking About Expanding Simple Sentences

Tell how you might expand each sentence about the westward expansion by adding an adjective to describe a noun.

1. Settlers cleared forests.
2. Indians helped travelers.
3. The settlers built cabins.
4. Explorers climbed mountains.

Tell how you might expand each sentence by adding an adverb to describe each verb.

5. Pioneers used rafts.
6. Families packed belongings.
7. Pioneers found danger.
8. Oxen pulled wagons.

Writing Expanded Sentences

Expand each sentence about the westward expansion by adding an adjective to describe a noun. Write your new sentence.

1. People left cities.
2. Emigrants suffered hardships.
3. Traders found wilderness.
4. Roads rattled pots.
5. Wagons had sides.
6. Wagon trains crossed trails.
7. People built rafts.
8. Horses forded rivers.
9. Shouts warned travelers.
10. Wagons formed circles.

Expand each sentence by adding an adverb to describe each verb. Write your new sentence.

11. Farmers sought gold.
12. Adventurers left families.
13. Travelers found danger.
14. People sought gold.
15. Travelers drank water.
16. Wagons broke wheels.
17. Scouts climbed rocks.
18. Scouts saw water.
19. People wore homespun.
20. People built fires.
21. Women drove teams.
22. Children read books.

Writing Simple Sentences with Adjectives and Adverbs

Imagine that you are a pioneer traveling west in a covered wagon. Perhaps you are struggling across the Appalachians or the Rocky Mountains. You might be part of a long wagon train crossing the Great Plains. These trips took months and were filled with hardships, danger, adventure, and discovery. Write three sentences about your trip with adjectives that describe each noun. Then write three sentences using adverbs to describe the verbs.

Edit Your Sentences

1. Did you begin your sentences with capital letters?
2. Did you use colorful adjectives to describe your nouns?
3. Did you use adverbs that tell *when, where,* or *how* to describe your verbs?
4. Is your punctuation correct?

Editing Symbols

- ¶ indent
- ≡ capitalize
- ∧ add
- ℘ delete
- / lower case

Sample Answers 1. People from the East left cities.
11. Farmers sought gold everywhere.

Expanding Simple Sentences with Prepositional Phrases

Thinking About Expanding Simple Sentences

A *simple sentence* has a subject part and a predicate part. You can write a complete sentence with only a few words.

Prospectors rushed.

Prospectors is the subject part, and *rushed* is the predicate part. The sentence is complete. However, it does not give much information. You can expand, or build, the sentence by adding prepositional phrases. A *prepositional phrase* is a group of words beginning with a preposition and ending with a noun or pronoun.

With prepositional phrases, you can give your readers specific details about *when, where,* and *how* something occurred. Prepositional phrases also provide a variety of ways to build lively word pictures.

Remember that a prepositional phrase can act as an adjective that describes a noun. A prepositional phrase that describes an adjective is called an *adjective phrase.*

Prospectors <u>in search of gold</u> rushed.

The prepositional phrase *in search of gold* is an adjective phrase that describes the noun *prospectors.*

A prepositional phrase can act as an adverb that describes a verb. A prepositional phrase that describes a verb is called an *adverb phrase.*

Prospectors rushed <u>to California</u>.

The prepositional phrase *to California* is an adverb phrase that describes the verb *rushed.* It tells *where* the prospectors rushed.

Quite often the prepositional phrase comes immediately after the word it describes. However, sometimes you can vary your sentence structure so that the prepositional phrase begins the sentence.

People discovered gold in 1849. In 1849 people discovered gold.

When you start a sentence with a prepositional phrase, make sure the sentence does not sound awkward as a result.

Awkward: <u>Toward the mill on John Sutter's land</u>, miners streamed.
Better: Miners streamed <u>toward the mill on John Sutter's land</u>.

Talking About Expanding Simple Sentences

Tell how to expand each sentence about the gold rush by adding an adjective phrase that describes a noun.

1. A peddler sold his wares.
2. The cook made flapjacks.

Tell how to expand each sentence by adding an adverb phrase that describes the verb.

3. Weary miners slept.
4. The mule plodded.

Writing Expanded Sentences

Expand each sentence about the gold rush by adding an adjective phrase that describes a noun. Write your new sentence.

1. The mule carried supplies.
2. The prospector found a map.
3. People rushed to Pikes Peak.
4. People prospected for gold.
5. Miners found nuggets.
6. Workers earned hundreds.
7. Prices soared.
8. Miners scooped gravel.

Expand each sentence by adding an adverb phrase that describes the verb. Write your new sentence.

9. Wagon trains traveled.
10. Gold gleamed.
11. Men panned gold.
12. Prospectors climbed.
13. The din echoed.
14. Prospectors found gold.
15. Miners paid for everything.
16. Men scraped rocks.

Writing Simple Sentences with Prepositional Phrases

Imagine you are a "forty-niner." Now you have joined thousands of gold seekers, scraping gold dust out of rocks with a jackknife, or getting your boots wet in the rivers. Write three sentences using an adjective phrase to describe a noun. Then write three sentences using an adverb phrase to describe the verb.

Edit Your Sentences

1. Did you use adjective phrases to describe your nouns?
2. Did you use adverb phrases to describe your verbs?
3. Did you use correct spelling and punctuation?

Editing Symbols

¶	indent
≡	capitalize
∧	add
℘	delete
/	lower case

Sample Answers 1. The mule carried supplies for the prospectors.
9. Wagon trains traveled over rough territory.

Combining Simple Sentences to Build Compound Sentences

Thinking About Building Compound Sentences

You can connect or contrast related thoughts by combining two separate sentences into one sentence. Using compound sentences is another way to vary your writing. A *compound sentence* is a sentence that contains two or more simple sentences joined by the coordinating conjunctions *and, but,* or *or.*

Remember that each of the coordinating conjunctions will give your compound sentence a slightly different meaning. When you use the correct conjunction, you will make your meaning as clear as possible.

And means in addition to

But means with this exception or on the contrary

Or introduces an alternative or another possibility

Remember to put a comma before the conjunction when you form a compound sentence.

The Union Pacific Railroad began laying track from the East, and the Central Pacific began building from the West.

President Lincoln signed the Pacific Railroad Act in 1862, but work did not begin until 1863.

Central Pacific workers laid tracks over mountains, or they blasted tunnels through them.

If there already are commas within the parts of a compound sentence, use a semicolon to separate the parts.

Rails, locomotives, and other supplies had to come 15,000 miles around Cape Horn; but the Central Pacific pushed steadily east.

If a compound sentence does not have a coordinating conjunction between the two parts of the sentence, use a semicolon to separate the parts.

The two engines puffed up to touch noses; a photographer recorded the historic moment.

Talking About Building Compound Sentences

Tell how to combine each pair of sentences into a compound sentence. Tell which conjunction is appropriate.

1. Chinese immigrants worked in the West. Irish immigrants labored in the East.
2. Blizzards howled. Snow sheds protected the tracks.

Building Compound Sentences

Write each pair of sentences as one compound sentence. Put commas and semicolons where they belong.

1. Work began in 1863. Workers finished the railroad in 1869.
2. The work was dangerous. Soldiers protected them.
3. Engineers built bridges. Miners dug tunnels.
4. Surveyors went ahead. Workers could not find the best routes.
5. Supplies came by boat. They came by freight wagon.
6. Tent camps sprang up. They soon disappeared.
7. One track began at Sacramento. The other started from Omaha.
8. The tracks met at Promontory. The East and West were joined.

Writing Compound Sentences

Imagine you are a worker laying track for the first transcontinental railroad. You might be tunneling through a mountain or pounding spikes across the dusty plains. Write six compound sentences. Put commas and semicolons where they belong.

Edit Your Sentences

1. Did you use capital letters correctly?
2. Does each main clause in your compound sentences have a subject and a predicate?
3. Did you choose the best coordinating conjunction to make your meaning clear?
4. Did you put commas and semicolons where they belong?

Editing Symbols

¶	indent
≡	capitalize
∧	add
ℓ	delete
/	lower case

Sample Answer 1. Work began in 1863, and workers finished the railroad in 1869.

Combining Simple Sentences to Build Complex Sentences

Thinking About Adverb Clauses

Because of the variety of relationships between the clauses in a complex sentence, you can express more complicated ideas. Thus complex sentences provide another way to vary the structure and rhythm of your writing.

A *complex sentence* is a sentence that has an independent clause and one or more subordinate clauses. An *independent clause* has one subject part and one predicate part. It expresses a complete thought, and it can stand alone. A *subordinate clause* is a group of words that has a subject part and a predicate part, but it cannot stand alone. It does not express a complete thought. It is always combined with an independent clause.

Some subordinate clauses are adverb clauses. An *adverb clause* tells *where, when, why, how,* or *under what conditions.* It is made up of a subordinating conjunction, a subject, and a predicate.

Subordinating conjunctions are words that join an adverb clause to an independent clause. Read the list below.

When		**Where**	**How**	**Why**	**Under What Conditions**	
when	since	where	as	as	although	whether (or not)
before	until	wherever	as if	because	as long as	while
whenever	after		as though	since	if	
while	as				though	
as long as					unless	
as soon as					whereas	

- Read the following sentences. Notice how each adverb clause is used. Also notice that a comma follows the subordinate clause when the subordinate clause introduces the sentence.

When: After Congress passed the Homestead Act, thousands came West.

Where: Wherever they found rich land, settlers staked claims.

How: The house stood against the sky as if it grew out of the land.

Why: Many turned to farming because they did not find gold.

Under What Conditions: Unless they found food, the family would starve in winter.

Talking About Building Complex Sentences

Tell how you would combine each pair of simple sentences as a complex sentence with an adverb clause. Use a subordinating conjunction that tells *when, where, how, why,* or *under what conditions.* Use commas where needed.

1. Settlers built homes out of earth.
   There were few trees.
2. Sod houses were warm in winter.
   They were dark and dusty.

Building Complex Sentences with Adverb Clauses

Write each pair of simple sentences as a complex sentence with an adverb clause. Use a subordinating conjunction that tells *when, where, how, why,* or *under what conditions.* Use commas where needed.

1. Homesteaders had 160 acres.
   The law allowed that much land.
2. The railroads were built.
   People came on the train.
3. Women worked hard at home.
   They also helped in the fields.
4. Women preserved food.
   Food must last all winter.
5. Winters were bitter cold.
   Women stored meat outside.
6. Families or neighbors were sick.
   Women did the nursing.
7. People made "coffee" from bran.
   It tasted rather strange.
8. Some people returned to the East.
   They had tried extremely hard.

Writing Sentences

Imagine that you are a homesteader somewhere in the Great Plains. A blizzard is raging. You have buffalo robes to keep you warm. Your cellar is well stocked with preserved food. Write six complex sentences about your experiences. Use an adverb clause in each sentence.

Edit Your Sentences

1. Did you use capital letters correctly?
2. Does each of your sentences contain an independent clause and an adverb clause?
3. Did you use commas correctly?

Sample Answer 1. Homesteaders had 160 acres because the law allowed that much land.

Editing Symbols

¶ indent
≡ capitalize
∧ add
ℓ delete
/ lower case

Formal and Informal Writing Styles

Thinking About Writing Styles

If you were going to a picnic, what would you wear? What would you wear if you were invited to a fancy restaurant? Chances are you wouldn't wear the same clothes for both occasions. One occasion is casual; the other is more formal. Casual and formal situations exist in writing, too. You may use one style of writing in a business letter and another in a letter to a friend. The style you choose will depend on the occasion and your audience.

When you prepare a business letter, a report, a formal invitation, or a formal lecture, use language that is especially clear. You should also use complete sentences and a more formal vocabulary.

When you write casual letters to friends, use a casual style. Such a style makes use of short sentences and ordinary words.

- Read each letter. The business letter on the left is written in a formal style. The casual letter on the right is written in an informal style.

13 West 316 Street
New York, NY 10099
January 9, 1984

Reservation Clerk
Williamsburg Manor
41 Williamsburg Square
Williamsburg, VA 23185

Dear Reservation Clerk:

Please reserve one double room at the rate of $50 per day for six nights beginning April 7. Enclosed is my check for $300. Please send confirmation of my reservation.

Sincerely,
Cynthia Morton
Cynthia Morton

Williamsburg Manor
41 Williamsburg Square
Williamsburg, VA 23185
April 10, 1984

Dear Elena,

I can't believe it! We're actually here in colonial Williamsburg. Seeing how people lived in Colonial times is fascinating. The dogwoods are in bloom here, and they're gorgeous! Tomorrow we're going to Yorktown to see where General Cornwallis surrendered.

Your friend,
Cindy
Cindy

Talking About Writing Styles

Tell which wording is a more appropriate response to each situation.

1. Your friend just won a trip to Europe. You write, saying:
   A. That's fantastic!
   B. Your luck in winning this delightful prize is phenomenal.
2. You work at a historic landmark. The president of the Historical Society asks you to work on Saturday evening. You write, saying:
   A. Sure, you can count on me!
   B. I would be glad to work Saturday evening from 7 to 10 P.M.

Writing in a Formal Style

Read each sentence written in an informal style. Write the same idea in a formal manner. Use complete sentences.

1. I had a super time running around Colonial Williamsburg.
2. We were up with the sun every morning.
3. Thanks a bunch for the souvenirs.
4. The story tickled my funnybone.
5. See you around.
6. They worked like horses in the old days.
7. Those old-time storms were really something.
8. My brother spilled the beans about the party.
9. My uncle hit the roof.
10. The trip was out of sight.

Writing Sentences

Imagine that you met a famous person from American history. Write three sentences of a letter inviting this person to dinner. Then write three sentences of a note to your friend describing the dinner.

Edit Your Sentences

1. Did you use a formal style in your sentences to the famous person?
2. Did you use an informal style in your sentences to your friend?
3. Are your spelling and punctuation correct?

Editing Symbols

¶	indent
≡	capitalize
∧	add
ℓ	delete
/	lower case

Sample Answer 1. I had a wonderful time touring colonial Williamsburg.

Avoiding Unnecessary Words

Thinking About Unnecessary Words

When you edit your writing, watch for long-winded phrases that can be reduced to one or two words. Watch for expressions that use unnecessary words.

Remember that the adjectives *this* and *these* point out people or things that are nearby. *That* and *those* are adjectives that point out people or things that are farther away. Do not use the words *here* or *there* when using adjectives that point out.

RIGHT: This painting is by Frederic Remington.

WRONG: This here painting is by Frederic Remington.

Avoid using the word **a** where it is not needed.

RIGHT: Remington painted this kind of painting.

WRONG: Remington painted this kind of a painting.

Remember that *these* and *those* describe plural nouns.

I like these kinds of sculptures. (plural, more than one kind)

He makes those sorts of sculptures. (plural, more than one sort)

Sentences that begin with *there is* (*are, was, were*) or *it is* (*was*) are weak sentences with unnecessary words.

WEAK: There were bears crashing through the forest ahead.

BETTER: Bears crashed through the forest ahead.

Also avoid extra pronouns that repeat information.

WRONG	**RIGHT**
Remington he is a famous artist.	Remington is a famous artist.
Many people they like his work.	Many people like his work.
This statue it is of a horse.	This statue is of a horse.

All of the pronouns crossed out in the sentences on the left are unnecessary. Each pronoun means the same thing as the noun it follows.

Finally do not use wordy phrases that can be cut to just one word.

for the purpose of → for	in order to → to
by means of → with, by	along the lines of → like
in view of the fact that → because	on the occasion of → when
in the time of → during	despite the fact that → although

Talking About Unnecessary Words

Read each sentence. Tell which word or words in parentheses correctly completes each sentence.

1. The artist ___ painted the Old West. (Remington, Remington he)
2. ___ painting shows his realistic style. (This here, This)
3. ___ of paintings show the Old West. (Those kind, Those kinds)
4. Remington went West ___ adventure. (to seek, for the purpose of seeking)

Writing Sentences That Avoid Unnecessary Words

Choose the words in parentheses that correctly complete each sentence. Write the sentence.

1. ___ drawing by Remington shows a Texas ranger. (That there, That)
2. ___ you see any Remingtons, call me. (If, In the event that,)
3. ___ grew up in New York. (Remington he, Remington)
4. This ___ painting shows the Old West. (kind of, kind of a)
5. ___ on the plains. (It was raining, Rain fell)
6. Remington wrote articles ___ the West. (about, in respect to)
7. In this painting the horses ___ . (they are galloping, are galloping)
8. The artist ___ an expert on horses. (was, he was)
9. ___ paintings are very dramatic. (Those there, Those)
10. ___ of paintings show American Indians. (Those kinds, Those kind)

Writing Sentences

Frederic Remington is famous for his paintings and articles of the Old West. If you were an artist and writer, what aspects of modern life would you choose to paint or write about? Write six sentences describing modern life as if you were a journalist.

Edit Your Sentences

1. Did you use capital letters correctly?
2. Did you check each sentence for unnecessary words or phrases?
3. Is your punctuation correct?

Editing Symbols

- ¶ indent
- ≡ capitalize
- ∧ add
- ℘ delete
- / lower case

Sample Answer 1. That drawing by Remington shows a Texas ranger.

Avoiding Fragments and Run-ons

Thinking About Fragments and Run-ons

A *sentence* is a group of words that states a complete idea. A sentence has a subject part and a predicate part. The *subject part* names whom or what the sentence is about. The *predicate part* tells what action the subject does or what the subject is or is like.

- Read each group of words below. Only item 2 is a complete sentence.

1. A group of women.	3. From cities in the East.
2. They plowed the fields.	4. Rode in covered wagons.

The other groups of words are not complete sentences. Each is only part of a sentence, or a *sentence fragment.* A predicate part is missing in 1. A subject part is missing in 4. A subject part and a predicate part are missing in 3. This group of words is only a prepositional phrase.

- Notice how you can correct the sentence fragments above by adding a subject part or a predicate part or both parts, if necessary.

1. A group of women searched for opportunity and a better life.
3. From cities in the East, they streamed into Kansas.
4. Over the Long Trail, they rode in covered wagons.

Sometimes the word *and* is used to join too many ideas in a sentence. A sentence with too many ideas that run on and on is called a *run-on sentence.*

> In 1868 Mrs. Inman and her baby traveled to Kansas by train and it was stuck in a blizzard for 36 hours and Mrs. Inman fried bacon in a wash basin and sliced the mince pies she had packed and fed everyone.

Run-on sentences should be rewritten as shorter sentences.

> In 1868 Mrs. Inman and her baby traveled to Kansas by train. It was stuck in a blizzard for 36 hours. Mrs. Inman fried bacon in a wash basin, sliced the mince pies she had packed, and fed everyone.

Run-on sentences also occur when commas are used between sentences instead of periods.

> Nature was the settlers' worst enemy, tornadoes destroyed everything, winters brought furious blizzards.

A correct way to write the run-on sentence is shown below.

Nature was the settlers' worst enemy. Tornadoes destroyed everything. Winters brought furious blizzards.

Talking About Fragments and Run-ons

Read each sentence fragment about the westward expansion. Tell how you would reword each fragment to make a complete sentence.

1. Built a small cabin
2. With great excitement
3. A kettle over the fire
4. With the wind howling

Writing Sentences That Avoid Fragments and Run-ons

Rewrite each sentence fragment about the westward expansion to make a complete sentence.

1. Had few supplies
2. The howling of wolves
3. From the well
4. Covered with grasshoppers
5. Used calico muslin
6. Floods in the spring

Rewrite this run-on sentence to make it correct.

7. Kansas settlers were hospitable, they welcomed passing travelers, they enjoyed exchanging news and gossip, strangers received a good meal and a place to sleep.

Writing Sentences

How do you think your family would fare as pioneers? Imagine you are settlers on a new planet. Write six complete sentences telling how you would deal with the following: food, water, weather conditions, aliens, loneliness, and danger.

Edit Your Sentences

1. Did you begin each sentence with a capital letter?
2. Does each sentence have one or more subjects and one or more predicates?
3. Did you avoid unnecessary words or phrases?

Editing Symbols

¶	indent
≡	capitalize
∧	add
ℓ	delete
/	lower case

Sample Answer 1. People working on the frontier had few supplies.

Unit Review

WRITING AND EDITING SENTENCES

Write each sentence adding an adjective to describe a noun. *pages 292-293*

1. Pioneers needed tools.

2. Fires warmed cabins.

3. Families hunted game.

4. Wagons followed trails.

Write each sentence adding an adverb to describe the verb. *pages 292-293*

5. Pioneers faced danger.

6. The river rose.

7. The traveler woke.

8. The child ate.

Write each sentence adding an adjective phrase to describe a noun. *pages 294-295*

9. Miners sought riches.

10. Miners lived in tents.

11. Rumors flew.

12. Nuggets filled the pockets.

Write each sentence adding an adverb phrase to describe the verb. *pages 294-295*

13. Fortune hunters came.

14. Some returned.

15. The miner shouted.

16. Gold was discovered.

Write each pair of sentences as one compound sentence. Put commas and semicolons where they belong. *pages 296-297*

17. The steam hissed.
The whistle blew.

18. She boarded the train.
She jumped off.

19. The train might stop there.
It might go to Topeka.

20. The train was in a snowdrift.
It could not move.

Write each pair of simple sentences as a complex sentence. Use the subordinating conjunction that tells *when, where, how, why,* or *under what conditions*. Use commas where needed. *pages 298-299*

21. Daniel Boone grew up in Pennsylvania.
Friendly Indians lived nearby.

22. Boone had little formal education. Quick thinking saved him many times.

23. Boone connected old Indian trails. He completed the Wilderness Road.

24. Boone explored Kentucky.
He was a famous pioneer.

25. Boone did not like killing.
He fought when necessary.

26. He built a fort on the Kentucky River. The river joined the Wilderness Trail.

27. Boone was a wise pioneer.
Settlers asked him for help.

Read each sentence written in an informal style. Write the same idea in a formal manner. Use complete sentences. *pages 300-301*

28. Please drop in for dinner Saturday at six.
29. We had a great time at your ranch.
30. Crossing a river in a covered wagon was a real pain.
31. "Paint Your Wagon" is a super musical about gold miners.

Write the correct word or words in parentheses for each sentence. *pages 302-303*

32. I like ___ picture. (that kind of a, that kind of)
33. ___ across the plains. (Snow flew, It was snowing)
34. ___ paintings are by Remington. (These, These here)
35. ___ , the train was disabled. (Due to the fact that there was a blizzard, Because of the blizzard)
36. Many people ___ Western movies. (like, they like)
37. ___ of movies are exciting. (Those kinds, Those kind)

Rewrite each sentence fragment to make a complete sentence. *pages 304-305*

38. Faced danger and disease
39. From the oven
40. Brave women in log cabins
41. Courageous explorers

Rewrite this run-on sentence to make it correct. *pages 304-305*

42. People who settled the West faced many dangers, they had to be resourceful and they had to fight loneliness, and they survived and built a new world from the Appalachians to the Pacific.

Exploring Language

You can combine words to make compound words. Match each word in the first column with a word in the second column to make a compound word. Write each new word.

barber	vine
deer	shop
flag	side
grape	pole
loud	skin
lumber	speaker
mountain	jack

A scuba diver hovers over the seabed.

Our perceptions of the world are corrected by our knowledge.

ARTHUR KOESTLER
British philosopher (1905-1983)

17

WRITING AND EDITING PARAGRAPHS

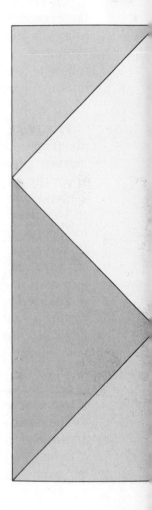

The Writing Process

Thinking About the Writing Process

The major purpose of all writing is to develop a clear message for the reader. Whether you are writing a single paragraph or a composition, you need to plan carefully how you will develop your message. Writing is a *process* — a series of steps — that professional writers follow to create a message. By following the same process, you will improve your own writing.

Prewriting In this step you plan your ideas for writing. First think about the audience for your writing. The people who will read your message are your *audience*. For example, you are the audience when you write an entry in your diary. In a friendly letter, your audience is a friend. For a school assignment, your audience may be your teacher. If you write a letter to the editor of a newspaper, you are writing to people in the community, an unknown audience. Remember to vary your writing *style,* your choice of words and tone, depending on your audience. Use a formal style for special occasions and an informal or friendly style for everyday situations.

Then consider the purpose for your message. Your *purpose* for writing is the reason for which you are writing to your audience. Do you want to *entertain, inform,* or *persuade* your audience? Once your purpose is clear in your own mind, your writing will be more effective.

Next consider what form your writing will take. Will it be a report, a letter, or a composition?

The final part of the prewriting process is to jot down your ideas and organize them. You can get ideas for writing from many sources. You may get ideas from friends, movies, television, or books. You may be given ideas by teachers. Your own personal experiences are an excellent source for ideas for writing. After gathering your ideas, jot them down in note form. Then decide how to organize them.

Writing In this step you will compose your message. Focus on getting all your ideas on paper. This first copy is called a rough draft. You will learn specific suggestions for writing as you progress through this section of your book.

Editing In this step you reread your rough draft and edit it, making changes to clarify the message. All writers, beginners or professionals, edit their rough drafts. You may get some excellent suggestions for editing your work by asking others to read your draft. These suggestions will help make your message clear to your readers. Finally you rewrite your rough draft, incorporating the changes made during the editing. Then you create a final copy to be shared with your audience.

Talking About the Writing Process

For the following writing situations, tell who the audience is, the purpose of the writing, and the kind of style that would be used.

1. Alphabet picture book
2. Newspaper editorial
3. Complaint to a company
4. A letter home from camp
5. A report on diabetes
6. An adventure story

What is the writer's purpose in the following examples?

7. Mystery story
8. Election poster
9. Driver's manual
10. Newspaper editorial
11. Encyclopedia article
12. Science fiction story

Writing About the Writing Process

For the following writing situations, write who the audience is, what the purpose is, and what writing style is appropriate.

1. You are writing a children's story for a first grade class.
2. You are writing a letter to the editor of the local paper urging people to support fund raising for a new running track.
3. You are entering a composition contest sponsored by a teenage magazine. The topic is "Family Life in a Changing World."
4. You are asked to write a "how-to-do-it" article on building a rabbit hutch for a 4-H newsletter.
5. You are writing a short story for your school literary magazine.
6. You must write an essay on American Indians for a history test.
7. You write a newsy letter to your cousin.
8. You write to your aunt, who is recovering from an operation.
9. You are writing a gossip column for your school newspaper.
10. You write a letter to the school board requesting new gym lockers.

Sample Answer 1. children; to entertain; formal/informal

Paragraph Structure

Thinking About Paragraph Structure

When you read a book or a magazine, the sentences are usually grouped into paragraphs. A *paragraph* is a group of sentences that tells about one main idea. A paragraph may have three kinds of sentences.

A *topic sentence* is a general sentence that states the main idea of a paragraph. Often the topic sentence is the first sentence in the paragraph. Occasionally it comes at the end of the paragraph.

The *concluding sentence* summarizes the main idea of the paragraph. It comes at the end of the paragraph. In some paragraphs the concluding sentence can also be the topic sentence of the paragraph.

Detail sentences present information or ideas that develop or support the topic sentence of the paragraph. The purpose of the detail sentences is to prove that what you said in the topic sentence is true. The detail sentences support the topic sentence with specific statements. In this unit you will learn to develop topic sentences with detail sentences that give events or explanations in time order, concrete descriptive details, facts, comparisons, and reasons.

Because a paragraph is a group of sentences about a single idea, all of the detail sentences must relate to, or develop, the topic sentence. The detail sentences also relate to each other. Logical connecting words show the reader how the details are connected to each other. Some logical connecting words are *first, similarly,* and *finally.*

Unity in a paragraph means that all the sentences relate to, or develop, the main idea expressed in the topic sentence. When a sentence in a paragraph does not relate to the main idea, the paragraph is confusing.

Talking About Paragraph Structure

Read these paragraphs and answer the questions that follow.

A. A river or stream is created from a melting glacier. First the glacier forms in a high mountain valley until the ice mass is about 100 feet deep. Then the glacier begins to move slowly, usually just a few inches a day. As the glacier moves into the lower areas of the valley, the ice melts. Once the glacier is melted, a river has been born.

B. Ten years ago the town of Dover had 7,000 visitors during the summer. Four years ago there were 18,000 summer guests. Last year 25,000 people spent their summers in Dover. It is clear that Dover is becoming an increasingly popular summer vacation spot.

1. What is the topic sentence in each paragraph? Where is it?
2. Does either paragraph have a concluding sentence? What is it?
3. Do all the details relate to each topic sentence? Does each paragraph have unity?
4. Which kinds of details are used to develop each topic sentence: time order, descriptions, facts, comparisons, or reasons?
5. What logical connecting words are used in each paragraph?

Writing About Paragraph Structure

Read these paragraphs and answer the questions that follow.

A. Without reduced "student" ticket prices, most students would rarely go to concerts or plays. Half-price tickets allow students to discover fine music and the magic of the theater. As a result, their education is greatly enriched. Student tickets should be available for sports, too. Student price policies for concerts and theater help build an audience who will enjoy and support the arts all their lives.

B. Putting on stage makeup is a complicated business. First smooth on a thin layer of cold cream. Next smooth on a thin layer of skin-colored greasepaint. Then add eye makeup, lip color, and some rouge or wrinkle lines, if you need them. Clown makeup is also hard to put on. Finally dust your face with powder to remove the shine and set the makeup. The ability to put on makeup skillfully is part of an actor's art.

1. Write the topic sentence of each paragraph.
2. Write the concluding sentence of each paragraph, if there is one.
3. Write the detail sentence in each paragraph that does not belong.
4. Write which kinds of detail sentence are used to develop each topic sentence: time order, descriptions, facts, comparisons, or reasons.
5. Write the logical connecting words used in each paragraph.

A Narrative Paragraph in Time Order

Thinking About a Narrative Paragraph

Have you ever written a mystery or adventure story? Perhaps you have written an account of a special assembly for your school newspaper. This type of writing is called narrative writing. In *narrative* writing, the writer tells, or narrates, a real or imaginary story.

A *narrative paragraph* tells a story about a real or imaginary experience or incident. The topic sentence in a narrative paragraph introduces the main idea of the incident. The detail sentences in the paragraph are usually arranged in time order, or chronological order, the actual order in which the details occurred. Logical connecting words such as *first, next,* and *after* are used in the detail sentences to make clear the sequence of events in the incident. You can achieve unity by making sure that each detail sentence is related to the main idea.

- Read this narrative paragraph. Notice how it is organized.

> Twenty students at Mayfair School have won an award for brightening their neighborhood. The students first suggested the idea a month ago. After getting buckets, brushes, and paint, the class chose work areas. Next they painted houses and stores. The students finished their project yesterday. Afterward several local merchants offered the students summer jobs.

The first sentence in this narrative paragraph is the topic sentence. The detail sentences state events in the story in the order in which they happened. The underlined logical connecting words help clarify the order of events in the paragraph.

Talking About a Narrative Paragraph

Look again at the narrative time order paragraph above.

1. What is the main idea introduced in the topic sentence?
2. Where is the main idea stated?
3. In what order are the detail sentences arranged?
4. How do the logical connecting words help make the story clear to the reader?
5. Does the paragraph have unity? Why?

Practicing a Narrative Paragraph

The notes below relate events in a real story. Read the notes and organize them in an appropriate time order.

- Life preserver thrown to boy.
- Lifeguard sees swimmer in trouble.
- Boy thanks lifeguard.
- Lifeguard pulls swimmer to shore.

Now you are ready to write a narrative paragraph.

1. The topic sentence will be *A lifeguard at Jones Beach saved a drowning boy today.* Write the topic sentence. Indent the first word.
2. Look at your notes. Write a detail sentence explaining each event. Use logical connecting words to make the time order clear.

Edit Your Paragraph

Read your paragraph. Use these check questions to edit your paragraph. Then write a final copy of your paragraph.

1. Does the topic sentence tell the main idea of the paragraph?
2. Are the detail sentences related to the main idea?
3. Do you use logical connecting words to make the order of events clear?
4. Do you use correct capitalization and punctuation?

Editing Symbols

¶	indent
≡	capitalize
∧	add
ℓ	delete
/	lower case

INDEPENDENT WRITING

A Narrative Paragraph in a Journal

Prewriting In a journal or diary you may tell about experiences that have happened to you. Choose an important incident in your life. The incident may be getting a 10-speed bicycle, winning an award, or meeting a person who becomes your best friend. Make notes about the events. Then organize your notes in a time-order sequence.

Writing Write a narrative paragraph for your journal that tells about an important incident in your life. First write a topic sentence that describes the incident. Then use your notes to write detail sentences. Explain the events in the order in which they happened. Use logical connecting words to make the time order clear.

Editing Use the check questions above to edit your paragraph.

Editing Paragraphs

Thinking About Editing a Paragraph

Editing is an important step in the writing process. *Edit* means to think about your writing and decide on the changes you will make to insure that your message is clear to your audience. Following these steps can help you become a better writer:

1. Read your rough draft carefully. If possible, have another person read it.
2. Write the changes on your rough draft.
3. Make a final copy incorporating all the changes.

As you edit, you should keep certain questions in mind for every paragraph or composition you write. These check questions will help you to know if you have been successful in determining your purpose in writing, your audience, and your style of writing.

- Is my purpose for writing to entertain, persuade, or inform?
- Who is my audience? Is my style of writing appropriate for this audience?
- Is the message of my writing clear as well as interesting to my audience?

As you edit each paragraph, ask yourself specific check questions that are related directly to the structure of a paragraph. These check questions will help you to know if your paragraph has unity, or if it is written about one idea, and if you used logical connecting words to relate your detail sentences to one another.

- Does the topic sentence tell the main idea of the paragraph?
- Are the detail sentences related to the main idea and to each other?
- Do you use logical connecting words to show how the detail sentences are related to each other?

Writers, editors, and some teachers use editing symbols to indicate changes in the rough draft. You may find these symbols useful as you edit your writing.

Talking About Editing a Paragraph

Look at this narrative paragraph. The writer edited it to show corrections and changes. Notice how the editing symbols are used.

¶ Mayfair School's spruce-up Campaign spread to other schools in town. First West Side school began its ~~own~~ own program. students there painted nearby ~~neary~~ apartments. Next Central High students painted their school walls. Later more schools ~~scools~~ followed the example set by mayfair. Finally The town mayor announced that all ~~all~~ the students would receive awards. The Awards were presented at special assemblies in each school. ~~Athletic awards were presented at a later time.~~ student leaders explained the campaign and described the projects they had completed. the mayor made a brief ~~breif~~ speech and then presented the awards.

Editing Symbols

¶ indent
≡ capitalize
∧ add
ℓ delete
/ lower case

1. Why did the writer use the editing symbol for a new paragraph?
2. What are the misspelled words in the paragraph?
3. What letters were changed to capitals or lower case?
4. What words did the writer delete or leave out?
5. Why did the writer delete the sentence about the athletic awards?
6. What words were added to the paragraph?

Editing and Rewriting a Paragraph

Rewrite the following paragraph, making the necessary changes. Leave out ideas that do not belong. Add logical connecting words. Correct the spelling and punctuation.

Last week my family and I visited one of New York citys newst museums. This museum is a huge gigantic world war II Aircraft Carrier the U.S.S. *Intrepid* and first we saw models of fighter plains on display on the hanger deck I sat in a fighter plane cockpit. We were mad because we forgot our camera. We saw two movies. One showed training on a modern nucular-powered carrier, the other showed the history of the the *Intrepid.* I climbed to the bridge and sat in the captains chair. We had a snack in the cafeteria, and and visited the gift shop. the *Intrepid* a fasinating experience.

An Expository Paragraph in Time Order

Thinking About an Expository Paragraph

Every paragraph has a purpose. A paragraph whose purpose is to explain an event or give directions is called an *expository paragraph.*

The topic sentence in an expository paragraph introduces the main idea. The detail sentences explain the directions or the sequence of steps in the event. As in a time-order paragraph, the detail sentences are usually arranged in chronological order. You may use order words in the detail sentences so that your readers can follow the sequence of steps. Some logical connecting words are *first, second, next, then, finally,* and *last.* Others are *before, after, soon,* and *once.* You may use a concluding sentence to summarize or restate the main idea of the paragraph.

• Read this paragraph. Notice the underlined time-order words.

> A friend of mine tried to coax a skunk out of her cellar. First she scattered a trail of bread crumbs up the cellar stairs to the outside entrance. Next she closed the inside door and made sure that the outside entrance was open for the night. Then in the morning she checked her cellar and found that a second skunk had followed the bread crumbs down into the cellar. Now she had two skunks. At last she decided to lay a plank over the stairs. Finally the two clumsy climbers were able to walk up the planks and out of the cellar.

The first sentence in this expository paragraph is the topic sentence. It introduces the event that will be explained. The detail sentences explain the steps in the event in chronological order. The last sentence is a concluding sentence, summarizing the explanation.

Talking About an Expository Paragraph

1. What is the main idea of the paragraph?
2. In what order are the detail sentences arranged?
3. Look at the order words. What other order words could have been used?
4. Why did the writer use a concluding sentence?

Practicing an Expository Paragraph

You are going to write an expository paragraph that gives directions for completing a job application. Read these notes that explain the steps in the directions. Organize the notes in chronological order.

- Complete each item.
- Read application.
- Write neatly.
- Check application.

Now you are ready to write an explanatory paragraph.

1. The topic sentence will be: *Follow these directions when completing a job application.*
2. Use your notes and write a detail sentence for each step of the directions. Try to use adverbs to make your sentences interesting. Use connecting words to clarify the sequence of steps in the directions.

Edit Your Paragraph

Use these questions to edit your paragraph. Use the editing symbols to mark corrections. Make a final copy of your paragraph.

1. Does the topic sentence tell the main idea?
2. Are the detail sentences in chronological order?
3. Do you use logical connecting words?
4. Did you use adverbs correctly in your sentences?
5. Did you use correct punctuation and capitalization?

Editing Symbols

¶ indent
≡ capitalize
∧ add
℘ delete
/ lower case

INDEPENDENT WRITING

An Expository Paragraph

Prewriting The elementary school is holding a "Hobby Day" to introduce various hobbies to the children. You must submit an expository paragraph explaining your hobby to the principal. Write notes that explain the steps involved in doing your hobby. Organize your notes in chronological order. Decide which logical connecting words you will use.

Writing Write an expository paragraph explaining your hobby to the elementary school principal. The topic sentence will introduce your hobby. Use your notes to write the detail sentences in chronological order for the paragraph.

Editing Use the check questions above to edit your paragraph.

A Descriptive Paragraph

Thinking About a Descriptive Paragraph

Using clear descriptions will make your writing more interesting to your audience, or readers. A good *descriptive paragraph* creates vivid word pictures that describe scenes, objects, or people.

The first step in preparing to write a description is to become a good observer. Use your five senses to improve your powers of observation. Choose an object or scene you might describe. Think about how it looks, tastes, smells, sounds, and feels. If you are writing about people, observe them closely in different situations.

The second step is to choose precise words. Precise nouns are important because they name the parts of an object, the things that you observe in a scene, or the qualities you observe in a person. Verbs explain the actions you observe. Your choice of adjectives and adverbs will help your reader see the subject of your description vividly.

The final step is to organize your descriptions into a paragraph. The topic sentence will state what you are describing or your opinion concerning what you have observed. The detail sentences will state your observations.

- Read this descriptive paragraph.

The blazing <u>sun</u> is as hot as fire. The sand is a warm <u>blanket</u> underfoot. At the same time a cool <u>wind</u> sweeps gently across your face. The <u>air</u> smells sweet and refreshing. A child's laughter rings in your ears. Meanwhile people splash each other playfully in the foamy, blue <u>waters</u>. Nothing is more special than a <u>day</u> at the beach.

Talking About a Descriptive Paragraph

Read the descriptive paragraph again.

1. How are the writer's observations related to the five senses?
2. Why do you think the writer placed the topic sentence last?
3. Notice the underlined nouns. What adjectives describe these nouns?
4. What verbs are used? What adverbs did the writer select?
5. What other adverbs and adjectives could the writer have chosen?
6. What figures of speech did the writer use?

Practicing a Descriptive Paragraph

Write a descriptive paragraph about your best friend. The paragraph should describe some of the qualities you like best in your friend.

Use the sentences below to describe your friend. First choose the most appropriate word on the right to complete each sentence. Select the word that best describes your friend. If you think of a better word than those suggested, use it. You may want to use the dictionary.

1. I have a ___ friend.	capable/smart/talented
2. My friend possesses a wonderful ___ .	personality/smile/outlook on life
3. I feel ___ when I am with my friend.	confident/happy/relaxed
4. For these reasons my friend is ___ to me.	important/special/comforting

Now you are ready to write the sentences in paragraph form. Begin your paragraph with the topic sentence. Indent the first word.

Edit Your Paragraph

Read the paragraph again. Use these check questions to edit your paragraph. Then write a final copy of your paragraph.

1. Does the topic sentence tell the main idea?
2. Are the detail sentences related to the main idea and each other?
3. Do you use precise nouns, verbs, and adjectives?
4. Do you use correct capitalization and punctuation?

Editing Symbols

- ¶ indent
- ≡ capitalize
- ∧ add
- ℘ delete
- / lower case

INDEPENDENT WRITING

A Descriptive Paragraph in a Sports Report

Prewriting You are a sports correspondent on the planet Earth for an intergalactic newspaper. You have been assigned to write a paragraph describing the Intergalactic Olympics being held on Earth. Choose an event or a player. Think about how things might look, feel, and sound. Make notes about vivid images to use in writing your descriptive paragraph.

Writing Write a descriptive paragraph about a sports event or about a player. Choose words that describe your topic vividly.

Editing Use the check questions above to edit your paragraph.

An Expository Paragraph of Facts

Thinking About a Paragraph of Facts

A paragraph of facts is a useful type of paragraph. Reporters write paragraphs of facts for their news articles. You use paragraphs of facts for reports in school subjects such as social studies or science. Writing that uses facts to inform or explain is called *expository* writing.

A *paragraph of facts* gives information based on facts about a specific subject. A *fact* is something that has happened or that people know to be true. Facts must be based on evidence that can be proven through research or personal observation. The topic sentence presents the main idea. The detail sentences give specific facts that prove that the topic sentence is true. Use the answers to the questions *who, what, when, where, why,* and *how* to select facts for the detail sentences.

You have a choice of two different ways to present facts. In a narrative paragraph you may present facts in chronological order. Facts in a news story are usually presented in order of importance. In this way the reader receives the most important information first.

Logical connecting words help make the sequence of facts clear to the reader. Some logical connecting words are *when, after, although, first, finally, eventually, at the same time,* and *yesterday.*

Talking About a Paragraph of Facts

Read this paragraph of facts. Notice the underlined logical connecting words. Then answer the questions that follow.

Two joggers plunged into an icy lake in Prospect Park yesterday afternoon to rescue a 13-year-old boy who had fallen through thin ice into the lake. The joggers, Miguel Ortiz, 24, and Elizabeth Siegel, 31, had been running separately on the path circling the lake <u>when</u> they heard cries for help. They lay flat on the ice and pulled Thomas Kane, 13, of Brooklyn, to safety. The three were taken by ambulance to Kings County Hospital. The two joggers were released <u>immediately.</u> Thomas was released <u>after</u> being treated for shock and exposure. <u>Later</u> police found that signs warning of thin ice had been covered by snow.

1. What is the topic sentence in the paragraph?
2. Do all of the detail sentences support the topic sentence?
3. In what order are the facts presented?
4. Does the story answer the questions *who, what, when, where, why,* and *how*?

Practicing a Paragraph of Facts

Now you will write a paragraph of facts. The notes below give facts about a student who won an award. Read the notes carefully.

Who: Tamayo Li 7th grade student at Summit School
What: Presented certificate for perfect attendance
Where: School awards assembly
When: Friday, May 27, 1983
How: Attended school every day
Why: Tamayo's reasons for winning: Has good health, enjoys school

1. Use this topic sentence: *Tamayo Li won an important award this week.*
2. Using the notes above, write detail sentences that give facts about Tamayo's award.

Edit Your Paragraph

Read your paragraph again. Use the check questions to edit it. Then make a final copy.

1. Do your detail sentences develop the main idea in the topic sentence?
2. Do your sentences answer the questions who, what, when, where, why, and how?
3. Did you use correct capitalization and punctuation?

Editing Symbols

¶	indent
≡	capitalize
∧	add
ℓ	delete
/	lower case

INDEPENDENT WRITING

A Paragraph of Facts in a News Report

Prewriting You are assigned to report on important events at your school. Plan a factual paragraph based on an event that happened recently at your school. The subject of the event could be sports, a class field trip, or activities of the science or drama club. Use the answers to the questions *who, what, when, where, why,* and *how* to make notes of the facts about your event.

Writing Write a paragraph of facts about an important event that happened at your school. The topic sentence should identify the event. Use your notes to write detail sentences for the paragraph.

Editing Use the check questions above to edit your paragraph.

An Expository Summary Paragraph

Thinking About a Summary Paragraph

The purpose of a *summary paragraph* is to summarize the important facts about a subject.

A summary paragraph is similar to a paragraph of facts. The topic sentence in a summary paragraph introduces the subject of your research. The detail sentences may be arranged in order of importance, with the most important facts presented first.

Suppose you are writing a summary paragraph about why people moved to Newtown. You have surveyed 100 new residents and interviewed the town mayor. The results are found below.

Interview

Q: What is Newtown's employment rate?

A: Over 90% of the adult population is working. There are many places of employment here.

Q: What is the weather like?

A: The temperature generally stays around 70° all year.

Q: How high are the taxes?

A: Newtown's land taxes are low, and there is no state income tax.

Q: What is the school system like?

A: Our schools rate among the nation's best. Nearly 80% of our high school graduates attend college.

Survey Results

Reason for Moving to Newtown	Number of People
Pleasant climate	18
High employment	23
Friends nearby	11
Low tax rate	17
Good school system	20
Convenient public transportation	7
Large shopping centers	4

Talking About a Summary Paragraph

Read this paragraph and answer the questions that follow.

People move to Newtown for a variety of reasons. Many people live in Newtown because of the many places of employment. Many residents are attracted by the school system, one of the nation's best. Others come for the climate, which stays warm all the year. Some residents move to benefit from the low land taxes.

1. What is the topic sentence in the summary paragraph?
2. What facts from the survey were included in the summary?
3. What facts from the survey were left out of the summary?
4. What information from the interview was included in the summary?
5. What information from the interview was left out of the summary?

INDEPENDENT WRITING

A Summary Paragraph for a Report

Prewriting You are going to write a summary paragraph for a report based on the information presented below. Select the most important information. Make notes on the facts you have chosen.

Interview: Director of Recreation

Q: Where can people fish in Cooper City?

A: We have two lakes outside the city containing bass and trout.

Q: How many television channels are there?

A: We have six channels, and cable is coming soon.

Q: What libraries do you have?

A: We have two public libraries and one college library.

Q: Does Cooper City have museums?

A: We have an art museum and a science museum.

Survey Results: 100 residents

Favorite Leisure Activity	Number of People
golf	4
television	17
bowling	5
movies	10
theater	9
museums	14
reading	16
concerts	10
fishing	15

Writing Write a summary paragraph using the information above and your notes.

Editing Edit your paragraph and make a revised copy.

1. Did you include only the important information from the survey and the interview?
2. Are your detail sentences arranged in order of importance?
3. Did you use correct capitalization and punctuation?

A Persuasive Paragraph of Reasons

Thinking About a Persuasive Paragraph of Reasons

You have learned that all your writing should have a purpose. You may wish to entertain your audience or tell facts. Your purpose may be to persuade your readers that your opinion about an issue or idea is important and valid.

The purpose of a *persuasive paragraph* is to state your personal opinion about an issue or idea and to present reasons that support your opinion. You should consider all available information before forming your opinion. Your opinion should be based on solid reasons in order to prove to your audience that your opinion is valid.

The topic sentence in a persuasive paragraph expresses your opinion about an idea or issue. The detail sentences in the paragraph state your supporting reasons. You may write a concluding sentence that restates or emphasizes the opinion expressed in the topic sentence.

- Read the following persuasive paragraph. It was written by a student.

> The students at our school should be allowed to run the school cafeteria. First students know better than anyone else what they like to eat. Also many students have learned how to prepare food in home economics classes. Now would be the perfect time for them to put their knowledge to work. The work would teach students a sense of responsibility. This program has been successful in other schools. It is time to give students a chance to run the school cafeteria.

Talking About a Paragraph of Reasons

Look again at the above paragraph.

1. What is the topic sentence of the paragraph?
2. What reasons does the writer give to support the opinion?
3. If you disagree with the writer's opinion, what reasons could you give to support your own opinion?
4. What is the concluding sentence? How does it relate to the topic sentence of the paragraph?

Practicing a Paragraph of Reasons

Write a persuasive paragraph about some problem you feel students face in school. Give your honest opinion about the problem.

1. Write a topic sentence that expresses your feelings regarding the problem students face in school.
2. Now write a detail sentence that supports your opinion. Explain how the problem affects you personally.
3. If other students have discussed the problem, write detail sentences telling what you have heard from them. (You should not use others' names without permission. Either get permission or use expressions such as "Another student has said," or "other students feel that.")
4. Write a concluding sentence for your paragraph.

Edit Your Paragraph

Read your paragraph again. Use these check questions to edit your paragraph. Then make a revised copy.

1. Does your topic sentence state your opinion?
2. Do your detail sentences give valid reasons for your opinion?
3. Does your concluding sentence restate or emphasize your main idea?
4. Did you use correct punctuation and spelling?

Editing Symbols

¶	indent
≡	capitalize
∧	add
ℓ	delete
/	lower case

INDEPENDENT WRITING

A Paragraph of Reasons in an Advertisement

Prewriting Advertisements in newspapers and magazines are examples of persuasive writing. Think of a new product that would be useful or entertaining. Plan a persuasive paragraph that can be used as an advertisement for your product. Make notes about your opinion of the product and supporting reasons for that opinion.

Writing Write a persuasive paragraph about a product of your choice. The topic sentence should state your opinion of the product and also interest people in buying it. State your supporting reasons in detail sentences. You may want to write a concluding sentence.

Editing Use the check questions above to edit your paragraph.

An Expository Paragraph of Comparison

Thinking About a Paragraph of Comparison

How are the games of rugby and football alike? Compare the prices of designer jeans and discount store jeans. Give three ways the Congress of the United States is similar to the Parliament of the United Kingdom. Where have you heard these ideas before? You probably recognize them as the kinds of writing assignments you do everyday in school. These assignments require you to write a paragraph of comparison.

The first step in planning a paragraph of comparison is to select the two things to be compared. Of course, you may compare more than two things in your paragraph. Then you must think of the ways in which the things are alike. You will want to make notes of those ways.

The purpose of a *paragraph of comparison* is to present the similarities, the likenesses, of two or more things. The topic sentence in the paragraph will introduce the main idea, the things being compared. The detail sentences present the specific ways the things are alike. Certain logical connecting words are helpful in signaling your reader that you are presenting similarities. These logical connecting words are *both, resemble, each, similar to, like,* and *in the same way.* You may use a concluding sentence to summarize the main idea of the paragraph.

Talking About a Paragraph of Comparison

Read this paragraph and answer the questions that follow.

Ice skating and roller skating are similar in many ways. Both types of skating may be done outdoors or indoors, on special rinks. Skaters on wheels or blades enjoy skating to music, and both compete in the same ways. Speed-skating, dance routines, and roller or ice hockey are all popular competitive sports. Whether you zoom around a hardwood floor or glide over smooth ice, you will enjoy exercise that strengthens your legs and improves balance and stamina.

1. What is the topic sentence of the paragraph?
2. What logical connecting words are used? What other words might have been used?
3. How many similarities are mentioned?
4. How does the concluding sentence tie the paragraph together?

Practicing a Paragraph of Comparison

Now you will write a paragraph of comparison. Look at the notes below. They tell some ways in which apples and pears are alike.

> *Similarities*
> Excellent low calorie snack foods: 100 calories per piece.
> Produce both yellow and red fruit.
> Grow on trees about 40–50 feet high.
> Have white blossoms on trees in the spring.

1. Use this topic sentence: *Apples and pears are very similar fruits.*
2. Write a detail sentence telling the similarity of these fruits as a snack food.
3. Write two or three sentences comparing the color, size of the tree, and the blossoms of the apples and pears.

Edit Your Paragraph

Read your paragraph again. Use the check questions to edit your paragraph. Then make a revised copy.

1. Does the topic sentence introduce the two things being compared?
2. Do the detail sentences tell the ways the things are alike?
3. Did you use correct punctuation and spelling?

Editing Symbols

¶	indent
≡	capitalize
∧	add
℘	delete
/	lower case

INDEPENDENT WRITING

A Paragraph of Comparison in a Friendly Letter

Prewriting You are a seventh grader in the year 3000. Write a letter to your pen pal on the planet Xando. Compare the recreational habits of people on Earth with the people on Xando. Choose a topic and then imagine what life might be like in the year 3000. Jot down notes on the similarities. Then organize your notes.

Writing Write a paragraph of comparison about the topic you chose or about another topic. Be sure your topic sentence states what you are comparing. Use logical connecting words in your detail sentences. Write a concluding sentence that summarizes your main ideas.

Editing Use the check questions above to edit your paragraph.

Unit Review

WRITING AND EDITING PARAGRAPHS

For the following situations, write who the audience is, what the purpose is, and what style is appropriate. *pages 310-311*

1. You are writing to a friend who has recently moved. You are reporting all the latest news and gossip.
2. You are writing invitations to the faculty for a teacher recognition day sponsored by the student council.
3. You are writing a humorous report for the school newspaper of the costumes worn for "Dress as Your Favorite Character Day."
4. You are entering a contest sponsored by a political group. You will write a composition on your choice for the next President.

5. Choose one of the following topics or think of your own. Write a narrative paragraph in time order. Remember that your detail sentences should support your topic sentence. Use logical connecting words to make the time order clear. *pages 312-315*

a. My first airplane trip
b. How I tried out for the team
c. My proudest moment
d. How I met my best friend

6. Rewrite the following paragraph. Edit it and make the necessary changes. Leave out ideas that do not belong. Add logical connecting words. Correct the spelling and punctuation. *pages 316-319*

Direct marketing is the Process in which companys advertise directly to customers and customers purchase products directly from the companies, and Customers do not need to go to a store to shop. Stores are more fun to shop in, however. Mail Catalogs Telephone Sales and television ads are examples of direct marketing. Direct marketing is growing fast because companys use it reach only those people they think will buy there product.

7. Imagine that you are a reporter for your local newspaper. You are asked to write a paragraph of facts on one of the following events, or you may choose your own event. *pages 322-323*

a. Fire destroys a warehouse
b. High school football team wins championship

c. Meteor falls through roof of house

d. Lion escapes from circus

Make notes of facts that answer the questions *who, what, where, when, why,* and *how.* The topic sentence should identify the event. Detail sentences should support the topic sentence. Use logical connecting words to make the sequence of events clear.

8. Write a persuasive paragraph of reasons about one of the following topics, or choose one of your own. *pages 326-327*

a. You are running for class president. Write a campaign speech.

b. The Student Council should sponsor and run a school store.

c. The school should buy computers for use in all grades.

d. Your grade should raise money for a trip to Washington, D.C.

Your topic sentence should state your opinion about a problem or issue. State your supporting reasons in your detail sentences. Write a concluding sentence that sums up your point of view.

Careers

A *computer programmer* writes the instructions that tell computers what to do. First the programmer reads a description of the tasks the computer is required to do. The description tells what information must go into the computer (input), what processing is needed, and what information must come out of the computer (output). Then the programmer makes two diagrams. The first shows how all parts of the job will fit together. The second breaks the job down into a series of steps. A programmer uses one or more of several special computer languages to write the instructions. The machine reads the instructions and stores the information on tape.

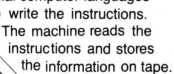

Mother Teresa, Nobel prize winner for her social work in India, receives an honorary degree from Harvard in 1982.

No one can do inspired work without genuine interest in his subject and understanding of its characteristics.

ANDREAS FEININGER
American photographer
and artist (1906-)

18

WRITING AND EDITING COMPOSITIONS

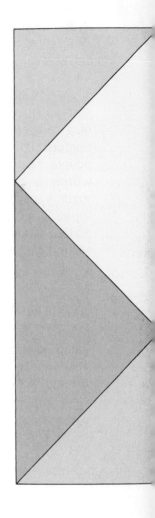

Prewriting: Selecting and Limiting a Topic

Thinking About Purpose and Audience

A composition is a piece of writing on a particular topic. The process of writing a composition is divided into three stages. The stages are prewriting (thinking and planning), writing, and editing.

As you begin to think about your composition, the very first things you must consider are the purpose and the audience. The *purpose* of a composition may be to inform, to persuade, or to entertain your readers. You must also consider who your audience will be. The people who read your composition are the *audience*. Suppose you are writing a composition for your school newspaper. You want to persuade your fellow students to adopt your point of view about a specific topic. Your purpose is to persuade. Your audience is your schoolmates. Knowing this information will help you to choose a style of writing that will be appropriate to your audience.

Thinking About Composition Topics

Now you are ready to choose a topic. The first step in writing a composition is selecting a topic. If your teacher assigns a specific topic, make sure you understand the assignment before you begin writing. At other times you may be asked to choose your own topic for a composition. Then select a topic with which you are familiar. Write about a subject that interests you. Your familiarity and interest in the subject matter will help make the composition a good one.

Once you have chosen your topic, you need to limit it. *Limiting* the topic means narrowing it to a more specific subject. Suppose your assignment calls for a composition of two or three paragraphs, and you decide to write about sports. The topic of "Sports" is too general. You can not write about all sports in your paper.

Limit your topic to a particular sport. If you choose "Baseball," the topic still is too broad. You need to limit the topic even further. If you focus on a particular incident or person, your final topic could be "The Most Exciting Baseball Game I Ever Played" or "My Favorite Baseball Coach." These subjects can be covered in two or three paragraphs.

Here is how the process of limiting a topic looks in chart form:

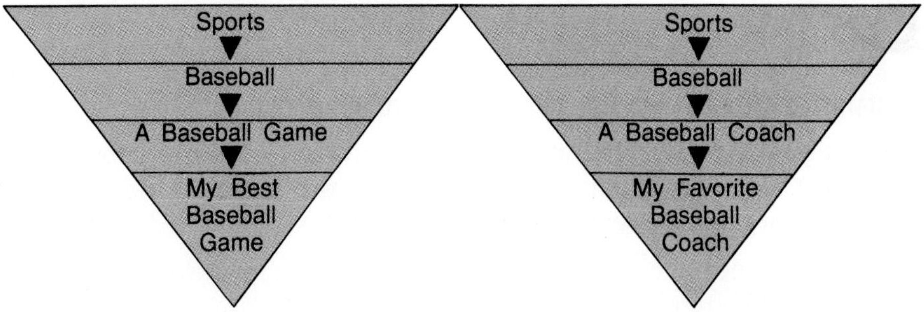

The following chart suggests how general topics can be limited for a composition of two or three paragraphs.

Too General	**Limited Topic**
Music	How to Find Good Music on the Radio
Food	The Best Possible Thanksgiving Dinner
Hobbies	Why I Collect Baseball Cards
Animals	What I Saw at the Zoo

Talking About Topics

Read each topic below. Tell whether the topic is **appropriate** for a composition or if it **needs to be limited.** If it needs to be limited, state the reason.

1. Tests
2. My Best Science Project
3. Why I Like to Play the Piano
4. How Scientists Predict the Weather
5. Science
6. The World of Music
7. The Best New Television Shows This Season
8. Career Studies

Writing Composition Topics

Each topic below is too general for a composition. Assume you are asked to write a composition of two or three paragraphs. Narrow each topic more specifically. Write the title of your new topic.

1. Food
2. The World of Books
3. My Family
4. Inventions
5. Animals
6. Responsibility
7. Vacation Time
8. School Rules
9. Traveling

Prewriting: Brainstorming and Organizing Ideas

Thinking About Ideas for a Composition

Once you have selected and limited the topic for your composition, you must consider what you will say in the paper. One kind of composition requires research.

Another kind of composition is based on your own experiences or opinions. This type of composition does not require you to locate information in the library. You begin work on this type of composition by brainstorming. *Brainstorming* means listing all the ideas that immediately come to mind about the topic on a piece of paper.

Next you categorize your notes. *Categorizing* is organizing the ideas that are alike into groups. Finally you review the notes in each group. You may discover that some ideas do not relate directly to the topic, or that some notes repeat others in the list. By *eliminating* these unnecessary details, you will be left with the details that will be used in the composition.

When you actually write your composition, you will develop each group of notes into one paragraph. The number of categories you create tells you how many paragraphs your composition will contain.

Imagine you are writing a composition entitled "How to Get a Job." These are some notes you might jot down while brainstorming.

go to employment agency
bring a résumé to interview
keeping a job may be hard or easy
call friends who have jobs
dress appropriately for interview

look in newspaper want ads
pay attention to interviewer
prepare questions to ask interviewer
do not let mind wander at interview
do not wear unattractive clothes

Notice how the ideas can be categorized and how some can be eliminated.

Finding available jobs
go to employment agencies
call friends who have jobs
look in newspaper want ads

Going through the interview
bring a résumé to interview
dress appropriately for interview
pay attention to interviewer
prepare questions to ask
interviewer

Talking About Ideas for a Composition

Look at the original set of notes for the composition. Then look at the way the ideas have been organized in the second set.

1. In the second set of notes, what are the two headings under which the details have been listed?
2. Which details appear in the first set of notes, but not in the second?
3. Why do you think the detail about "keeping a job may be hard or easy" was eliminated in the second set?
4. Why do you think the detail about "do not let mind wander at interview" was eliminated?
5. Why do you think the detail about "do not wear unattractive clothes" was eliminated?

Writing Ideas for a Composition

In each group of ideas below, one idea could serve as a heading, or category topic, for the others. Write the idea that could be the heading in each group.

1. Listens to my problems; spends time with me; qualities of my best friend; has good sense of humor; helps me in school.
2. Earned money delivering newspapers; saved money in bank; shopped around for nicest bike; compared prices; purchased bike; how I bought a bicycle.
3. Painted my walls; straightened books on shelves; fixing up my room; put posters on walls; rearranged my closet; rearranged furniture.

In each group of items, one detail does not belong. Write the detail that does not belong.

4. Arrived at mountain slope; rented a pair of skis; rode lift to top of slope; hope to go fishing; skied down a trail through the woods.
5. Grades fairly; gets tests back quickly; doesn't embarrass anyone; builds model planes as a hobby; leads interesting class discussions.
6. Like to run laps around gym; enjoy working out on exercise mats; do not care for television; enjoy playing ball with other students; look forward to using gym equipment.

Prewriting: Writing a Thesis Statement and an Outline

Thinking About Thesis Statements and Outlines

Organizing is an important part of any composition. Once you have decided what details to include in your composition, you need to organize them. The best way to do so is by developing an outline.

In an outline, the main ideas are written next to Roman numerals **I** and **II.** The supporting details for each main idea are written next to letters **A, B,** and so on, under the Roman numeral.

In addition to making an outline, you should develop a *thesis statement.* A thesis statement is a sentence that summarizes all the main ideas in the outline. Since it expresses the central idea of the entire composition, the thesis statement begins the first paragraph.

Here is an outline for a two-paragraph composition entitled "My Best Baseball Game":

I. Performed well at bat
- **A.** Hit home run in first inning
- **B.** Hit triple in third inning
- **C.** Hit double in eighth inning

II. Performed well in the field
- **A.** Made shoestring catch
- **B.** Set up triple play
- **C.** Caught a line drive

The two main ideas of the composition are indicated next to Roman numerals I and II in the outline. A possible way to phrase the thesis statement for the outline is: *In the best baseball game I ever played, I performed well both at bat and in the field.*

Talking About Thesis Statements and Outlines

The following details belong in an outline for a two-paragraph composition entitled "How To Do Well on Tests." Tell how the details should be organized and how the thesis statement might be phrased.

1. Answer harder questions later
2. Review notes several times

3. Preparing yourself before the test
4. Read textbook carefully.
5. Review all answers before handing in paper.
6. Answer easier questions first.
7. Using your test time wisely
8. Takes notes on material to be tested

Writing Thesis Statements and Outlines

Read each group of main ideas from an outline. Write a thesis statement that summarizes all the main ideas.

1. **I.** I enjoy stories that have surprise endings.
II. I enjoy stories that contain interesting characters.

2. **I.** Scouting offers you a chance to be outdoors.
II. Scouting enables you to work toward an achievement.

3. **I.** The first step in gardening is buying seeds.
II. The next step in gardening is planting the seeds.
III. The third step in gardening is watering the seeds.

4. **I.** You save money by bringing your own lunch to school.
II. You don't waste time in line when you bring your own lunch.
III. You can prepare your favorite food when you bring your own lunch.

The following details belong in an outline for a two-paragraph composition entitled "How to Plan a Party." Write the details in their proper order in outline form. Then write a thesis statement that summarizes the main ideas.

5. Count the number of people who say they will attend.
6. Set out the food on tables before people arrive.
7. Preparing the right amount of food.
8. Buy enough food for all those who will attend.
9. Determining the number of people.
10. Make a list of food you will serve at the party.
11. Send out invitations to everyone on the list.
12. Make a list of people you wish to invite.

An Expository Composition

Thinking About an Expository Composition

An *expository composition* explains, or clarifies, a subject. Most of the factual writing that you do in your schoolwork is expository writing. Since your textbooks explain different subjects, they are written in an expository style. History books are also examples of expository writing.

When you write an expository composition, you begin by selecting and limiting your topic. Then you brainstorm for ideas, organize your notes, and eliminate unnecessary details. From your notes, you develop an outline and thesis statement. Then you follow the outline as you write each paragraph of the composition.

You have learned how to develop the main idea of a paragraph. Your supporting details may give narrative information, descriptions, explanations, facts, comparisons, or reasons. Look over your notes and your outline. Then choose the kind of paragraph development that will present each group of ideas in the best way.

In a short composition the first sentence in the opening paragraph is the thesis statement. This sentence states the central idea of the entire composition. The second sentence states the main idea of the paragraph. Detail sentences support the main idea. You may end the paragraph with a concluding sentence that summarizes the main idea.

In a two-paragraph composition, the second paragraph is related to the first. You need to show the reader how they are related. You do so by using a transitional device. A *transitional device* is a word or phrase that begins a new paragraph. The word or phrase shows how the ideas in the new paragraph are connected to previous ideas. Here are some transitional devices:

to begin with	in addition to	similarly
a second (or third)	besides	on the other hand
another	moreover	however
a further	equally important	a final

The last paragraph of the composition begins with a transitional device and also states the main idea of the second paragraph. The detail sentences support the main idea. In addition the final paragraph ends with a conclusion. The *conclusion* is a sentence that summarizes the points you have made in the entire composition.

Now read the following outline and the two–paragraph expository composition based on the outline.

Exercising Without Joining the Team

Thesis Statement: *People who do not like team sports enjoy jogging and bicycle riding as a means of having fun while exercising.*

I. Jogging
- **A.** Need shoes
- **B.** Run miles
- **C.** Improve feeling
- **D.** Get second wind

II. Bicycle riding
- **A.** Provide exercise
- **B.** Build stamina
- **C.** Enjoy view
- **D.** Take long trips

Exercising Without Joining the Team

thesis statement	People who do not like team sports enjoy jogging and bicycle riding as a means of having fun while exercising.
main idea **details (facts)**	To begin with jogging is one of the most popular ways to keep in shape. The only equipment you need is a pair of running shoes and a willing pair of legs. Many joggers run as much as several miles daily. People who jog in the morning claim they feel better all day long. The exercise gives them a "second wind" that carries them until evening.
concluding sentence	Because jogging is one of the simplest ways to exercise, you can see joggers on city and country roads at almost any time of day or night.
transition/ main idea **details (reasons)**	Another popular form of exercise is bicycle riding. This activity provides good exercise for legs, lungs, and heart. It helps build stamina, the ability to endure fatigue and hardship. Bike riders can enjoy the view as they pedal along a scenic path. Friends even travel together on long cross-country trips.
conclusion	So grab your running shoes or bicycle and enjoy your fun and exercise — even when you're not on a team.

Talking About an Expository Composition

Look at the two-paragraph composition about exercise.

1. What is the thesis statement? Where does it appear?
2. What is the main idea in each paragraph?
3. What kinds of details support the main idea in each paragraph?
4. What is the concluding sentence of the first paragraph?
5. What transitional device begins the second paragraph?
6. What sentence is the conclusion of the entire composition?

Writing the First Paragraph of a Composition

Read each group of sentences. Each group comes from the first paragraph of a composition, but the sentences are out of order. Write a paragraph for each group. Begin each paragraph with the thesis statement. Then write the main-idea sentence. Finally write the detail sentences.

1. **a.** I began the collection by buying stamps from stores and dealers.
   b. Then I used the profits from the sale to buy more stamps.
   c. My hobbies are collecting stamps, records, and old magazines.
   d. When I got two of the same stamp, I sold the duplicate.
   e. The hobby I like most is buying, selling, and trading stamps.

2. **a.** First I had to locate home owners who wanted their lawns mowed.
   b. Mowing lawns was the most profitable of the three jobs.
   c. After I mowed each lawn, I collected the payment.
   d. Next the owners and I had to agree on how much I would be paid for the mowing.
   e. Last summer I mowed lawns, delivered newspapers, and sold juice to earn money for a new radio.

3. **a.** Three serious problems today are pollution, inflation, and crime.
   b. Factories must reduce the smoke coming from their chimneys.
   c. One challenge is lessening the amount of air pollution.
   d. Also, car manufacturers should seek ways to eliminate the harmful fumes that automobiles produce.
   e. Last, it is the duty of all private citizens to use household products that do not contaminate the air.

Write the first paragraph of an expository composition, using the following outline.

Caring for My Dog

Thesis statement: *I care for my dog by feeding it, bathing it, walking it, and teaching it obedience.*

I. Feeding
- **A.** Rinse out food dish
- **B.** Pour in dry dog food
- **C.** Mix in water
- **D.** Set out separate dish of water

Writing About the Last Paragraph of a Composition

Read the paragraph below. Then answer the questions that follow.

In addition to thinking about the quality of sound when buying a piano, you must consider the amount of available space. If you don't have much room, you may want to buy a type of vertical piano instead of a grand piano. Vertical pianos come in various sizes and have strings that run up and down. An old-fashioned upright stands about five feet tall and is the biggest of the verticals. Since 1935 smaller pianos have become popular because they fit into modern apartments and homes. The spinet is the smallest vertical piano, measuring less than 39 inches high. A console stands between 39 and 41 inches high. Most pianos sold today are verticals. Whether you buy a grand piano or vertical, you must consider the quality of the sound and your available space.

1. What transitional device introduces the paragraph?
2. What is the main idea in the paragraph?
3. How many detail sentences are there? What kinds of details are they?
4. What sentence is the conclusion of the entire composition?
5. The opening paragraph of the composition does not appear. However, the conclusion indicates what was discussed. What was the topic in the opening paragraph of the composition?

Writing an Expository Composition

Thinking About an Expository Composition

Now you will write a two-paragraph expository composition. The title is "Learning to Be Responsible." Read the following outline for a two-paragraph composition.

Learning to Be Responsible

Thesis statement: *Responsibility can be learned at school and in the home.*

I. At school
- **A.** Arriving at classes on time
- **B.** Paying attention in class
- **C.** Completing assignments on time
- **D.** (Provide your own detail.)

II. In the home
- **A.** Keeping room tidy
- **B.** Taking care of clothes
- **C.** Helping clean after meals
- **D.** (Provide your own detail.)

Practicing an Expository Composition

Use the outline to write a two-paragraph composition entitled "Learning to Be Responsible." Follow these steps:

1. Write the title of the composition at the top of your paper.

2. a. Begin the first paragraph with this thesis statement: *Responsibility can be learned at school and in the home.*

b. Continue the first paragraph with a sentence that states the main idea of the paragraph.

c. Now write four detail sentences that support the main idea.

d. Conclude the first paragraph with a sentence that summarizes your ideas or emphasizes your attitude in the paragraph.

3. a. Begin the second paragraph with a sentence that states the main idea of the paragraph. Use a transitional device to connect your second paragraph to the first one.

b. Continue the second paragraph by writing four detail sentences that support the main idea.

c. Conclude the second paragraph with a sentence that summarizes the two main ideas in your composition.

Edit Your Composition

Read over your expository composition. Use the editing symbols to mark corrections, and use these questions to check your work.

1. Is the entire composition about one main subject?
2. Does each paragraph have a main idea, thesis statement, and supporting details?
3. Do the main ideas and details follow the outline?
4. Does each paragraph end with a concluding sentence?

Editing Symbols

¶	indent
≡	capitalize
∧	add
℘	delete
/	lower case

INDEPENDENT WRITING

An Expository Composition

Prewriting Suppose that your local Junior Chamber of Commerce is sponsoring a contest. They are requesting compositions about improving programs for teenagers. You are going to write a two-paragraph composition explaining one of the following topics or a topic of your own.

How to Earn Money	A Good Youth Program
How to Get a Summer Job	How to Find Volunteer Work

First narrow your topic to a specific subject. Now brainstorm for ideas. Jot down all the ideas you can think of about your topic. Next categorize your notes and eliminate ideas you do not want to use. Finally make an outline. Put your main ideas next to Roman numerals I and II and list your supporting details for each paragraph.

Writing First write a thesis statement that expresses the main idea of the composition. Use the thesis statement as the first sentence. Then write a sentence that tells the main idea of your first paragraph. Write your detail sentences. Be sure to follow your outline.

Begin your second paragraph with a transitional sentence. This sentence shows the reader how the ideas in the first paragraph are connected to the ideas in the second and states the main idea of your second paragraph. Then write your detail sentences. Your last sentence should be a conclusion that sums up the main ideas.

Editing Refer to the checklist at the top of the page, and correct your composition. Recopy your work if necessary.

A Persuasive Composition

Thinking About a Persuasive Composition

A *persuasive composition* persuades someone to accept your point of view. Editorials in a newspaper are examples of persuasive writing.

A persuasive composition is similar in many ways to an expository composition. You begin by selecting and limiting your topic. Then you brainstorm for ideas, organize your notes, develop an outline, and write a thesis statement.

Follow the outline as you develop each paragraph. Decide what kind of paragraph development will convince your readers to agree with your opinion. Details that state facts, examples, or reasons will make readers more sympathetic to your position.

Remember that the first sentence in the first paragraph is the thesis statement. The thesis statement expresses the central idea of the entire composition. The second sentence gives the main idea of the first paragraph. Detail sentences support the main idea. You may end the paragraph with a concluding sentence. The concluding sentence summarizes the main idea or emphasizes your attitude in the paragraph.

If you are writing a three–paragraph composition, both the second and third paragraphs are related to the first. You need to show how they are related by using a transitional device.

The final paragraph of the composition also has a transitional device, a main idea, and supporting details. The final paragraph ends with a conclusion that summarizes and emphasizes your attitude.

Now read the following outline and persuasive composition.

An Indoor Pool for the New High School

Thesis statement: *An indoor swimming pool for the gym of our new high school would benefit the students, provide advantages for the region, and be cost effective.*

I. Benefit students
- **A.** Add to program
- **B.** Swim meets
- **C.** Swim lessons
- **D.** Water safety

II. Provide advantages
- **A.** Open to residents
- **B.** Open evenings
- **C.** Year round
- **D.** Attract new residents

III. Be cost effective
- **A.** Fees reduce cost
- **B.** Guest fees
- **C.** Lesson fees
- **D.** Part of gym

An Indoor Pool for the New High School

thesis statement	An indoor swimming pool in the gym of our new high school would benefit the students, would provide advantages for the region, and would be cost effective.
main idea	First of all an indoor swimming pool would benefit students in many ways.
details (reasons)	Swimming could be added to our gym program. Our school could participate in swim meets. Swimming lessons could be offered as an elective. Water safety courses in lifesaving and boating could also be included.
transition/ main idea	In addition to these benefits for students, an indoor pool would provide important advantages for our towns.
details (reasons)	The pool would be open to town residents. Evening hours would make it possible for people to swim after work. Since the pool would be indoors, people could swim laps for health all year round; and families could enjoy swimming together even in the winter.
concluding sentence	Because a high school with an indoor pool provides so many benefits, it might even attract people to move into one of our towns.
transition/ main idea	Despite the benefits to our students and to our towns, many people feel that a pool would cost too much.
details (reasons)	We can reduce costs by charging pool fees for residents. Guests and nonresidents would also pay a fee. Young children would pay for swimming lessons on weekends. In addition the pool can be easily installed in the basement of the new gym wing.
conclusion	Taking a long-range view, the benefits to students and residents of adding an indoor pool to the new high school will far outweigh the cost.

Talking About a Persuasive Composition

Look again at the persuasive composition.

1. Where does the thesis statement appear in the composition?
2. What is the main idea in each paragraph?
3. What kinds of details support the main idea in each paragraph?
4. What transitional devices begin the second and third paragraphs?
5. What sentence is the conclusion of the entire composition?

Writing a Persuasive Composition

Thinking About a Persuasive Composition

Now you will write a persuasive composition.

Why Time off from School Is Important

Thesis statement: *Students need time off from school so that they can catch up on their rest, pursue individual interests, and participate more in social activities.*

I. Rest
- **A.** Get extra sleep
- **B.** Store energy
- **C.** Relax the mind
- **D.** (Provide your own detail.)

II. Individual Interests
- **A.** Read books
- **B.** Watch TV/movies
- **C.** Write stories
- **D.** (Provide your own detail.)

III. Social Activities
- **A.** Hold parties
- **B.** Play ball
- **C.** Take trips
- **D.** (Provide your own detail.)

Practicing a Persuasive Composition

Use the outline as a guide to writing a three-paragraph persuasive composition entitled "Why Time off from School Is Important." You may change the details in the outline. Follow these steps:

1. Write the title of the composition at the top of your paper.

2. a. Begin the first paragraph with the thesis statement.
b. Continue with a sentence that states the main idea.
c. Write four detail sentences that support the main idea.
d. You may end the paragraph with a concluding sentence that summarizes the main idea or emphasizes your attitude.

3. a. Begin the second paragraph with a sentence that states the main idea of the paragraph. Start with a transitional device.
b. Write four detail sentences that support the main idea.
c. You may end the second paragraph with a concluding sentence.

4. a. Begin the third paragraph with a sentence that starts the main idea of the paragraph. Start with a transitional device.
b. Write four detail sentences that support the main idea.
c. Complete the last paragraph with a conclusion that summarizes all the main ideas in the composition and emphasizes your attitude.

Edit Your Composition

Read your composition. Use the editing symbols to mark corrections.

1. Is the entire composition about one main subject?
2. Do the main ideas and details follow the order of the outline?
3. Do you begin with the thesis statement?
4. Do you use transitional devices?
5. Does the last paragraph have a conclusion?

Editing Symbols

¶	indent
≡	capitalize
∧	add
℘	delete
/	lower case

INDEPENDENT WRITING

A Persuasive Composition

Prewriting You have decided to write a three–paragraph composition to the Editor of your local newspaper. You will persuade the readers to accept your point of view on one of the topics below or on a subject of your own choosing.

A Larger (or Smaller) Budget for Our Sports Program

Our Town/City Needs (topic)

After you have chosen a topic and limited it, brainstorm for ideas. Categorize your ideas and decide on three main topics. Put your main topics beside Roman numerals I, II, and III. List the details that support each main idea. Choose the details that will persuade your readers to accept your point of view.

Writing Start your letter with the greeting, *To the Editor.* Begin your first paragraph with a thesis statement that expresses the central idea of your composition. Continue to write three paragraphs, following your outline. Decide what kind of paragraph development will present your ideas most forcefully to your readers. You may want to use important facts, examples, or valid reasons to make readers more sympathetic to your position. Remember to use transitional devices to help your readers move smoothly from one paragraph to the next. At the end of your third paragraph, write a conclusion that summarizes your main idea or emphasizes your attitude toward your subject.

Editing Use the checklist at the top of the page, and correct your composition. Recopy your work if necessary.

Unit Review

WRITING AND EDITING COMPOSITIONS

Each topic below is too general. Narrow each to make it suitable for a two– or three–paragraph composition. Write the title of your new topic. *pages 334-335*

1. Pets	**3.** Holidays	**5.** Parties
2. Cooking	**4.** Baby-sitting	**6.** Friends

In each group of items below, one idea could serve as the heading for the others. Write the idea that could be the heading. *pages 336-337*

7. Like different shows; parents limit viewing hours; television and my family; three television sets in my house; watch old movies.

8. Focus must be sharp; do not cut off heads; how to take good pictures; adjust lens opening to light; compose picture well.

In each group of items, one detail does not belong. Write the detail that does not belong. *pages 336-337*

9. Weighed in luggage at counter; received seat number; smiled at pilot; held breath at takeoff; watched the city lights sparkle below; read magazine; bought souvenirs at open air market.

10. Stood in line three hours; bought two tickets; rushed to seats; cheered for rock group; listened to music; waited at stage door; practiced guitar for three hours.

Read each group of main ideas from an outline. Write a thesis statement that summarizes all the main ideas. *pages 338-339*

11. I. The first step in windsurfing is to climb onto the sailboard.
II. The next step in windsurfing is to pull the sail up out of the water.
III. The third step in windsurfing is to hold the sail steady.

12. I. A reporter writing a story takes many notes.
II. A reporter puts the most important facts first.
III. A reporter writes fast to meet the deadline.

13. The following details belong in an outline for a two-paragraph expository composition entitled "How to Vote Intelligently." Write the details in the proper order. Then write a thesis statement that summarizes the main ideas. Finally write the first paragraph of the composition. *pages 340-345*

1. Learn as much as you can about the pros and cons of each issue.
2. Decide for whom you will vote and why.
3. Learning about the issues
4. Find out how the candidates stand on important issues.
5. Decide whether you will vote *yes* or *no* and why.
6. Knowing the candidates
7. Find out what referendum questions will be on the ballot.
8. Study the past voting records of the candidates.

14. Write a two-paragraph persuasive composition using the thesis statement and outline given below, or write a persuasive composition on a topic you choose. *pages 346-349*

Solving the Video Game Problem

Thesis statement: *Because many people feel that arcade video games cause problems, our town council should study the effects on children and decide on regulations if necessary.*

I. Study effects on children
  A. Playing during school
  B. Spending money
  C. (Provide your own detail.)

II. Decide on regulations
  A. Supervision by parents
  B. Hours of operation
  C. (Provide your own detail.)

Exploring Language

When you use words in unexpected or unusual ways to create a picture or to make a comparison, you are using *figurative language.* In one kind of figurative language, names of parts of the body are used as verbs. These verbs are usually used in informal speech. Here are a few examples:

My friends are *footing* the bill for dinner.
I can't *stomach* the sight of liver.

An archaeologist works to reassemble mosaics at Mt. Zion, Jerusalem.

Attempt the end, and never stand to doubt;
Nothing's so hard but search will find it out.

ROBERT HERRICK
American novelist and educator
(1868-1938)

19

WRITING AND EDITING A RESEARCH PAPER

A Research Report

Most likely, much of the writing you have done up to now has come out of your own knowledge and opinions. Sometimes you might be assigned to write a research report. A research report involves finding out information on a subject using outside sources. The assignment requires careful preparation. Use the following steps to help make your assignment as easy as possible.

Prewriting

1. Choose a topic.
2. Locate your research sources.
3. Take complete notes on your sources.
4. Outline your report and write a thesis statement.

Writing

5. Write a draft of the report.

Editing

6. Edit your draft of the report.
7. Make a clean copy of your edited draft.
8. Prepare a bibliography of your sources.

Thinking About a Research Report

Read this research report about nutrition, which was written by a student named Jody. Notice how Jody followed the Prewriting, Writing, and Editing steps to write her research report.

1. Jody planned to write a research report for her Life Sciences class about three sources of nutrition: proteins, minerals, and vitamins.
2. Jody went to the library to locate resource material on her topic. She used the library card catalog to find a book on nutrition. She also used an encyclopedia, an almanac, and a dictionary.
3. Jody took notes on the information. Here are the notecards she made.

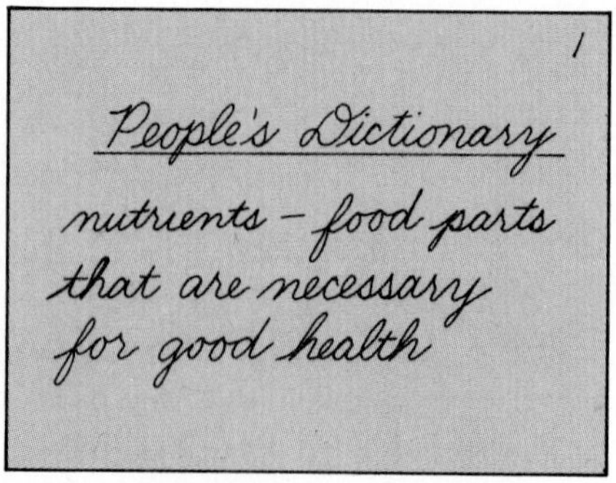
1
People's Dictionary
nutrients – food parts
that are necessary
for good health

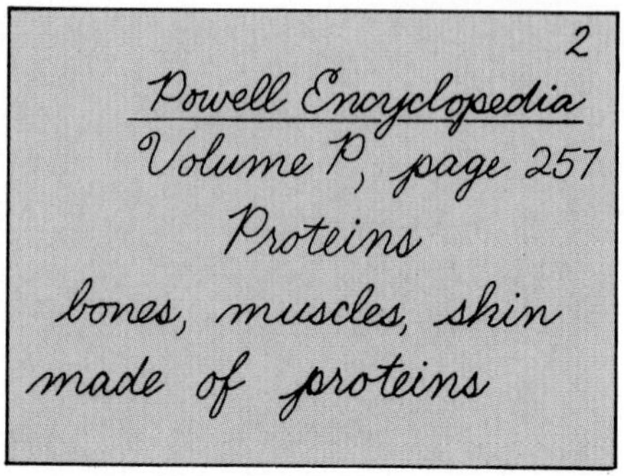
2
Powell Encyclopedia
Volume P, page 257
Proteins
bones, muscles, skin
made of proteins

3
Powell Encyclopedia
Volume M, page 154
Minerals
calcium important
part of bones and teeth

4
Powell Encyclopedia
Volume V, page 143
Vitamins
body can't make vitamins
vitamin A - skin/bones
vitamin C - body tissue

5
Nutrition R. A. Mann
Proteins
provide energy, page 76

6
Nutrition R. A. Mann
Minerals
iron important part
of blood, page 52

7
Nutrition R. A. Mann
Proteins
found in cheese, eggs,
fish, meat, milk, grains,
vegetables, page 77

8
Everyfact Almanac
Vitamins
4500 units vitamin A
45 units vitamin C
Daily amount for 13 yr. old
page 15

9
Everyfact Almanac
Vitamins
raw tomato (1 whole)
2200 units vitamin A
46 milligrams vitamin C
page 15

10
Everyfact Almanac
Minerals
1200 milligrams calcium
18 milligrams iron
Daily amount for 13 yr. old
page 14

4. Look again at Jody's notecards. Notice that Jody has given each notecard a number and a topic heading: minerals, vitamins, and proteins. Because all her notes belong to one of these three topics, Jody decided to write her report in three paragraphs.

Jody also wrote a thesis statement. A *thesis statement* is a sentence that summarizes the main ideas in an essay.

Here is the thesis statement and outline Jody wrote for her report.

Three Important Nutrients

Thesis statement: *Three important nutrients, or food parts that are necessary for good health, are protein, minerals, and vitamins.*

I. Proteins
- **A.** Proteins for bones, muscles, skin
- **B.** Proteins for energy
- **C.** Foods with protein
- **D.** Daily requirement of protein

II. Minerals
- **A.** Calcium for bones, teeth
- **B.** Iron for blood
- **C.** Foods with minerals
- **D.** Daily requirement of minerals

III. Vitamins
- **A.** Body's dependence on food for vitamins
- **B.** Vitamins A, C for skin, bones, tissue
- **C.** Food with vitamins
- **D.** Daily requirement of vitamins

5., 6., and 7. Then Jody made a draft of her report, edited it, and made a revised copy. All three paragraphs in the report were about the same main subject. Each paragraph had its own topic sentence and detail sentences. Here is the report she wrote:

Three Important Nutrients

Three important nutrients necessary for good health are proteins, minerals, and vitamins. Proteins provide energy and are necessary for growth and maintenance of the body. Bones, muscles, and skin are made up largely of proteins, and proteins also provide energy. Proteins are found mostly in cheese, eggs, fish, meat, and milk.

A second important nutrient is minerals. Calcium is essential for strong bones and teeth. Iron is an important part of blood. A 13 year old needs 1200 milligrams of calcium and 18 milligrams of iron daily.

Finally, vitamins are necessary for good health. The body cannot make vitamins, so it finds them in food. Vitamin A is needed for healthy skin and bones, and vitamin C helps maintain body tissue. A raw tomato provides 2200 units of vitamin A and 46 milligrams of vitamin C. Daily requirements for a 13-year-old are 4500 units of vitamin A and 45 units of vitamin C. In order for people to stay healthy, they should eat foods that provide sufficient proteins, minerals, and vitamins.

8. Jody compiled bibliography cards as she read and took notes. A *bibliography* is a list of the sources of information used in preparing a report. Here are Jody's bibliography cards.

After Jody made a copy of her edited report, she added a bibliography to acknowledge where she had found her information.

Bibliography

Mann, R.A., Nutrition, New York, Spiral Books, 1976.

"Nutrients," Powell Encyclopedia, Vol. 18, Chicago, Powell Books Inc., 1972.

"Nutritional Values of Common Foods," Everyfact Almanac, Los Angeles, Sommers Publishing Co., 1979.

People's Dictionary, New York, The People's Press, 1975.

Talking About a Research Report

Look again at the steps Jody followed to write her report.

1. What other resources could Jody have used to learn about nutrients?
2. What information was written on each notecard?
3. What was the thesis statement of the entire report? What was the topic sentence in each paragraph?
4. Are Jody's bibliography cards written correctly? What information did she include on each one?

Reviewing Research Skills

A research report is based on careful study of a particular subject. Here is a checklist of steps that will help you plan, organize, and write a research report.

Prewriting Steps

1. Select a topic or subject that is narrow enough for a short paper.
2. Locate your research sources. Compile a list of several types of sources you could use to find information on your topic. Begin your reading with general reference works such as encyclopedias and periodicals. Consult the card catalog and periodical indexes in a library to locate a list of specific sources. You can also obtain information from nonprint sources such as films or interviews.

   Prepare a bibliography card for each reference source. Include on each card the author's name, the title, the place of publication, the publisher's name, and the copyright date. If the source is an article, include the author's name, the title of the article and book or periodical, the volume, and page numbers. Remember to keep the cards in alphabetical order.

   Skim the pages of books or articles to be sure the source will provide you with helpful material related to your topic.
3. Take notes on information that you think may be useable. Summarize the information on notecards. Give each notecard a number and a topic heading. Be sure to summarize in your own words. Record each reference source on one notecard. Use quotation marks if you quote an author directly. Include on the notecard the author's name and the title of the source. After each note write the page number on which that information was found.
4. Study your notecards and consider how to arrange them into a thesis statement and outline. Arrange the notecards into groups with related headings. Based on what you have learned, write a thesis statement that states the main idea of your topic.

   Write your outline with Roman numeral divisions to indicate the main topics. Use the same kind of words or phrases, or parallel sentence structure to name them. Include capital letters beneath these main ideas to show supporting ideas or subtopics. These, too, should have parallel grammatical structure.

Writing Steps

5. Using your outline and thesis statement as a guide, write a draft of your report.

Editing Steps

6. Read your report. Consider your reader. Will the person who reads your report understand it? Do you need to find more facts to support your thesis statement? Do you use logical connecting words to help your reader follow as you move from one subtopic to the next? Does each paragraph have unity? Are your spelling and punctuation correct?
7. After you have edited your draft, make a clean copy. Then write a bibliography listing all the sources of information that you used.

Talking About Research Skills

Discuss these questions in relation to a two-paragraph report on the topic of "The Life Cycle of the Butterfly."

1. Name three sources that might help you research this topic.
2. How would you go about compiling a bibliography?
3. What related subjects might help you find information on butterflies?

Practicing Research Skills

Write the answers to these questions in relation to a two-paragraph report on "The Life Cycle of the Butterfly."

1. List all the things you can see that are wrong with this notecard.

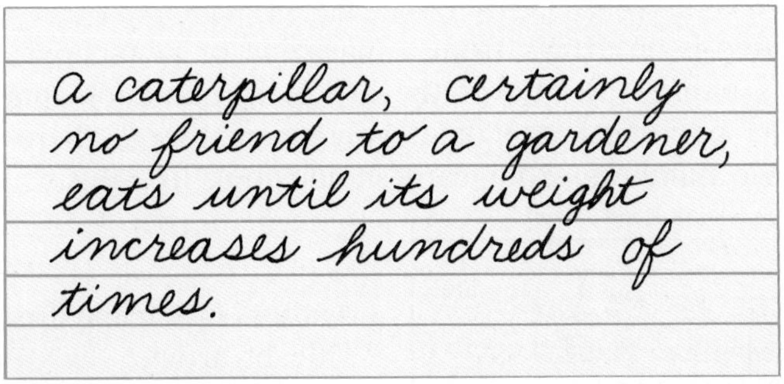
a caterpillar, certainly
no friend to a gardener,
eats until its weight
increases hundreds of
times.

2. Arrange these main topics and subtopics in outline form.
   1. Caterpillar hatches
   2. Caterpillar makes pupa
   3. From egg to pupal stage
   4. Caterpillar sheds skin
   5. From pupa to butterfly
   6. Hard shell forms
   7. Female lays egg
   8. Butterfly cracks shell
3. Write a bibliography card for this article: "Caterpillar in the Garden," by G. Roth in the *Garden Observer.* May, 1978, pages 23 to 26.

Developing a Bibliography

Whenever you do research, you collect information from a variety of books and articles. These books and articles make up your bibliography. A *bibliography* is an alphabetical list of books and articles you use to write your research report. You will probably make two bibliographies, a beginning and final one.

A beginning bibliography contains a list of books, articles, and other materials that look like helpful sources for your report. You compile this bibliography by using the card catalog and periodical indexes. Here are some guidelines for making a bibliography.

1. Keep a set of bibliography cards. The 3 x 5 file cards are a good size.
2. If your source is a book, write the author's name. Put the last name first. Put a comma after the name. Then write the title of the book, the city in which it was published, the name of publisher, and the year of publication. Your card should look like this:

> Fawcett, Julia
> Australia, Land Down Under,
> New York,
> University Books, 1982.

Author, last name first
Title
Place of publication
Name of publisher
Date of publication

3. If your source is an article from a magazine or newspaper, include the author's name, the title of the article in quotation marks, the name of the periodical, the date, volume number if there is one, and the page numbers. Your card should look like this:

> Hailey, Thomas, "Through
> the Outback and Back,"
> The New York Times Magazine
> May 21, 1983 pp. 26-31.

Author, last name first
Title of article
Periodical name
Date and page numbers

Keep your bibliography cards in alphabetical order. As you do your research, you may add new cards and get rid of cards for books or articles you do not need.

Here is a bibliography you might compile for a report on native plants and animals of Australia:

"Australia-Animals," *The All-Purpose Encyclopedia,* Vol. 1, Houston, College Press, 1978.

Harrison, Peter, *Australia's Flora and Fauna,* New York, Eastern Press, 1978.

Lamartine, Hannah, *Animals of Australia,* San Francisco, Foster Publications, 1977.

Notice that the first item listed above does not begin with an author's name. When using a source such as an encyclopedia article that does not identify the author, begin your listing with the title of the article. Put quotation marks around the title.

Talking About a Bibliography

Discuss how you would prepare a bibliography card for each.

1. A book entitled *Rome in the Dark Ages* by Peter Llewellyn, published in New York and Washington by Praeger Publishers in 1971

2. An article entitled "Invisible Plants" by Clara Jacobs and printed in a magazine, *Weekend Botanist,* in May, 1977, on pages 22 to 26

Practicing a Bibliography

Write a bibliography card for each book or article.

1. An article entitled "Bionics for Tomorrow," written by David Greenley in a magazine called *Tomorrow's Science* in January, 1976, pages 18 to 23

2. A book entitled *The View from Morningside, One Family's New York* by Constance Tabor Colby, published by J. P. Lippincott Co. in Philadelphia and New York in 1978

3. An article entitled "New Ideas About the Ice Age" by Robin J. Weekly, published in a magazine called *Science for Everyone* in February, 1978, pages 21 to 26

A Research Report

Now you are ready to write your own research report using the *Prewriting, Writing,* and *Editing* steps. The steps below are numbered to help you follow them.

Prewriting

1. *Select a topic.* Limit your topic to a subject that can be covered adequately in three paragraphs.

2. *Locate your reference sources.* Use the library for resource materials such as encyclopedias, almanacs, and atlases, to gather information on your topic. Make use of the card catalog to locate books and the *Readers' Guide to Periodical Literature* to find information in magazine articles. You can also get information from nonprint media as well as interviews and surveys. Skim the written sources and decide which ones will be useful to your report. Write a bibliography card for each reference source that you will use in your report.

3. *Take complete notes on your sources.* Keep your notes brief and exact. Write notes about *one* topic from *one* source on each 3″ X 5″ index card. Be sure to write the title and author of the source at the top of each card. Write a number and a topic heading on each notecard to help you organize the information you find for your outline. Put quotation marks around any sentences that are quoted exactly from a source. Next organize all the notecards with the same topic heading into one group. Then arrange the groups into the best possible order.

4. *Write a thesis statement and outline.* Think back on what you have learned from your research and write a sentence that summarizes the main ideas of the topic. This sentence will be the thesis statement for your report.

Now write an outline of the main ideas that you will use to develop your thesis statement. The main headings of the outline will present the main topics while the subheadings will list the details that support the main headings. Use Roman numerals to indicate the main headings in your outline and capital letters to indicate subheadings.

Writing

5. *Write a draft of the report.* Reread your thesis statement and, using your outline as a guide, begin writing your report. Do not worry about correct spelling and punctuation at this point. Write down your report as if you were telling a friend about your research. State the information in the order that it occurs in your outline.

Editing

6. *Edit your draft of the report.*

Edit Your Research Report

Read your report. Use the editing symbols to mark corrections. Also use this checklist of questions. Then make a good copy of your report.

1. Does your outline have main headings? Do the subheadings relate to each main heading?
2. Does your report follow the outline you developed?
3. Does the report have a thesis statement, transitional devices, and a conclusion?
4. Are all the paragraphs about the same main subject?
5. Does each paragraph have its own topic sentence?
6. Did you indent the first word of the new paragraph?
7. Did you use capital letters and punctuate correctly?
8. Are all your words spelled correctly?

Editing Symbols

¶	indent
≡	capitalize
∧	add
ℓ	delete
/	lower case

What actions are unfolding behind this reader's languid posture?

Every time I open a book, I risk my life. . . .
Every work of imagination offers another view of life, an invitation to spend a few days inside someone else's emotions.

ANATOLE BROYARD
American author and critic (1920-)

20

WRITING BOOK REPORTS, LETTERS, AND FORMS

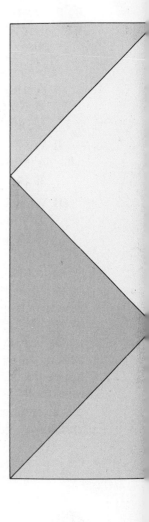

A Book Report

Thinking About a Book Report

Writing a book review can add to your enjoyment of a book. It may help you remember the book for a long time. Also, your review lets you share the book with friends.

A book review should include the following information:

I General information about the book
- **A** Title and author
- **B** Kind of book
- **C** Setting

II What the book is about
- **A** Main characters
- **B** Plot

III What you think about the book
- **A** Your opinion
- **B** Reasons for your opinion

Your first paragraph should tell the title of the book, the author's name, and the kind of book. It should also describe the setting, or where and when the story takes place. The second paragraph should briefly describe the main characters, and summarize the plot. The plot is the action of the story. Do not describe every small detail of the action. Just tell about the important events in the order in which they happened. Do not give away the ending of the story. If you do, you may spoil the surprise for others who might read the book. In the last paragraph, give your opinion of the book. Make your opinion convincing by backing it up with good reasons.

Read the example of a book review that follows.

The Call of the Wild is an exciting adventure novel written by Jack London. It takes place in Alaska at the time of the Klondike gold rush.

The main characters in *The Call of the Wild* are a dog named Buck and his master, John Thornton. Buck, half Saint Bernard and half Scotch Shepherd, is kidnapped from his comfortable home in California to be a sled dog in Alaska. John Thornton is a gold prospector who saves Buck from his cruel owner in Alaska. The story begins when Buck is kidnapped and goes on to describe his life as a sled dog. In Alaska Buck is beaten, starved, and forced to work until he almost dies of exhaustion. He becomes a fierce fighter and battles his way to the position of lead dog. After he is rescued by John Thornton, Buck's life improves.

I enjoyed *The Call of the Wild* for three reasons. First Jack London describes the setting so realistically that I could actually see the frozen wastelands and primitive Alaskan mining towns. Second the author makes the reader think of Buck as a person. Finally the story is filled with adventure.

INDEPENDENT WRITING

A Book Report

Prewriting First choose a book that you have read and enjoyed. Look at the outline on page 366. Make notes about your book in outline form. Be sure to make notes for each item of the outline.

Writing Write a book review of the book you have chosen. Start with an introductory paragraph that gives the book's title and author. Remember to underline the title. Also tell the reader what type of book it is. (Is it a novel, a biography? Is it science fiction, adventure?) Briefly describe the setting, or time and place, of the story.

Your second paragraph should tell about the main characters and the plot. Write a topic sentence that lists the names of the most important characters. Next write detail sentences about each one. Give only important descriptions. Leave out minor details. Then summarize the plot. Write one sentence that tells what the book is about. Write detail sentences that tell about the most important events in the order in which they occur in the book.

In the last paragraph, tell your opinion of the book. The topic sentence should state whether you liked the book or not. Detail sentences should give reasons for your opinion.

Edit Your Book Report

Read your report. You may use the editing symbols and the questions below to check your work. Then make a revised copy of the report.

1. Does each topic sentence give the main idea of the paragraph?
2. Do your detail sentences tell more about the topic sentences?
3. Did you capitalize and punctuate correctly?
4. Did you indent each new paragraph?

Editing Symbols

¶	indent
≡	capitalize
∧	add
ℓ	delete
/	lower case

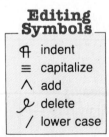

A Friendly Letter

Thinking About a Friendly Letter

We communicate with people in many ways. Often we speak with others in person. Sometimes we talk to individuals by telephone.

Letters are frequently the best way to communicate with friends. Writing allows you time to say exactly what you mean. Also, a letter can be read over to keep thoughts fresh. Letters written to friends and family are called *friendly letters*.

- Read the friendly letter below. Notice how it is organized in five main parts.

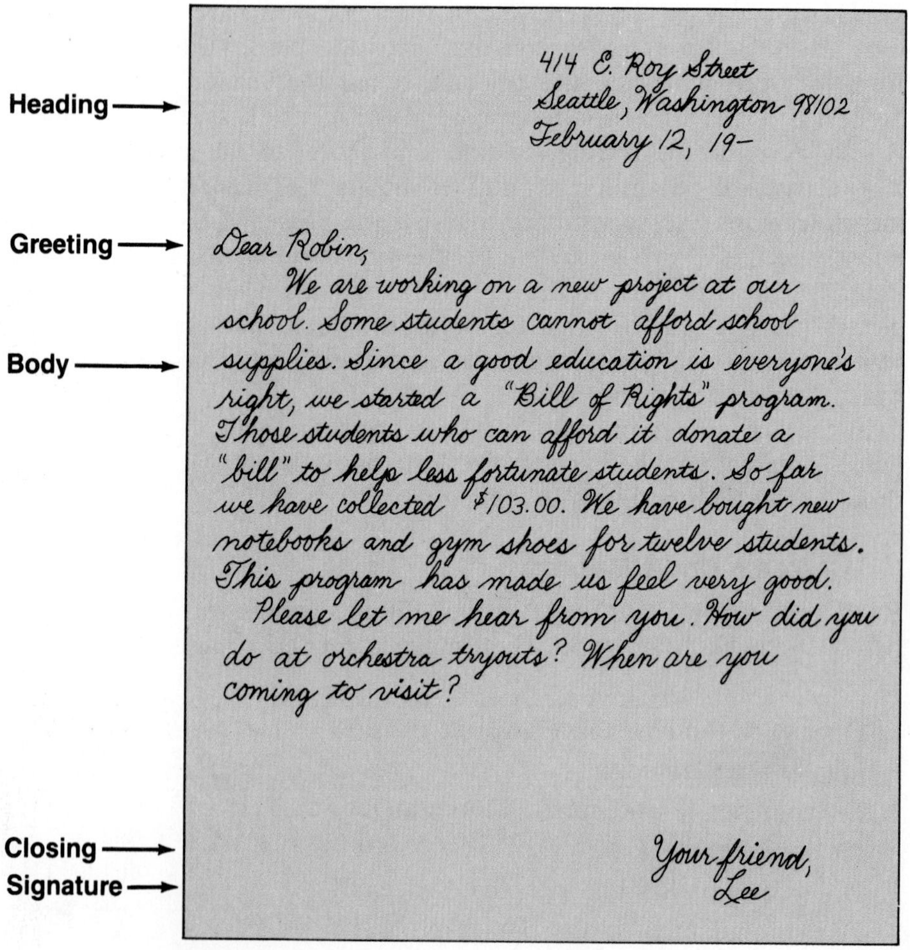

414 E. Roy Street
Seattle, Washington 98102
February 12, 19–

Dear Robin,

We are working on a new project at our school. Some students cannot afford school supplies. Since a good education is everyone's right, we started a "Bill of Rights" program. Those students who can afford it donate a "bill" to help less fortunate students. So far we have collected $103.00. We have bought new notebooks and gym shoes for twelve students. This program has made us feel very good.

Please let me hear from you. How did you do at orchestra tryouts? When are you coming to visit?

Your friend,
Lee

Talking About a Friendly Letter

Read Lee's friendly letter again.

1. The *heading* includes the writer's address and the date. This heading goes in the upper right corner of the page. Where is a comma used in the address? Where is a comma used in the date?
2. You say "hello" to your friend in the *greeting* of the letter. Why do you think Lee wrote his friend's first name only in the greeting?
3. The *body* of the letter contains the message. Remember to indent all paragraphs. The first paragraph of Lee's letter describes his school project.
   a. What is the topic sentence of the paragraph?
   b. How many detail sentences are in the first paragraph?
   c. Do you think the "Bill of Rights" program is explained well? Why or why not?
   d. What words describe nouns in the first paragraph?
   e. What action words are in the first paragraph?
4. You say "goodbye" to your friend in the *closing* of the letter. Where is the closing placed in Lee's letter? Where is a comma used in the closing?
5. Your *signature* goes beneath the closing. Why do you think Lee signed his first name only?

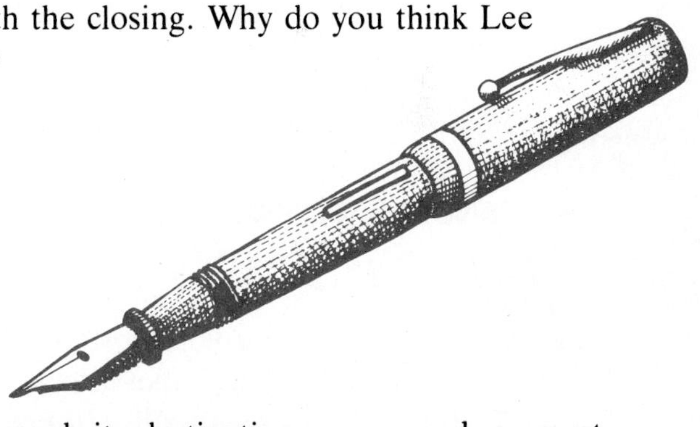

In order for your letter to reach its destination, your envelope must be addressed in a certain style.

The return address goes in the upper left hand corner of the envelope. It should indicate your name as well as your address.

The name and address of the person to whom you are writing are placed just below and to the right of center on the envelope. The address of the envelope should be the same as the inside address of the letter, including any titles. Always use the Zip Code in the address.

Writing a Friendly Letter

You have learned that a friendly letter is another way to communicate with friends and family members.

A friendly letter uses an informal writing style. Since a letter reflects the person who wrote it, your letter should be organized and neat.

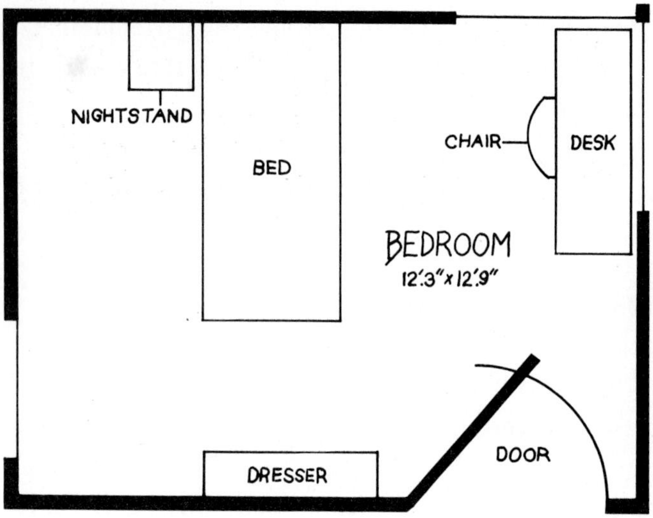

INDEPENDENT WRITING

A Friendly Letter

Prewriting Suppose you move to a different city. Write a letter to a friend. Use the diagram above to get ideas, if you wish. First you need to study the room carefully. Notice all the details. Then jot down notes that describe how your room looks.

Writing Write a letter to your friend. Follow the form on page 368 of this book. Begin your letter with a topic sentence. The body of your letter will be a descriptive paragraph that tells about the furniture, the walls, or the size of your room. Then write a second short paragraph. In it suggest that your friends write a description of their rooms and send it to you.

Terry Bisbee

Edit Your Letter

Editing is an important step in the writing process. Read your letter over. Use the editing symbols to mark corrections. Refer to the check questions below to help you edit your letter. Make any changes that will improve your letter so that your message is precise and clear. Then write a revised copy of your letter.

1. Does your letter have a heading, greeting, body, closing, and signature?
2. Does the topic sentence of each paragraph state the main idea?
3. Do the detail sentences tell more about the topic sentence?
4. Did you use colorful words to describe your room?
5. Did you end the last paragraph of your letter with a concluding sentence?
6. Is each new paragraph indented?
7. Did you use commas properly in the heading, greeting, and closing?
8. Did you use correct capitalization and punctuation in your sentences?

Editing Symbols

- ¶ indent
- ≡ capitalize
- ∧ add
- ℓ delete
- / lower case

A Business Letter

Thinking About a Business Letter

Sometimes you want to obtain information, make a complaint, or place an order. You might perform these tasks by phone. However, it is usually better to write a *business letter*. First your letter is a written record of your business. Also, a letter gives you time to express yourself clearly and politely.

The style of a business letter is a little different from the style of a friendly letter. A business letter is briefer and more formal. The letter should include all the necessary information.

- Read the following business letter.

Heading →

15 Maple Drive
Pine Bluff, Arkansas 60211
November 4, 19___

Inside address →

Adopt-a-Child Plan
P.O. Box 23
Chicago, Illinois 60645

Greeting →

Dear Adopt-a-Child Plan:

Body →

Our class learned about your organization in social studies. We would like to "adopt" a child in South America. Our teacher, Ms. Harriet Warren, is in charge. A committee of seventh graders will give money, write letters, and send holiday presents. Could you please send us more information about your organization?

We look forward to hearing about our new "family member." Thank you.

Closing →

Yours truly,

Signature →

Jerome Gross
Jerome Gross

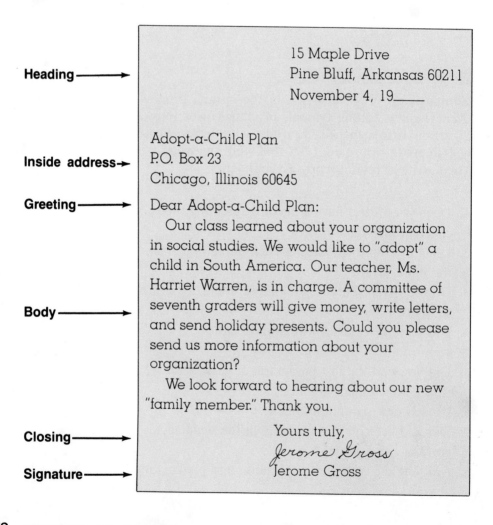

Notice the parts of a business letter.

1. **Heading.** The heading of a business letter is the same as in a friendly letter. It includes the writer's address and the date. Write the heading in the upper right corner of the page. Do not forget to use commas in the address and date.

2. **Inside Address.** Write the name and address of the person or company receiving the letter. Include the Zip Code. Put the inside address at the left margin of the letter.

3. **Greeting.** When writing to a company, use the greeting *Dear (name of company)*. When writing to a person, use *Dear Mr. (name), Dear Mrs. (name),* or *Dear Ms. (name)*. Put a colon (:) after your greeting.

4. **Body.** The body of your letter should be businesslike, clear, and polite. Even in a letter of complaint, complain politely. Remember to indent your paragraphs.

5. **Closing.** The correct closing for a business letter is *Yours truly* or *Very truly yours*. Place a comma after the closing of the letter.

6. **Signature.** Write your full name under the closing. If you type the letter, sign your name in ink. Also, type your name under the signature.

7. Be sure to address the envelope clearly. Write your own address in the upper left corner of the envelope.

Talking About a Business Letter

Read Jerome's business letter again.

1. What is the topic sentence in the first paragraph of the letter?

2. Do the detail sentences give more information about the main idea?

3. Why was it necessary for Jerome to write his own address in the letter?

4. Why do you think Jerome typed his name under his signature?

5. Do you think Jerome's letter was businesslike, clear, and polite? Give reasons for your answer.

Writing a Business Letter

Thinking About a Business Letter

As you know a business letter is a formal means of communication. In business, people expect a letter to have a certain style and form so that they can understand and reply to the letter quickly and accurately.

THE CRUISE OF YOUR LIFE

for ONLY $299.99

Attention travel lovers! Have you always wanted to take a long trip by ship? Have you been waiting for a journey that you could afford?

Well, wait no longer! Our ship, the S.S. Happiness, will sail next week on a cruise to the South Seas. You will sleep in a large, fancy cabin. The food will be prepared by the world's best chefs. And there will be a lot of entertainment on board.

All this can be yours for only $299.99. Sign up now. Send your money to Happiness Cruises, Inc., 11 Harbor Bay, Atlantic City, New Jersey 08243.

A Business Letter

Prewriting Suppose you read the preceding advertisement in a newspaper, and you signed up for the cruise. Several things, however, go wrong during the trip. Perhaps your room was very small. Maybe the food was terrible or there was no entertainment. You decide to write a business letter in which you ask for a refund. Make notes of the reasons why you were unhappy with the cruise.

Writing Write a business letter to Happiness Cruises, Inc. Follow the form for a business letter on page 372 of this book. Begin your first paragraph with a topic sentence. The body of your letter should be a paragraph of facts that accurately explains what happened and why you are dissatisfied with the cruise. In your second paragraph, ask for your money back. Write a topic sentence to express this idea. Then explain why you want your money back.

Edit Your Business Letter

Read your letter over. Look for any mistakes you might have made. You may use the editing symbols to mark your corrections. The questions below will help you edit your work. Then make a revised copy of your letter.

1. Does each topic sentence state the main idea of the paragraph?
2. Does each detail sentence give information about the topic sentence?
3. Did you write the heading and inside address correctly?
4. Did you use commas in the heading, inside address, and closing?
5. Did you use a colon in the greeting?
6. Did you indent the first word in each paragraph?
7. Did you use correct capitalization and punctuation in your sentences?

Editing Symbols

¶	indent
≡	capitalize
∧	add
ℓ	delete
/	lower case

Thinking About Business Forms

Business forms are a way of life. A business form is a printed request for facts and information. Since business forms vary in purpose and style, it is important to read the directions carefully.

Be sure to use a pen when filling out a business form and print or write neatly all the information requested.

- Familiarize yourself with the two types of forms below. The first is a money order and the second is a bank deposit slip.

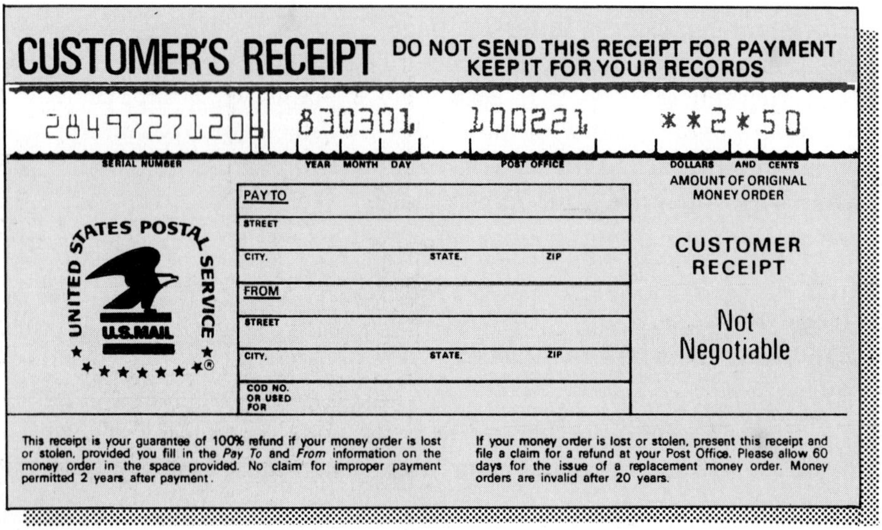

CUSTOMER'S RECEIPT DO NOT SEND THIS RECEIPT FOR PAYMENT KEEP IT FOR YOUR RECORDS

2849727120 | 830301 | 100221 | **2*50

SERIAL NUMBER | YEAR MONTH DAY | POST OFFICE | DOLLARS AND CENTS AMOUNT OF ORIGINAL MONEY ORDER

UNITED STATES POSTAL SERVICE U.S.MAIL

PAY TO

STREET

CITY, STATE, ZIP

FROM

STREET

CITY, STATE, ZIP

COD NO. OR USED FOR

CUSTOMER RECEIPT

Not Negotiable

This receipt is your guarantee of 100% refund if your money order is lost or stolen, provided you fill in the *Pay To* and *From* information on the money order in the space provided. No claim for improper payment permitted 2 years after payment.

If your money order is lost or stolen, present this receipt and file a claim for a refund at your Post Office. Please allow 60 days for the issue of a replacement money order. Money orders are invalid after 20 years.

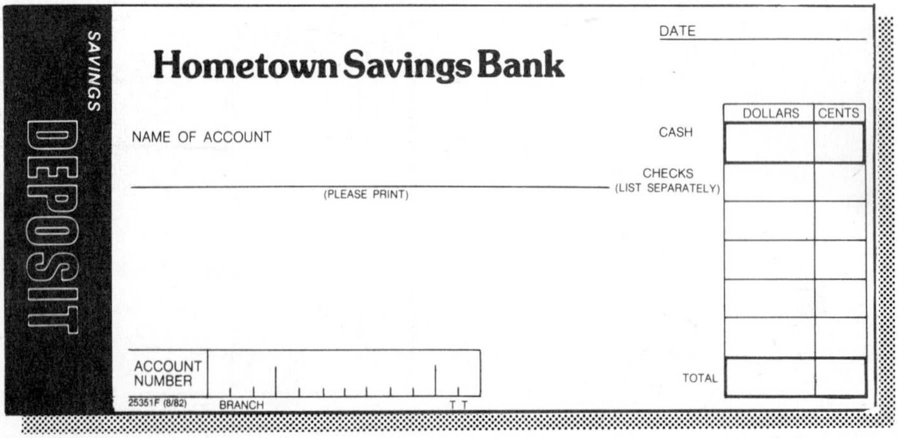

SAVINGS DEPOSIT

Hometown Savings Bank

DATE

NAME OF ACCOUNT

(PLEASE PRINT)

	DOLLARS	CENTS
CASH		
CHECKS (LIST SEPARATELY)		
TOTAL		

ACCOUNT NUMBER

25351F (8/82) BRANCH T T

• Study the following application for a Social Security number. Note the information requested.

DEPARTMENT OF HEALTH AND HUMAN SERVICES
SOCIAL SECURITY ADMINISTRATION

Form Approved
OMB No. 0960-0066

FORM SS-5 — APPLICATION FOR A SOCIAL SECURITY NUMBER CARD (Original, Replacement or Correction)

MICROFILM REF. NO. (SSA USE ONLY)

Unless the requested information is provided, we may not be able to issue a Social Security Number (20 CFR 422.103(b))

INSTRUCTIONS TO APPLICANT ▶ Before completing this form, please read the instructions on the opposite page. You can type or print, using pen with dark blue or black ink. Do not use pencil.

NAA 1 NAME TO BE SHOWN ON CARD — First | Middle | Last

NAB FULL NAME AT BIRTH (IF OTHER THAN ABOVE) — First | Middle | Last

ONA OTHER NAME(S) USED

STT 2 MAILING ADDRESS (Street/Apt. No., P.O. Box, Rural Route No.)

CTY STE ZIP CITY | STATE | ZIP CODE

CSP 3 CITIZENSHIP (Check one only)
- ☐ a. U.S. citizen
- ☐ b. Legal alien allowed to work
- ☐ c. Legal alien not allowed to work
- ☐ d. Other (See instructions on Page 2)

SEX 4 SEX
- ☐ MALE
- ☐ FEMALE

ETB 5 RACE/ETHNIC DESCRIPTION (Check one only) (Voluntary)
- ☐ a. Asian, Asian-American or Pacific Islander (Includes persons of Chinese, Filipino, Japanese, Korean, Samoan, etc., ancestry or descent)
- ☐ b. Hispanic (Includes persons of Chicano, Cuban, Mexican or Mexican-American, Puerto Rican, South or Central American, or other Spanish ancestry or descent)
- ☐ c. Negro or Black (not Hispanic)
- ☐ d. North American Indian or Alaskan Native
- ☐ e. White (not Hispanic)

DOB 6 DATE OF BIRTH ▶ MONTH | DAY | YEAR

AGE 7 PRESENT AGE

PLB 8 PLACE OF BIRTH ▶ CITY | STATE OR FOREIGN COUNTRY | FCI ☐

MNA 9 MOTHER'S NAME AT HER BIRTH — First | Middle | Last (her maiden name)

FNA FATHER'S NAME — First | Middle | Last

PNO 10 a. Has the person listed in Item 1 above or anyone acting on that person's behalf ever applied for a social security number card before? ☐ YES (2) ☐ NO (1) ☐ Don't know (1) If yes, when: MONTH | YEAR

b. Was a card received? ☐ YES (3) ☐ NO (1) ☐ Don't know (1) **If you checked yes to a or b, complete items c through e; otherwise go to Item 11.**

SSN c. Enter Social Security Number ☐☐☐–☐☐–☐☐☐☐

NLC d. Enter the name shown on the most recent social security card

PDB e. Date of birth correction (See Instruction 10 on page 2) ▶ MONTH | DAY | YEAR

DON 11 TODAY'S DATE ▶ MONTH | DAY | YEAR

12 Telephone number where we can reach you during the day. Please include the area code. ▶ HOME | OTHER

ASD **WARNING: Deliberately furnishing (or causing to be furnished) false information on this application is a crime punishable by fine or imprisonment, or both.**

13 YOUR SIGNATURE

14 YOUR RELATIONSHIP TO PERSON IN ITEM 1 ☐ Self ☐ Other (Specify) ____________

WITNESS (Needed only if signed by mark "X") | WITNESS (Needed only if signed by mark "X")

DO NOT WRITE BELOW THIS LINE (FOR SSA USE ONLY) | DTC | SSA RECEIPT DATE:

SSN ASSIGNED ☐☐☐–☐☐–☐☐☐☐ | NPN

DOC | NTC | CAN | BIC | SIGNATURE AND TITLE OF EMPLOYEE(S) REVIEWING EVIDENCE AND/OR CONDUCTING INTERVIEW.

TYPE(S) OF EVIDENCE SUBMITTED | ☐ MANDATORY IN PERSON INTERVIEW CONDUCTED | DATE | DATE

IDN | ITV | DCL

Form SS-5 (7-82) 3

Talking About Business Forms

1. Why is it important to fill out a form neatly?
2. Why is it important to read over your completed form?
3. What business forms, if any, have you ever filled out? What information did they require?

Unit Review

WRITING BOOK REPORTS, LETTERS, AND FORMS

1. Write a friendly letter. Use a *descriptive paragraph* for the body of the letter. Try to include colorful words to describe nouns and action words. Remember that a letter also has a *heading*, a *greeting*, a *closing*, and a *signature*. Edit your letter carefully for capitalization and punctuation. Select one of the topics below or use one of your own. *pages 368-371*

A new movie	A sporting event
A new pet	A trip to the city/country
A museum exhibit	A concert

2. Write a business letter. Use the information below to write your letter. The *body* of your letter should be a *factual paragraph*. The letter should also include all the necessary information. Remember that a business letter is briefer and more formal than a friendly letter. Be sure to include a *heading*, an *inside address*, a *greeting*, a *closing*, and a *signature*. Edit your letter carefully for capitalization and punctuation. *pages 372-375*

You have heard that the American Museum of Natural History has tours for groups of students. Your science class will be studying dinosaurs next month and would like to visit the museum. The address of the museum is: 79th Street at Central Park West, New York, New York 10024.

The names of many inventions are acronyms. An *acronym* is a word made from the initial letters of other words. Look at these acronyms. Unimportant words are not used in some acronyms.

SAM: **Surface to Air Missiles**
SCUBA: **Self-Contained Underwater Breathing Apparatus**
RADAR: **Radio Detection and Ranging**
LASER: **Light Amplification by Stimulated Emission of Radiation**

Can you find an acronym for a postal number code in the following words?
Zone Improvement Plan

Exploring Language

COMPOSITION

Write each pair of sentences as one compound sentence. Put commas, conjunctions, and semicolons where they belong. *pages 296-297*

1. Modern ranch work presents new challenges.
Ranchers adapt to new developments.
2. The cowhand's skills include a knowledge of horses and livestock.
Beginners quickly learn to mend fences and to rope cattle.
3. The ranchers needed open spaces for grazing their cattle.
The sheepherders wanted to fence the open grasslands.
4. Most cowhands live on their employer's ranch.
They camp out on the range.
5. Jeeps move quickly over the range.
Horses carry cowhands into rugged areas.
6. Sometimes huge trucks carry the cattle to market.
The cowhands transport cattle by rail.
7. The covered wagon era included cattle drives.
The early cattle drives were often slow and dangerous.
8. Animal scientists study ways to improve cattle.
Ranchers profit from their research.
9. Modern ranchers use helicopters.
The cowhands easily locate their livestock from the air.
10. Helicopters keep the herds together.
The cattle stray into deserted parts of the range.

Write each pair of sentences as one complex sentence using an adverb clause. Put commas in where needed. *pages 298-299*

11. Cattle were driven east.
They reached Sedalia, Missouri.
12. The trip took two or three months.
Bad weather or trail hazards forced the drive to stop.
13. The cowboys gathered for dinner.
They herded the cattle into the pasture.

Section Review

14. Cattle could be purchased cheaply.
Prices fell at the end of the Civil War.
15. The Chisholm Trail was a popular route.
Many trails were well known.
16. Cattlemen made huge profits.
They drove their cattle east.
17. Cattle trails always shifted.
Fenced farmlands broke the trail routes.
18. Cowboys drove four million cattle east.
The railroad reached Texas.
19. Smaller cattle drives continued.
Train service improved rapidly.
20. Cattle were driven slowly during the morning.
The steers needed special attention.

Rewrite each sentence fragment to make a complete sentence. *pages 304-305*

21. The old fishing boats.
22. Is mending a hole in a large net.
23. Through the sky above the harbor.
24. The clangs of bells on the buoys.
25. Climbed the rigging of the boat.
26. For a short trip down the coast.
27. The captain's crew.
28. Remove the barnacles.
29. Of seagulls along the beach.
30. Hundreds of shrimp.

Rewrite these run-on sentences to make them correct. *pages 304-305*

31. Law students already have a degree from a four-year college, they study all areas of the law for several more years, most students

often work as assistants in law firms near their school, they also attend local court sessions.

32. A degree in law enables a person to enter many different fields of work and you may wish to represent anyone from a doctor to an athlete and you may even run for public offices such as senator or state representative.

33. Rewrite the following paragraph. Edit it and make the necessary changes. Correct the spelling and the punctuation. *pages 316-317*

the romans were not the first people in italy with an advanced culture. A groups calle the etruscans farmed built cities their as early as 1800 B.C. the etruscans were a peaceful people They traided their beautifully crafted pottery and tools with other mediterranean cultures, From citys in Crete, etruscan ships carried grain wine and precious mettals to all parts of the world. By studying the paintings on the remaining buildings constructed by the etruscans, we can learn alot about there activitys and organization.

34. Write a persuasive paragraph of reasons for an editorial in your school newspaper. Write about one of the following topics, or choose one of your own. *pages 326-327*

1. The school dance should be held downtown and not in the gymnasium.
2. The eighth grade should organize a clothing drive for the needy.
3. Janitorial service within school grounds should be improved.
4. The school board should allow a larger recreation area to be built.
5. All students should study a musical instrument before graduating.
6. The school and the community should sponsor a volunteer center.

Section Review

35. Write a two-paragraph persuasive composition using the thesis statement and outline given below. *pages 346-347*

How to Publish a School Newspaper

Thesis statement: *In order to publish a school newspaper, we must first organize a newspaper club and then write the articles for the newspaper.*

I. Organizing the newspaper club
- **A.** Discuss ideas with faculty advisor
- **B.** Get permission to use school supplies
- **C.** Find other students for staff
- **D.** (Add your own detail.)

II. Writing the Newspaper
- **A.** Brainstorm to decide the content
- **B.** Choose writers for each article
- **C.** Set up publication schedule
- **D.** (Add your own detail.)

36. Suppose that you bought a tape recorder from the Sounds Alive Company. However several things are wrong with the cassette. Perhaps the rewind button doesn't work. Maybe the shoulder strap wasn't included in the package, or the volume button doesn't turn. You have decided that you want your money back.
The address of the company is 1955 Fairmont Terrace, York, Pennsylvania 17402.

Write a business letter. Use the information above to write your letter. The body of your letter should be a paragraph of facts stating why you want your money back. The letter should also include all the necessary information. Be sure to include a *heading*, an *inside address*, a *greeting*, a *closing*, and a *signature*.
Edit your letter carefully. *pages 372-375*

Section Review

37. Look at how the following business form was filled out. Then write the answer to each question below.

READ-ON MAGAZINE

11 issues: $14.97
and your choice of 2 FREE BOOKS.

(check one) ☐ Please enter my new subscription to Read-On for 11 issues at the thrifty $14.97 price.

☐ I am a subscriber now. Extend my current subscription for 11 more issues at $14.97

(check two) Send me the 2 FREE BOOKS checked below:

☑ Rainy Day Activity Book
☑ Puzzles and More Puzzles
☑ The Read-On Student Atlas

(check one) ☐ Payment enclosed. Add ONE EXTRA ISSUE to my subscription at no charge.

☑ Bill me, payable in 30 days.

PLEASE PRINT

Mary — last name   *Johnson* — first name

39 Grove St., — street address

Ames, Iowa — city, state/province   *63801* — zip code

3541

1. What information has the person omitted at the top of the form?
2. What mistake has the person made indicating the free books she desires?
3. How has the person incorrectly checked the box regarding payment?
4. What two errors has the person made in writing her name?
5. How has the address been filled in incorrectly on the form?

The novels and stories of Willa Cather (1873-1947) describe her strong sense of place—often the Midwest.

Fiction reveals truths that reality obscures.

JESSAMYN WEST
American writer (1907-   )

21

WRITING AND APPRECIATING A SHORT STORY

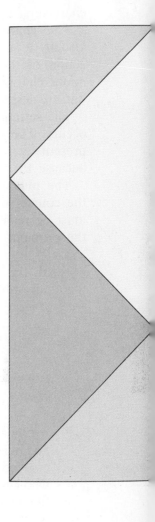

A Short Story

Thinking About a Short Story

Every short story has three basic elements. These elements are characters, setting, and plot.

The **characters** in short stories are usually people or animals. Usually a short story has one *main character* who participates in the action of the story. Often there are *minor characters* as well. The minor characters participate in the action or help the action to occur but are less important than the main character.

The **setting** of a short story is the time and place in which the action occurs. The story may take place anywhere or any time in the past, present, or future. The location and the time usually change very little because the story is so brief.

The **plot** is the *series of events* that takes place in a story. During the course of these events the main character faces a *problem* which must be resolved. The events that follow lead up to the resolution of the problem. By the end of the story, the problem has been settled.

Read the following short story. Notice that the setting works together with the plot to develop a problem for the main character.

Survival

Linda Roper loved to travel. Since her childhood, she and her family had traveled often to different places. Linda enjoyed visiting new areas. She also liked meeting the people who lived there. But today Linda was on a trip by herself. She was driving through the desert for the first time. She would reach her aunt and uncle's house in a few hours. Linda was fascinated by the tall rocks and the wide blanket of white sand that covered the desert. The early morning sun beat down intensely. Linda was thankful that her car had air conditioning. She smiled as she viewed this new region.

Suddenly the car jolted. Linda heard a funny noise. The engine sputtered and then gave out. Linda tried to start the engine, but nothing happened. She waited several minutes and tried again. Again it failed. Linda began to feel the extreme heat of the desert sun. She honked her horn, hoping a passing motorist would hear her. However, no one else was nearby. As the hours dragged on, Linda felt hotter and hotter. She was thirsty, but no water was left in her canteen. She hoped her aunt and uncle would send for help soon. In the meantime, Linda got out of the car. She took a stick and wrote "HELP" in giant letters in the sand.

The next morning Linda was awakened by the sound of roaring engines. At first Linda was not sure where she was, but she quickly remembered. Linda got out of the car and saw a plane flying overhead. She rushed to get a mirror from the car. Then she flashed the mirror to make a reflection in the sky. The plane seemed to fly away but soon it came closer and landed. Linda never felt happier as the pilot helped her to the plane. Later Linda promised her aunt and uncle that she would never travel alone in the desert again.

Talking About a Short Story

1. Who is the main character? Who are the minor characters?
2. Describe Linda's personality. What did you learn about her by her thoughts and actions.
3. What is the setting of the story? Do the time and location remain the same throughout the story?
4. How is the setting described in the first paragraph? Which words helped you picture the setting the best?
5. What problem does Linda face in the story? How is the problem settled?
6. Tell why this story could or could not have taken place in any other setting.
7. Did you like the ending of the story? What might be a better ending?
8. Why did the author call the story "Survival"?

Outlining a Short Story

Thinking About an Outline

You may find it useful to make an outline before you write a short story. The outline helps you develop and organize ideas you will use. The outline should work like a rubber band. It should be able to "stretch" to fit the package it holds. However, a helpful outline generally organizes the information in the following way.

Title

I. Beginning
- **A.** Introduce the main character
- **B.** Describe the setting
- **C.** Present the first event of the plot

II. Middle
- **A.** Write a step-by-step sequence of events
- **B.** Introduce minor characters as the action continues
- **C.** Describe the problem that the main character faces

III. Ending
- **A.** Present the final event of the plot
- **B.** Describe the main character's reaction

Look at the middle part of the outline again. Notice that the events, the characters, and the problem are listed separately. This separate listing will encourage you to develop the action, the problem, and the characters more fully by directing your attention to each one individually. As you write, however, keep in mind that the characters, setting, and action all work together to develop the problem. You may introduce minor characters during several different events. You may also include several events after you have introduced the problem. Remember, though, that all the events should help lead up to the solution of the problem. The final event in the plot is the event that settles the problem for the main character.

Look at the ideas on the next page. You might use them to develop a short story.

Characters	Settings	Problems
a scientist	a castle	surviving a storm
a pilot	an abandoned warehouse	finding food or shelter
an inventor	a laboratory	escaping from captivity
an artist	a space station	avoiding the enemy
a strange creature	a city of the future	searching for someone
a stowaway	a museum	finding a path home
a boy or girl	a run-down shack	overcoming an emotion
a hermit	a submarine	making friends

Writing an Outline

Develop an outline for a short story. Use the ideas presented for characters, settings, and problems; or suggest ideas of your own. Then follow the steps below to organize the ideas for the story in an outline.

1. First write *I. Beginning*. Then decide on the main character's name, age, and unusual characteristics. Also decide what your character will be doing. For example, *A. Kim, 15, adventurous and outgoing, witnesses the landing of a spaceship.* Next choose a setting and describe it briefly, such as *B. Dark meadow behind old, abandoned farmhouse*. Now decide on the first event in the plot. For example, *C. Spaceship door opens. Alien being comes out.*
2. Next write *II. Middle*. Then develop a series of events, such as *A. Kim enters the ship, trips over a wire, and becomes invisible*. Now develop the minor character and show how the character affects the action of the story. For example, *B. Cosmo, wrinkled alien being, motions to Kim in sign language*. Also identify the problem the main character faces. You might write *C. Kim, frightened, is unable to escape from ship.*
3. Now write *III. Ending*. Consider all possible events for ending the story. Then choose the best idea, and describe the event briefly. For example, *A. Cosmo makes Kim visible, releases her.* Finally, think about the main character's reaction. Does the person learn anything from the experience? If so, describe it in the B part of the ending, such as *B. Kim, relieved, realizes that Cosmo is really friendly.*
4. When your outline is complete, copy it on your own paper. Keep the outline as you will need it for the next lesson.

Practicing a Short Story

Thinking About a Short Story

Use the ideas you have organized in your outline to write a short story. Describe the characters as you imagine them, and include additional events that further develop the story in the outline.

Writing a Short Story

1. Begin the first paragraph by introducing the main character. Describe the character clearly and tell what the person is doing. Next describe the setting briefly. Use clear and colorful adjectives. Now present the first event in the plot.
2. In the second paragraph develop the events in the story in sequence. As you describe the events, introduce the minor characters. Include descriptions of the characters. Next describe the problem that the main character faces in the story.
3. In the third paragraph present the final events that settle the problem. If you include more than one event, be sure to use the last event in the series to solve the problem. Finally describe how the main character feels at the end of the story. Show what the person has learned from the experience.

Edit Your Short Story

Read over your story. Ask yourself the following questions as you edit your writing. Make the changes you feel will improve the story. Then copy the edited story on a new sheet of paper.

1. Does your story have a beginning, a middle, and an ending?
2. Do you describe your main character clearly? Do you introduce minor characters and show how they affect the events in the story?
3. Do you describe the setting of the story vividly?
4. Do you present the events in a logical order? Do you describe a problem for the main character?
5. Does the final event in the story settle the problem for the main character?
6. Do you describe how the main character feels about the solution?
7. Does your story have a title?
8. Have you spelled all the words and punctuated the sentences correctly. Do your subjects and verbs agree in number?

Appreciating a Short Story

You know that a good short story has *characters,* a *setting,* and a *plot.* Events by themselves do not make a good story. The writer must develop all three elements. These elements work together to create a problem and lead up to its resolution. The resolution is brought about by the last event in the story.

In the story that follows, notice that characters, setting, and events all contribute to the development of a problem. Observe how the writer resolves the problem with the final event of the story.

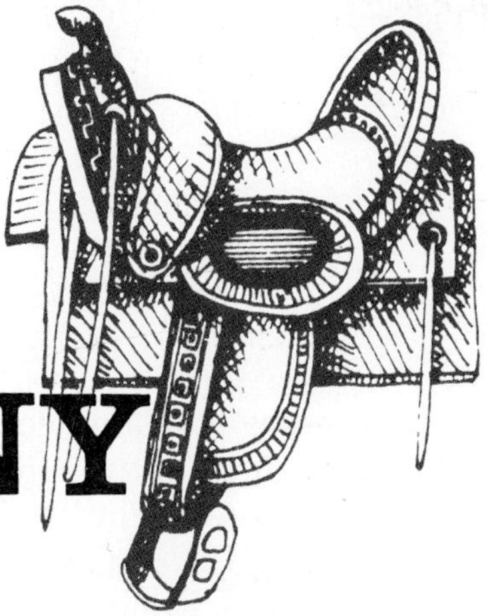

JENNY

by Sam Savitt

This happened in upper New York State, around the year 1867, and I'll tell you the story just the way it was told to me.

Dr. Kraft Payson Kimball lived in Burville, a small village just outside of Watertown, New York, but his practice carried him over a good part of the northwest corner of Jefferson County. He made his rounds by horse and buggy most of the time, but whenever the roads were too muddy or snow covered, he rode a little brown mare named Jenny. The doctor told everyone she had Morgan and Arabian ancestry, but most of all she had a whole lot of good, everyday horse sense.

Now, people who spend many hours on horseback, like cowhands or cavalry officers or country doctors, have learned through necessity the knack of sleeping in the saddle. Doc Kimball was no exception. Many nights, after a long day of house calls, his good mare Jenny would carry him home while he slept in the saddle. She would plod along quietly, undisturbed by the things that spook most horses, and stop only when she arrived at the doctor's house.

This year the snow had lain deep all winter, and now, in April, with the addition of the constant spring rains, the roads became almost impassable. Jim McKay, who lived up near Saint Lawrence, had a tree fall on him, and when Jim's boy brought the news, Doc Kimball quickly saddled Jenny and rode out to the McKay place. He set two broken legs, and it was well after dark before he was ready to ride for home.

"You can't go out on a night like this, Doc," pleaded Mrs. McKay. "Stay over with us. You can head back in the morning with a good hot breakfast under your belt." But Doc Kimball wouldn't hear of it. He had some pretty sick patients down near Rutland. Besides, the rain had slowed down to a drizzle, and he could count on old Jenny to get him back home.

There were twelve miles to go. The doctor settled into the saddle and, with his head tucked into the upturned collar of his oilskin slicker, promptly dozed off.

He didn't know how long he'd slept, but he was startled awake suddenly when Jenny came to a halt. He found he was sitting on his horse beside the picket fence in front of his own house. The yellow light streaming through the open door fell across his stable boy Billy, who was holding Jenny's bridle and peering anxiously up into the doctor's face.

"Are you all right, Doc?" Billy's voice quavered.

"Of course I'm all right—why shouldn't I be?" the doctor answered. He slid to the ground and began unfastening his saddlebag.

"Which way did you come home?"

Billy's question was so intent and irregular that the doctor stopped what he was doing and looked searchingly at the boy.

"The way I always do," he answered softly. "Down Cumberland Road and across Brownville Bridge." He paused to sling the saddlebag across his shoulder.

"Why do you ask, Bill? You know darned well the route I take—it's the only one there is."

"But that's impossible, Doc." Billy's words came slowly and disbelievingly. "Brownville Bridge washed out over four hours ago!"

Next morning Dr. Kimball and Billy went down to the river crossing. Sure enough, the bridge was gone. Only one old rotten beam still spanned the swirling waters. But there in the mud, in the early light, they could see the hoofprints of old Jenny. The doctor and the boy traced them to the crumbling bank and stood in awe and amazement as their eyes unfolded the story of last night.

Old Jenny, in the stormy darkness, with the doctor asleep in the saddle, had crossed the single narrow beam to bring him safely home.

Talking About a Short Story

Look back at the story again.

1. Who are the main characters in the story? Who are the minor characters?
2. What is the problem that Jenny faces in the story?
3. What is the setting of the story?
4. How does Jenny solve the problem? How do we find out about the solution?

INDEPENDENT WRITING

A Short Story

Prewriting There are many different characters, settings, and events that can be used to develop a short story. Good writers may consider several combinations of these elements before they decide which ones they will use. Look back at the suggestions for characters, settings, and problems on page 389. You may have some other ideas

which you now could add to this list, too. Choose a new combination of these elements, and develop some thoughts about each one.

Imagine what your character or characters actually look like. Think about what kind of characters they are. What is the setting? What does it look like? What is unusual or noteworthy about the setting as you imagine it? What is the problem that the main character faces? What kinds of events could contribute to the development of this problem for this character in this particular setting? What characters or events could help resolve the problem before the end of the story?

When you have developed some thoughts about your characters, setting, problem, and events, begin writing an outline for a short story. Use the form of outline suggested on page 388 to help you organize your information logically. As you complete the outline with information about characters, setting, and plot, include any additional ideas that develop the story even further.

Writing Write a short story, using the ideas you have organized in your outline. Select adjectives that will make your descriptions clear and colorful. Be certain that you present your events in a logical order. Check the steps provided for writing a short story on page 390 to remind yourself of how to begin.

Editing Read over your short story. Ask yourself the questions provided for editing a short story on page 390 as you review your writing. Make the changes you feel will improve the story. Then copy the edited story on a new sheet of paper.

Thornton Wilder (1897-1975) won Pulitzer Prizes for both his fiction and drama.

A work of art does not exist without its audience.

RICHARD HAMILTON
British artist (1922-)

22

WRITING AND APPRECIATING A PLAY

A Play

Thinking About a Play

A play, like a short story, has characters, setting, and plot. A play, however, is not written in a series of paragraphs. Instead, it is written in a script. The author, or playwright, uses play form, which includes three different kinds of writing.

In a play most of the story is revealed in conversations between characters. These conversations between characters are called **dialogue.** Even though the characters are speaking, the playwright does not use quotation marks. Instead, the name of the character who is speaking appears before his or her speech, or *lines*.

During a play, the characters make gestures and move around the stage. The playwright tells how and where the characters move in **stage directions.** These directions are written in parentheses and usually appear along with the dialogue.

Usually a play is divided into sections called **scenes.** A scene focuses on one dramatic event and therefore has a clear beginning and ending. At the beginning of the scene, the playwright writes a brief description of the setting and of the characters who are present. If this information changes during the scene, however, it is written as a stage direction.

- Read the following example of a scene from a play.

Life or Death

Cast of Characters

KING GOLDTHRONE, King of Meadowland
HURLEY, a prisoner
TAKIT, GRASPA } guards to the king

Scene: A dark, dusty cell in the basement of the palace. (Hurley sits on a small bed, his face buried in his hands. He is a young man about 30 years old. His clothes are ragged. Suddenly two guards appear.)

TAKIT: Prisoner, arise!

GRASPA: The king is here to see you. (Hurley stands up as King Goldthrone enters his cell. The king is an old man with a mean face.)

KING: So, you are the spy in Meadowland. Well, you must be ready to pay for your crime!

HURLEY: But I tell you I am *not* a spy. You have made a mistake.

KING: That's what they all say. You must die, Hurley. But to show you I am fair, I hold in my hand two slips of paper. One says *Life* and the other says *Death.* If you choose the *Life* slip, I will let you go. (King holds out his hand.)

HURLEY: (aside to audience) What shall I do? The king has probably written *Death* on both slips to make sure I can't win. (Suddenly Hurley snaps his fingers as if struck with an idea. He takes one slip from the king.)

KING: (laughing) Now open the paper and see what it says. (Hurley quickly swallows the paper.)

HURLEY: Sorry, your majesty, but I have swallowed the paper I chose. Now, look at the paper you have left in your hand. If it says *Death,* that proves I must have chosen *Life.* (The king opens the remaining slip.)

KING: Very clever, you scoundrel. This slip does say *Death.* (to audience) Rats! (to Hurley) You are a free man. Guards, take him away.

TAKIT: Yes, your majesty.

GRASPA: This way out, Hurley. (The guards lead Hurley away.)

Talking About a Play

Look at the examples of a scene from a play.

1. Who are the characters in the scene you just read? Where in the script do you find descriptions of the characters with speaking parts?
2. In which part of the script do you find a description of the setting?
3. In which part of the script do you learn about the plot?
4. Where in the script do you learn what each character does during the scene?
5. Why did the playwright call the play "Life or Death"? What other titles would be appropriate?

Outlining a Play

Thinking About an Outline

Before you actually begin writing a scene from a play, you need to develop ideas about the setting, the characters, and the plot. An outline helps you in organizing and writing the scene.

Title

I. Scene
  A. Describe the setting for the scene.
  B. Describe the characters present and what they are doing as the scene opens.
II. Beginning
  A. Introduce the main characters.
  B. Explain the problem the main character faces.
III. Middle
  A. Write a step-by-step sequence of events.
  B. Introduce minor characters.
IV. Ending
  A. Describe the final event of the scene.
  B. Tell how each character feels about the ending.

In a scene from a play, the problem is usually introduced in the beginning of the dialogue. The writer then uses dialogue and stage directions to show how the characters feel about the problem. The remaining dialogue focuses on how the characters will resolve the problem. In the outline you do not have to write the exact words that each character will say. Simply list the sequence of events and describe the dialogue. List which characters speak and make brief notes about what each one will say. Use the final portion of dialogue to solve the problem. Look at these ideas for developing a scene from a play.

Characters	Settings	Problems
a knight	a zoo	helping another person
a sales clerk	an airplane	asking directions
a student	a circus	handling a customer complaint
a driver	a department store	interviewing for a job
a prince, princess	an attic	finding an escape route
a pilot	a school	trying out for the team
a magician	a laboratory	performing for an audience
an animal trainer	a traffic jam	communicating in a foreign country
a scientist	a castle	learning to be a leader

Writing an Outline

Develop a scene for a play. Use the ideas provided for characters, settings, and problems; or suggest ideas of your own. Then prepare an outline for the scene, following the steps given below.

1. First write *I. Scene.* Then choose a setting and describe it briefly. For example, *A. It is a typical hospital room with a bed, a cabinet, and a wall lamp over the bed.* Next describe the characters present as the scene opens, such as *B. The patient, wrapped in bandages, is lying in the bed. The doctor, a middle-aged woman, is taking the patient's pulse. A police investigator stands at the foot of the bed and taps his foot impatiently against the floor.*
2. Next, write *II. Beginning.* Then decide which character will introduce the problem and how you want that character to reveal the problem. For example, *A. Investigator asks series of questions trying to learn who the patient is.* Now describe how each character feels about the problem, such as *B. The patient is unable to answer the questions and is upset. The doctor shows concern for the patient's health.*
3. Now write *III. Middle.* Then develop a step-by-step sequence of events. Describe the dialogue in which the events will be revealed. For example, *The investigator asks questions about other topics, hoping to bring back the patient's memory.* Also introduce minor characters and show how the minor character affects the action of the story, such as *B. A young nurse pokes her head into the room and announces that she must change the patient's bandages. The look on the patient's face shows that he is startled.*
4. Last write *IV. Ending.* Consider all possible ways to solve the problem. Then choose the best idea, and describe the dialogue, such as *A. The patient, on hearing the word "bandages," recalls that he was going to hear a band play at the time of the accident and now remembers who he is.* Finally describe how each character reacts to the solution. For example, *B. The patient is excited and tries to get up; the doctor is relieved that his confusion is over; the police officer announces that he must report the discovery to headquarters.*
5. Keep the outline as you will need it for the next lesson.

Practicing a Play

Thinking About a Play

Write a scene for a play building on the ideas you have organized in your outline. Develop the scene further by adding stage directions and by expanding the dialogue.

Writing a Scene from a Play

1. Write *Scene,* and describe the setting and the characters present, using the notes you made in your outline. Be sure to indicate what the characters are doing as the scene opens.
2. For the beginning of the scene, write the name of the character who speaks first and add a colon. (You will need to repeat this step each time a character begins speaking.) Then write the lines of dialogue. Make certain that the problem is clearly stated early in the scene.
3. For the middle develop the dialogue step by step from the sequence of events in your outline. Introduce the minor characters to further develop the action of the scene.
4. In the ending bring the scene to a close, using final dialogue that shows how the problem is solved. Include final stage directions that show what the characters are doing and how they feel about the change in the situation.

Edit Your Play

Read over your scene, and ask yourself the following questions as you edit your writing. Make the changes you feel will improve the scene. Then copy the edited version on a new sheet of paper.

1. Have you introduced the scene with a description of the setting and the characters present as the scene begins?
2. Does one of your characters state the problem clearly in the first few lines of dialogue?
3. Do the dialogue and stage directions develop the sequence of events in a clear and logical order?
4. Do you use the final dialogue to show how the problem is solved?
5. Do you include final stage directions to show what your characters are doing and how they feel as the scene ends?
6. Does your title suit the scene you have written?

Appreciating a Play

Like a short story, a play has characters, a setting, and a plot. Unlike other forms of writing, however, the story within the play is revealed through dialogue and stage directions.

As you read the following play, think about the characters, setting, and plot. Notice how the playwright uses dialogue to introduce the problem, to reveal the characters' thoughts and feelings, and to solve the problem.

A Garden Grows on Spring Street

Steven Otfinoski

CHARACTERS: CARLOS, LINDA, HENRY, JOEY, FRED, BOBBY, ANITA, MR. SANCHEZ, MRS. ROBINSON

SCENE: An ordinary spring day on Spring Street. (*Young people from the neighborhood have gathered on the vacant dirt lot at the corner — their favorite meeting place.*)

CARLOS: Well, what are we going to do today?

LINDA: How about a game of stickball?

JOEY: We always play stickball. Let's do something different.

HENRY: What else *can* we do here?

ANITA: We could have a party.

BOBBY: That's a great idea! We can have an outdoor party.

FRED: You can't have a party outside unless you get permission from the block association.

HENRY: And how are we going to get permission for a party now?

ANITA: It doesn't have to be for now. We could plan a party for everyone on the block.

LINDA: We could bring food and hire a band to play music. People from other streets around here have done it.

JOEY: But those things cost money. Who's going to pay for it?

LINDA: We could raise money, couldn't we?

FRED: How are we going to do that? We don't have anything to sell.

CARLOS: Yes, we do. We can turn this lot into a community garden.

HENRY: What good will that do? We can't sell the lot. It doesn't belong to us.

CARLOS: The people on Avenue A turned their lot into a garden last summer. They divided the land into plots and rented out the space. People on the street who wanted to plant a garden rented the plots and grew vegetables on them.

JOEY: It sounds like a lot of hard work, and we would still need permission from the block association.

ANITA: So what? We haven't got anything else to do, and at least it would be something different.

LINDA: We could even keep one of the plots for a garden of our own.

HENRY: I think the whole idea's crazy, and it's too complicated.

BOBBY: It's a way to raise money for a party, Henry.

JOEY: And our folks would like it because they would save money growing their own vegetables.

FRED: When I want vegetables, I'll go to the supermarket.

HENRY: Right! If you guys are going to turn into a bunch of farmers, count us out. Let's go, Fred. (*Henry and Fred leave.*)

CARLOS: Well, I think it's a good idea.

ANITA: So do I. Let's go speak with members of the association about setting up the garden.

(*A few days later Mrs. Robinson is talking to Mr. Sanchez in his hardware store on Spring Street.*)

MRS. ROBINSON: I don't know what this country is coming to, Mr. Sanchez. Food prices are getting higher all the time.

MR. SANCHEZ: That's the truth.

MRS. ROBINSON: And have you seen what the kids are doing to this neighborhood? They're making a mess of that corner lot!

MR. SANCHEZ: Yes, I've been meaning to ask them what they are doing over there. (*Joey, Linda, and Carlos enter the store.*)

LINDA: Hi, Mrs. Robinson, Mr. Sanchez.

JOEY: We'd like to buy some vegetable seeds.

MR. SANCHEZ: Vegetable seeds?...I think you'll find them on the rack behind the door. What do you want with seeds, Carlos?

CARLOS: We're starting a community garden on the corner.

MRS. ROBINSON: Then it's you who've taken over that vacant lot.

JOEY: That's right. We have permission from the block association, and we've divided up the lot into sixteen small garden plots.

LINDA: Anyone in the neighborhood who wants to have a garden can rent a plot and grow vegetables on it.

CARLOS: (*looking at seed packages on the rack*) Carrots, radishes, beans, and tomatoes...that ought to do it.

MRS. ROBINSON: Well, I suppose it is cheaper to grow your own vegetables than to buy them in the store.

JOEY: A lot cheaper, Mrs. Robinson.

MR. SANCHEZ: And how many plots did you say you've rented?

CARLOS: Almost all of them. There are only three left.

MRS. ROBINSON: I'll take one!

MR. SANCHEZ: Me, too!

(*Three weeks pass. The garden on Spring Street is beginning to take shape.*)

ANITA: (*inspecting the plot*) Let's see...we put the beans here, I think. (*Henry and Fred enter.*)

HENRY: And how are the farmers doing today?

BOBBY: Just fine, Henry.

FRED: How come I don't see anything growing then?

BOBBY: It takes time. Vegetables don't pop up overnight, you know.

HENRY: If they pop up at all, it'll be a miracle! Come on, Fred. Let's leave these sod busters to do their dirty work. (*They leave.*)

ANITA: They won't think it's so funny when we start selling vegetables.

BOBBY: Mrs. Robinson, have you finished weeding your plot?

MRS. ROBINSON: Yes, I have, Bobby.

BOBBY: But there are still some weeds in it.

ANITA: Over there where you planted your radishes last week.

MRS. ROBINSON: Then those must be...

EVERYONE: OUR FIRST SPROUTS! (*They all stare at the sprouts in awe.*)

CARLOS: I'd say the Spring Street Garden is officially under way.

(*A fence has been built to protect the gardens. One night in August, two figures approach the fence.*)

FRED: I don't know about this, Henry. It's one thing to make fun of the garden, but wrecking it could get us into a lot of trouble.

HENRY: No one's going to know we did it. Besides, these farmers deserve it for ruining our lot. (*Fred watches as Henry climbs over the fence and drops down inside. He turns his flashlight on the plants.*) I think I'll start with the tomato plants. (*Henry is about to grab the nearest plant, but suddenly he stops.*) Wow! Look at the size of those tomatoes! And they're so red!

FRED: (*peering through the fence*) What are those little green plants over there on the left? And look at all those beans. I wonder how they ever did it. (*Fred turns suddenly and sees the other gardeners all standing behind him glaring.*)

ANITA: Those bushy green plants are carrots, Fred. Carrots grow in the dirt, not above it...I think you'd better leave now.

JOEY: That's right. It took a lot of hard work to get this garden growing; and we're not going to let you ruin it for us now.

HENRY: (*climbing back over the fence*) All right. I admit I was wrong. I guess I was really just jealous. All of you have been so busy, and Fred and I felt left out. We never thought you'd really grow anything here anyway.

CARLOS: It is amazing, isn't it, Henry?

FRED: I know you're probably really angry with us, but do you think Henry and I could help you get ready for the block party?

JOEY: Hey! I forgot that the party was our reason for starting the garden in the first place.

BOBBY: That's right. We've become so involved with growing vegetables that we didn't need any other reason for having a garden.

ANITA: Growing something by ourselves has been enough of a reason.

MRS. ROBINSON: Well, you've done a fine job, kids. We all have. I'd like to help out with preparing food for the party. I think everyone will want to contribute food from the gardens.

HENRY: Then maybe you could call the party a "harvest festival."

MR. SANCHEZ: You know, Henry, for someone who takes so long to catch on, you've really got some good ideas!

Talking About a Play

1. In which part of the script do you find a description of the setting?
2. In which part of the script do you learn the plot?
3. When you read the dialogue, how do you know which character is speaking?
4. Which part of the script tells where the characters move during the scene?
5. When you read the script, how do you learn about the problem that one or more characters face?
6. Which part of the script reveals how the characters solve the problem? What changes occur by the end of the play?

INDEPENDENT WRITING

A Play

Prewriting A good play is like a good story. It holds the reader's attention because it is interesting and convincing. The characters, setting, and plot are believable even though they are not necessarily from the real world as you know it. They seem believable because the writer has developed a complete picture of the people, places, and events.

Look at just some of the ideas that playwrights use to develop a picture for their writing on page 400. Choose a new combination of characters, setting, and problem, or work with ideas you have thought about. Develop a complete picture of these elements. Let your mind become like a camera that shows what your characters and setting look like. First think about what kind of characters they are. Next identify any unusual or noteworthy details about them and about the setting. Then consider the problem your characters face and decide what conversations would occur as a result of the problem. Finally imagine possible endings for the scene.

When your image of the scene seems real and believable to you, begin writing an outline of the details. Use the form of outline suggested on page 400 to help you organize the information logically.

Writing Use the ideas you have organized in your outline to write a play. Check the steps provided for writing a scene on page 402 to remind yourself of how to begin. Be sure that one of your characters states the problem clearly at the beginning of the scene. Then develop believable dialogue for your characters from the notes you have made about their conversation. Do not rush your dialogue to get to the end of the scene quickly. Remember that in normal conversations, people may make several different comments before they finish expressing an idea completely.

Editing Read through your script and ask yourself the questions provided for editing a scene on page 402 as you review your play. Make the changes you feel will improve the story you tell. Then copy the edited script on a new sheet of paper.

Poet Gwendolyn Brooks received the Pulitzer Prize in 1950.

Poetry is life distilled.

GWENDOLYN BROOKS
American poet (1917–   )

23

WRITING AND APPRECIATING POETRY

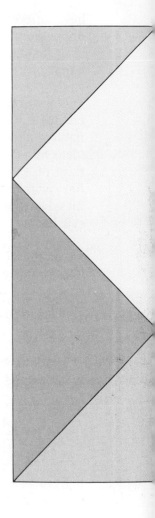

Poetry

Thinking About Haiku and Couplets

Poetry is much like music. Like music, poems create moods and have different forms. Poets choose the form that will best express their impressions, feelings, or ideas. Sometimes a poem describes just one brief moment the poet has experienced. At other times poetry is humorous.

One form of poetry is haiku. A *haiku* is a Japanese verse form that creates a vivid word picture. A haiku often describes something in nature, although it can be used to describe various other events and ideas as well. A haiku has a feeling of fleeting, delicate beauty like the flash of a butterfly or the haunting song of a flute. A haiku has three lines with a total of seventeen syllables. The first line has five syllables; the second line has seven syllables; and the third has five syllables.

Another form of poetry is the couplet. A *couplet* consists of two lines that rhyme at the end. The lines usually have the same number of beats, or syllables. In couplets, some beats are stressed, or emphasized.

Read the following examples of haiku. Notice the arrangement of syllables and the subject described.

Falling Flower
Moritake

The falling flower
I saw drift back to the branch
was a butterfly.

The Kite
Kubonta

The tight string broke and
the loose kite fell fluttering,
losing its spirit.

River
Meisetsu

A river leaping,
tumbling over rocks roars on...
as the mountain smiles.

A Better View
Masahide

Since my house burned down,
I now own a better view
of the rising moon.

Ogden Nash is famous for creating humorous verses by twisting grammar, misspelling words, and making up words. Read these verses about animals. Notice that each verse is made up of two rhyming couplets.

The Octopus

Tell me, O Octopus, I begs,
Is those things arms, or is
they legs?
I marvel at thee, Octopus;
If I were thou, I'd call me Us.

The Panther

The panther is like a leopard.
Except it hasn't been peppered.
Should you behold a panther
crouch,
Prepare to say Ouch.
Better yet, if called by a
panther,
Don't anther.

The Rhinoceros

The rhino is a homely beast,
For human eyes he's not a feast.
Farewell, farewell, you old
rhinoceros.
I'll stare at something less
prepocerous.

The Ostrich

The ostrich roams the great
Sahara.
Its mouth is wide, its neck is
narra.
It has such long and lofty legs,
I'm glad it sits to lay its eggs.

Talking About Poetry

1. In "Falling Flower" what subject is described? Which line tells what the poet really saw?
2. What picture comes to your mind when you read "River"?
3. In "The Kite" why does the poet say that the kite loses its spirit?
4. In "A Better View" what subject is described? What is the poet's attitude about the burned-down house?
5. In "The Octopus" how does the poet misuse grammar to make a couplet rhyme?
6. In "The Rhinoceros" which new word did the poet make up to emphasize the rhyme?
7. In "The Panther" and "The Ostrich," which words did the poet misspell in order to emphasize a rhyme?
8. Reread all four verses correcting the grammar and the words. Are the verses still funny?

Imagery and Figures of Speech

Thinking About Images, Similes, Metaphors, and Personification

How can you paint pictures with words? Just as a painter uses color and line to create visual images, a poet creates pictures in the mind with special tools: words that create images. *Images* are pictures that come to mind when you read the words. They develop from the way a poet describes a person, a place, an object, an animal, or an action.

Sometimes poems describe what you have already experienced by seeing, touching, tasting, hearing, and smelling. The use of words to appeal to one or more of the five senses is called *imagery.* It is writing that creates images by describing something so vividly you can see it in your mind.

Some poems create images by presenting comparisons, or similarities, between two things that are different. In poetry, similes, metaphors, and personification are all called *figures of speech* because they use words in an unusual way to create specific, vivid images.

A *simile* is a comparison of two different things using the words *like* or *as*.

That fullback is like a bull. That fullback is as strong as a bull.

A *metaphor* is a comparison of two different things without using the words *like* or *as*.

That fullback is a bull.

Similes and metaphors always compare ideas from two different categories. You cannot, for example, create a simile or metaphor by comparing one person with another. Instead, you must compare the person with something that is not another human being, such as a bull. When you picture that fullback carrying the football through the opposing team, you picture a bull.

Personification is the giving of life or personality to an object or idea that is not alive.

With how sad steps, O Moon, thou climb the skies;
How silently, with how wan [pale] a face. *(Sir Philip Sidney)*

In this example, the moon is given the qualities and feelings of a person: the ability to climb, the emotion of sadness, and a face.

Talking About Images and Figures of Speech

Tell which senses are appealed to in the following lines of poetry. Some appeal to more than one sense.

1. His eyes were like fireballs fearfully blazing.
2. I lay my hand upon the stile; the stile is lone and cold.
3. My love is like a melody.
4. When all at once I saw a crowd, a host, of golden daffodils.

Find the simile, metaphor, or personification in each of the following lines of poetry.

5. And the muscles of his brawny arms are strong as iron bands.
6. The road was a ribbon of moonlight over the purple moor.
7. O, my love is like a red, red rose.
8. Hope is a tattered flag.
9. She [the sunset] sweeps with many colored brooms and leaves the shreds behind. Oh housewife of the evening west, come back and dust the ponds!
10. The seasons played around his knees like children 'round a sire.
11. And life is color and warmth and light.
12. I think that I shall never see a poem lovely as a tree.

Writing Poems with Images and Figures of Speech

1. Write a short, unrhymed poem in which every line begins with "I wish." Use a color or sound image in each line. For example, one line might be, "I wish I could slide down a rainbow."
2. Write a short, unrhymed poem in which each line is a simile or metaphor that compares two different things. For example, you might write, "Happiness is like a flower that has just bloomed." Below are two lists of suggested things to compare. Use any combination you like, or think of your own.

a person you know	an animal
a feeling (happiness, sadness, fear, or another feeling)	something in nature (a flower, a tree, the sun)
a season	a taste

Rhyme, Alliteration, Onomatopoeia

Thinking About Rhyme, Alliteration, Onomatopoeia

Just as poets can create picture images with words, they can use words to create sound effects. One of the major differences between poetry and prose, or stories, is the way words are used to create sounds that emphasize the meaning of the poem. Poets often use the following techniques to create sound effects.

A **rhyme** is the repetition of a similar sound in two or more words. Words such as *gold-behold-old* and *care-chair-solitaire* rhyme.

When the beginning consonant sound in words repeats in the lines of a poem, the repetition is called **alliteration.** Examples of alliteration are *babbling brook* and *snakes slither swiftly through the whispering grass.* Read the second example again, but read it in a whisper. Notice how the repetition of the letter *s* in five words suggests the hissing sound that snakes make.

Some words are formed to imitate the sound they name, such as *fizz, whiz, pop, clank, bop, zoom.* Other words, which are normally connected with an idea or action, already imitate the sound they name, too. These are ordinary words, such as *whistle, slap, sweep,* and *crunch.* They have real meanings, and their sounds when pronounced out loud reinforce those meanings. The imitation of sounds with words is called **onomatopoeia.**

- Read these stanzas from "The Little Black-Eyed Rebel" by Will Carleton. This is a story poem, or ballad, written in couplets. It is based on a true story of a Philadelphia girl, Mary Redmond. She helped the Continental Army during the American Revolution by smuggling letters containing important news through the enemy lines.

The Little Black-Eyed Rebel

Will Carleton

A boy drove to the city, his wagon clattered down
The road; 'twas laden with fresh apples for the British-governed town;
And the little black-eyed rebel, so innocent and sly,
Was watching for his coming from the corner of her eye.

For she knew that 'neath the lining of the coat he wore that day,
Were long letters from the husbands and the fathers far away,
Who were fighting for the freedom that they meant to gain or die;
And a tear like silver glistened in the corner of her eye.

But the treasures—how to get them? crept the question through her mind,
Since keen enemies were watching for what prizes they might find;
So she thought, and then she walked up to the wagon old and red;
"May I have a dozen apples for a kiss?" she sweetly said.

Clinging round his brawny neck, she clasped her fingers white and small,
And then whispered, "Quick! the letters! thrust them underneath my shawl!
Carry back again this package, and be sure that you are spry!"
And she sweetly smiled upon him from the corner of her eye.

Talking About Rhyme, Alliteration, and Onomatopoeia

1. Name the pairs of words in the poem that rhyme.
2. Which lines form couplets?
3. Read the lines in stanzas 2 and 3 again, and identify the words and sounds that are examples of alliteration.
4. Find an example of onomatopoeia in the first stanza of the poem.
5. Find a simile in the second stanza.

Writing Poems with Alliteration and Onomatopoeia

Write 10 lines about things that could never happen. Use alliteration or onomatopoeia in each line. For example, you might write, "A frog could never wear feathers like a pheasant." Here are some topics and words you can use, or choose your own.

Animals	**Things**	**Nature**	**Others**
sheep	jet	brook	bell
chicks	boat	grass	drum
horse	car	sea	balloon
pup	chair	wind	teeth
kitten	pie	rain	feet
hen	spoon	thunder	hands
crow	diamond	lightning	hammer
fish	shoe	ice	shovel

Practicing Haiku and Couplets

Thinking About a Haiku

Write a haiku that expresses a feeling, an impression, an idea, or describes a brief moment that you remember. Your experience may have been with a person, a place, an object, or an animal. Choose from the topics listed on page 420, or you may choose one of your own.

Remember that a haiku is written in three lines. The pattern of syllables is 5-7-5, and there is usually no rhyme. Follow these steps to write your haiku.

Writing a Haiku

1. Begin by making notes on the subject you have chosen. Jot down descriptions of your subject. Create vivid word pictures by using images that appeal to one of the five senses.
2. Next create a simile for your subject. Compare it with a subject from an entirely different category. Remember to use *like* or *as*.
3. Now decide upon a metaphor for your poem. Think of something altogether different that reminds you of your subject. Then write a sentence stating that your subject *is* the other thing.
4. Finally examine the ideas that you have written down, and select one or two that best express your subject. Develop the idea or ideas into one or two complete sentences. Write the sentence or sentences in the form of a haiku. If you wish, write your poem as a description following the structure of "Falling Flower" or "River" on page 410.
5. Write a title for your poem.

Edit Your Haiku

Read your haiku aloud, asking yourself the following questions as you review your writing. Make the changes you feel will improve the poem. Then copy the edited version on a new sheet of paper.

1. Does the poem convey your impression of an experience or feeling that you had?
2. Does the poem create vivid word pictures with images that appeal to one of the five senses or by using a striking simile or metaphor?
3. Are the ideas in the poem expressed in complete sentences?

Thinking About Couplets

Write two couplets that describe an animal. Choose a topic from the list below, or you may choose a topic of your own.

elephant	whale	sea horse	eagle
giraffe	shark	penguin	toucan
unicorn	swordfish	flamingo	myna bird

Writing Couplets

1. Begin by making notes that describe your subject. Write five descriptions of your subject, based on information from each of your five senses.
2. Next select two descriptions that you could develop into alliteration with an additional word or two. Write down several words you might add to your description to create alliteration.
3. Now decide what sounds are connected with the words you have used in your descriptions. Think of words that imitate these natural sounds. Add them to your description.
4. Use the ideas you have developed to write your couplets. Establish a rhythm for your couplets. Try to write lines that have the same number of syllables. The strongest beats in both lines should be the same. If the beats do not match, find words to replace the ones you have used. Make your end words rhyme. If you like, follow the structure of one of Ogden Nash's verses, replacing some of the words. For instance, you might follow the structure of "The Panther" by writing, "The ___ is like a ___ . Except ___ ."

Edit Your Couplets

Read your couplets aloud. Ask yourself the following questions as you review your writing. Make the changes you feel will improve the couplets. Then copy the edited version on a new piece of paper.

1. Do the couplets use images that appeal to one of the senses to create a vivid word picture?
2. Do they reinforce the image with alliteration of beginning sounds?
3. Have you used onomatopoeia to reinforce your image?
4. Do the lines end with words that rhyme?

Appreciating Poetry

Every language in the world has its own poetry. Long before Shakespeare, people used poetry to describe the beauty of nature, their feelings about loneliness and love, drama and adventure, and moments of human experience. Poems challenge you to see, taste, hear, feel, and smell through the words the poet chooses for sounds and images.

Japanese haiku express an idea vividly with only a few words of description. As you read the poems that follow below, notice that each haiku captures the experience of the writer by creating a picture image of one brief moment.

The Wind
Roseanne Harris

Whispers of the wind
Entice fields of wheat to sway
In gentle rhythm.

Melody of Life
Roseanne Harris

A bird, broken winged
Sang a melody of life
Outside my window.

Talking About Haiku

Look at the haiku again.

1. What subject is described in each poem?
2. Tell which words in each poem appeal to one of the five senses.
3. Find an example of alliteration in each haiku above. Tell the words that develop this particular sound effect.
4. Identify the one example of onomatopoeia in the lines above. Explain why this word demonstrates this type of sound effect.

Couplets are two lines of poetry that have exactly the same rhythm and that rhyme at the end. This poem is a series of couplets that tell a story. A poem that tells a story is called a *ballad*.

from
Casey at the Bat
Ernest Lawrence Thayer

The outlook wasn't brilliant for the Mudville nine that day;
The score stood four to two, with but one inning more to play;
And so, when Cooney died at first, and Burrows did the same,
A sickly silence fell upon the patrons of the game.

A straggling few got up to go in deep despair. The rest
Clung to the hope which springs eternal in the human breast;
They thought, if only Casey could but get a whack, at that,
They'd put up even money now, with Casey at the bat.

But Flynn preceded Casey, as did also Jimmy Blake,
And the former was a pudding, and the latter was a fake;
So upon that stricken multitude grim melancholy sat,
For there seemed but little chance of Casey's getting to the bat.

But Flynn let drive a single, to the wonderment of all,
And Blake, the much-despised, tore the cover off the ball;
And when the dust had lifted, and they saw what had occurred,
There was Jimmy safe on second, and Flynn a-hugging third

Then from the gladdened multitude went up a joyous yell;
It bounded from the mountaintop, and rattled in the dell;
It struck upon the hillside, and recoiled upon the flat;
For Casey, mighty Casey, was advancing to the bat.

There was ease in Casey's manner as he stepped into his place;
There was pride in Casey's bearing, and a smile on Casey's face;
And when, responding to the cheers, he lightly doffed his hat,
No stranger in the crowd could doubt 'twas Casey at the bat,

Ten thousand eyes were on him as he rubbed his hands with dirt;
Five thousand tongues applauded when he wiped them on his shirt;
Then while the writhing pitcher ground the ball into his hip,
Defiance gleamed in Casey's eye, a sneer curled Casey's lip.

Talking About Couplets

1. How many couplets does each stanza from "Casey at the Bat" contain?

2. How many stressed beats does each line in a couplet have?

3. Find examples in the poem of images that appeal to one of the five senses.

4. Ernest L. Thayer creates a humorous effect by using fancy language to describe an ordinary event. Find examples.

5. Find examples of the following in the poem: alliteration, onomatopoeia, metaphor.

INDEPENDENT WRITING

A Haiku

Prewriting Japanese haiku captures in a fragile and lovely way a fleeting moment of experience: a butterfly lighting on your glasses; a moment of companionship between two people; a fish shattering the moon's reflection in a lake; a moment of peace, of excitement, of beauty—moments caught for a second and swiftly gone.

Remember that a haiku has a special form. It has seventeen syllables. The first and third lines have five syllables; the second line has seven syllables. The pattern is 5-7-5.

Think of a moment in your past that you would like to develop in a haiku. Your experience may have been with a person, a place, an object, or a season. Choose a topic from the box below or use one of your own choosing.

People	Animals	Seasons	Weather	Places	Objects
friend	dog	spring	rain	home	souvenir
teacher	kitten	fall	snow	zoo	photograph
parent	horse	winter	ice	circus	food
grandparent	snake	summer	heat	sports field	tree
(other)	tiger		wind	outdoors	fence
			(other)	(other)	television

Jot down notes about the subject you have chosen. Follow steps 1 to 3 on page 416 to develop the images, similes, and metaphors you will use in your haiku.

Writing Use steps 4 and 5 for Writing a Haiku on page 416 to help you develop your ideas. Keep in mind the attitude or feeling that you wish to convey as you organize your ideas. Make certain that you use colorful words in your descriptions in order to create vivid picture images. Then use complete sentences to capture that moment from the past in a haiku.

Editing Read your poem to yourself, and ask the questions provided for editing a poem on page 416 as you read. Make the changes you feel will improve your writing. Then copy the edited version of the haiku on a new sheet of paper.

INDEPENDENT WRITING

Couplets

Prewriting Couplets are a form of poetry that rely heavily on sound effects. Remember that the two lines of a couplet have a matching rhythm, and they end with words that rhyme. A *rhyme* is the repetition of the end sound in two or more words. Remember that a poem can be made up of many couplets. If the poem tells a story, it is called a *ballad.*

Think about writing a ballad using couplets about an experience you have had or about an incident in the life of someone you know. If you prefer, you may choose your own topic. The incident may be real, fictional, sad, or humorous. Choose a person, a place, and a situation from the list below to get ideas for your ballad. Or create your own ideas. Then follow steps 1–3 on page 417 to create your descriptions.

People	Places	Situations
yourself	camp	hopelessly lost
friend	school	mistaken identity
parent	sports event	a school play
relative	store	a scary incident
mail carrier	supermarket	an exciting game
store clerk	outdoors	cooking dinner
police officer	home	trying to impress someone

Writing Follow step 4 on page 417 for Writing Couplets to write your poem. Then use the ideas you developed to write the rest of the poem. Make certain that your words create sound effects as well as vivid picture images. Express each thought in a complete sentence. To establish the rhythm for your ballad, you might like to follow the structure of "The Little Black-Eyed Rebel," which begins on page 414 or "Casey at the Bat," which begins on page 418. As you continue, add your own words to make the ballad your own. For instance, you might begin, "The outlook wasn't brilliant for ___ that day."

Editing Read your couplets aloud, and ask yourself the questions provided for editing a poem on page 417 as you read. Make the changes you feel will improve your writing. Then copy the edited version of your ballad on a new sheet of paper.

Review: Four Kinds of Sentences, pages 4-5

Write each sentence. Capitalize and punctuate each one correctly. Label each one **declarative, interrogative, imperative,** or **exclamatory.**

1. we toured Washington, D.C., on our week's vacation
2. what a long time a tour of that great city would take
3. tell the class about the most interesting parts of the trip
4. shall I begin with the city's history or with modern topics

Sentences and Sentence Fragments, pages 6-7

Write each group of words that forms a complete sentence. Underline the complete subject once and the complete predicate twice. If the group of words is not a complete sentence, write **fragment**.

1. Eight different cities or towns before the Revolution.
2. Leaders in Congress selected a site on the Potomac River.
3. President Washington chose lands between Maryland and Virginia.
4. An area of large estates and farms.

Complete and Simple Subjects, pages 8-9

Write each sentence. If a sentence is interrogative, reword it as a declarative sentence. Then underline the complete subject of each sentence. Draw a second line under the simple subject. Write the word **You** if it is the understood subject of an imperative sentence.

1. Describe P.C. L'Enfant's plans for Washington's construction.
2. Did L'Enfant choose Jenkins Hill for the site of the Capitol?
3. The modern Capitol stands on this small hill.
4. Was the location of the President's home a part of L'Enfant's plan?

Complete and Simple Predicates, pages 10-11

Write each sentence. Reword each interrogative sentence as a declarative sentence if you need to. Then underline the complete predicate of each sentence. Draw a second line under the simple predicate.

1. L'Enfant's designs required marble buildings and large parks.
2. Would very wide avenues give the capital a Parisian appearance?
3. Investigate L'Enfant's ideas for a monument to George Washington.
4. Did these enormous projects seem costly to the young nation?

Subject-Verb Agreement, pages 12-13

Write each sentence using the correct form of the verb in parentheses.

1. The city ____ four sections. (has, have)
2. Many streets ____ between the major sections. (runs, run)

3. Avenues _____ the city from east to west. (crosses, cross)
4. Three dollars _____ a reasonable price for a tour of the city. (is, are)

Compound Subjects and Predicates, pages 14-15

Write each sentence using the correct form of the verb or verbs.

1. Modern Washington _____ and _____ on L'Enfant's ideas. (understands, understand/expands, expand)
2. Parks or a monument _____ grace to the city. (adds, add)
3. Legislators and ambassadors _____ and _____ in structures rich with history. (lives, live/works, work)
4. The Potomac and the Anacostia Rivers _____ by the city. (flows, flow)

Compound Sentences, pages 16-17

Write each sentence. Label it as a **simple** or a **compound sentence.** Draw one line under each subject. Draw two lines under each verb. If it is a compound sentence, draw a line between the two simple sentences.

1. Washington, D.C., contains the White House and the Congress of the United States; it also has many cultural activities.
2. Either a museum or a gallery has an American art exhibition.
3. The huge Smithsonian Institution attracts and educates visitors.
4. Several hospitals perform valuable research in Washington, D.C. and the Walter Reed Center serves this function well.

Complex Sentences, pages 18-19

Write each sentence. Draw one line under the independent clause and two lines under the subordinate clause. Then write the subordinating conjunction that begins each subordinate clause.

1. While Washington, D.C., has many parks, most cultural events take place in buildings such as Constitution Hall.
2. More outdoor events occur as the warm months of the year arrive.
3. If visitors prefer nature exhibits, they can find them in the city.
4. Roosevelt Island is a wildlife park though a city surrounds it.

Review: Nouns, pages 26-27

Write the nouns in each sentence. Write **common noun** or **proper noun** after each noun. Then write **concrete noun** or **abstract noun**.

1. The history of cities tells much about social development.
2. The earliest cities were probably in Egypt and Mesopotamia.
3. Such centers also developed in China and in Central America.
4. The modern metropolis is the result of fifty centuries.

Additional Exercises

Nouns in the Subject and Predicate, pages 28-29

Write each sentence. Draw a line between the subject part and the predicate part. Label each noun as a **common noun** or a **proper noun.**

1. Most large ancient cities began as small towns on trade routes.
2. Farmers of the Middle East became merchants and builders.
3. With better agriculture the populations of the towns increased.
4. Shops, markets, and temples attracted new settlers quickly.
5. Soon the cities of Asia, Europe, and America became important.

Plural Nouns and Irregular Plurals, pages 30-31

Write each sentence using the correct form of the noun in parentheses.

1. The architecture of many ____ varies to suit the location. (city, cities)
2. The ____ and ____ of Egypt built enormous pyramids in the flat deserts. (man, men / woman, women)
3. Egyptian designs have many ____ and ____ in them. (3, 3's / 7, 7's)
4. Is *Knossos* spelled with three ____? (c, c's)

Possessive Nouns, pages 32-33

Write each sentence and add an apostrophe in the right place. Write whether the word with an apostrophe is a **singular possessive noun,** a **plural possessive noun,** or a **contraction.**

1. Athens steep hills served as protection for its citizens.
2. The Greek peoples designs became a model for later cities.
3. Troys high towers commanded a view of two great seas.
4. Babylons protected by two rivers.

Distinguishing Plurals and Possessives, pages 34-35

Write each sentence. Underline the word in parentheses that correctly completes the sentence. Write whether it is a **plural noun, singular possessive noun,** or **plural possessive noun.**

1. Many (cities, cities') find new life after great destruction.
2. Both Athens and Rome outlived several (wars, wars') effects.
3. A natural (disaster's, disasters') result is often new growth.
4. Scholars also treasure old (ruin's, ruins') historical uses.
5. Some of (Jerusalems', Jerusalem's) sections still draw scholars.

Collective Nouns, pages 36-37

Write each sentence. Underline the collective noun. Write whether the meaning of the collective noun is **singular** or **plural.**

1. The whole fleet is very important for the seaside city.

2. The group of ships, one by one, deliver vital supplies.
3. The flock feeds a huge population.
4. The herd arrive at different piers on the harbor.
5. The entire crowd at the dock await their imported goods.

Review: Verbs, pages 42-43

Write each sentence. Underline each action verb. If there is a direct object, underline it twice. Then write whether the verb is **transitive** or **intransitive.**

1. Several of the weary ticket sellers rested before the game.
2. Inside the huge stadium the ice glistened.
3. Usually a play-off hockey game thrills the crowd.
4. The coaches of both teams studied their opponents.

Linking Verbs, pages 44-45

Write each sentence. Draw one line under each verb. Then write whether it is an **action verb** or a **linking verb.** If it is a linking verb, write whether it is followed by a **predicate noun** or a **predicate adjective.**

1. One young hockey player scored the first goal.
2. Number 19 is the youngest player in the entire league.
3. The noise from the wild crowd was very loud.
4. The determined center hit the puck toward the goal.

Verbs with Predicate Nouns or Direct and Indirect Objects, pages 46-47

Write each sentence and draw a line under each verb. Write whether it is a **linking verb** or an **action verb.** Write whether each underlined word in the predicate part is a **predicate noun,** a **direct object,** or an **indirect object.**

1. The Montreal Canadians were the champions for many years.
2. The powerful defense players showed the fans their skills.
3. A skillful defense player blocked the sudden slapshot.
4. The play gave the other team time for a line change.

Distinguishing Action and Linking Verbs, pages 48-49

Write each sentence. Draw a line under each verb. Then write whether each verb is used as an **action verb** or as a **linking verb.**

1. The tall man with the mustache looked angry.
2. The goalie feels each strap on his protective gear.
3. He looked to his right for a pass from the goalie.
4. The enthusiastic crowd grew more enthusiastic during the game.

Present, Past, and Future Tenses, pages 50-51

Write each sentence. Use the correct tense of the verb in parentheses. Then write whether the form of the verb is in the **present, past,** or **future** tense.

1. Right now the ice machine ____ the rink. (clean)
2. The players ____ for the next few minutes. (wait)
3. That last game ____ the surface of the ice. (damage)
4. The machine constantly ____ new ice. (create)
5. Soon the players ____ on a smooth surface. (skate)

Making Subjects and Verbs Agree, pages 52-53

Write each sentence. Use the correct form of the verb in parentheses.

1. Both the manager and the coach ____ the game. (understand, understands)
2. Either an official or a celebrity ____ out the first ball. (throw, throws)
3. A former player and her friends ____ the game. (watch, watches)
4. Neither the players nor the manager ____ the reporters. (see, sees)
5. There ____ a lot of noise in the crowded dressing room. (is, are)

Principal Parts, Helping Verbs, and Verb Phrases, pages 54-55

Write each sentence. Use the helping verb in parentheses to complete each sentence. Then underline each participle and write whether it is a **present participle** or a **past participle.**

1. Polly ____ earned nine points for a bull's-eye. (is, has)
2. Georgia ____ counting five points for the arrow on the blue ring. (is, has)
3. The scorer ____ awarding the archer one point. (was, had)
4. Those archers ____ played until dusk every day this week. (are, have)

Present and Past Progressive, pages 56-57

Write each sentence using the present progressive tense of the verb.

1. Some of the gymnasts ____ over the floor. (tumble)
2. That athlete ____ backward and forward on the mat. (flip)
3. Several athletes ____ warm-up exercises on the mats. (do)

Write each sentence using the past progressive tense of the verb.

4. King Charles II of Britain ____ out prizes. (hand)
5. Archers from all over the world ____ for tournaments. (practice)
6. One archer ____ her own arrows in the distant target. (hit)

Present and Past Perfect, pages 58-59

Write each sentence using the present perfect tense of the verb.

1. The gymnasts ____ hard on their programs. (work)
2. The sports reporter ____ eagerly for an interview with the champ. (wait)
3. Many photographers ____ that nimble gymnast on film. (capture)

Write each sentence using the past perfect tense of the verb.

4. Americans ____ crude bows and arrows before 1860. (use)
5. By 1880 archery ____ into a relaxing sport. (turn)
6. Several bands of archers ____ clubs or associations. (form)

Irregular Verbs, pages 60-63

Write the past tense and the past participle of each verb.

1. say
2. creep
3. tear
4. choose
5. teach
6. drink
7. wear
8. write
9. swim
10. seek
11. break
12. throw

Review: Pronouns, pages 70-71

Write the second sentence of each pair. Replace the underlined word or words with a pronoun. Write whether you have used a **subject pronoun** or an **object pronoun.**

1. Myths are stories. <u>Myths</u> describe unusual adventures or strange events.
2. One myth is about the hero Jason. <u>Jason</u> leads a group of heroes.
3. The heroes look for the golden fleece. <u>The fleece</u> is priceless.
4. Jason calls the men the Argonauts. <u>Jason</u> names <u>the heroes</u> after their ship, the *Argo*.

Possessive Pronouns, pages 72-73

Write each sentence. Find the possessive noun, and replace it with a possessive pronoun. Then write whether the possessive pronoun is used **before a noun** or if it can **stand alone.**

1. Characters in myths vary. A myth's characters may be superhuman.
2. The characters rule the world. All events are in the characters' control.
3. Zeus is the most important Greek god. Zeus' powers are very strong.
4. One powerful goddess is Aphrodite. Aphrodite's powers control love.
5. Another goddess is Athena. Power over wisdom and war are Athena's.

Pronouns and Antecedents, pages 74-75

Write the second sentence of each pair using the correct pronoun for each blank. Then write the antecedent for each pronoun.

1. Jupiter is the leader of the Roman gods. ____ rules the heavens.
2. Minerva is a Roman goddess. ____ controls all matters of wisdom.
3. Some myths explain the history of Rome. ____ was founded by twins.
4. The twins were placed in a basket at birth. ____ were adopted by a wolf.
5. Romulus and Remus built Rome. They built ____ in honor of the wolf.

Pronouns as Objects of Prepositions, pages 76-77

Write the second sentence in each pair. Use the correct pronoun.

1. Many old temples still stand. Statues stand inside ____ . (they, them)
2. The temples are centuries old. They seem awesome to ____ . (me, I)
3. Cambodia's Angor Wat is very ancient. Dense jungle grows all around ____ . (they, it)
4. Interested Americans can study Angor Wat. Pictures and articles are available to ____ . (us, we)

Indefinite Pronouns, pages 78-79

Write each sentence using the correct word in parentheses.

1. Some ____ that a myth is only a fanciful story. (say, says)
2. Everyone ____ the imaginative quality of myths. (understand, understands)
3. Others put forward ____ different opinions. (their, her)
4. Each ____ cautiously with new research. (proceed, proceeds)

Reflexive and Intensive Pronouns, pages 80-81

Write each sentence using the correct pronoun in parentheses.

1. Most people in myths take ____ seriously. (them, themselves)
2. Sometimes a goddess finds ____ in difficulties. (herself, her)
3. The human hero ____ might come to her aid. (him, himself)
4. ____ may feel sympathy for the characters. (You, Yourself)
5. The gain of such awareness fascinates ____ . (me, myself)

Interrogative Pronouns, pages 82-83

Write the second sentence of each pair below using the correct word.

1. ____ do Romulus and Remus appreciate? (Who, Whom)

2. ____ the Greek goddess of war and wisdom? (Whose, Who's)
3. With ____ do the Greek Argonauts sail? (who, whom)
4. ____ influence controls the heavens in Roman myths? (Whose, Who's)

Review: Adjectives, pages 88-89

Write each sentence. Draw one line under each adjective. Draw two lines under the noun or pronoun each adjective describes. If a linking verb connects the subject and adjective, circle the predicate adjective.

1. Edgar Degas was famous for his art.
2. He painted people in familiar everyday poses.
3. He chose ordinary subjects such as dancing.
4. The graceful movements fascinated him.

Articles, page 90

Write each word or group of words with the indefinite article that belongs before it.

1. bronze statue
2. ivory earring
3. paintbrush
4. sculptor's chisel
5. easel
6. hour's work
7. happy day
8. usual event
9. unnecessary expense

Proper Adjectives, page 91

Write the following list of words. Capitalize where necessary.

1. canadian bacon
2. young writer
3. appalachian mountains
4. old radio
5. african art
6. south american country

Comparative and Superlative Adjectives, pages 92-93

Write each sentence using the correct form of the adjective in parentheses.

1. Some colors look ____ together than others. (bad, worse, worst)
2. Blue colors seem ____ than red colors. (cool, cooler, coolest)
3. Orange is ____ than yellow. (warm, warmer, warmest)
4. Some of the ____ paintings in the world are still lifes. (good, better, best)
5. The ____ painting of the two is framed in wood. (small, smaller, smallest)

More Comparative and Superlative Adjectives, pages 94-95

Write each sentence using the correct word in parentheses.

1. John Constable is the ____ famous of all landscape painters. (more, most)
2. He painted ____ interesting landscapes than anyone. (more, most)
3. Constable was ____ famous than Jean-Baptiste Camille Corot. (less, least)
4. The colors of the countryside are ____ beautiful in late afternoon than in morning. (more, most)
5. The early morning is the ____ attractive of all. (less, least)

Demonstrative Adjectives and Pronouns, pages 96-97

Write each sentence using the correct word in parentheses.

1. ____ is a painting by the Frenchman Claude Monet. (This, These)
2. ____ six paintings show the very same bridge. (That, Those)
3. ____ shows the bridge in the light of dawn. (That, Those)
4. The bridge looks very different in ____ shadows. (those, them)
5. Was ____ his inspiration for the paintings? (that, those)

Review: Adverbs, pages 102-103

Write each adverb. Write the word the adverb describes. Write whether it is an **action verb,** an **adverb,** or an **adjective.**

1. The waltz began slowly.
2. The instruments played loudly.
3. Some dancers moved especially gracefully.
4. One couple was unusually clumsy.
5. They tripped accidentally.
6. The huge lights were particularly attractive.

Comparative and Superlative Adverbs, pages 104-105

Write each sentence. Use either the comparative or superlative form.

1. The fifth flutist plays the ____ of all. (better, best)
2. The best singer practiced the ____ of all. (more frequently, most frequently)
3. He follows the music ____ than I do. (more carefully, most carefully)
4. High notes appear ____ in your part than in Sarah's. (more often, most often)
5. The cellist sits ____ to the violinist than I do. (closer, closest)

Intensifiers, pages 106-107

Write each sentence. Underline each intensifier once and the word it describes twice. Write whether the word described is an **adjective** or an **adverb.**

1. The school band was certainly excellent.
2. The band marched quite precisely.
3. The leader dressed very nicely.
4. Rather eagerly the horses pranced up the road.

Adverbs and Adjectives, pages 108-109

Write each sentence. Write whether the underlined word is an **adjective** or an **adverb.** Then write the word it describes.

1. The explorers worked <u>fast</u> at the designated site.

2. The first explorer found a wall.
3. The next discovery surprised them.
4. They sat down on the wall first.
5. Next they laughed very loud.

Using Adverbs and Adjectives, pages 110-111

Write each sentence using the correct word in parentheses. Then write whether the word is an **adverb** or an **adjective.**

1. That climb looks ____ . (impossible, impossibly)
2. We ____ climbed the steep hill. (careful, carefully)
3. The girl seemed ____ after the climb. (sick, sickly)
4. She made her way ____ to the car. (slow, slowly)

Avoiding Double Negatives, pages 112-113

Write each sentence using the correct word in parentheses.

1. Hardly ____ people ever climbed that mountain. (no, any)
2. Nobody ____ called that adventure an easy one. (ever, never)
3. There isn't ____ clear path up the mountainside. (any, no)
4. Scarcely ____ will grow on those snowy peaks. (nothing, anything)
5. That adventure, without your skills, ____ hardly possible. (is, isn't)

Review: Prepositions and Prepositional Phrases, pages 118-119

Write each sentence. Draw a line under each prepositional phrase. Draw two lines under the object.

1. Paris is an important center of fashion.
2. Many top clothes designers work in Paris.
3. Models from other countries work there, too.
4. Some interesting shops are found along the Champs Élysées.

Prepositional Phrases as Adjectives and Adverbs, pages 120-121

Write each sentence. Draw one line under each prepositional phrase. Draw two lines under the word each phrase describes. Write **adjective phrase** or **adverb phrase** for each prepositional phrase.

1. The noises of the city do not disturb the tourists.
2. The tourists and I traveled around the Greek countryside.
3. We saw a statue inside the temple.
4. The temple is a structure of fragile beauty.
5. Japan lies near the Asian coast.

Agreement in Sentences with Prepositional Phrases, pages 122-123

Write each sentence using the correct form of the verb.

1. The history of the horse ____ interesting. (is, are)
2. Horses in European history ____ very important. (was, were)
3. These animals, through the ages, ____ in paintings of farm life. (appear, appears)
4. The labor of agriculture still ____ on the horse in many lands. (depend, depends)

Identifying Conjunctions, pages 124-125

Write each sentence. Underline each conjunction and write whether it is a **coordinating conjunction,** a **correlative conjunction,** or a **subordinating conjunction.** Draw two lines under any prepositions.

1. Both pewter and bone were popular materials for buttons.
2. The collector didn't keep the button because it was damaged.
3. The button was valuable, and collectors admired it.
4. Although old buttons are interesting, many types aren't rare.
5. The shop owner buys and sells antique buttons.

Interjections, pages 126-127

Write each sentence. Underline the interjection in each and place the proper punctuation mark after each.

1. Tut-tut You must be exaggerating about the cost of that button.
2. Fiddlesticks my button-collecting magazine didn't arrive.
3. This button was worn by a famous general. No kidding
4. Hey is this button really made of solid gold?

Review: Clauses and Sentences, pages 132-133

Write each sentence using the correct punctuation. Write whether it is a **simple sentence** or a **compound sentence.** Then draw one line under each complete subject and two lines under each complete predicate.

1. The old steel plow digs deeply into the rich earth.
2. A crow watches from a tree it is waiting for the seeds.
3. The young farmer plows and plants and the field is watered.
4. Several birds and some insects help the new crop.

Complex Sentences, pages 134-135

Write each sentence. Underline the subordinate clause. Draw two lines under the subordinating conjunction that begins each subordinate clause.

1. Until we had an alphabet, people communicated through pictures.
2. Picture writing was useful, although it had limitations.
3. While most ideas were intelligible, finer meanings were less clear.
4. Phoenician traders refined the symbols as they traveled widely.

Adverb Clauses, pages 136-137

Write each sentence. Draw one line under the adverb clause and two lines under the subordinating conjunction. Write the word the clause modifies. Then write whether that word is a **verb,** an **adjective,** or an **adverb.**

1. Before we learn a language, we communicate with gestures.
2. People add meaning to their words whenever they gesture.
3. Some can say more with gestures than they can with language.
4. Wherever they perform, mimes find an appreciative audience.

Appositives, pages 138-139

Write each sentence. Underline the appositive phrase in each. Add commas where necessary. Draw two lines under the noun or pronoun the appositive phrase identifies.

1. Alan an excellent acrobat wants to become a professional clown.
2. He studies with Marie an excellent clown.
3. He improves his coordination a necessary skill for a clown.
4. Balance an important skill on the high wire adds to a clown's act.

Participles in Verb Phrases and as Adjectives, pages 140-141

Write each sentence. Draw one line under the verb phrase in each sentence. Draw a second line under the helping verb or verbs.

1. Celia has brought a very young raccoon home from the forest.
2. The baby raccoon was wandering alone in the open meadow.
3. Celia and her parents have discussed the best plan of action.

Write each sentence. Underline the participle in each sentence. Write whether it is used as part of a verb phrase or as an adjective.

4. This orphaned raccoon feeds hungrily on fresh warm milk.

5. Celia is listening to its chatter during the late hours.
6. Celia's parents are contacting the local zoo about the raccoon.

Gerunds and Gerund Phrases, pages 142-143

Write each sentence. Write whether the underlined word is the **main verb** in a verb phrase, a participle used as an **adjective,** or a **gerund.** Write whether the gerund is the **subject** of the sentence or the **direct object** of the verb.

1. Celia has been taking the young raccoon back into the woods.
2. Exercising is important for the animal.
3. Celia's friends enjoy a visit with this appealing pet.
4. They like watching while the raccoon washes its food.

Write each sentence. Underline the gerund phrase in each.

5. The zoo has scheduled special visiting times for Celia.
6. Caring for such animals is a particular skill of the zoo's.

Infinitives and Infinitive Phrases, pages 144-145

Write each sentence. Write whether the underlined words in each are an **infinitive** or a **prepositional phrase.** Then write whether each infinitive is the **simple subject** of the sentence or the **direct object** of the verb.

1. To rake leaves on a Saturday is fun for the Singer family.
2. A certain part of the job belongs to each of them.
3. Frank always wants to rest.

Write each sentence. Underline the infinitive phrase in each.

4. The Singers like to share the work on a cool autumn day.
5. To play touch football after work is their goal.

Parts of Speech in Sentences, pages 146-147

Write each sentence. Write each underlined word and its part of speech.

1. A company invented a special camera.
2. It transfers drawings to celluloid sheets.
3. The process is easier and faster than the old process.
4. One movie shows dozens of spotted puppies repeatedly.
5. Hey, the camera repeats the group across the whole sheet!

Review: Beginning and Ending Your Sentences, pages 164-165

Write each sentence. Capitalize and punctuate each one correctly. Write **declarative, interrogative, imperative, exclamatory,** or **interrogative** for each one.

1. look at the big strawberries in the clay basket
2. michael and i run back to the greenhouse
3. how plump the strawberries are
4. where do white strawberries come from

Capitalizing Proper Nouns and Proper Adjectives, pages 166-167

Write each sentence using capital letters where they are needed.

1. A group of new york students met outside the united nations.
2. Two were african students, and three were australian students.
3. A girl from brazil asked the american if he had been born in new york.
4. They all took a course called *english 2*.
5. Three asian students joined the group on november 9, 1983.

Commas I, pages 168-169

Write each sentence using commas where necessary. Give a reason by writing **series, address, date, interrupting word** or **expression, appositive,** or **person's name.**

1. The art of setting type by the way is changing rapidly.
2. Well new technology is increasing its speed and accuracy.
3. Writers of the past often wrote set and printed their books.
4. Walt Whitman a poet of lasting quality did such a job himself.
5. Whitman worked in Brooklyn New York for several typesetters.

Commas II, pages 170-171

Write each sentence and underline the subordinate clause. Use commas where necessary. Give the reason.

1. When a manuscript is ready editors prepare it for the printer.
2. Editors know the design of the book and they add directions to the printer.
3. Editors and printers agree on a design before the printers begin work.
4. After the computer receives the program the first copies of the manuscript are printed.

Semicolons and Colons, pages 172-173

Write the sentences below. Punctuate them correctly using semicolons and colons.

1. Pictures, reports, and stories about the case filled the news and some people followed the case carefully.
2. The best television news program was on at 330 P.M. each day.
3. Some individuals expressed opinions certain newspapers published editorials.
4. Three people testified at the trial the police officer, the defendant, and I.

Quotation Marks and Italics, pages 174-175

Write the sentences below correctly. Use quotation marks, punctuation marks, and italics correctly.

1. Have you read Tolkien's Lord of the Rings, Jean asked Wendy.
2. No, I haven't Jean answered but please tell me about it, Wendy
3. Well, Wendy began it continues the story begun in The Hobbit
4. Oh yes said Jean I enjoyed that book about Bilbo Baggins

Other Punctuation Marks, pages 176-177

Write each sentence. Use a hyphen, dash, or parentheses where necessary.

1. My uncle Guglielmo 1899 1981 was an Italian immigrant to America.
2. He arrived at Ellis Island, New York with others, of course, in 1910.
3. Most of the people with him were exfarmers and craftspeople.
4. Guglielmo he had several skills found work quickly in New England.
5. Soon around 1915 he and other immigrants bought a small farm.

Abbreviations, pages 178-179

Change each word group, using capital letters and punctuation marks. Abbreviate each underlined word. Write the new phrase.

1. boise, <u>idaho</u>
2. <u>doctor</u> florence <u>rena</u> sabin
3. <u>wednesday</u>, <u>september</u> 2
4. <u>thomas</u> <u>alva</u> edison, <u>senior</u>
5. 850 high park <u>boulevard</u>
6. <u>betty</u> j. meggers, <u>doctor of philosophy</u>
7. 2 park <u>place</u>

Contractions, pages 180-181

Write each sentence. Use an apostrophe where necessary.

1. Russ father owns a small restaurant, and its successful.
2. Theyre working together now at the restaurants sandwich counter.
3. "Theres plenty of bread for all these workers lunches," says Russ father.
4. A secretary says that its her sandwich.

Using the Table of English Spellings, pages 188-189

Use the dictionary and the Table of English Spellings to correct the spelling of the underlined word in each sentence. Then write each sentence correctly.

1. A horse-drawn wagon on a superhighway seems an <u>anakronism</u>.
2. The general delivered an <u>ultamatum</u> to the enemy camp.
3. Sheila's essay contained a few <u>superfluis</u> statements.
4. Kenny was <u>ambivelent</u> about joining the school track team.

Spelling Rules I, pages 190-191

Read each pair of words. Write the correctly spelled word in each pair. Check your answers against the spelling rules in the lesson.

1. abusing, abuseing
2. terribley, terribly
3. reducate, reeducate
4. fronteir, frontier

Add the prefix or suffix to each word. Write the new word. Check your answers against the spelling rules in the lesson.

5. enhance + ing
6. replace + able
7. abate + ment
8. care + ful
9. ir + rational
10. judge + ment

Spelling Rules II, pages 192-193

Read each pair of words. Write the correctly spelled word in each pair. Check your answers against the spelling rules in the lesson.

1. spotless, spottless
2. curryed, curried
3. pited, pitted
4. coverring, covering

Add the suffix to each word. Write the new word. Check your answers against the spelling rules in the lesson.

5. rally + ing
6. opus + es
7. sorry + est
8. cut + er
9. river + s
10. dry + ing

Irregular Plural Nouns, pages 194-195

Write the correct plural form or forms of each word. Check your answers against the spelling rules in the lesson.

1. studio
2. man
3. cliff
4. solo
5. species
6. hero
7. series
8. life
9. lasso
10. woman
11. veto
12. child

Words Often Confused I, pages 196-197

Write each sentence using the correct word in parentheses.

1. The department store ____ was very crowded. (aisle, isle)
2. Many shelves were empty of their ____ . (wares, wears)
3. ____ could not keep the shoppers away. (Reign, Rain)
4. Anna was ____ confused by the many bargains. (holy, wholly)
5. She asked her mother to ____ her. (council, counsel)
6. ____ difficult to choose from the wide selection of clothes. (It's, Its)
7. ____ trying on a matching skirt and sweater. (She's, She)

Words Often Confused II, pages 198-199

Write each sentence using the correct word in parentheses.

1. Michael is fixing the ____ wheel on his bike. (lose, loose)
2. He wonders ____ he should remove the wheel. (whether, weather)
3. The wheel, of course, must be ____ . (strait, straight)
4. ____ did he put that special wrench? (Where, Were, Wear)
5. Michael thought all the tools ____ in the box. (where, were, wear)
6. He takes old ____ bolts off the wheel rim. (led, lead)
7. Now he senses his brother's ____ behind him. (presence, presents)

Words in Context, pages 204-205

Read each sentence carefully. Write what you think the underlined word means.

1. The dark old house gave us an <u>eerie</u> feeling.
2. The driver <u>veered</u> to avoid a bump.

3. The adaptation of the book made an interesting play.
4. My brother spliced together each strand of old rope.
5. Rosa wanted to plant some tomato sprouts, but the tomato seeds had not yet germinated into tiny plants.

Words with Multiple Meanings, pages 206-207

Read each sentence. Write each underlined word. Then write the meaning of the underlined word as it is used in each sentence. Use the dictionary if necessary.

1. Andy will fill himself at the neighborhood picnic today.
2. The building company sought fill for the swampy land area.
3. Doctor Forbes asked her assistant to fill the prescription.
4. The music from Nancy's guitar fills the concert hall.
5. Wind fills the sails of each boat during the yacht race.

Prefixes, pages 208-209

Write a word with a prefix that can replace the underlined words in each sentence. Write each sentence using the new word.

1. Sandra has been rather not involved with school activities.
2. The seats of the outdoor theater are arranged in a half a circle.
3. These historical facts seem related among.
4. That train on one rail runs extremely quietly.
5. The high-jump athlete made a better than other humans effort.
6. It is not probable that Gary will see you after the show.

More Prefixes, pages 210-211

Write a word with a prefix that can replace the underlined words in each sentence.

1. It seemed destined before that Joan would find that dog.
2. Toni stated again her words for her many listeners.
3. Charles is doing very well in the after operative room.
4. The new merchant will sell at a lower price his competitor.
5. Alan piled together his latest poems and short stories.
6. Do not look over the important work done by this painter.

Noun Suffixes, pages 212-213

Add the suffix in parentheses to each word below. Write the word. Check the spelling in your dictionary.

1. astronomy (er)
2. great (ness)
3. resist (ance)
4. develop (ment)
5. connect (ion)
6. improve (ment)
7. judge (ment)
8. busy (ness)
9. art (ist)

Adjective Suffixes, pages 214-215

Read each sentence. Look at the underlined adjective. Write the meaning of the adjective.

1. Andrew is always regardful of safety regulations.
2. Some bothersome details keep Jill from completing the work.
3. That action by the opposing player was contemptible.
4. A beautiful sunset ended the final day of our trip.
5. The diver drove sharks away with repellent chemicals.
6. Donna is quite creative with some clay and a sculpting tool.

Roots, pages 216-217

Write the word in each sentence that contains one of the roots below. Then underline the word root and write the meaning of the word. Use the dictionary if necessary.

sign *vis* *pos* *pend* *port* *voc* *cess* *cep*

1. The interception of the pass discouraged the quarterback.
2. Martha's comments on the book seemed significant to the class.
3. Len had a difficult time defending his position on the field.
4. An immense vista of fields and hills appeared around the bend.
5. The soldiers looked forward to the cessation of hostilities.
6. Charles finally won a place in the vocal section of the band.
7. Large ripe pears hung like pendants from the many trees.
8. Butterflies in the field seemed to be portents of spring.

Synonyms, pages 218-219

Write each sentence. Use the word in parentheses that better completes the sentence. Think carefully about which word gives the clearer meaning.

1. Norman Rockwell sometimes paints funny scenes. (good, hilarious)
2. Many of his well-known paintings first appeared as magazine covers. (nice, famous)

3. Most of his paintings are lifelike. (realistic, good)
4. In one, the kind sheriff has a gift for a lost boy. (friendly, nice)
5. Another painting shows an attractive young woman fixing a car. (pretty, nice)

Antonyms, pages 220-221

Choose the antonym of the underlined word in each sentence. Then write the sentence with the antonym.

1. Frank constantly improves at his carpentry. (never, always)
2. He spends hours on the many details of his ornate designs. (complex, simple)
3. Frank is versatile and builds several kinds of things. (repetitious, varied)
4. Impressed customers offer complimentary prices for furniture. (insulting, pleasing)
5. This rewarding work gives Frank satisfaction. (worthwhile, futile)
6. A regular customer has just arrived. (unfamiliar, usual)

Verbs Often Confused, pages 222-223

Write each sentence using the word in parentheses that correctly completes the sentence.

1. Will you ____ your harmonica to the party? (take, bring)
2. ____ me have one of those blue pencils, please. (Let, Leave)
3. My friend ____ young children how to read. (teaches, learns)
4. Jeanne ____ the stack of newspapers on the ground. (lied, laid)
5. Anita ____ from the sofa. (raised, rose)

Words Often Confused, pages 224-225

Write the word in parentheses that completes each sentence correctly.

1. Donna studies the ____ through books, films, and museums. (passed, past)
2. I would ____ your dinner invitation, but I have to work tonight. (except, accept)
3. This river changes its ____ during rainy seasons. (course, coarse)
4. Two police officers ran ____ the governor's car. (besides, beside)

TABLE OF CONTENTS

Handbook

I. Grammar and Usage

Sentences

DEFINITION

A **sentence** is a group of words that expresses a complete thought. Every sentence begins with a capital letter. page 4 ADDITIONAL EXERCISES, page 422

Many pioneers built log cabins. They covered the walls with bark.

A **sentence fragment** is a group of words that is only part of a sentence. It does not express a complete thought. page 6 ADDITIONAL EXERCISES, page 422

Settlers of the frontier. sentence fragment

Worked for weeks on their cabins. sentence fragment

Settlers of the frontier worked for weeks on their cabins. complete sentence

PARTS OF SENTENCES

The **complete subject,** or **subject part,** of a sentence names whom or what the sentence is about. The complete subject part of a sentence may be more than one word. page 6 ADDITIONAL EXERCISES, page 422

A blacksmith forged horseshoes. A skilled carpenter made furniture.

The **complete predicate,** or **predicate part,** of a sentence tells what action the subject does. Sometimes it tells what the subject is or is like. The complete predicate may be more than one word. page 6 ADDITIONAL EXERCISES, page 422

Scouts blazed trails through the forests of the frontier.

The notches on the trees along the trail were helpful to other travelers.

The **simple subject** is the main word or group of words in the complete subject. page 8 ADDITIONAL EXERCISES, page 422

Many families traveled west toward the frontier in colonial times.

The Mississippi River was the western border of the frontier at that time.

Handbook

The **simple predicate** is the main word or group of words in the complete predicate. page 10 ADDITIONAL EXERCISES, page 422

The scouts had explored the frontier. They knew the territory well.

A **compound subject** has two or more simple subjects that have the same predicate. The subjects are joined by *and* or *or.* page 14 ADDITIONAL EXERCISES, page 423

Buffalo and deer roamed the plains. Cattle or sheep live there now.

A **compound predicate** has two or more verbs that have the same subject. The verbs are connected by *and* or *or.* page 14 ADDITIONAL EXERCISES, page 423

Settlers sent and received letters by pony express.

Pony express riders delivered or picked up letters at each stop.

An **independent clause** has one subject part and one predicate part. It expresses a complete thought and it can stand alone. page 18 ADDITIONAL EXERCISES, page 423

People traveled more comfortably after the stagecoach was introduced.

Passengers rode inside the coach while a driver managed the horses.

A **subordinate clause** is a group of words that has a subject part and a predicate part, but it cannot stand alone. It does not express a complete thought. It is always combined with an independent clause. Subordinate clauses often begin with these subordinating conjunctions: *after, because, since when, although, before, though, where, as, if, until, while,* and *unless.* Use a comma after a subordinate clause that introduces a sentence. page 18 ADDITIONAL EXERCISES, page 423

The stagecoach stopped frequently because the journey was long.

After the sun had set, stagecoach drivers often continued the journey.

An **adverb clause** is a subordinate clause that tells more about a verb, an adjective, or an adverb in the independent clause. page 136 ADDITIONAL EXERCISES, page 433

Richard left early because of the bad weather.

While Carol worked, Richard saw several movies.

An **appositive** is a noun or pronoun that is placed next to another noun or pronoun to identify it or to give additional information about it. An appositive often includes modifiers. An appositive is set off from the rest of the sentence with commas. page 138 ADDITIONAL EXERCISES, page 433

My favorite dessert, carrot cake, can be very sweet.

This recipe, Ken's Texas Chili, looks simple.

KINDS OF SENTENCES

A **declarative sentence** is a sentence that makes a statement. A declarative sentence ends with a period. page 4 ADDITIONAL EXERCISES, page 422

A buffalo bug chews clothes.

A carpet beetle eats rugs and carpets.

An **interrogative sentence** is a sentence that asks a question. An interrogative sentence ends with a question mark. page 4 ADDITIONAL EXERCISES, page 422

Do museum beetles live in a museum?

Why do fireflies glow in the night?

An **exclamatory sentence** is a sentence that expresses strong feeling. An exclamatory sentence ends with an exclamation mark. page 4 ADDITIONAL EXERCISES, page 422

How I love to catch fireflies!

What an exciting ballgame it was!

An **imperative sentence** is a sentence that gives a command or makes a request. An imperative sentence ends with a period. page 4 ADDITIONAL EXERCISES, page 422

Shut the door please.

Listen to the night noises.

A **simple sentence** is a sentence that has one subject part and one predicate part. page 16 ADDITIONAL EXERCISES, page 423

Some animals sleep through the winter.

A hamster takes naps all winter.

A **compound sentence** is a sentence that contains two or more simple sentences joined by *and, or,* or *but.* It has at least two subjects and two predicates. page 16 ADDITIONAL EXERCISES, page 423

Bats sleep during the day, and hummingbirds sleep at night.

Many frogs sleep in the winter, but desert frogs sleep in the summer.

I need to sleep ten hours at night, or I fall asleep at lunch.

A **complex sentence** is a sentence that has an independent clause and one or more subordinate clauses. page 18 ADDITIONAL EXERCISES, page 423

As cold weather sets in, some animals begin hibernation.

Animals in hibernation sleep until warm weather arrives.

Parts of Speech

NOUN

A **noun** is a word that names a person, place, thing, or idea. page 26 ADDITIONAL EXERCISES, page 423

The tired cowboys led their horses to the pasture before dinner.

They sang a song about the beauty of the sunset over the open range.

A **concrete noun** is a noun that names things you can see or touch. page 26 ADDITIONAL EXERCISES, page 423

Look at the horse. Its saddle is leather.

An **abstract noun** is a noun that names ideas and feelings that cannot be seen or touched. page 26 ADDITIONAL EXERCISES, page 423

The speed of the horse is remarkable. Hunger drove it on.

A **common noun** is a noun that names any person, place, thing, or idea. page 26 ADDITIONAL EXERCISES, page 423

The pony galloped down the road. Clouds float across the sky.

A **proper noun** is a noun that names a specific person, place, thing, or idea. page 26 ADDITIONAL EXERCISES, page 423

Some horses come from Arabia.

One breed was named after Justin Morgan.

A **singular noun** names one person, place, thing, or idea. page 30 ADDITIONAL EXERCISES, page 424

A ballad tells a story about a cowboy.

A cowboy sings the sad song.

A **plural noun** names more than one person, place, thing, or idea. page 30 ADDITIONAL EXERCISES, page 424

Most cowboys wore special boots with spurs at the heels.

Leather chaps protected their legs from rough winds.

A **possessive noun** is a noun that names who or what has something. page 32 ADDITIONAL EXERCISES, page 424

People often call the saddle a cowboy's home.

Charles Russell's paintings show scenes from cowboy life.

A **collective noun** names a group of people or things. The noun has a singular meaning when you speak about a group that acts as a unit. The noun has a plural meaning when you want to show that each member of the group acts separately or individually. page 36 ADDITIONAL EXERCISES, page 424

The audience applauds the performers at the rodeo.
(audience= it, singular)

The audience leave the rodeo at different times.
(audience= they, plural)

A **predicate noun** is a noun that follows a linking verb. It tells what the subject is. page 46 ADDITIONAL EXERCISES, page 425

The tall cowboy is the winner.

He becomes the national champion.

VERB

An **action verb** is a word that names an action. It may contain more than one word. page 48 ADDITIONAL EXERCISES, page 425

Dancers first performed ballet in 1581.

They danced for the French royalty.

The **direct object** of a verb receives the action of the verb. It answers the question *whom*? or *what*? after an action verb. page 46 ADDITIONAL EXERCISES, page 425

John Glenn orbited the earth. Magellan sailed the seas.

A **transitive verb** is a verb that has a direct object. page 42 ADDITIONAL EXERCISES, page 425

Dancers wore elaborate costumes. Masks covered their faces.

An **intransitive verb** is a verb that does not have a direct object. page 42 ADDITIONAL EXERCISES, page 425

In the first ballets dancers sang. Dance critics complained later.

A **linking verb** is a verb that connects the subject part with a noun or an adjective in the predicate part. It tells what the subject is or is like. page 44 ADDITIONAL EXERCISES, page 425

Songs were important in early ballets.

Dancing grew more popular later.

The **present tense** of a verb names an action that happens now. page 50 ADDITIONAL EXERCISES, page 426

Dancers practice every day. The exercise strengthens their muscles.

The **past tense** of a verb names an action that already happened. page 50 ADDITIONAL EXERCISES, page 426

Isadora Duncan started dancing in the early 1900s.

She rebelled against the traditional training for ballet.

The **future tense** of a verb names an action that will take place in the future. page 50 ADDITIONAL EXERCISES, page 426

Isadora Duncan's influence will always affect the forms of dance.

Dancers will try new forms of expression in dance because of her.

A **participle** is a verb form that can follow a helping verb in a verb phrase. The participle is the main verb in the verb phrase. The **present participle** is formed by adding *-ing* to most verbs. The **past participle** is formed by adding *-ed* to most verbs. The past and past participles are the same for most verbs. pages 54, 140 ADDITIONAL EXERCISES, pages 426, 433

The world is applauding Ms. Duncan.

People have recognized her skill.

People are praising her creativity.

Once only Europeans had applauded.

A **helping verb** helps the main verb to name an action or make a statement. page 54 ADDITIONAL EXERCISES, page 426

Ballet has changed since that time.

Dancers have created new styles.

A **verb phrase** consists of one or more helping verbs followed by a main verb. It names the action or tells what the subject is or is like. page 54 ADDITIONAL EXERCISES, page 426

Isadora Duncan has influenced dance.

She had been criticized at first.

The **present progressive tense** of a verb names an action or condition that is continuing in the present. It consists of a helping verb *am, is,* or *are* and the present participle of the main verb. page 56 ADDITIONAL EXERCISES, page 426

Dancers are seeking their own interpretations of Greek art now.

Performers are creating new forms of expression in dance.

The **past progressive tense** of a verb names an action or condition that continued for some time in the past. It consists of the helping verb *was* or *were* and the present participle of the main verb. page 56 ADDITIONAL EXERCISES, page 426

Isadora Duncan was offering her own style of dance to the world.

Dancers were criticizing her form of dance at that time.

The **present perfect tense** of a verb names an action that happened at an indefinite time in the past. It also names an action that started in the past and is still happening in the present. page 58 ADDITIONAL EXERCISES, page 427

The art of Greece has inspired many dancers throughout the centuries.

Dancers have used classical art as an inspiration for their work.

The **past perfect tense** of a verb names an action that has happened before another past action. page 58 ADDITIONAL EXERCISES, page 427

The pictures of nature and Greek characters had inspired Ms. Duncan.

She had imitated the freedom of movement and expression of the Greeks.

A **gerund** is a verb form ending in *-ing* that is used as a noun. page 142 ADDITIONAL EXERCISES, page 434

Running is a great exercise.

The students enjoy running.

A **gerund phrase** is a group of words that includes a gerund and other words that describe the gerund. page 142 ADDITIONAL EXERCISES, page 434

Going to the movies is fun.

Watching a play is also enjoyable.

An **infinitive** is formed from the word *to* together with the basic form of a verb. The infinitive is often used as a noun in a sentence. page 144 ADDITIONAL EXERCISES, page 434

To sightsee is interesting.

Many people try to see everything.

An **infinitive phrase** is a group of words that includes an infinitive and other words that describe the infinitive. page 144 ADDITIONAL EXERCISES, page 434

To see everything is difficult.

To really enjoy a trip one should see the highlights.

Handbook

Irregular verbs form the past tense and past participle in different ways. One group simply changes one vowel to form the past and past participle. page 60 ADDITIONAL EXERCISES, page 427

Verb	Past	Past Participle
become	became	(have, has) become
begin	began	(have, has) begun
come	came	(have, has) come
drink	drank	(have, has) drunk
ring	rang	(have, has) rung
run	ran	(have, has) run
shrink	shrank	(have, has) shrunk
sink	sank	(have, has) sunk
sing	sang	(have, has) sung
spring	sprang	(have, has) sprung
swim	swam	(have, has) swum

A small group of irregular verbs has the same spelling in its past and past participle forms as the verb itself. page 60 ADDITIONAL EXERCISES, page 427

Verb	Past	Past Participle
bet	bet	(have, has) bet
burst	burst	(have, has) burst
cut	cut	(have, has) cut
put	put	(have, has) put
set	set	(have, has) set

Several irregular verbs have the same past and past participle forms. page 60 ADDITIONAL EXERCISES, page 427

Verb	Past	Past Participle
bring	brought	(have, has) brought
buy	bought	(have, has) bought
catch	caught	(have, has) caught
creep	crept	(have, has) crept
fling	flung	(have, has) flung
lay	laid	(have, has) laid
lend	lent	(have, has) lent
lose	lost	(have, has) lost
say	said	(have, has) said
seek	sought	(have, has) sought
sit	sat	(have, has) sat

Verb	Past	Past Participle
sting	stung	(have, has) stung
swing	swung	(have, has) swung
teach	taught	(have, has) taught
think	thought	(have, has) thought

Two special verbs that you see and use often are *be* and *have.* page 62 ADDITIONAL EXERCISES, page 427

Verb	Past	Past Participle
be	was, were	(have, has) been
have, has	had	(have, has) had

Other irregular verbs do not follow a pattern of any sort. The past participles for these irregular verbs generally end in **n.** Most of them require other spelling changes also. page 62 ADDITIONAL EXERCISES, page 427

Verb	Past	Past Participle
bite	bit	(have, has) bitten
blow	blew	(have, has) blown
break	broke	(have, has) broken
choose	chose	(have, has) chosen
do	did	(have, has) done
draw	drew	(have, has) drawn
drive	drove	(have, has) driven
eat	ate	(have, has) eaten
fall	fell	(have, has) fallen
fly	flew	(have, has) flown
freeze	froze	(have, has) frozen
get	got	(have, has) gotten
give	gave	(have, has) given
go	went	(have, has) gone
grow	grew	(have, has) grown
know	knew	(have, has) known
ride	rode	(have, has) ridden
see	saw	(have, has) seen
shake	shook	(have, has) shaken
speak	spoke	(have, has) spoken
steal	stole	(have, has) stolen

Verb	Past	Past Participle
take	took	(have, has) taken
tear	tore	(have, has) torn
throw	threw	(have, has) thrown
wear	wore	(have, has) worn
write	wrote	(have, has) written

PRONOUN

A **pronoun** is a word that takes the place of a noun.
page 70 ADDITIONAL EXERCISES, page 427

The campers paddled their canoes. They paddled toward the island. One camper had bought the food. She had placed it in her canoe.

A **subject pronoun** is used as the subject of a sentence.
page 70 ADDITIONAL EXERCISES, page 427

Avery and I started a campfire. We gathered firewood first.

An **object pronoun** is used as the object of a verb or of a preposition. page 70 ADDITIONAL EXERCISES, page 427

The other campers waited for us. They thanked me for the wood.

A **possessive pronoun** is a pronoun that shows who or what has something. A possessive pronoun may take the place of a possessive noun. page 72 ADDITIONAL EXERCISES, page 427

We cooked our dinner over the fire.
The pot for the food was mine.

An **antecedent** is the noun or group of words to which a pronoun refers. page 74 ADDITIONAL EXERCISES, page 428

Michelle arrived at the island first. She reached it quickly.

An **indefinite pronoun** is a pronoun that does not refer to a particular person, place, or thing. page 78 ADDITIONAL EXERCISES, page 428

Someone started to sing a song. Several began to sing along.

A **reflexive pronoun** points the action of the verb back to the subject. page 80 ADDITIONAL EXERCISES, page 428

We warmed ourselves beside the fire.
My dog occupied itself with a bone.

An **intensive pronoun** is a pronoun that adds emphasis to a noun or pronoun already named. page 80 ADDITIONAL EXERCISES, page 428

He himself prepared the entire meal.

Joan and I ourselves ate the whole thing.

An **interrogative pronoun** is a pronoun used to introduce an interrogative sentence. page 82 ADDITIONAL EXERCISES, page 428

Who will gather more wood?

Whose job is it?

Whom did we ask?

Demonstrative pronouns point out something and they take the place of nouns. page 96 ADDITIONAL EXERCISES, page 430

This is my flashlight.

That is your flashlight.

ADJECTIVE

An **adjective** is a word that modifies, or describes, a noun or pronoun. page 88 ADDITIONAL EXERCISES, page 427

Waves lap against the sandy shore.

A **predicate adjective** is an adjective that follows a linking verb. It describes the subject by telling what it is like. pages 44, 88 ADDITIONAL EXERCISES, pages 425, 429

Picnics usually are fun.

People seem relaxed after picnics.

A and **an** are called **indefinite articles** because they refer to one of a general group of people, places, things, or ideas. Use **a** before words beginning with a consonant sound. Use **an** before words beginning with a vowel sound. page 90 ADDITIONAL EXERCISES, page 429

An automobile stops beside the lake.

A passenger climbs out of the car.

The is called a **definite article** because it identifies specific people, places, things, or ideas. page 90 ADDITIONAL EXERCISES, page 429

The girls take food from the basket.

They admire the view of the lake.

A **proper adjective** is an adjective formed from a proper noun. A proper adjective is capitalized. page 91 ADDITIONAL EXERCISES, page 429

The Monday luncheon featured Italian food.

The **comparative form** of an adjective compares two people or things. You often add *-er* to an adjective to make the comparative form. page 92 ADDITIONAL EXERCISES, page 429

One girl is hungrier than her friends.
Her lunch is bigger than the others.

The **superlative form** of an adjective compares more than two people or things. You often add *-est* to an adjective to make the superlative form. page 92 ADDITIONAL EXERCISES, page 429

She eats the fastest of the three. They climb the tallest tree of all.

Use the words *more* and *most*, or *less* and *least*, before adjectives of three or more syllables to form the comparative and superlative. Add *-er* and *-est* to some two-syllable adjectives. Use *more* and *most*, or *less* and *least* with others. Do not use *more* and *most*, or *less* and *least* before adjectives that already have *-er* or *-est* added to them. page 94 ADDITIONAL EXERCISES, page 429

The view of the lake is lovelier from the tree than from the ground.
The lake is more suitable for picnics than others in the area.
This is the most beautiful lake of any in the state.

A **demonstrative word** is an adjective when it is used to modify a noun. page 96 ADDITIONAL EXERCISES, page 430

These girls enjoyed this picnic.
That view from those trees was lovely.

A **participle** can be used as an adjective to describe a noun or a pronoun. page 140 ADDITIONAL EXERCISES, page 433

Hunted animals roamed the frontier.
Working families farmed the land.

ADVERB

An **adverb** is a word that modifies, or describes, a verb, an adjective, or another adverb. page 102 ADDITIONAL EXERCISES, page 430

The people stood silently. They very carefully studied the problem.

Use the **comparative form** of the adverb to compare two actions. page 104 ADDITIONAL EXERCISES, page 430

I stayed longer at the park than Betsy.

The runner moved faster than the other runner.

Use the **superlative form** of the adverb to compare more than two actions. page 104 ADDITIONAL EXERCISES, page 430

Sam stayed the longest of anyone.

The winner moved the fastest of all the runners.

Use the words *more* and *most* before most long adverbs ending in *-ly* to form the comparative and superlative. page 104 ADDITIONAL EXERCISES, page 430

Karen moved more slowly than I.

She moved the most slowly of all.

Use the words *less* and *least* before both short and long adverbs to form the comparative and superlative. Do not use *more* or *most*, or *less* or *least* before adverbs that already have *-er* or *-est* added to them. page 104 ADDITIONAL EXERCISES, page 430

I drove less frequently than Jan.

Meg drives the least frequently of all.

An adverb that emphasizes or intensifies an adjective or an adverb is called an **intensifier.** Some adverbs that are used as intensifiers are *very, quite, too, almost, so, surely, somewhat, partly, totally, scarcely, hardly, barely, wholly, slightly, unusually.* page 106 ADDITIONAL EXERCISES, page 430

The task seemed difficult.

The task seemed extremely difficult.

PREPOSITION

A **preposition** is a word that relates a noun or pronoun to another word. page 118 ADDITIONAL EXERCISES, page 431

I walked beside the river. My dog leaped into the water.

A **prepositional phrase** is a group of words that begins with a preposition and ends with a noun or pronoun. The noun or pronoun is called the **object of the preposition.** page 119 ADDITIONAL EXERCISES, page 431

The duck near my dog was quacking.

A duck swam toward my dog.

An **adjective phrase** is a prepositional phrase that modifies, or describes, a noun or a pronoun. page 120 ADDITIONAL EXERCISES, page 431

The duck in the water startled him.

The sight of my dog made me laugh.

An **adverb phrase** is a prepositional phrase that may modify, or describe, a verb. page 120 ADDITIONAL EXERCISES, page 431

He raced from the water quickly.

I whistled to my dog.

CONJUNCTION

A **conjunction** is a word that joins other words or groups of words. page 124 ADDITIONAL EXERCISES, page 432

Cats and dogs make good pets. Cats are quiet, and dogs are loving.

A **coordinating conjunction** is a single word used to connect parts of a sentence such as words, phrases, or clauses. *And, but, or, for,* and *nor* are used as coordinating conjunctions. page 124 ADDITIONAL EXERCISES, page 432

She likes dogs but hates cats.

He adores all animals, and he has many different pets.

Correlative conjunctions are pairs of words used to connect parts of sentences such as words, phrases, or clauses. page 124 ADDITIONAL EXERCISES, page 432

He has not only a dog but also several cats.

Both my sister and my brother like pets.

A **subordinating conjunction** is a word or group of words that joins a subordinate clause to a main clause in a sentence. page 124 ADDITIONAL EXERCISES, page 432

Although dogs are popular pets, some people are afraid of them.

He goes to the zoo because he likes the unusual animals.

INTERJECTION

An **interjection** is a word or group of words that expresses strong feeling. An interjection has no grammatical connection to any other words. page 126 ADDITIONAL EXERCISES, page 432

Great! How amazing!

CONTRACTION

A **contraction** is a word made up of two words combined into one by leaving out one or more letters. pages 112, 180 ADDITIONAL EXERCISES, pages 431, 437

It's a great book. (It is)

We're waiting for you. (We are)

II. Mechanics

Capitalization

Use a **capital letter** to begin the first word of every sentence. pages 4, 164 ADDITIONAL EXERCISES, pages 422, 435

Who was the greatest musician?

Some people think Bach was the best.

Use a **capital letter** to begin important words in proper nouns. pages 166 ADDITIONAL EXERCISES, pages 435

Johann Sebastian Bach composed music in the early 1700s.

Orchestras throughout the United States of America perform his music.

Use a **capital letter** to begin an adjective formed from a proper noun. page 166 ADDITIONAL EXERCISES, page 435

Bach composed German church music.

European composers studied his music.

Punctuation

Use a **period** at the end of a declarative sentence or an imperative sentence. pages 4, 164 ADDITIONAL EXERCISES, pages 422, 435

Bach is famous for his development of the fugue.

Notice how different instruments repeat the same melody in a fugue.

Use a **question mark** at the end of an interrogative sentence. pages 4, 164 ADDITIONAL EXERCISES, pages 422, 435

Is Bach famous for his fugues?

Did Bach play the organ?

Handbook

Use an **exclamation mark** at the end of an exclamatory sentence. pages 4, 164 ADDITIONAL EXERCISES, pages 422, 435

How talented Bach's relatives were!

How unusual they were!

Use an **exclamation mark** after an interjection when it stands alone. Use a **comma** to separate an interjection from the rest of a sentence when it is part of the sentence. page 164 ADDITIONAL EXERCISES, pages 422, 435

Oh! Of course! Alas, I cannot.

Add an **apostrophe** and **s** to form the possessive of most singular nouns. page 32 ADDITIONAL EXERCISES, page 424

Pearl's record is new.

She left it at her friend's house.

Add an **apostrophe** to form the possessive of plural nouns that end with **s**. page 32 ADDITIONAL EXERCISES, page 424

The girls' hobby is fun.

They share their friends' records.

Add an **apostrophe** and **s** to form the possessive of plural nouns that do not end with **s**. page 32 ADDITIONAL EXERCISES, page 424

The children's records are lost.

They left them in the men's store.

Use an **apostrophe** in a contraction to show that one or more letters are missing. pages 112, 180 ADDITIONAL EXERCISES, page 437

The music isn't over yet.

We won't turn the radio off.

Use a **comma** to separate each noun, verb, or adjective in a series of three or more nouns, verbs, or adjectives. page 168 ADDITIONAL EXERCISES, page 435

Hayden, Mozart, and Beethoven were talented composers.

The musicians composed, performed, and conducted their works.

Their music was vivid, beautiful, and exciting.

Use **commas** to separate the different items in addresses and dates. Use a **comma** after the last part of the address or date when it appears in the middle of a sentence. page 168 ADDITIONAL EXERCISES, page 435

J.S. Bach was born on March 21, 1685, in Eisenach, Germany.

His son Carl Philipp Emanuel Bach was born in Weimar, Germany.

Use **commas** to set off words such as *well, yes,* and *no* when they begin a sentence. page 168 ADDITIONAL EXERCISES, page 435

Yes, C.P.E. Bach was a composer.

No, he never wrote an opera.

Use **commas** to set off expressions such as *by the way, of course,* and *however* when they interrupt a sentence. page 168 ADDITIONAL EXERCISES, page 435

His brother J. C. Bach, however, did write operas.

His compositions, by the way, were influenced by Italian composers.

Use **commas** to set off appositives when they interrupt a sentence with information. page 168 ADDITIONAL EXERCISES, page 435

J. S. Bach, a talented organist, is best known as a composer.

Bach's musical combinations, both complex and simple, convey various moods.

Use **commas** to set off a person's name when you address the person directly. page 168 ADDITIONAL EXERCISES, page 435

Pei, have you heard Bach's Brandenburg Concertos?

Did you know, Larry, that he composed the six concertos in one year?

Use a **comma** after the salutation of an informal letter and after the closing of all letters. page 168 ADDITIONAL EXERCISES, page 435

Dear Don, Sincerely,

Use a **comma** before *and, or,* or *but* when they join simple sentences. page 170 ADDITIONAL EXERCISES, page 435

Bach won recognition for his music, but his relatives were gifted, too.

Bach had twenty children, and two of them became composers.

Use a **comma** after an adverb clause that introduces a sentence. page 170 ADDITIONAL EXERCISES, page 435

When he composed music, he avoided mere showiness.

As the concert ended, the audience cheered with delight.

Use a **semicolon** to separate the parts of a compound sentence if there are commas within one or both parts. page 172 ADDITIONAL EXERCISES, page 436

J. S. Bach composed oratorios, cantatas, and concertos; but his music was not appreciated during his lifetime.

Use a **semicolon** to separate parts of a compound sentence if they are not joined by *and, or,* or *but.* page 172 ADDITIONAL EXERCISES, page 436

Bach finally won recognition in the 1800s; the musician Felix Mendelssohn performed one of his compositions at a concert.

Use a **colon** between the hour and the minute when writing the time. page 172 ADDITIONAL EXERCISES, page 436

9:00 A.M. 3:30 P.M.

Use a **colon** after the greeting in a business letter. page 172 ADDITIONAL EXERCISES, page 436

Dear Dr. Mandell: Dear Caroco Manufacturing Co.:

Use a **colon** to show that a list of items will follow in a sentence. page 172 ADDITIONAL EXERCISES, page 436

The following music forms are popular today: rock and roll, country western, soul, and show tunes.

Use **quotation marks** to set off a speaker's exact statement. Commas and periods at the end of direct quotations always go inside the closing quotation marks. page 174 ADDITIONAL EXERCISES, page 436

"I want to go to the concert," said Nancy.

Mr. Charlson replied, "That's a good idea."

Use **italics** to set apart special names of things and titles of artworks. Underline these special words in your own writing to show that they are italicized. page 174 ADDITIONAL EXERCISES, page 436

Madame Bovary *Hamlet* *Business Week*

Use a **hyphen** after the prefix *ex-*. page 176 ADDITIONAL EXERCISES, page 436

ex-secretary ex-bicyclist

Use a **hyphen** when a prefix comes before a capital letter. page 176 ADDITIONAL EXERCISES, page 436

pre-Colombian mid-March

Use a **hyphen** to indicate that a person or thing existed between two dates. page 176 ADDITIONAL EXERCISES, page 436

Susan B. Anthony (1820-1906)

Use a **hyphen** to indicate a route from one place to another. page 176 ADDITIONAL EXERCISES, page 436

the New York-California flight

Use a **hyphen** to connect compound words that act as one word. page 176 ADDITIONAL EXERCISES, page 436

twenty-one father-in-law

Use a **dash** to show a sharp change, or an interruption, in the main thought of a sentence. page 176 ADDITIONAL EXERCISES, page 436

Sharon—my very good friend—has found a job.

Use **parentheses** to set apart extra information within a sentence. Parentheses are always used in pairs. page 176 ADDITIONAL EXERCISES, page 436

The Whitney Museum (a small building) has many modern art treasures.

Use a **period** after certain abbreviations: initials, titles, academic and professional titles, street names, days of the week, and most months. May, June, and July are never abbreviated. Do not use a period after the abbreviation of states. page 178 ADDITIONAL EXERCISES, page 436

M. M. Mandell
Rachel Lustiger, Ph.D.
Dr. Richard Alan
122 Sunset St.
Jan. 11, 1957
Sat., May 28, 1983

III. Spelling

Spelling Rules

Use a **Table of English Spellings** to help you find words that you know how to pronounce but do not know how to spell. page 188 ADDITIONAL EXERCISES, page 437

Write **i** before **e** except after **c** or when sounded like **a** as in *neighbor* and *weigh*. Notice these **ei** words: *either, leisure, neither, weird, ceiling, deceive, receipt, beige, eight, vein,* and *reign*. page 190 ADDITIONAL EXERCISES, page 437

chief relieve

Do not change the spelling of a word when you add a prefix to it. page 190 ADDITIONAL EXERCISES, page 437

tri + cycle = tricycle re + appear = reappear

When a word ends in **e,** generally keep the **e** when adding a suffix that begins with a consonant. page 190 ADDITIONAL EXERCISES, page 437

rare + ly = rarely   care + less = careless

When a word ends in **e,** generally drop the **e** when adding **-y** or a suffix that begins with a vowel. page 190 ADDITIONAL EXERCISES, page 437

lace + y = lacy   move + able = movable
survive + al = survival

When a word ends in **ce** or **ge,** keep the final **e** before adding a suffix that begins with **a** or **o.** page 190 ADDITIONAL EXERCISES, page 437

courage + ous = courageous   place + able = placeable

When a one-syllable word ends in **ie,** change the **ie** to **y** before adding **-ing.** page 190 ADDITIONAL EXERCISES, page 437

lie + ing = lying   tie + ing = tying

When a word ends in a consonant and **le,** drop the **le** and add **-ly.** page 190 ADDITIONAL EXERCISES, page 437

gentle + ly = gently   possible + ly = possibly
simple + ly = simply

When a word ends in a consonant and **y,** change **y** to **i** before adding a suffix. However, when you add a suffix to certain one-syllable words or when the suffix begins with *i,* do not change the *y* to *i.* page 192 ADDITIONAL EXERCISES, page 437

country + es = countries   happy + ly = happily
simple + ly = simply

When a word ends in a vowel and **y,** generally keep the **y** when adding a suffix. page 192 ADDITIONAL EXERCISES, page 437

birthday + s = birthdays   cowboy + s = cowboys

Double the final consonant before a suffix beginning with a vowel (1) if the word ends in one vowel and one consonant, and (2) if the word is only one syllable or is accented on the final syllable. page 192 ADDITIONAL EXERCISES, page 437

unusual + ly = unusually   plan + ed = planned

Do not double the final consonant if the stress does not fall on the last syllable. page 192 ADDITIONAL EXERCISES, page 437

open + ing = opening   cancel + ed = canceled

Do not double a final consonant before a suffix beginning with a consonant. page 192 ADDITIONAL EXERCISES, page 437

hope + less = hopeless   appoint + ment = appointment

To form the plural of most nouns, add **-s.** page 30 ADDITIONAL EXERCISES, page 424

can + s = cans   muffin + s = muffins   bag + s = bags

To form the plural of letters, numerals, signs, or words considered as words, add an **apostrophe** and **-s.** page 30 ADDITIONAL EXERCISES, page 424

n's   and's   l's   2's   t's

To form the plural of nouns ending in **s, ss, sh, ch, x,** and **z,** add **-es.** page 192 ADDITIONAL EXERCISES, page 437

dish + es = dishes   match + es = matches   circus + es = circuses

To form the plural of most nouns ending in a vowel and **o,** add **-s.** page 194 ADDITIONAL EXERCISES, page 438

radio + s = radios   stereo + s = stereos   cameo + s = cameos

To form the plural of most nouns ending in a consonant and **o,** generally add **-s,** but sometimes add **-es.** page 194 ADDITIONAL EXERCISES, page 438

piano + s = pianos   veto + es = vetoes   potato + es = potatoes

To form the plural of some nouns ending in **f** and all nouns ending in **ff,** add **-s.** page 194 ADDITIONAL EXERCISES, page 438

roof + s = roofs   cliff + s = cliffs   puff + s = puffs

To form the plural of some nouns ending in **f** or **fe,** and many nouns ending in **lf,** change the **f** to **v** and add **-s** or **-es.** page 194 ADDITIONAL EXERCISES, page 438

thief + es = thieves   wife + s = wives   elf + es = elves

Some nouns have irregular plural forms. They do not follow any spelling rule. page 194 ADDITIONAL EXERCISES, page 438

child—children	mouse—mice	tooth—teeth	foot—feet
woman—women	goose—geese	man—men	ox—oxen

Some nouns have the same form in both the singular and plural. page 194 ADDITIONAL EXERCISES, page 438

one sheep	one series	one deer	one species	a trout	one fish
many sheep	two series	four deer	ten species	a few trout	many fish

Words Often Confused

Many words in our language with similar sounds or similar spellings have different meanings. pages 196, 198 ADDITIONAL EXERCISES, page 438

Word	Meaning	Example
aisle (noun)	a passageway	The man walked down the center *aisle*.
isle (noun)	land surrounded by water, a small island	We visited a Pacific *isle*.
council (noun)	a group of advisers	The city *council* meets today.
counsel (verb)	to give advice	Our advisers will *counsel* us.
holy (adjective)	sacred	They celebrated a *holy* day.
wholly (adverb)	completely, entirely	The answer was not *wholly* accurate.
rain (noun)	condensed water vapor, falling from the sky	The Weather Service predicts *rain*.
reign (verb)	to rule, control	How long did the king *reign*?
serf (noun)	a kind of slave	The *serf* worked for the landlord.
surf (noun)	seawaves on the shore	The *surf* rose high during the storm.
wares (noun)	goods for sale	The merchants sold their *wares*.
wears (verb)	has on the body	Gail *wears* boots when she rides.
stake (noun)	a sharpened stick or post for driving into the ground	Use *stakes* to support the tent.
steak (noun)	a cut of meat or fish	We ate *steaks* for dinner.
presents (noun)	gifts	Jan received many *presents*.
presence (noun)	state of being in a place at a given time	Her *presence* at the meeting was upsetting.

Word	Meaning	Example
straight (adjective)	proceeding in same direction without curving or bending	He made a *straight* line across the page.
strait (noun)	narrow waterway connecting two larger bodies of water	We steered the boat through the *strait*.
loose (adjective)	not firmly tied	The bolt is *loose*.
lose (verb)	misplace, be deprived of	Don't *lose* the bolt.
quiet (adjective)	silent	It was a *quiet* night.
quite (adverb)	to a large extent	It was *quite* a dark night.
weather (noun)	atmospheric conditions	The *weather* has been very cold.
whether conjunction)	if	I don't know *whether* to go.
lead (verb)	(led) show the way (present tense)	The dogs *lead* the way.
lead (noun)	(led) a heavy metal	That *lead* pipe is in the way.
led (verb)	(led) showed the way (past tense)	Who *led* the way yesterday?
choose (verb)	select or pick out (present tense)	Please *choose* two cards.
chose (verb)	selected or picked out (past tense)	You *chose* two cards.
than (conjunction)	compared with	My bike cost less *than* yours.
then (adverb)	at that time	He *then* left the room.
wear (verb)	to have on	She will *wear* a suit.
where (adverb)	at what place	*Where* shall we meet?
were (verb)	plural past form of *be*	*Were* you meeting them?

IV. Vocabulary

A **prefix** is a letter or group of letters added to the beginning of a word. pages 208, 210, 212 ADDITIONAL EXERCISES, page 437

One group sat in a circle.
Another group sat in a semicircle.

Some people like bicycles.
Others like tricycles better.

Prefix	Meaning	Example
uni-	one	unicycle (one wheel)
mono-	one, single	monotone (a single tone)
bi-	two, twice	bicycle (two wheels)
tri-	three	triangle (three angles)
un-	not; the opposite of	uncomfortable (not comfortable)
im-	not; the opposite of	impossible (not possible)
in-	not; the opposite of	inaccurate (not accurate)
non-	not; the opposite of	nonproductive (not productive)
inter-	between, among	international (among nations)
semi-	half of, partly	semiprivate (partly private) semicircle (half of a circle)
auto-	self	autobiography (a biography of oneself)
super-	extra, beyond better than others of its kind	superhuman (better than other humans)
under-	below, lower in place, lesser in degree	underground (below the ground)
pre-	before	preview (see before)
re-	again	restart (start again)
over-	extra, beyond, above, over, more	overreach (reach beyond)
com-	with, together	compromise (promise with)
post-	after, in time or order	postgame (after the game)

A **suffix** is a letter or group of letters added to the end of a word. Adding a suffix sometimes changes the meaning of a word.

pages 212, 214, ADDITIONAL EXERCISES, page 440

Margaret collects coins.

Paul is also a coin collector.

Teresa has a large coin collection.

Suffix	Meaning	Noun
-ment	result	improvement, result of being improved
-ion	action or state	collection, state of being collected
-ance	the act of	acceptance, the act of accepting
-ence	the act of	dependence, the act of depending
-ful	full of, marked by	harmful (full of harm)
-less	lacking, without	spotless (without a spot)
-ish	like, suggesting	stylish (suggesting style)
-ous	marked by, given to	humorous (marked by humor)
-ent	doing, showing, tending	excellent (showing excellence)
-ant	doing, showing, tending	triumphant (showing triumph)
-ary	relating to	imaginary (relating to an image)
-y	showing, suggesting	rainy (showing rain)
-ive	tending to	expensive (tending to expense)
-able	able to, capable of being	agreeable (able to agree)
-ible	able to, capable of being	covertible (able to convert)
-some	showing, apt to	troublesome (showing trouble)

A **root** is the original word to which you add a suffix or prefix. Some are not words by themselves. page 216 ADDITIONAL EXERCISES, page 440

Root	**Meaning**	**New Words**
graph	write	autograph
scrib, scrip	write	scribble, script
sign	sign, mark	signal
port	carry	report, portable
cap, cep	take, receive	captive, reception
pel, puls	drive, push	compel, impulse
pend, pens	hang	impending, suspense
duc	lead	deduct
pos, pon	place, put	deposit
voc, vok	call, voice	vocal, revoke
spec	see, watch	spectator
vid, vis	see	visual
grad, gred, gress	step, walk	progress, gradual
cede, ceed, cess	go, surrender	recede
ped, pod	foot	pedestrian

A **synonym** is a word that is similar in meaning to another word. page 218 ADDITIONAL EXERCISES, page 440

The children skipped along the sidewalk (walked)

The team hiked up the steep trail. (climbed)

An **antonym** is a word having an opposite meaning of another word. page 220 ADDITIONAL EXERCISES, page 441

I agree with you. (disagree)

The train arrives at noon. (leaves)

Workbook

TABLE OF CONTENTS

Review: Four Kinds of Sentences pages 4-5

A **sentence** is a group of words that expresses a complete idea. Every sentence begins with a **capital letter.**

A **declarative sentence** makes a statement and ends with a **period (.).**

Athletes in foreign countries play many games.

An **interrogative sentence** asks a question and ends with a **question mark (?).**

An **exclamatory sentence** expresses strong feeling and ends with an **exclamation mark (!).**

How wonderfully that athlete plays soccer!

An **imperative sentence** gives a command or makes a request and ends with a **period (.).**

Read about sports in other countries.

Write each sentence. Capitalize and punctuate each sentence correctly. Then write **declarative, interrogative, imperative,** or **exclamatory** after each sentence.

1. what sport do Americans like best
2. many teams in Japan, Canada, and Latin America play baseball
3. each baseball team has nine players
4. what marvelous athletes professional baseball players are
5. hit a home run
6. the National League and the American League play in the World Series
7. which two teams play in the World Series
8. do most pitchers bat in the American League
9. many fans visit the Baseball Hall of Fame
10. where is Cooperstown
11. how I like baseball
12. please sign my baseball glove
13. pitchers puzzle batters with different pitches
14. do Japanese baseball teams play American teams
15. what great catches that outfielder makes
16. watch the all-star game in person
17. which is your favorite baseball team

Sentences and Sentence Fragments pages 6-7

A **sentence fragment** is a group of words that is only part of a sentence. It does not express a complete thought.

People on horseback.

The **complete subject,** or **subject part,** names whom or what the sentence is about. The complete subject of a sentence may be more than one word.

The **complete predicate,** or **predicate part,** of a sentence tells what action the subject does. Sometimes it tells what the subject is or is like. The complete predicate may be more than one word.

Two teams of four players | compete in polo.

Write each group of words that forms a complete sentence. Underline the complete subject once and the complete predicate twice. If the group of words is not a complete sentence, write **fragment**.

1. A regulation polo field.
2. The horses need a rest.
3. The horse's equipment.
4. Polo players carry mallets.
5. Weigh over 800 pounds.
6. The goal posts.
7. Polo resembles hockey.
8. Different playing fields.

Complete and Simple Subjects pages 8-9

A **complete subject** names whom or what the sentence is about and may be more than one word.
A **simple subject** is the main word or group of words in the complete subject.

Many athletes in America play soccer.

Write each sentence. Then underline the complete subject of each sentence. Draw a second line under the simple subject.

1. Only Americans use the term "soccer."
2. Teams of eleven people play on a rectangular field.
3. The team with the highest score wins the game.
4. Most players touch the ball only with their feet and chests.
5. Goalies also use their hands and arms.
6. Players kick the ball into the goal net.
7. Pelé designed many new plays for soccer.

Complete and Simple Predicates pages 10-11

The **complete predicate,** or predicate part, of a sentence tells what action the subject does, what the subject is, or what the subject is like.

The **simple predicate** is the main word or group of words in the complete predicate.

Rugby teams play with an oval-shaped ball.

Write each sentence. Underline the complete predicate of each sentence. Draw a second line under the simple predicate.

1. Athletes play rugby with rules similar to football.
2. Rugby players often carry the ball.
3. Players pass the ball to each other.
4. Players throw forward passes.
5. Officials divide the game into forty-minute halves.
6. The referee serves as the official timekeeper.

Subject-Verb Agreement pages 12-13

The form of the verb, or simple predicate, in each sentence must agree in number with the singular or plural subject in the sentence.

The child likes croquet. The children like croquet.

When the subject is singular in meaning, even though plural in form, use the form of the verb that agrees with the singular subject.

Rules of Croquet teaches people about croquet.

The United States has many croquet players.

Write each sentence using the correct form of the verb.

1. Many people ____ croquet. (plays/play)
2. A croquet set ____ wooden balls, mallets, and small metal arches. (has, have)
3. Croquet partners ____ each other. (helps/help)
4. Two people usually ____ a team. (forms/form)
5. *The Origins of Croquet* ____ me. (interests/interest)
6. A player usually ____ the ball once each turn. (hits/hit)
7. A few hours ____ quickly in croquet. (passes/pass)

Compound Subjects and Predicates

pages 14-15

A **compound subject** has two or more simple subjects that have the same predicate. The subjects are joined by *and* or *or*.

Canadians and Americans play lacrosse.

A **compound predicate** has two or more verbs that have the same subject. The verbs are connected by *and* or *or*.

The players throw or kick a ball into the goal.

When simple subjects are joined by *or*, the predicate part must agree with the nearer simple subject.

A defense player or attack players score goals.

Write each sentence using the correct form of the verb.

1. High schools and colleges often ____ lacrosse matches. (holds/hold)
2. Men or women ____ the game. (plays/play)
3. Only a referee or goalkeepers ____ the ball with their hands. (touches/touch)
4. Many fans ____ and ____ lacrosse matches. (watches/watch, enjoys/enjoy)
5. A player ____ or ____ the ball with the lacrosse stick. (scoops/scoop, throws/throw)
6. Lacrosse and polo ____ hockey. (resembles/resemble)
7. The team or players ____ padded gloves. (wears/wear)
8. A tennis player ____ or ____ the ball. (slices/slice, smashes/smash)
9. Cement, grass, or clay surfaces ____ the ball to bounce differently. (causes/cause)
10. The umpire or line judges ____ the shots in or out. (calls/call)
11. Old and young players ____ the sport. (enjoys/enjoy)
12. The people ____ and ____ at the players. (claps/clap, cheers/cheer)
13. The professional tennis player ____ and ____ well. (serves/serve, volleys/volley)
14. Robert and Francie ____ tennis every day. (plays/play)

Compound Sentences pages 16-17

A **simple sentence** is a sentence that has one subject part and one predicate part.

A **compound sentence** is a sentence that contains two or more simple sentences joined by a coordinating conjunction. It has at least two subjects and two predicates.

Professional football teams compete in weekly games, and the two best teams play in the Superbowl.

Coordinating conjunctions, such as *and*, *or*, or *but*, join two simple sentences. Use a **comma (,)** before the conjunction to separate the two parts of the new sentence. When there are already commas within the parts of a compound sentence, use a semicolon (;) to separate the two parts.

Players kick, pass, or run with the football; they try to make a touchdown.

Correlative conjunctions, such as *either . . . or* and *neither . . . nor* are conjunctions that work in pairs.

Write each sentence. Write whether it is a **simple sentence** or a **compound sentence.** If the sentence has a compound subject, draw one line under each simple subject. If the sentence has a compound predicate, draw two lines under each verb. If it is a compound sentence, draw a line between the two simple sentences.

1. Some people play touch football, but others play tackle.
2. Americans and Canadians play professional football.
3. Radio stations and TV channels broadcast football games.
4. Americans play football; Europeans play soccer.
5. Either college teams or professional teams play for TV audiences.
6. A punter kicks the ball, and the game begins.
7. A team scores a touchdown or kicks a field goal.

Complex Sentences pages 18-19

An **independent clause** has one subject part and one predicate part. It expresses a complete thought and it can stand alone. A **subordinate clause** is a group of words that has a subject part and a predicate part, but it cannot stand alone. It does not express a complete thought. It is always combined with an independent clause. Subordinate clauses are often signaled by subordinating conjunctions. Some subordinating conjunctions are: *although, as, after, because, before, if, since, though, until, when,* and *while.*

Some Olympic games take place in the summer while others take place in the winter.

A **complex sentence** is a sentence that has an independent clause and one or more subordinate clauses.

Although the athletes spent long hours in training, they lost almost every game.

Write each sentence. Draw one line under the independent clause and two lines under the subordinate clause. Circle the subordinating conjunction that begins the subordinate clause.

1. While some summer events occur in gymnasiums, other events take place in outdoor stadiums.
2. Before athletes arrive at the Olympic Games, they prove their abilities in national competitions.
3. Athletes often set new Olympic records every four years because they train hard and learn from former Olympians.
4. Since engineers improve ski equipment, ski racers ski faster with each new Olympiad.
5. Fans cheer the athletes as television cameras and photographers take pictures of the events.
6. After the International Olympic Committee sets the rules for each event, the games begin.
7. Athletes must practice their sport for many years until they become experts in their event.
8. Although individuals compete against each other in some events, national teams in basketball, hockey, and volleyball play against each other.

Review: Nouns pages 26-27

A **noun** names a person, place, thing, or idea.

A **concrete noun** names a thing that can be seen or touched. house car city

An **abstract noun** names feelings or ideas that cannot be seen or touched. love happiness kindness

A **common noun** names any person, place, thing, or idea. man street book anger

A **proper noun** names a specific person, place, thing, or idea. Amy Dallas Chrysler

Write the nouns in each sentence. After each noun, write **common noun** or **proper noun.** Then write **concrete noun** or **abstract noun.**

1. Tourists in California enjoy the weather of the state.
2. Motorists in Los Angeles drive on large freeways.
3. Many people like San Francisco for its hills.
4. Giant redwoods grow near the coast of the Pacific Ocean.
5. Wild animals live in Yosemite National Park.
6. People look at the Sierra Nevada Mountains in amazement.

Nouns in the Subject and Predicate pages 28-29

The **subject part** of a sentence names whom or what the sentence is about.

The Statue of Liberty | stands on an island in New York Harbor.

The **predicate part** tells what action the subject does. It may also tell what the subject is or is like.

The Hudson River | flows through New York State.

Write each sentence. Draw a line between the subject part and the predicate part. Write each noun. Write whether it is a **common noun** or a **proper noun.**

1. Tourists from all over the world travel to New York.
2. Many people spend their honeymoon at Niagara Falls.
3. Vineyards thrive near the Finger Lakes.
4. Swimmers enjoy sandy beaches on the Atlantic Ocean.
5. Baseball fans visit the National Baseball Museum.
6. The World Trade Center towers over other skyscrapers.

Workbook

RETEACHING AND ENRICHMENT

Plural Nouns and Irregular Plurals pages 30-31

A **plural noun** names more than one. To make most singular nouns plural, add **-s.** For some singular nouns, add **-es** to form the plural. The plural form of some other nouns follows no special rules.

river rivers   watch watches   man men

Write each sentence using the correct form of the noun.

1. Thousands of ____ ski in Vermont. (person, people)
2. ____ cover Green Mountains with snow. (Storm, Storms)
3. A ____ produces white cheddar cheese. (farmer, farmers)
4. How many ____ are there in cheddar? (ds, d's)
5. ____ watch the autumn leaves. (Visitor, Visitors)
6. The Green Mountains overlook Canada and three other ____. (state, states)

Possessive Nouns pages 32-33

A **possessive noun** is a noun that names who or what has something. Add an **apostrophe** and **s ('s)** to form the possessive of most singular nouns.

Florida's beaches attract thousands of visitors.

Add an **apostrophe (')** to form the plural of most plural nouns that end in *s*. Add an **apostrophe** and **s ('s)** to form the possessive of plural nouns that do not end in *s.*

The men's favorite beach lies north of the tourists' resort.

An apostrophe is also used in a contraction to show where the letters are left out.

Juan's going to Florida.

Write each sentence. Add apostrophes where needed. Write whether each word with the apostrophe is a **singular possessive, plural possessive,** or **contraction.**

1. Tourists purchases are essential to Floridas economy.
2. Disneyworlds one of many childrens favorite places.
3. Tourists visit Orlandos other attractions, too.
4. Everglades National Parks exotic animals enchant visitors.
5. Other states senior citizens often move to Florida.
6. Miamis warm climate attracts swimmers and scuba divers.
7. Cape Kennedys located near Cocoa Beach.

Distinguishing Plurals and Possessives pages 34-35

A **plural noun** is a noun that names more than one.

Many <u>states</u> have a strong tourist industry.

A **possessive noun** is a noun that names who or what has something.

Tourist <u>industries'</u> income helps state economies.

Write each sentence using the word in parentheses that correctly completes each sentence. Write whether the word in parentheses you used is a **plural noun** or a **possessive noun.**

1. ____ take pictures of buffalo in Yellowstone National Park. (Tourists, Tourists')
2. Wyoming has wildlife refuge ____. (areas, area's)
3. The ____ beauty amazes its visitors. (states, state's)
4. The ____ steam bursts from the ground. (geyser, geyser's)
5. Many ____ herd cattle. (ranchers, ranchers')
6. Huge water ____ drop from cliffs. (falls, falls')

Collective Nouns pages 36-37

A **collective noun** names a group of people or things. The noun has a singular meaning when you speak about a group that acts as a unit. The noun has a plural meaning when you want to show that each member of the group acts separately or individually.

The fleet enters the town's harbor. (singular, acts as unit)

The fleet sail in different directions. (plural, acts individually)

Write each sentence using the correct form of the verb.

1. The baseball team ____ their different positions. (take, takes)
2. The baseball team ____ onto the field at one time. (walk, walks)
3. The family ____ to the game in two cars. (goes, go)
4. The audience ____ the hall through different doors. (leaves, leave)
5. The class ____ for a student president. (votes, vote)

Review: Verbs pages 42-43

An **action verb** is a word that names an action.

Animals talk like human beings in fables.

A **transitive verb** is a verb that has a direct object. The **direct object** of a verb receives the action of the verb. It answers the questions *whom?* or *what?* after an active verb.

Aesop told clever fables.

An **intransitive verb** is a verb that does not have a direct object.

The animals spoke.

Write each sentence. Underline each action verb. If there is a direct object, underline it twice. Then write whether the verb is transitive or intransitive.

1. Aesop lived in ancient Greece.
2. Aesop recited his tales to many people.
3. His audiences repeated the stories for their friends.
4. People transmitted Aesop's fables orally for more than three hundred years.
5. Then a Greek writer collected the stories in a book.
6. Aesop used animals for many of his characters.
7. However Aesop really discussed human weaknesses.
8. Aesop criticized laziness and foolishness.
9. Each tale has a moral at the end.
10. The proverb offers useful advice for everyday experiences.
11. Almost everyone hears the story of the tortoise and the hare.
12. The hare and the tortoise race.
13. The hare runs far ahead of the tortoise.
14. The hare naps under a tree.
15. The tortoise plods along.
16. The hare awakens too late.
17. The tortoise wins the race.
18. The fable illustrates the value of slow and steady work.

Linking Verbs pages 44-45

A **linking verb** is a verb that connects the subject part with a noun or adjective in the predicate part. It tells what the subject is or is like. Some linking verbs are *be, taste, feel, smell, grow, sound, look, become,* and *turn.*

A **predicate noun** is a noun that follows the linking verb. It tells what the subject is.

A **predicate adjective** is an adjective that follows a linking verb. It describes the subject by telling what it is like.

The lion was [LV] a strong animal [PN].

The mouse seemed [LV] afraid [PA].

Write each sentence. Draw one line under each verb. Then write whether it is an **action verb** or a **linking verb.** If it is a linking verb, write whether it is followed by a **predicate noun** or a **predicate adjective.**

1. A great lion slept in the middle of a forest.
2. A mouse ran across the lion's nose.
3. The mouse was furry.
4. The lion suddenly awoke.
5. The mouse looked afraid.
6. The mouse asked the lion for mercy.
7. The lion seemed very kind.
8. The lion released the small mouse.
9. The mouse was grateful.
10. The mouse offered friendship to the lion.
11. The mouse and the lion became friends.
12. Later the lion fell into a hunter's net.
13. The lion felt helpless.
14. The mouse gnawed through the ropes of the net.
15. The lion was free at last.
16. The little mouse became the hero of the story.
17. A little friend became a great friend.
18. A little creature helped a very large one.
19. The moral of Aesop's story is clear.
20. This fable illustrates the value of friendship.

Verbs with Predicate Nouns or Direct and Indirect Objects pages 46-47

A **linking verb** is a verb that connects the subject part with nouns or adjectives in the predicate part. It tells what the subject is or is like.

A **predicate noun** is a noun that follows the linking verb. It tells what the subject is.

The young woman was [LV] a milkmaid [PN].

Action verbs are often followed by two kinds of objects. A **direct object** is a noun or pronoun that answers the question *whom*? or *what*? after an action verb. The direct object directly receives the action of the verb.

An **indirect object** is a noun or pronoun that tells *to whom* or *for whom* the action was done.

The milkmaid's mother gave [AV] her [IO] the milk [DO].

Write each sentence and draw a line under each verb. Write whether it is a **linking verb** or an **action verb.** Write whether each underlined word in the predicate part is a **predicate noun,** a **direct object,** or an **indirect object.**

1. The young woman put the pail of milk on her head.
2. The milkmaid took the milk to the market.
3. She usually sold a shopkeeper her milk.
4. The woman remembered the cost of her milk.
5. Aesop wrote the milkmaid's thoughts.
6. The money for the milk buys her mother a hen.
7. The hen gives us a nestful of eggs.
8. The eggs become chicks.
9. I supply the chicks with food.
10. Then the small chicks become chickens.
11. I sell the grocer all the chickens.
12. I take the money to the store.
13. I buy my mother a fine new dress.
14. My mother wears it proudly.
15. The milkmaid tossed her head backwards.
16. The milk became a puddle on the ground.
17. In the end the milkmaid gets nothing.
18. This fable illustrates the idea of not counting on things.

pages 48-49

Distinguishing Action and Linking Verbs

An **action verb** is a word that names an action. A **linking verb** connects the subject part with a noun or pronoun in the predicate part. It tells what the subject is or is like. Except for be and seem all verbs that are used as linking verbs can also be used as action verbs.

The carrots tasted (LV) good. The child tasted (AV) the carrots.

Write each sentence. Draw a line under each verb. Write whether it is used as a **linking verb** or an **action verb.**

1. A bird tasted some grapes on a vine.
2. A fox appeared near the grapevine.
3. The grapes appeared tasty to the hungry fox.
4. The fox looked at the grapes out of its reach.
5. The grapes smelled sweet and ripe.
6. The fox felt helpless.
7. Now the grapes seemed sour to the fox.
8. This fable illustrates the idea of denying the value of something out of reach.

Present, Past, and Future Tenses pages 50-51

The **present tense** of a verb names an action that happens now. The **past tense** of a verb names an action that already happened. The **future tense** of a verb names an action that will take place in the future.

A hare races to the old oak tree. (present)

The tortoise tried very hard. (past)

The quick rabbit surely will win the race. (future)

Write each sentence using the correct tense of the verb. Then write if it is in the **present, past,** or **future** tense.

1. In a few minutes I ____ you a fable. (tell)
2. I ____ the tale of the grasshopper and the ant. (read)
3. Long ago an ant and a grasshopper ____ on a field. (live)
4. The grasshopper ____ in the sun. (play)
5. However the industrious ant ____ food. (store)
6. In winter the grasshopper ____ the mistake. (realize)
7. Today this fable ____ the value of hard work. (illustrate)

RETEACHING AND ENRICHMENT

Workbook

Making Subjects and Verbs Agree pages 52-53

A **compound subject** joined by *and* or by *both . . . and* is always plural, and the verb must agree.

A monkey and a cat often make mischief.

Both the cat and the monkey like chestnuts.

When a sentence has a compound subject joined by *or*, by *either . . . or*, or by *neither . . . nor*, the verb must agree with the nearer object.

Either the cat's paw or the monkey's hands grab the chestnuts.

Neither the monkey's hands nor the cat's paw grabs the chestnuts.

Write each sentence. Use the correct form of the verb.

1. Neither monkeys nor a cat ____ fires. (likes, like)
2. The cat and the monkey ____ the chestnuts. (wants, want)
3. Both the monkey and the cat ____ the problem. (has, have)
4. Either all monkeys or only this monkey ____ clever. (is, are)
5. Either the cat's hunger or the monkey's actions ____ the cat. (encourages, encourage)

Principle Parts, Helping Verbs, and Verb Phrases pages 54-55

A **helping verb** helps the main verb to name an action or make a statement.

A **verb phrase** consists of one or more helping verbs followed by a main verb. It names the action or tells what the subject is or is like.

A bear had made a sudden noise.

Write each sentence using the correct form of the helping verb. Draw a line under each participle, and write whether it is a **present participle** or a **past participle.**

1. One boy ____ thinking only about himself. (is, has)
2. The other fellow ____ learned about bears. (is, had)
3. A smart young man ____ lying on the ground. (was, has)
4. The bear ____ approaching the still body. (was, has)
5. The bear ____ ignored the boy. (is, has)

Present and Past Progressive pages 56-57

The **present progressive** tense names an action that is in progress now. It consists of the helping verb *am*, *is*, or *are* and the present participle of the main verb.

The man is telling a fable.

The **past progressive** tense of a verb names an action that was happening or was in progress at some time in the past. It consists of the helping verb *was* or *were* and the present participle of the main verb.

The girl was enjoying the tale.

Write each sentence. Use the present progressive tense.

1. Now the TV ____ a fable of Aesop's. (show)
2. A happy, country mouse ____ dinner. (make)
3. It ____ for a city cousin. (wait)
4. It ____ the finest dishes and best food. (use)
5. It ____ simple, country food. (cook)
6. A cousin ____ to the house. (walk)
7. The city mouse ____ very elegant clothes. (wear)
8. The country mouse ____ the cousin. (greet)
9. The two mice ____ about old times. (talk)
10. They ____ all the food. (eat)

Write each sentence. Use the past progressive tense of the verb in parentheses to complete each sentence.

11. The next morning the city mouse ____ . (leave)
12. The city mouse ____ about the simple, country life. (complain)
13. It ____ life in the city. (explain)
14. The city mouse ____ elegant surroundings. (describe)
15. It ____ about exotic food. (tell)
16. It ____ the country mouse for company. (beg)
17. The country mouse ____ about a simple home. (think)
18. The country mouse ____ the amazing city. (imagine)
19. At last they ____ the city together. (visit)
20. Soon the city mouse ____ to the humble and safe, country
21. home. (return)
22. This fable ____ the value of appreciating one's own home. (illustrate)

Present and Past Perfect pages 58-59

The **present perfect** tense of a verb names an action that happened at an indefinite time in the past. It also names an action that started in the past and is still happening in the present.

A cat has frightened some mice.

The **past perfect** tense of a verb names an action that happened before another past action.

One mouse had escaped from the cat.

Write each sentence using the present perfect tense.

1. The cat ____ the mice. (chase)
2. The mice ____ from the cat. (scurry)
3. The mice ____ the dangerous cat. (discuss)
4. Each mouse ____ a suggestion. (make)
5. One mouse ____ throughout the meeting. (boast)
6. This mouse ____ of an idea. (think)
7. The other mice ____ carefully. (listen)
8. Many ____ to the plan. (agree)
9. They ____ it. (congratulate)
10. The mouse ____ a bell around the cat's neck. (suggest)
11. It ____ about itself. (boast)

Write each sentence. Use the past perfect tense of the verb in parentheses to complete each sentence.

12. Some mice ____ about the plan. (argue)
13. One wise old mouse ____ . (object)
14. It ____ from the start. (frown)
15. It ____ the plan. (reject)
16. This wise mouse ____ at the other mice. (laugh)
17. It ____ their intelligence. (question)
18. The mice ____ for another plan. (plead)
19. They ____ the first idea. (take)
20. They ____ the plan's faults. (ignore)
21. No mouse ____ to approach the cat. (dare)
22. The mice ____ putting a bell on the cat. (fear)
23. The cat ____ free. (stay)
24. This fable ____ the value of unworkable plans. (illustrate)

Irregular Verbs pages 60-63

Irregular verbs are verbs that form the past and past participle in different ways from most verbs. The best way to learn the forms of most irregular verbs is to study them carefully and to use them often. If you need help remembering these verb forms, look at the charts on page 60 and page 62.

Write each sentence using the past tense or the past participle. Remember to watch for *have* or *has.*

1. One morning a crow ____ a piece of cheese. (see)
2. It ____ the cheese in its beak. (put)
3. The bird ____ to a branch of a tree. (fly)
4. A crafty fox has ____ nearby. (creep)
5. The fox ____ hungry for the cheese. (grow)
6. The clever fox ____ to the crow. (speak)
7. The fox ____ under the branch. (go)
8. It ____ the crow several compliments. (give)
9. The crow ____ attentive to the fox's words. (become)
10. The fox ____ on the bird's pride. (bet)
11. It has ____ cheese before. (steal)
12. The fox ____ a pleasant smile. (wear)
13. The crow ____ in the fox's praises. (drink)
14. Flattery ____ the crow in its tracks. (freeze)
15. Compliments have ____ sense out of many people. (shake)
16. The fox ____ the crow's vanity for granted. (take)
17. Aesop ____ about everyone's faults. (write)
18. He ____ about people's good and bad qualities. (know)
19. The fox has ____ closer to the tree. (come)
20. The crow's head ____ with the fox's praises. (swim)
21. The bird ____ its common sense. (lose)
22. Finally the fox ____ the crow unawares. (catch)
23. The crow ____ out with a "caw." (burst)
24. The cheese ____ to the ground. (fall)
25. The fox ____ onto the cheese. (spring)
26. He hungrily ____ the morsel. (eat)
27. The bird ____ in shame. (shrink)
28. It ____ away on the wind as quickly as possible. (ride)

Review: Pronouns pages 70-71

A **pronoun** can take the place of one or more nouns.

Animals sometimes live in the ocean. They sometimes live in it.

A **subject pronoun** is used as the subject of a sentence.

Water covers most of the earth's surface.

It covers most of the earth's surface.

An **object pronoun** is used as the object of the verb or as the object of a preposition.

Oceanographers study the seas. Oceanographers study them.

Subject Pronouns		**Object Pronouns**	
I	we	me	us
you	you	you	you
it, she, he	they	it, her, him	them

Write each sentence. Replace the underlined word or words with a pronoun. Then write whether the pronoun you use is a **subject pronoun** or an **object pronoun.**

1. Three great oceans cover the earth.
2. Ocean water contains minerals and salts.
3. Some countries turn seawater into fresh water.
4. Andrea scuba dives off the Florida coast.
5. Fish and plant life interest Andrea.
6. Maps and charts guided many sailors across the oceans.
7. The ocean floor contains plains, canyons, and mountains.
8. Mrs. Parker studies ocean currents.
9. Ocean currents change slightly every year.
10. Scuba divers wear wet suits.
11. Large metal enclosures take people to the bottom of the ocean safely.
12. Ocean scientists measure the depths of oceans.
13. Paul photographs underwater life.
14. Many different kinds of fish watch Paul.
15. Divers breathe from tanks of air strapped to their backs.
16. Scientists measure the speed of sound in water.
17. Divers study the movement of waves and sand.
18. Scientists interpret the discoveries.

Possessive Pronouns pages 72-73

A **possessive pronoun** shows who or what has something and may take the place of a possessive noun. Possessive pronouns have two forms. One form is **used before a noun.** The other form is **used alone.**

Melanie got her dog in a pet shop. The dog is hers.

Write each sentence. Replace each underlined possessive noun with a possessive pronoun. Then write whether the possessive pronoun is **used before a noun** or if it **stands alone.**

1. Sand and gravel cover the turtle's aquarium.
2. The blue aquarium is Linda's.
3. The blue aquarium is the turtle's home.
4. Linda's brother Leo has three turtles.
5. Leo's turtles have separate homes.
6. These tanks are the turtles'.

Pronouns and Antecedents pages 74-75

When using pronouns, be sure you are clear and make sure that your pronouns agree with the nouns they replace.

I read about sponges. They interest me.

When using a pronoun, be sure that it refers to its **antecedent** clearly. Also be sure that the pronoun agrees with its antecedent in number (singular or plural) and gender (male, female, or neuter).

Tony and Molly share a hobby. He shares her interest in underwater life.

Write the second sentence of each pair using the correct pronoun for each blank. Then write the antecedent for each pronoun.

1. Marie collects sponges. ____ dives for them.
2. Small holes cover a sponge's body. ____ pull in water.
3. The sponge filters out food morsels. ____ eats the food.
4. Marie finds beautiful sponges. Their strange shapes interest ____ .
5. Dried sponges absorb water. People clean with ____ .

Pronouns as Objects of Prepositions

pages 76-77

> A **preposition** is a word that relates a noun or pronoun to another word. Use an object pronoun after a preposition.
>
> **Object Pronouns:** *me you him her it us you them*
>
> The dolphin grabs a fish from him.

Write the second sentence of each pair. Use the correct pronoun in parentheses.

1. Dolphins usually like people. They act friendly toward ____. (we, us)
2. Dolphins learn tricks very easily. Trainers teach difficult tricks to ____. (they, them)
3. These mammals communicate with clicking sounds. Scientists communicate with ____. (they, them)
4. Andy makes friends with some dolphins. They swim with ____. (he, him)
5. Andy throws a ball into the air. A dolphin catches the ball beside ____. (he, him)
6. Rena studies dolphins. She reads about ____. (they, them)
7. She outlines a report. The other students will listen to ____. (her, she)
8. Dolphins understand people's words or signals. Perhaps dolphins can talk to ____. (we, us)
9. Rena watches some scientists perform an experiment. The scientists have the dolphins swim to ____. (they, them)
10. Rena speaks some simple words aloud. The dolphins listen to ____. (she, her)
11. Rena needs Andy's help. Andy quickly moves beside ____. (her, she)
12. The dolphins watch Rena and Andy closely. The dolphins playfully splash water at ____. (they, them)
13. Andy laughs loudly. Rena laughs with ____. (he, him)
14. The scientists ask Andy a question. They get a surprising answer from ____. (he, him)
15. "The dolphins understand your words," says a scientist. "I am glad that you are with ____." (us, we)

Indefinite Pronouns pages 78-79

An **indefinite pronoun** is a pronoun that does not refer to a particular person, place, or thing. Most indefinite pronouns are singular. The verbs must agree with these singular pronouns.

Everyone talks about the danger of sharks.

Other indefinite pronouns are plural. The verbs must still agree with these plural pronouns.

Some see these creatures of the sea.

If you need help remembering the indefinite pronouns, see the lists of indefinite pronouns on page 78.

Write each sentence using the correct word in parentheses.

1. Many ____ the relatively gentle whale shark. (studies, study)
2. Others ____ about more dangerous sharks. (reads, read)
3. Some ____ the shark's food preferences. (analyzes, analyze)
4. Many ____ each other. (eats, eat)
5. Others ____ only small fish. (devours, devour)
6. Something ____ people about this habit. (bothers, bother)
7. Everyone ____ sharks. (avoids, avoid)
8. Many ____ close to popular beaches. (swims, swim)
9. Others ____ in the open seas. (remains, remain)
10. Several make the study of sharks ____ careers. (her, their)
11. Nothing ____ a shark except dolphins. (scares, scare)
12. Both ____ the same waters. (occupy, occupies)
13. Each ____ in its own way. (breathe, breathes)
14. Some ____ in city aquariums. (live, lives)
15. Everybody ____ at their large size. (gasp, gasps)
16. One ____ a young shark to the aquarium. (bring, brings)
17. Much ____ known about the young shark. (becomes, become)
18. Others lend ____ help to the workers. (their, his)
19. Nobody ____ nervous around the sharks. (seem, seems)
20. Several ____ the shark's slow movements. (study, studies)
21. One ____ the shark's sleep habits. (describes, describe)
22. No one ____ the shark's rest period. (understand, understands).
23. Few offer ____ explanations to the workers. (their, her)

Reflexive and Intensive Pronouns

pages 80-81

A **reflexive pronoun** points the action of the verb back to the subject.

Singular: *myself yourself herself himself itself*

Plural: *ourselves yourselves themselves*

We taught ourselves about whales.

An **intensive pronoun** is a pronoun that adds emphasis to a noun or pronoun already named. Intensive pronouns have the same form as the reflexive pronouns.

I myself saw a whale.

Reflexive and intensive pronouns should never be used where a subject pronoun or an object pronoun belongs.

Write each sentence using the correct pronoun.

1. Whales ____ have very sensitive hearing. (them, themselves)
2. A whale's eye cleanses ____ with tears of grease. (it, itself)
3. The captain ____ sighted a group of whales. (she, herself)
4. She told ____ about the near extinction of many whales. (us, ourselves)
5. We saw the whales ____. (us, ourselves)
6. A blue whale lifted ____ out of the water. (him, himself)
7. I took a picture of ____ with my camera. (him, himself)
8. ____ swam away from the ship. (He, Himself)
9. Blue whales ____ grow larger than dinosaurs or elephants. (them, themselves)
10. You ____ can see pictures of these whales. (you, yourself)
11. I ____ have seen whale bones in museums. (me, myself)
12. My sister positioned ____ beside the main exhibit. (her, herself)
13. The design ____ received much attention. (it, itself)
14. ____ designed the huge display of pictures. (He, Himself)
15. ____ required many miles of ocean travel. (It, Itself)
16. She ____ took many of the photographs. (her, herself)
17. We asked the director to show more to ____. (us, ourselves)
18. The director ____ gave us a guided tour of the exhibit. (he, himself)
19. Now we see these animals for ____. (us, ourselves)
20. The whale spouts as water washes over ____. (it, itself)

Interrogative Pronouns pages 82-83

An **interrogative pronoun** is a pronoun used to introduce an interrogative sentence.

Who is used as the subject of the verb.

Who studies the ocean?

Whom is used as the object of the verb or as the object of a preposition.

Whom did the dolphins obey? With whom did you study?

What and *which* are used to refer to things.

What do oceanographers study?

Whose is used to show possession. Do not confuse the contraction *who's* with the possessive pronoun *whose*.

Whose equipment is this? Who's studying dolphins?

Write the second sentence in each pair using the correct word in parentheses to complete the sentence.

1. The challenger first scientifically explored the ocean in 1872. ____ did the sailors aboard it discover? (Which, What)
2. Today many nations conduct scientific research of the ocean. ____ first explored the Arctic Ocean? (Which, What)
3. Jacques Cousteau made many scientific voyages in many oceans and seas. ____ broadcast many discoveries on television? (Who, To whom)
4. Cousteau's discoveries saved some fish and mammals from extinction. ____ Cousteau? (Whose, Who's)
5. Captain Cook discovered many islands in the South Pacific. ____ maps did later sailors and scientists follow? (Whose,Who's)
6. Oceanographers create new instruments and techniques. ____ sea currents have these techniques and instruments found? (Whose, Which)
7. They build special submarines for underwater exploration. ____ is the greatest depth in the world's oceans? (What, Who)
8. New species of sea animals have surfaced. ____ of these two creatures weighs the most? (Who, Which)
9. Two oceanographers took us aboard their ship. ____ equipment did they use in the work? (Who's, Whose)

Review: Adjectives pages 88-89

An **adjective** modifies, or describes, a noun or pronoun.

Millions of people enjoy the rhythmic sounds of jazz.

A **predicate adjective** is an adjective that follows a linking verb. It modifies, or describes, the subject by telling what it is like.

The sounds of jazz are rhythmic.

Write each sentence. Draw one line under each adjective. Draw two lines under the noun or pronoun each adjective describes. If a linking verb connects the subject and adjective, circle the predicate adjective.

1. Jazz seems intricate to some listeners.
2. Musicians often improvise beautiful melodies.
3. Listeners like different styles of jazz.
4. Jazz evolved from older forms of music.
5. Some musicians are famous.
6. Most styles of jazz are tuneful.

Articles and Proper Adjectives pages 90-91

Articles are special kinds of adjectives. **Indefinite articles** are most often used with a noun that has not been mentioned before. They refer to one of a general group of people, places, things, or ideas. The two indefinite articles are **a** and **an.**

a violin an oboe a drum an encore a composition

The is usually used with a noun that has been mentioned before.

The is called a **definite article** because it identifies a specific person, place, thing, or idea.

the violin the oboe the drum

A **proper adjective** is an adjective formed from a proper noun. A proper adjective is capitalized.

African rhythm American music French band

Write each pair or group of words with the indefinite article that belongs before it. Capitalize each proper adjective.

1. english folk song
2. japanese instrument
3. irish coffee
4. chicago jazz band
5. jam session
6. dallas concert

Comparative and Superlative Adjectives pages 92-95

The **comparative** form of an adjective compares two people or things. The **superlative** form of an adjective compares more than two people or things. You often add **-er** to an adjective to form the comparative and **-est** to form the superlative. Sometimes you use **more** and **most** to form the comparative and superlative of adjectives.

Adjective	Comparative	Superlative
hot	hotter	hottest
good	better	best
cheerful	more cheerful	most cheerful

Write each sentence using the correct form of the word in parentheses.

1. Maynard Ferguson plays the ____ possible notes on the trumpet. (high, higher, highest)
2. Alberta Hunter sings songs with the ____ catchy melodies. (more, most)
3. Eubie Blake lived a ____ life than most other jazz musicians. (long, longer, longest)
4. A jazz combo has ____ musicians than a big band. (few, fewer, fewest)
5. Charlie Parker played ____ melodies on the saxophone than anyone before him. (fast, faster, fastest)
6. Art Tatum was one of the ____ jazz pianists of all time. (good, better, best)
7. Ella Fitzgerald improvised ____ melodies with her voice. (impressive, more impressive, most impressive)
8. The Dixieland tunes of the 1920s seem ____ than many modern jazz tunes. (simple, simpler, simplest)
9. Lena Horne performs her songs on both stage and television with a ____ voice. (strong, stronger, strongest)
10. In a solo Count Basie plays the ____ notes of any jazz pianist. (few, fewer, fewest)
11. The audience grew the ____ attentive of all during Wes Montgomery's guitar solo. (more, most)

Demonstrative Adjectives and Pronouns

pages 96-97

The words *this, that, these,* and *those* are *demonstrative words* that "demonstrate," or point out, people, places, or things. The words *this, that, these,* and *those* are **demonstrative adjectives** when they point out something and when they describe nouns. Do not use *here* or *there* when using a demonstrative adjective. Do not use *them* in place of the demonstrative adjective *those.*

this composition　　that recording
these arrangements　　those songs

The words *this, that, these,* and *those* are **demonstrative pronouns** when they take the place of nouns.

This is my favorite composition.
That is my favorite arrangement.
These are her best recordings.
Those are my favorite songs.

Write each sentence using the correct word or words.

1. George and Ira Gershwin wrote ____ songs in the 1930s. (that, those)
2. ____ was one of the most popular shows on Broadway. (Them, That)
3. ____ is an original program from the Gershwin show on Broadway. (This, These)
4. Jazz musicians and singers still play many of ____ Gershwin songs. (them, those)
5. Cole Porter wrote ____ song for a Hollywood movie. (that, those)
6. Eubie Blake played ____ songs during a recent television performance. (them, those)
7. Many jazz artists play ____ song by Richard Rodgers. (this, them)
8. ____ are the best compositions Scott Joplin ever wrote. (These, This)
9. Bix Biderbeck originally composed ____ pieces for the piano. (those, that)
10. One jazz musician arranged ____ piece by Bix Biderbeck for five guitars. (these, this)

Review: Adverbs pages 102-103

An **adverb** is a word that modifies, or describes, a verb, an adjective, or another adverb.

Columbus gallantly sailed from Spain in 1492.

Write each adverb. Then write the word it describes. Write whether the word described is an **action verb**, an **adverb**, or an **adjective**.

1. Columbus led some extremely dangerous voyages.
2. He looked hard for an easier route from Europe to India.
3. King Ferdinand and Queen Isabella of Spain kindly paid for his trip.
4. He and his crew sailed westward in the *Nina, Pinta,* and *Santa Maria.*
5. Severe storms sometimes menaced the ships.
6. The journey delivered them safely to the New World.
7. He quite mistakenly reached America.
8. He made four very adventurous voyages to the New World.
9. The explorer boldly claimed discovery of a western route to India.
10. Unfortunately, Columbus mistook the West Indies for islands near China.
11. Later, other sailors discovered his very large error.
12. He accidentally landed on the shores of South America on his third voyage.
13. Columbus never realized his discoveries of new lands.
14. The Queen died immediately before Columbus could report his adventures.
15. At fifty-three Columbus was very sick.
16. He suffered terribly from arthritis.
17. King Ferdinand stubbornly refused to see him on his return to Spain.
18. Columbus very sadly died alone.
19. Americans celebrate Columbus' discovery of America annually.
20. Now we proudly remember his accomplishment.

Comparative and Superlative Adverbs

Use the **comparative form** of the adverb to compare two actions.

Balboa explored the New World later than Columbus.

Use the **superlative form** of the adverb to compare more than two actions.

The ship brought Balboa farthest of all Spanish travelers.

Write each sentence. Use the comparative or superlative form in parentheses to complete the sentence.

1. Balboa lived ____ than Columbus. (later, latest)
2. His travels brought him ____ into America than Columbus' voyages. (farther, farthest)
3. Balboa claimed the new discovery ____ than any other explorer. (more quickly, most quickly)
4. This Spanish explorer knew the South American continent ____ of all the settlers. (better, best)
5. However Balboa's Indian guides knew the territory ____ than he did. (better, best)
6. Among all the other settlers the Indians trusted Balboa ____ . (more, most)
7. Balboa liked some settlers ____ than others. (more, most)
8. People discovered gold and pearls ____ than they discovered the Pacific Ocean. (later, latest)
9. Of all pursuits wealth and fame attracted Balboa ____ . (more, most)
10. In 1509 the first Spanish expedition left for South America ____ than Balboa left. (sooner, soonest)
11. Because of debts, the authorities allowed the sailors to leave ____ than Balboa. (earlier, earliest)
12. The Spanish explorer traveled to the South American mainland ____ than the first colonizers. (later, latest)
13. The Darien settlement elected Balboa governor ____ of all his companions. (sooner, soonest)
14. At first Ferdinand considered Pedrarias ____ than Balboa for the position of governor. (better, best)

Intensifiers pages 106-107

An adverb that emphasizes or intensifies an adjective or adverb is called an **intensifier**.

Meriweather Lewis and William Clark <u>very</u> <u>bravely</u> explored the Louisiana Territory in 1804.

Write each sentence. Underline each intensifier once and the word it describes twice. Write whether the word described is an **adjective** or an **adverb**.

1. The United States government bought the somewhat unfamiliar territory in 1803.
2. The expedition quite relentlessly traveled to the Pacific Coast.
3. The men made a very dangerous journey by boat, horseback, and foot.
4. They quite diligently gathered information about animals, plants, and minerals of the Northwest.
5. Lewis and Clark kept very meticulous journals.
6. During their journey they saw an exceedingly large number of buffalo.
7. Clark very carefully mapped the expedition's routes to the coast.
8. Indians helped the enormously bold men of the expedition.
9. Both Lewis and Clark spoke Indian languages rather well.
10. As they traveled by boat, Lewis very frequently went ashore.
11. The country rather reluctantly gave up hope for the explorers.
12. Lewis and Clark quite miraculously returned to St. Louis in 1806.
13. They arrived in St. Louis as extremely famous individuals.
14. Lewis became governor of the Louisiana Territory almost immediately.
15. Clark explored the very beautiful Yellowstone River.
16. Thomas Jefferson rather enthusiastically supported the expedition.

Adverbs and Adjectives pages 108-109

Some words can be used as either adjectives or adverbs. You can tell the difference between a word used as an adjective and a word used as an adverb by the way it is used in a sentence. An *adjective* describes a noun or a pronoun. An *adverb* describes a verb.

The first European reached the Hudson River in 1609.

Molly Pitcher first fought in the Revolutionary War in 1788.

Write each sentence. Then write whether the underlined word is an **adjective** or an **adverb**. Write the word it describes.

1. Henry Hudson first searched for a passage to the East.
2. Hudson sailed a straight path from Amsterdam to North America.
3. The ship's crew worked hard during the voyage to Canada.
4. His men suffered from a hard voyage through bad weather.
5. Hudson's last crew mutinied on the fourth voyage.
6. He discovered Hudson Bay last.
7. His far journey led him along the North American coast.
8. The explorer made a fast trip into Chesapeake Bay.
9. Hudson headed right into trouble on his last voyage.
10. He ran far into the cold Canadian waters.
11. Molly Pitcher was the first heroine of the American Revolution.
12. She was first named Mary Ludwig.
13. In 1769 she began an early marriage to John Hays.
14. Hays joined the Revolutionary army early in 1775.
15. Molly carried pitchers of water daily to the soldiers.
16. The soldiers appreciated her kindly deed.
17. They kindly named her Molly Pitcher.
18. The short Battle of Monmouth took place on June 28, 1778.
19. On a hot day in late summer the soldiers went to battle.
20. Molly walked next to the soldiers toward the battlefield.
21. Her husband suffered a stroke late in the battle.
22. Molly's next idea made her a hero.
23. She fought hard during the rest of the battle.
24. After the war her sickly husband died.
25. Molly later married a soldier named George McCauley.
26. The government recognized her deep feelings of patriotism.

Using Adverbs and Adjectives pages 110-111

Use a **predicate adjective** after a linking verb. Use an **adverb** to describe an action verb.

The first sailing expedition around the world was difficult for the crew of Ferdinand Magellan. (adjective)

Magellan cleverly navigated the journey. (adverb)

Write each sentence using the correct word. Write whether it is an **adverb** or an **adjective**.

1. A journey around the earth in 1519 seemed ____. (impossible, impossibly)
2. The King of Portugal treated Magellan ____. (bad, badly)
3. The King of Spain ____ employed Magellan. (eager, eagerly)
4. Magellan was ____ as a navigator and seaman. (brilliant, brilliantly)
5. He ____ proved the round shape of the earth. (actual, actually)

Avoiding Double Negatives pages 112-113

A **contraction** is a word made up of two words combined into one by leaving out one or more letters. Use an **apostrophe (')** in a contraction to show that one or more letters are missing.

is not → isn't   can not → can't   will not → won't

Two negative words in the same sentence make a double negative. Do not use a double negative in a sentence.

Incorrect: The Polo brothers couldn't never hire other merchants.

Correct: The Polo brothers could never hire other merchants.

Write each sentence using the correct word in parentheses.

1. Hardly ____ traveled as far on land during the Middle Ages as Marco Polo. (nobody, anybody)
2. No member of Marco's family ____ had such a long stay in China. (never, ever)
3. No relatives ____ recognize Marco on his return. (couldn't, could)
4. Scarcely anyone ____ traveled to China from Europe. (had, hadn't)
5. No one ____ believe Marco's stories of China. (could, couldn't)

Review: Prepositions and Prepositional Phrases pages 118-119

A **preposition** is a word that relates a noun or pronoun to another word.

Many people eat exotic foods in restaurants.

A **prepositional phrase** is a group of words that begins with a preposition and ends with a noun or pronoun as its object.

Some chefs find international recipes in cookbooks.

Write each sentence. Draw a line under each prepositional phrase. Draw two lines under the object.

1. Mrs. Nelson makes enchiladas with a special filling.
2. First she prepares the filling from chicken and cheese.
3. Mrs. Nelson moistens the tortillas between her fingers.
4. Around the filling she wraps a soft corn tortilla.
5. She heats the enchiladas on a frying pan.
6. She creates a red sauce out of tomatoes and peppers.
7. Mrs. Nelson pours the sauce over the enchiladas.
8. Then she bakes the enchiladas in the spicy sauce.
9. Finally she serves the enchiladas to her family and friends.
10. Felicia dislikes bread from the supermarket.
11. She makes bread with no preservatives.
12. Bread made from pure ingredients is her preference.
13. Therefore Felicia bakes whole wheat bread at her apartment.
14. First she combines flour and yeast in a bowl.
15. She heats milk with brown sugar, shortening, and salt.
16. Then Felicia combines all these ingredients in a larger bowl.
17. She kneads the dough on the counter.
18. Then she shapes the mixture into a circular shape.
19. Now the bread is covered and left in the dark.
20. After one hour she continues.
21. She divides the dough into two parts.
22. Felicia shapes each piece into a loaf.
23. Next she puts the dough in a pan.
24. She cooks the dough in the oven.
25. After forty minutes she removes the bread.

Prepositional Phrases as Adjectives and Adverbs pages 120-121

An **adjective phrase** is a prepositional phrase that modifies, or describes, a noun or pronoun.

Recipes from different countries taste delicious.

An **adverb phrase** is a prepositional phrase that modifies, or describes, a verb.

Mr. Thompson cooks with famous international recipes.

Write each sentence. Draw one line under each prepositional phrase. Draw two lines under the word each phrase describes. Write **adjective phrase** or **adverb phrase** for each prepositional phrase.

1. Mr. Thompson follows a recipe from Italy.
2. He makes linguine noodles with a special tomato sauce.
3. First Mr. Thompson cuts tomatoes on a cutting board.
4. Then he chops basil leaves into tiny pieces.
5. Mr. Thompson combines the ingredients in a bowl.
6. He adds cheese, black pepper, and a clove of garlic.
7. Mr. Thompson adds olive oil and salt to the mixture.
8. He boils the linguine noodles in a large pot.
9. Then he pours the sauce over the linguine.
10. Dr. Furey uses a recipe from Hong Kong.
11. He looks through many cookbooks.
12. He chooses a won ton soup recipe from a good book.
13. First he places the chicken on the counter.
14. Then he cuts various vegetables into small pieces.
15. He combines the chicken, vegetables, and cups of water.
16. He puts these ingredients in a pot.
17. Now Dr. Furey makes the dumplings with special dough.
18. First he prepares the filling for the dumplings.
19. Then he combines scallions and spices with meat.
20. He takes the dumpling dough from the package.
21. Each slice of dough is a thin, square sheet.
22. He places some filling in each slice.
23. He drops the dumplings in the boiling soup.
24. Then he serves the soup to the hungry family.

Agreement in Sentences with Prepositional Phrases pages 122-123

A verb must agree in number with its subject. When a prepositional phrase comes between the subject and the verb, make sure the verb agrees with the subject of the sentence and not with the noun in the prepositional phrase.

Chefs in one famous restaurant attend special cooking courses in Switzerland.

Write each sentence using the correct form of the verb.

1. Mrs. Gibson, in several classes each day, ____ people her famous international recipes. (teaches, teach)

2. Cooking wines from France ____ a richness to many European dishes. (adds, add)

3. A cookbook with international recipes ____ Mrs. Gibson's students. (helps, help)

4. Several dozen eggs in the refrigerator ____ for Mrs. Gibson's students. (waits, wait)

5. The students in one class ____ a delicious soufflé recipe from the south of France. (practices, practice)

6. Many ingredients in the saucepan ____ into a delicious meal. (combines, combine)

7. Mrs. Gibson in her cookbook ____ the step-by-step instructions for a cauliflower and sour cream soufflé. (writes, write)

8. Many students from Mrs. Gibson's class ____ the recipe for French onion soup. (likes, like)

9. A good cook with the right ingredients ____ the soup very quickly. (makes, make)

10. Fresh onion bits under bread and cheese ____ in boiling water. (simmers, simmer)

11. Vegetables on a cutting board ____ a tasty and attractive salad. (becomes, become)

12. Mrs. Gibson with her special seasonings ____ a light salad dressing. (makes, make)

13. The students in her class ____ down for the wonderful meal of salad, soup, and soufflé. (sit, sits)

14. All the students, with fork and spoon in hand, ____ the delicious dinner. (enjoys, enjoy)

Identifying Conjunctions pages 124-125

A **coordinating conjunction** is a word used to connect parts of a sentence such as words, phrases, or clauses.

I like Chinese food and Greek food.

Correlative conjunctions are pairs of words used to connect parts of sentences such as words, phrases, or clauses.

Both Chinese and Americans enjoy Chinese food.

A **subordinating conjunction** is a word or group of words that joins a subordinate clause to a main clause in a sentence.

I drank the wonton soup before I ate the chop suey.

Write each sentence. Underline each conjunction and write whether it is a **coordinating conjunction**, a **correlative conjunction**, or a **subordinating conjunction**.

1. The Allan family went to a restaurant and ate dinner.
2. Neither they nor anyone else in the restaurant disliked the food.
3. Whenever she has a chance, Mrs. Allan uses a wok.
4. Both Mrs. Allan and Mr. Allan enjoy cooking.
5. Although the family likes international recipes, they also enjoy new dishes.
6. Mr. Allan likes Chinese food, but he especially likes Chinese vegetables.

Interjections pages 126-127

An **interjection** is a word or group of words that expresses strong feeling. An interjection has no grammatical connection to any other words.

Wow! This food tastes great.

Write each sentence. Underline the interjection in each, and place the proper punctuation mark after each interjection.

1. Gee I like this food.
2. Ouch I burned my tongue.
3. Oops I dropped a spoon.
4. Hey Where are you going?
5. Alas I have to go home.
6. Yippee We'll come back soon.

Review: Clauses and Sentences pages 132-133

Every sentence has two parts. The **complete subject** names whom or what the sentence is about. The **complete predicate** tells what action the subject performs, what the subject is, or what the subject is like.

Many astronomers search for a tenth planet in our solar system.

A **compound subject** has two or more simple subjects that have the same complete predicate.

Telescopes on earth and equipment in space comb the skies.

A **compound predicate** has two or more verbs that share the same subject.

Some gravitational force affects Uranus and Neptune and causes irregularities in their orbits.

A **compound sentence** is a sentence that contains two or more simple sentences joined by *and, or,* or *but.* It has two or more subjects and two or more predicates. Use a comma before the conjunctions *and, but,* or *or* when you form a compound sentence.

Scientists look through telescopes, and they track two pioneer spacecraft near Pluto.

Write each sentence using correct punctuation. Write whether it is a **simple sentence** or a **compound sentence.** Then draw one line under each complete subject. Draw two lines under each complete predicate. Circle any compound subject or predicate.

1. Irregularities in the orbit of Uranus led scientists to the discovery of Neptune about 150 years ago.
2. William Pickering and Percival Lowell predicted the discovery of the tenth planet in the late nineteenth century.
3. Clyde Tombaugh discovered Pluto in 1930 but Pluto did not affect the orbits of Uranus and Neptune.
4. The first space telescope traveled into space in 1983 and detected infrared light.
5. American, British, and Dutch technicians launched the infrared telescope into an orbit above the North Pole.

Complex Sentences pages 134-135

An **independent clause** has one subject part and one predicate part. It expresses a complete thought, and it can stand alone.

A **subordinate clause** is a group of words that has a subject part and a predicate part. It cannot stand alone because it does not express a complete thought. It is always combined with an independent clause.

A **complex sentence** is a sentence that has an independent clause and one or more subordinate clauses.

While the Earth orbits the Sun, the Sun and the solar system travel through the galaxy.

Write each sentence. Underline the subordinate clause. Draw two lines under the subordinating conjunction that begins each subordinate clause.

1. Because the sun contains gases, parts of the sun rotate in less time than other parts.
2. While the sun seems very large and bright, most other stars dwarf our sun in actual size.
3. Although sunspots appear as dark spots to us, they actually rage as storms in the sun's atmosphere.
4. Light from the star nearest to our sun takes four years to reach earth since the star is so far away.
5. Although the sun radiates visible light, it also generates invisible rays of energy.
6. While ultraviolet rays cause suntanning, infrared light changes to heat.
7. As sunspots move across the sun, they produce great magnetic effects.
8. When the sunspots produce magnetism, they affect radio receivers on earth.
9. If we did not have the sun's light and heat, the earth would become a dead planet with no life or atmosphere.
10. While the earth takes 24 hours to rotate, the sun makes one rotation on its axis in about 25 days.
11. After the sun radiates light, it takes the light over eight minutes to reach earth.

Adverb Clauses pages 136-137

An **adverb clause** is a subordinate clause that tells more about a verb, an adjective, or an adverb in the independent clause.

Adverb clauses are introduced by subordinating conjunctions such as *after, as, as if, as though, before, since, than, until, when, whenever, where, wherever,* and *while.* Like adverbs, adverb clauses tell *how, when,* or *where* the action takes place.

After astronauts land on Mars, scientists will understand more about the red planet.

Write each sentence. Draw one line under the adverb clause and two lines under the subordinating conjunction. Write the word or words the clause modifies. Then write whether that word is a **verb,** and **adjective,** or an **adverb.**

1. Before astronomers and space probes explored Mars, many people speculated about intelligent life there.
2. Space probes sent back more valuable information about Mars than scientists could discover from Earth.
3. While Earth has a thick atmosphere of oxygen, nitrogen, and other elements, Mars' atmosphere consists mostly of carbon dioxide.
4. When scientists discovered the lack of water and oxygen there, they doubted the existence of intelligent life on Mars.
5. Since the Martian surface probably contains important ores and metals, people from Earth may eventually mine the planet.
6. Earth revolves around the Sun faster than Mars does.
7. While the Earth has a strong gravitational pull, Mars has only about one third of the Earth's gravity.
8. Although a person weighs 150 pounds on Earth, he or she would weigh only about 50 pounds on Mars.
9. Astronomers observe Mars closely whenever Mars comes closest to Earth in its orbit around the Sun.
10. Until scientists visit Mars, we will not know for sure about the existence of any life on the planet.

Appositives pages 138-139

An **appositive** is a noun or pronoun that is placed next to another noun or pronoun to identify it or to give additional information about it. Use commas to set an appositive off from the rest of the sentence.

Write each sentence. Underline each appositive phrase and put commas where they are needed. Draw two lines under the noun or pronoun the appositive phrase identifies.

1. Our Sun one star out of billions warms the Earth.
2. The Earth the third planet closest to the Sun rotates with the other eight planets around the Sun.
3. Mercury the closest planet to the Sun revolves the fastest.
4. The solar system also contains comets balls of rock and ice.
5. Light from the nearest star Proxima Centauri takes over four years to reach earth.
6. Our solar system a collection of rotating objects also revolves.
7. Astronomers specialized scientists study our solar system.
8. Twelve moons orbit Jupiter the largest planet in the solar system.
9. Jupiter's atmosphere a thick mass of frozen gases hides its surface from such investigation.
10. Jupiter is one of the Jovian planets a group of planets vastly larger than all others.
11. The *Voyager* probes several years in the making flew past these Jovian planets and out into deep space.
12. Their instruments each a set of carefully designed cameras and sensors sent back a huge amount of new data.
13. These probes will continue their journey into space a trip of uncountable millions of miles.
14. These *Voyager* ships will be the first artificial objects to leave the solar system the home of humanity.
15. The ships also carry time capsules collections of pictures and languages into the universe.
16. Our Sun a rather ordinary star may later attract new visitors.

RETEACHING AND ENRICHMENT

Workbook

Participles in Verb Phrases and as Adjectives pages 140-141

A **verb phrase** is one or more helping verbs followed by a main verb. It names the action or tells what the subject is or is like.

Astronomers have studied our galaxy.

A **participle** can be used as an adjective to modify or describe a noun or a pronoun.

Our sun lies in a rotating galaxy.

Write each sentence. Underline the participle in each sentence. Write whether it is used as part of a **verb phrase** or as an **adjective.**

1. People have traveled as fast as the speed of sound.
2. Our enduring solar system travels within our galaxy.
3. The Milky Way is rotating around the center of the universe.
4. A greatly reduced map might show the billions of galaxies in the universe.
5. Our sun lies within a spiraled arm of the Milky Way galaxy.
6. Scientists call clustered galaxies a supergalaxy.
7. Spiral galaxies have resembled hugh pinwheels.
8. Studies have announced the possibility of interstellar travel.
9. Designers are considering different ideas for the propulsion systems of huge ships.
10. Only a very advanced kind of engine could drive a ship close to the speed of light.
11. Highly refined nuclear engines would require a ship many city-blocks in length.
12. Another kind of engine is becoming more likely for the future.
13. Scientists have noticed the very small "kick" which results from the creation of light.
14. Millions of released atomic particles could drive a spaceship at very high speed.
15. Only with such amazing velocity could astronauts come and go between the stars in one lifetime.

Gerunds and Gerund Phrases pages 142-143

A **gerund** is a verb form ending in **-ing** that is used as a noun.

Flying is fun.

A **gerund phrase** is a group of words that includes a gerund and other words that describe the gerund.

Most astronauts enjoy flying the space shuttle.

Write each sentence. Write whether the underlined word is the **main verb** in a verb phrase, a **participle** used as an adjective, or a **gerund**. Write whether the gerund is the **subject** of the sentence or the **direct object** of the verb.

1. The first space shuttle started flying from another aircraft.
2. Leaving the earth's atmosphere takes tremendous speed.
3. A floating shuttle in space orbits the earth.
4. Once out of the earth's gravitational pull, the shuttle was floating in space.
5. Sailing a space shuttle through space takes great skill.
6. Astronauts have been flying shuttles since the mid 1970s.
7. The launching of the *Columbia* began the first shuttle mission in space.
8. The shuttles mark the beginning of a new period in space flight.
9. Until now, the United States was building a new spacecraft for each necessary mission.
10. The growing costs of these spaceships made the shuttle a vital part in the future of exploration.
11. America is using its shuttle again and again for various missions and experiments.
12. The shuttle recently began ferrying new satellites into orbit.
13. The repairing of old satellites is also part of its job.
14. A meeting in orbit between the shuttle and a satellite requires precision and well-made plans.

Infinitives and Infinitive Phrases pages 144-145

An **infinitive** is formed from the word *to* together with the basic form of the verb. It is often used as a noun in a sentence.

An **infinitive phrase** is a group of words that includes an infinitive and other words that describe the infinitive.

Edmund Halley tried to predict the return of the comet.

Write whether the underlined words in each sentence are an **infinitive** or a **prepositional phrase.** Then write whether each infinitive is the **simple subject** of the sentence or the **direct object** of the verb.

1. Scientists predict Halley's comet to return in 1986.
2. Halley's comet last returned to our skies in 1910.
3. Astronomers like to discover new comets.
4. To predict correctly requires scientific knowledge.
5. The tail of a comet never points to the sun.
6. Some scientists choose to become astronomers.
7. To understand astronomy requires a high degree of scientific knowledge.
8. Comets return to our view on varying timetables.
9. To understand the timetables requires complex mathematics.
10. Comets are known to travel along immense, elliptical paths.
11. Some comets begin to turn around when passing by the sun.
12. Their long journeys to the stars and back start again while they fade from our view.
13. To realize the length of a comet's journey took many centuries of careful observation.
14. The task of marking the return of each comet fell to each succeeding generation of scientists.
15. Most observers want to see a particular comet return quickly.
16. Most comets fail to appear in time.
17. To see Halley's comet return in 1986 is lucky for us.

Parts of Speech in Sentences pages 146-147

A part of speech is a category naming the job that a word performs in a sentence.

Every word in a sentence is one of the following **eight parts of speech:**

A **noun** names a person, place, thing, or idea.

An **action verb** names an action. A **linking verb** tells what a subject is or is like.

A **pronoun** takes the place of one or more nouns.

An **adjective** describes a noun or pronoun.

An **adverb** describes a verb, an adjective, or another adverb.

A **preposition** relates a noun or pronoun to another word.

A **conjunction** connects words or groups of words.

An **interjection** expresses strong feeling or surprise.

Write each underlined word and its part of speech.

1. Meteors are pieces of stone and metallic material.
2. Friction with the air makes meteors hot and very bright.
3. They hurtle into the Earth's atmosphere.
4. Wow! The Great Meteor Crater of Arizona is the hugest crater I have ever seen.
5. Thousands of bright meteorites enter the earth's atmosphere every day.
6. Meteorites are parts of meteors not yet burned up.
7. Meteors look like shooting stars in the sky.
8. The Earth encounters a great number of meteors every year.
9. The famous Tunguska meteorite crashed into the Earth in Siberia in 1908.
10. It flattened forests and scorched a 20-mile area of land.
11. Stony meteorites and iron meteorites are two kinds of meteorites.
12. Many different stony minerals with particles of iron make up stony meteorites.
13. Iron meteorites consist chiefly of iron and nickel.
14. Oh my, the largest meteorite at Hoba West in Southern Africa weighs about 60 tons.

Review: Beginning and Ending Your Sentences; Capitalizing Proper Nouns and Adjectives pages 164-167

A **declarative sentence** is a sentence that makes a statement. Use a **period** at the end of a declarative sentence.

An **interrogative sentence** is a sentence that asks a question. Use a **question mark** at the end of an interrogative sentence.

An **imperative sentence** is a sentence that gives a command or makes a request. Use a **period** at the end of an imperative sentence.

An **exclamatory sentence** is a sentence that expresses strong feeling. Use an **exclamation mark** at the end of an exclamatory sentence.

An **interjection** is a word or group of words that expresses strong feeling. Use an **exclamation mark** after an interjection when it stands alone. Use a **comma** to separate an interjection from the rest of a sentence when it is part of the sentence.

A **proper noun** names a specific person, place, thing, or idea. Capitalize the important words in a proper noun.

A **proper adjective** is an adjective formed from a proper noun. Capitalize proper adjectives.

Write each sentence or group of words. Capitalize and punctuate each one correctly. Then write **declarative, interrogative, imperative, exclamatory,** or **interjection.**

1. did a tornado damage that house on wilfred st.
2. the shifting of warm and cold air causes tornadoes
3. what a mess
4. how quickly that twister moved through orangetown
5. watch out for heavy black clouds over kansas skies
6. over one hundred tornadoes hit the american midwest every year
7. can these storms drive straw into trees
8. never underestimate the power of an iowa tornado
9. a tornado has great speed and a strong lifting force
10. tornadoes in the atlantic look like waterspouts
11. awesome

Commas pages 168-171

Use a **comma** to separate each noun, verb, or adjective in a series of three or more nouns, verbs, or adjectives.

The hurricane struck with speed, force, and viciousness.

Use **commas** to separate the different items in addresses and dates. Use a comma after the last part of the address or date when it appears in the middle of a sentence.

The storm hit Smithtown, Iowa, on April 2, 1985.

Use a **comma** to set off words such as **well, yes,** and **no** when they begin a sentence. Use **commas** to set off expressions such as **by the way, of course,** and **however** when they interrupt a sentence. Use **commas** to set off a person's name when you address the person directly. Use **commas** to set off appositives when they interrupt a sentence with more information.

Yes, the storm just barely missed my home town.

The hurricane, however, damaged a town nearby.

Mr. Mayor, ask the governor for disaster relief aid.

Hurricane Adam, the first storm of the year, traveled northward.

Use a comma before **and, or,** or **but** when they join simple sentences.

Hurricane Betsy hit our town, but it injured no one.

Use a **comma** after an adverb clause that introduces a sentence.

When great storms occur in the North Pacific, people call them typhoons.

Write each sentence. Use commas where necessary. Give the reason.

1. Well just what is a hurricane?
2. Angie a hurricane is a storm with wind speeds over 75 mph.
3. The storm heaves whirls and destroys.
4. The hurricane blows furiously but it has a calm center.
5. When hurricane winds push ocean water a storm tide may occur.
6. A hurricane a region of low air pressure carries great force.
7. A storm tide hit Galveston Texas in 1900.
8. Hurricanes typhoons and tropical storms pose dangers.
9. The eye of a storm the center may measure 20 miles across.

Semicolons and Colons/Quotations and Italics

pages 172-175

Use a **semicolon** to separate the parts of a compound sentence if there are commas within one or both parts.

Some people dislike snow, wind, and cold; but other people like winter weather.

Use a **semicolon** to separate the parts of a compound sentence if they are not joined by *and, or,* or *but.*

Snow always appears as six-sided crystals; no two crystals are exactly alike.

Use a **colon** between the hour and minute when writing the time.

Use a **colon** to show that a list of items will follow.

Here are some winter sports: skating, skiing, and tobaggoning.

Use a **colon** after the greeting in a business letter.

Quotation marks are used to set apart a speaker's exact words in a sentence.

Italics are a special slanted kind of print. Use italics to set apart special names of things and titles of artworks. When you write these special words, you underline them in your writing to show that they are italicized.

H.M.S. <u>Invincible</u>   <u>Mona Lisa</u>   <u>The Los Angeles Times</u>

Write the sentences below. Punctuate them correctly using semicolons, colons, quotation marks, or italics.

1. My Mexican friend said, I have never seen snow.
2. Warren Witheral wrote a book called How the Racers Ski.
3. The snow began falling at 1000 p.m.
4. Andy likes summer, spring, and fall but he dislikes winter.
5. This is a list of areas of large snow accumulation the Rocky Mountains, the Sierra Nevada, and the Alps.
6. The New York Times predicted snow for New England.
7. The winter of 1978 taught New Englanders a lesson the entire region realized the power of a major storm.
8. New England's highways became impassable, said Debbie.
9. For nearly a week most travelers were on foot but at home Debbie read Tolstoi's War and Peace.

Other Punctuation Marks pages 176-177

Always use a **hyphen** after the prefix *ex-*. A hyphen is also used when a prefix comes before a capital letter.

ex-councilman   mid-December   pro-American

The **hyphen** is used between two dates to show the length of a person's lifetime or a thing's existence.

Abe Lincoln (1809-1865)

A **hyphen** indicates the starting point and ending point in a journey.

New York-Miami train   Los Angeles-Chicago flight

Some words require **hyphens** as part of their spelling.

brother-in-law   twenty-five   French-Canadian

The **dash** shows an abrupt change, or interruption, in the main thought of a sentence.

Weather—all kinds of weather—affects our lives.

Parentheses are used to set off extra information within a sentence.

Air pressure (the weight of air pushing on the earth) varies from time to time and from place to place.

Write each sentence. Use a hyphen, dash, or parentheses where necessary.

1. The hailstorm delayed the Dallas Chicago flight.
2. The sun shines on the earth at different angles a 90 degree angle at the equator, and makes a region relatively warm or cool.
3. The ex weather reporter taught the class about the different kinds of clouds.
4. Weather forecasting developed significantly during the administration of President Kennedy 1961 1963.
5. Pro Weather Bureau advocates encourage the use of more satellites in tracking storms.
6. Meteorologists predicted a pre April hurricane near Florida.
7. The atmosphere traps sunshine sunshine is radiation in the form of short waves much as a greenhouse does.
8. Forty eight tornadoes hit the Midwest last year.
9. Humidity water vapor makes a hot day seem even hotter.

Abbreviations/Contractions pages 178-181

Capitalize the important words in proper nouns. Also capitalize the abbreviations and initials that are sometimes used in place of proper nouns.

Judith Beth Selner—J. B. Selner

Some common nouns become proper nouns when used with names. These words include *mister, doctor, reverend, junior,* and *senior.* They are capitalized and abbreviated when used with names.

Mr. Armand Cortez Dr. B. S. Jones Ms. Mary F. Carter

Professional and academic degrees are abbreviated and used after a person's name.

Doctor of Medicine—Marcus Welby, M.D.

Doctor of Philosophy—H. Bufalmaco, Ph.D.

Some abbreviations are used in charts and lists, but not in sentences.

Sunday—Sun. August—Aug.

Proper names of streets may be abbreviated in addresses.

Street—St. Road—Rd. Place—Pl. Court—Ct.

State names are abbreviated in addresses on envelopes.

Iowa—IA California—CA

A contraction is a word made up of two words combined into one by omitting one or more letters. Use an apostrophe in a contraction to show where letters are missing.

they're I've he's who's

Write each item. Use capital letters and punctuation. Add apostrophes where necessary. Abbreviate each underlined word.

1. <u>reverend</u> <u>mark</u> <u>david</u> powell
573 market <u>street</u>
fleming, <u>alabama</u>
2. <u>mistress</u> <u>alice</u> <u>fay</u> thomas
1120 <u>saint</u> stephen's <u>court</u>
chicago, <u>illinois</u>
3. im the one whos lucky.
4. <u>wednesday</u>, <u>august</u> 15
5. <u>doctor</u> <u>jeanne</u> marashian
584 alliance <u>avenue</u>
kansas city, <u>missouri</u>
6. well see you if youre there.
7. <u>clara</u> dale <u>doctor of philosophy</u>
236 <u>avenue</u> of the americas
new york city, <u>new york</u>

Using the Table of English Spellings

pages 188-189

The *Table of English Spellings* helps you find words that you know how to pronounce but do not know how to spell.

TABLE OF ENGLISH SPELLINGS

Sound	Spelling	Sound	Spelling
/a/	hand, have, laugh, plaid	/o/	lock, watch
/ā/	paper, rate, rain, pay, eight, steak, veil, obey, ballet, straight, gauge	/ō/	so, bone, boat, know, soul, foe, beau, oh, mauve, sew
/ä/	father	/ô/	off, fall, author, jaw, bought, caught, broad
/är/	car, heart, sergeant	/oi/	foil, toy
/âr/	dare, hair, where, pear, their, prayer	/ôr/	fork, war, ore, oar, four, door
/b/	bit, rabbit	/ou/	out, now, bough
/ch/	chin, nature, batch, question, cello	/p/	pill, happy
/d/	dive, ladder, would, failed	/r/	ray, parrot, wrong, rhyme
/e/	met, bread, many, said, friend, leopard, aesthetic, says, heifer	/s/	song, city, mess, scene, listen, psychology, waltz, sword
/ē/	he, city, bee, beach, athlete, machine, field, receive, key, Caesar, amoeba, people	/sh/	nation, shin, special, mission, expansion, machine, sugar, tissue, conscience, ocean
/ėr/	fern, turn, thirst, worst, earth, courage, amateur, myrtle	/t/	ten, bitter, topped, doubt, two, ptomaine, yacht, thyme
/f/	fine, phone, off, half, laugh	/th/	thin
/g/	go, stagger, vague, guard, ghost	/u/	sun, son, touch, come, flood, does
/h/	he, whom	/u̇/	full, look, should, wolf
/hw/	wheel	/ü/	tool, luminous, who, flute, soup, jewel, true, lose, fruit, maneuver, canoe
/i/	bit, myth, give, damage, build, been, pretty, carriage, busy, women	/ū/	music, use, few, feud, cue, view, beautiful, adieu
/ī/	fine, tiger, try, high, tie, dye, eye, stein, height, buy, aisle	/v/	vine, halve, of
/ir/	clear, cheer, here, cashier, souvenir, weird	/w/	we, queen
/j/	magic, jump, ledger, graduate, adjust, exaggerate, soldier	/y/	onion, yes
/k/	cat, key, tack, chord, account, mosquito, Iraq, walk	/z/	has, zoo, xylophone, fuzz, scissor, czar, tsar
/kw/	quit	/zh/	division, treasure, garage, azure, equation
/l/	line, hall, isle	/ə/	summon, alone, April, moment, furious, circus, oxygen, ancient, bargain, surgeon
/m/	mine, hammer, climb, salmon, hymn	/ər/	better, color, dollar, augur, picture, giraffe
/n/	nice, gnome, knee, funny, pneumonia		
/ng/	sing, link, tongue		

Read each sentence. Use the dictionary and the Table of English Spellings to correct the spellings of the underlined word in each sentence. Then write each sentence correctly.

1. J.S. Bach wrote musical compositions called fewgues.
2. He performed for famus people.
3. Mozart and other musicians played the harpsicord.
4. Mozart composed operas and simphonies.
5. The great orkestras of Europe performed his works.
6. Beethoven played in concert halls for the general public and arristocrats.
7. Composers today copy many of Beethoven's musical caracteristics.
8. Deafness unfortunately aflicted Beethoven for half of his life.
9. People of all nations recognize the geenius of Beethoven.
10. He wrote string quartets for violin, viola, piano, and chello.

Spelling Rules pages 190-193

Knowing spelling rules will help improve your spelling. Write *i* before *e* except after *c* or when sounded as *a* as in *neighbor* and *weigh.*

brief chief

A **prefix** is a letter or group of letters added to the beginning of a word. Do not change the spelling of a word when you add a prefix to it.

re+turn → return mis+spell → misspell

A **suffix** is a letter or group of letters added to the end of a word. A number of rules help you spell correctly when you add a suffix to a word.

retire+ment → retirement retire+ing → retiring

courage + ous courageous ice + y icy tie + ing tying

pity + ful pitiful swim + ing swimming

Refer to the spelling rules on pages 190 and 192.

Read each pair of words. Write the correctly spelled word.

1. belief, beleif
2. careing, caring
3. receive, recieve
4. weird, wierd
5. arrangement, arangement
6. arriveal, arrival
7. lieing, lying
8. capabley, capably
9. crying, criing
10. crammed, cramed
11. watchs, watches
12. sauces, saucees
13. unoticed, unnoticed
14. mistake, misstake
15. truely, truly
16. sincerely, sincerly
17. sillyer, sillier
18. changing, changeing

Add a prefix or suffix to each word. Then write the word.

19. snow + y
20. terrible + y
21. put + ing
22. un + touched
23. careless + ly
24. coy + ly
25. majority + es
26. care + ful
27. hive + s
28. un + tie
29. re + write
30. write + er
31. make + er
32. cover + ing
33. ir + responsible
34. awe + ful
35. abuse + ed
36. win + er

Irregular Plural Nouns pages 194-195

To form the plural of most nouns, add **-s.** To form the plural of nouns ending in *s, ss, x, z, ch,* and *sh,* add **-es.**

book→books toss→tosses fox→foxes bush→bushes

To form the plural of most nouns ending in a vowel and *o,* add **-s.**

solo→solos cello→cellos

To form the plural of most nouns ending in a consonant and *o,* generally add **-s,** but sometimes add **-es.**

photo→photos echo→echoes hero→heroes

Some words that end with a consonant and *o* can be made plural by adding either **-s** or **-es.**

volcano→volcanos or volcanoes

To form the plural of most nouns ending in *f* and all nouns ending in *ff,* add **-s.**

belief→beliefs gulf→gulfs cliff→cliffs

To form the plural of some nouns ending in *f* or *fe,* and many nouns ending in *lf,* change **f** to **v** and add **-s** or **-es.**

life→lives leaf→leaves calf→calves

Some nouns have irregular plural forms.

child→children mouse→mice man→men foot→feet

Some nouns have the same form in the singular and plural.

sheep→sheep moose→moose

Use a rule to form the plural of each word. Then write the correct plural form or forms of each word.

1. piano
2. bluff
3. sheaf
4. patio
5. deer
6. woman
7. veto
8. mango
9. cat
10. boss
11. box
12. wife
13. shelf
14. trout
15. elf
16. tooth
17. volcano
18. splash
19. cuff
20. radio
21. cameo
22. child

Words Often Confused pages 196-199

Some words sound alike. However, they have different meanings and are spelled differently. The **possessive pronoun** *its* takes the place of a noun in a sentence. The **contraction** *it's* is a short form of *it is.*

The cat licks its paws. It's very fond of people.

Possessive nouns and contractions are often confused.

Sam's friend plays the piano. (friend of Sam)

Sam's playing the piano. (Sam is)

Write each sentence using the correct word in the blank.

1. I like snow and ____. (rain, reign)
2. Queen Victoria's ____ lasted from 1837 to 1901. (rain, reign)
3. I never ____ anything anywhere. (lose, loose)
4. The cat worked the collar ____. (lose, loose)
5. Jean enjoys cold ____. (whether, weather)
6. I will decide ____ I can finish in time. (whether, weather)
7. Adam ____ a ski jacket and gloves. (wears, wares)
8. The ski shop sells ____ to customers. (wears, wares)
9. ____ quickly becoming cloudy. (Its, It's)
10. ____ on her way to the skating rink. (Stacey's, Staceys)
11. People ride the waves on special ____ boards. (surf, serf)
12. The king badly mistreated the ____. (surf, serf)
13. David received several ____ over the holidays. (presence, presents)
14. David's ____ at the party made the party enjoyable. (presence, presents)
15. The ship navigated through the stormy ____. (strait, straight)
16. It then sailed a ____ course across the ocean. (strait, straight)
17. Please ____ which path to take. (chose, choose)
18. You ____ the wrong path. (chose, choose)
19. ____ the way through the woods. (Lead, Led)
20. The campers hammered the ____ in the ground for their tent. (steak, stake)
21. Jan cooked the ____ on the grill. (stake, steak)
22. The poem was not ____ understandable. (holy, wholly)
23. The Vatican contains Christian ____ objects. (holy, wholly)

Prefixes pages 208-211

A **prefix** is a letter or group of letters added to the beginning of a word.

The students learned about co̲operation among nations.

The students learned about i̲n̲t̲e̲r̲national cooperation.

The underlined words in each sentence below are the definition of another word. Choose a word with a prefix that can replace the underlined words. Write each sentence using one new word that you choose.

1. The United Nations began in the after war era.
2. During the before war period there was a similar organization called the League of Nations.
3. In some people's opinion war is not humane.
4. The United Nations provides the nations of the world with a not violent way to resolve international problems.
5. UNICEF was established to help children in lesser developed countries.
6. Facts on world hunger emphasize again the importance of helping developing countries.
7. Few people today feel extra confident about solving world hunger easily.
8. A fast and easy solution is not possible.
9. Occasionally United Nations representatives attend not productive meetings.
10. The Secretary General piled together a list of United Nations' accomplishments.
11. Communications technology helps link together the nations of the world.
12. In some people's opinion, the United Nations is a partly political organization.
13. Solutions to some world problems demand better than human efforts.
14. The Charter provides one form rules for membership.
15. Many international problems remain not resolved.
16. Some nations display two-colored flags outside the United Nations building.

Noun Suffixes/Adjective Suffixes pages 212-215

A **suffix** is a letter or group of letters added to the end of a word. Adding a suffix sometimes changes the meaning of the word. Some suffixes change a noun, verb, or adjective into a new noun. Other suffixes change a noun or a verb into a new adjective.

create (original verb)   creator (new noun)

creative (new adjective)

Read each sentence pair below. Add the suffix in parentheses to the underlined word. Write the second sentence in each pair using the new word. Write whether the new word is a **noun** or an **adjective.**

1. American visitors <u>tour</u> Europe, Asia, and Africa. Many countries make money from ____ . (-ism)
2. A reporter must <u>investigate</u> a topic thoroughly. An ____ reporter is a curious person. (-ive)
3. <u>Rain</u> and clouds sometimes darken the skies over New York. However a ____ day rarely affects a tourist's good time. (-y)
4. The United Nations complex, the Empire State Building, and many museums <u>impress</u> visitors. These ____ sights bring many tourists to New York. (-ive)
5. Georgia O'Keeffe <u>paints</u> our western landscape. She is a famous ____ . (-er)
6. In some western states a bright <u>sun</u> in a cloudless sky follows a snowstorm. I like ____ days. (-y)
7. The <u>beauty</u> of our national parks impresses many visitors. Everyone finds them ____ . (-ful)
8. Every tourist likes the glitter and <u>imagination</u> of Hollywood movies. The movie stars and their ____ characters capture our attention. (-ary)
9. Tourists like the <u>cute</u> cartoon characters at Disneyland. The ____ of Mickey Mouse amused generations of children. (-ness)
10. Tourists from cold climates <u>enjoy</u> the Florida sun. They bathe in the warm sunlight on the ____ Florida coast. (-able)

Roots pages 216-217

The original, or base, word to which you add a prefix or suffix is called a **root.**

Root	**Meaning**	**New Word**
graph	write	autograph
port	carry	report
duc	lead	deduct

Write each word below. Write the meaning of the root and then the meaning of the word. Use your dictionary if necessary.

1. video
2. scribe
3. photograph
4. succeed
5. pedestal
6. export
7. vocation
8. accept
9. repulse
10. spectacle
11. pendulum
12. graphic
13. reduce
14. regression
15. propel

Write the words in the sentences that contain the following roots: **sign, graph, pend, duc, port, grad, cap, pel, voc, vis.** Then write the meaning of each word.

16. Ellen read a biography of the French king, Louis XIV.
17. The book reported on the king's great wealth and power.
18. Tourists in France gaze at Louis' famous and spectacular mansion at Versailles.
19. American visitors enjoy other wondrous sights of France.
20. Pedestrians watch for cars on the Champs-Elysee in Paris.
21. The Statue of Liberty invokes friendship between France and the United States.
22. This present from France to the United States captures the spirit of liberty in both countries.
23. Workmen transported the statue from France to America in dozens of crates.
24. Alexandre Eiffel designed another famous architectural wonder about one hundred years ago.
25. Tourists ascend the Eiffel Tower gradually by foot or in elevators.
26. The huge wrought-iron skeleton captivates thousands of tourists a year.
27. Progress in engineering made the great structure possible.

Synonyms pages 218-219

> A **synonym** is a word that is similar in meaning to another word.
>
> Japan has a rich and interesting culture.
>
> Japan has a rich and fascinating culture.

Write each sentence. Use the word in parentheses that best completes each sentence. Think carefully about which word gives the clearest meaning.

1. Baseball ____ most sports fans in Japan. (thrills, interests)
2. Japanese music may sound ____ to western listeners. (different, foreign)
3. Many Japanese orchestras play western music ____. (skillfully, well)
4. Kabuki theater ____ Japanese audiences. (entertains, pleases)
5. Western dramas also ____ to the Japanese. (call, appeal)
6. ____ paintings capture onlookers' attention. (Nice, Delicate)
7. Some Japanese wear ____ kimonos. (robelike, Japanese)
8. Many people wear ____ western business suits, too. (familiar, common)
9. Westerners find Japanese culture ____. (unique, unusual)

Antonyms pages 220-221

> Words that are opposite in meaning are called **antonyms.**
>
> up→down start→finish over→under in→out

Choose an antonym for the word to the left of the parentheses. Write the word and its antonym.

1. easy (simple, difficult)
2. fun (somber, merry)
3. asleep (tired, awake)
4. dark (light, shadow)
5. pretty (ugly, gorgeous)
6. tension (strain, relaxation)
7. careful (wary, careless)
8. delicious (repulsive, tasty)
9. noisy (loud, quiet)
10. numerous (few, many)
11. north (west, south)
12. frigid (cold, warm)
13. famous (unknown, noted)
14. towering (tall, tiny)
15. push (pull, shove)
16. throw (eject, catch)
17. play (frolic, work)
18. foreign (native, alien)
19. courteous (civil, rude)
20. basement (cellar, roof)

Verbs Often Confused pages 222-223

> Some verbs are often confused.
>
> The man teaches the students British history.
>
> The students learn some interesting things.
>
> Refer to the list of verbs on page 222.

Write each sentence correctly using the word in parentheses.

1. The English king did not always ____ down the law. (lie, lay)
2. One student ____ her hand. (raises, rises)
3. The class ____ about the development of the constitutional monarchy. (taught, learned)
4. Today the king or queen in Britain ____ on the throne but performs mostly ceremonial duties. (sits, sets)
5. The Prime Minister and the House of Commons ____ the laws. (sit, set)
6. The first American patriots ____ many democratic ideas from some British democratic ideas. (taught, learned)
7. British tradition ____ Americans about the power of the people. (taught, learned)
8. The teacher ____ many questions about the similarities between Britain and the United States. (rised, raised)
9. Tony ____ in an article on Britain yesterday. (took, brought)
10. He ____ it on the class bulletin board. (left, let)
11. Carrie now ____ some facts from it for her report. (takes, brings)
12. She ____ at the teacher's desk during her short talk. (set, sat)
13. Many hands ____ into the air with questions about democracy in Britain and America. (raised, rose)
14. Leo ____ books out of the library on the difference between the U.S. Congress and the British Parliament. (took, brought)
15. Carrie's answer then ____ several minutes. (takes, took)
16. Carrie ____ out a few photographs and articles on the desk for the use of the class. (laid, lay)
17. She has ____ the class thoroughly. (learned, taught)
18. In a democracy, justice ____ in the hands of citizens. (lies, lays)
19. The teacher ____ the class learn about the history of democracy. (left, let)

RETEACHING AND ENRICHMENT

Workbook

Words Often Confused pages 224-225

> Many English words share similar sounds but have different spellings and meanings.
>
> America accepts the friendship of its neighbor to the north, Canada.
>
> American tourists need passports in all countries except in Canada.
>
> Refer to the list of words on page 224.

Write the word that correctly completes each sentence.

1. Canada and the United States have similar governments ____. (two, too, to)
2. Farmers grow many different crops on the ____ of the western provinces of Canada. (planes, plains)
3. Canada and the United States have cooperated closely in the ____. (passed, past)
4. The ____ elements in their friendship are common goals and traditions. (principle, principal)
5. Both countries follow the ____ of democracy. (coarse, course)
6. Tourists like Ottawa, the ____ of Canada. (capitol, capital)
7. One student found both countries ____ each other on the map. (beside, besides)
8. Canadians ____ many American TV shows on their stations. (accept, except)
9. Many people went ____ Montreal during the 1980 Summer Olympics. (two, too, to)
10. The United States and Canada share other interesting landmarks ____ the five Great Lakes. (besides, beside)
11. Niagara Falls lies between the two nations along the ____ of the Niagara River. (coarse, course)
12. Artificial canals provide the ____ links between cities along the Great Lakes. (principle, principal)
13. What are the ____ largest cities in the area? (to, two, too)
14. None of the Lakes are connected to the sea ____ Lake Ontario. (accept, except)
15. Engineers dug the St. Lawrence Seaway from the ____ and rocky soil. (course, coarse)

Mechanics of Note-Taking and Writing an Outline pages 242-245

When you write a report, you should take careful and accurate notes from each source of information. Write notes on notecards, starting with the title of the source, and the author's name. Write each main idea and its supporting details on a separate notecard. Use phrase notes. After each note, write the page number on which the information was found. Arrange your notes in an outline. Decide which notes will be the main ideas, or main topics. Group your supporting details, or subtopics, for each main idea under each main topic.

Read the paragraphs below. Take notes and then organize them within the given outline form. Write a three-paragraph report.

Water is a unique substance because it exists in three different forms within earth's normal temperature range: as a liquid, as a solid in ice, and as a gas in water vapor.

The first example of this fact is seen in the properties of ice. While most liquids contract when frozen, water expands. Water molecules in ice are far apart, and they move slowly. Air becomes trapped between the molecules, making ice lighter than water. This fact leads to a vital and unique conclusion about water as ice. If ice sank, away from the sun's rays, more and more ice would pile up each winter. Soon the earth would become very cold and hostile to life forms.

Water is also unique in its liquid state. No other substance is so vital to every form of life, and those forms of life are themselves mostly water. Water is also one of the few substances that can be used over and over again. There is no more or less water on Earth today than there ever was, or will be.

Finally water in its gaseous state (water vapor) serves several purposes. Substances can be dissolved in water and then collected after water evaporates. Steam, of course, drives many machines. Clouds (water vapor) release rain to feed the Earth's life forms. No other substance plays such vital roles. Water is unique because it has three forms: ice, liquid, gas.

I. Ice	II. Liquid	III. Gas
A.	A.	A.
B.	B.	B.
		C.

Workbook

RETEACHING AND ENRICHMENT

Understanding Verbal Analogies pages 252-253

Analogy questions test your ability to understand relationships between words and ideas.

cat : kitten : : mother:

a. mommy **b.** father **c.** child

When stated in the form of a sentence, this analogy is really asking, "Cat is to kitten as mother is to which of the following words?" In order to choose the correct answer, you must carefully consider the relationship between the words in the first word pair. Your answer must express a relationship similar to the one expressed in the sample. Several types of relationships frequently appear on analogy tests. Look at these examples.

Word : Synonym	gigantic : huge : : muddy: unclear
Word : Antonym	victory : defeat: : joy: sorrow
Whole : Part	house: door : : car : wheel
Worker : Tool	writer : pen : : carpenter : hammer
Raw Material : Product	gasoline: oil : : linen : flax

Read each numbered pair of words and the choices that follow. Then write the pair of words that are related to each other in the same way the original pair of words are related.

1. Opponent : enemy : : ally :
a. acquaintance b. stranger c. friend

2. calm : stillness : : excitement :
a. peacefulness b. happiness c. commotion

3. skillful : clumsy : : deft :
a. awkward b. dumb c. large

4. smooth : rough : : hot :
a. steam b. burn c. cold

5. scale: notes : : rainbow :
a. circle b. rain c. colors

6. play: scenes : : book :
a. plot b. chapters c. characters

7. artist: brush : : carpenter:
a. hammer b. wood c. house

8. needle: sew : : pencil :
a. sharpen b. write c. break

Parts of a Dictionary pages 278-279

A dictionary contains an alphabetical list of words and their meanings. *Unabridged* dictionaries give the most complete information available about words in the English language.

Abridged dictionaries are shortened. They contain a selection of the most common words. In both kinds of dictionaries, each word listed is called an *entry word.* Entry words may be divided by dots or spaces into syllables. When you write, you may need to divide a word at the end of a line. You can check the dictionary to see where to divide it. If a word has no dots or spaces, it has only one syllable and cannot be divided.

Look at the sample dictionary entries below.

heart (härt) *n.* **1.** in man and other animals having a backbone, the hollow, muscular organ that pumps the blood through the body by beating regularly. **2.** the heart considered as the center of a person's innermost feelings, thoughts, or emotions: *He spoke from his heart when he thanked them for their help.* **3.** the center or innermost part of anything. **4.** the main, vital, or most important part. **5.** anything shaped like the heart.—by heart. by or from memory: *to know a poem by heart*

ri val (rī'vəl) *v.t.*, **1.** to try to equal or do better than; compete with. **2.** to compare favorably with or be the equal of: *Joan rivals her sister in beauty.* [Going back to Latin *rīvālis* a person who uses water from the same brook as another; because such people often quarreled about the use of the water.]

Use the sample dictionary entries to answer each question. Write your answers.

1. How many definitions does *heart* have?
2. What is the most common definition of *heart*?
3. What part of speech is *heart*?
4. What sample sentence is given for definition 2?
5. Write a sample sentence for the third definition of *heart.*
6. What idiom is given for *heart*?
7. What part of speech is *rival*?
8. What is the derivation of the word *rival*?

Dictionary: Words with More Than One Definition pages 280-281

Some words have more than one meaning. In order to decide which meaning of a word best fits in the sentence you are reading, you must consider the *sentence context.* Knowing the other words in the sentence helps to make the meaning of an unfamiliar word clear.

Look at the sample dictionary entries below.

par·ty (pär′tē) *n.* **1.** a gathering of people for pleasure or entertainment: *Everyone had a good time at the birthday party.* **2.** a group of people gathered together for some common purpose: *A search party was organized to find the lost child.* **3.** a group of people organized to gain political influence or control: *Each political party selected its candidate for the office of President.*

pass (pas) *v.* **1.** to go or move; proceed: *The waitress passed from table to table.* **2.** to go or move by: *A flock of birds passed overhead.* **3.** to come to an end; cease: *As time went on, his sorrow passed.* **4.** to complete an examination, trial, or course of study successfully or satisfactorily: *The student passed after taking the test over again.* **5.** to be approved or ratified: *The bill passed easily in the Senate.*

per·son·al·i·ty (pur′sə nal′ə tē) *n.* **1.** the sum of the traits, habits, attitudes, and behavior of a person that makes him or her different from all others. **2.** attractive personal qualities: *She was popular at school because of her personality.* **3.** a person, especially one who is well-known or distinguished: *He is a famous television personality.*

Write each sentence below. Then use the sample entries above to choose the appropriate meaning for each italicized word. Write the number of the definition after the sentence.

1. The *party* will choose its candidate at the convention.
2. Our foreign exchange student has *personality.*
3. The bill *passed* in the House, but not in the Senate.
4. We planned a surprise *party* for our teacher.
5. *Personalities* from television appeared at the benefit.
6. A *party* of volunteers helped clean up the mess.
7. A train *passed* in the night, whistling mournfully.

Workbook

RETEACHING AND ENRICHMENT

Expanding Simple Sentences with Adjectives and Adverbs pages 292-293

You can add adjectives to a simple sentence to describe the nouns in the subject and predicate parts of the sentence.

Skillful workers build tall skyscrapers.

You can also add adverbs to a simple sentence to describe verbs. Adverbs may tell *when, at what time, how long, how often, where,* or *how* something happened.

Today workers build skyscrapers. (when)

Workers often build skyscrapers. (how often)

Workers build skyscrapers everywhere. (where)

Workers continuously build skyscrapers. (how long)

Workers build skyscrapers quickly. (how)

Expand each sentence by adding an adjective to describe a noun. Write your new sentence.

1. Workers dig a hole.
2. Trucks bring supplies.
3. Workers walk beams.
4. Cars park on the streets.
5. Traffic clogs streets.
6. People watch workers.
7. People sit on benches.
8. The sun glares.
9. Workers eat lunches.
10. They construct buildings.
11. Welders use blowtorches.
12. Marble slabs go on walls.
13. Windows lean on the fence.
14. People watch the machines.
15. Beams sit on the ground.
16. Scaffolding protects us.
17. Buildings cover the area.
18. Workers wear hats.
19. He buys a hot dog.
20. Noise drowns out talking.

Expand each sentence by adding an adverb to describe each verb. Write your new sentence.

21. A crane swings.
22. Construction continues.
23. The styles change.
24. Work starts.
25. Workers labor.
26. A skyscraper rises.
27. The men check blueprints.
28. They follow instructions.
29. Cement trucks park.
30. The construction ends.
31. A decorator plans.
32. She designs.
33. The supervisor shouts.
34. The workers argue.
35. Carpenters hammer.
36. Machines move.
37. Workers cut wires.
38. Engineers measure wires.

Expanding Simple Sentences with Prepositional Phrases pages 294-295

A **prepositional phrase** is a group of words beginning with a preposition and ending with a noun or pronoun. A prepositional phrase that describes a noun is called an **adjective phrase.**

We saw the controls of the steam shovel.

A prepositional phrase that describes a verb is called an **adverb phrase.**

The driver climbed into the crane.

Expand each sentence by adding an adjective phrase that describes a noun. Write your new sentence.

1. Stone formed the facade.
2. A worker inspected a beam.
3. Steel arrived at the site.
4. The building has many floors.
5. People watched the workers.
6. Many people rent offices.
7. The workers build stores.
8. They build a restaurant.
9. I saw skyscrapers.
10. Elevators are swift.
11. Skyscrapers reflect clouds.

Expand each sentence by adding an adverb phrase that describes the verb. Write your new sentence.

12. The driver climbed.
13. The hammer pounded.
14. The workers labored.
15. That woman drilled.
16. This man shouted.
17. People hurried.
18. The wind blew.
19. The noise blared.
20. I watched.
21. They installed pipes.
22. The lights shine.

Combining Simple Sentences to Build Compound Sentences pages 296-297

A **compound sentence** is a sentence that contains two or more simple sentences joined by the coordinating conjunctions *and, but,* or *or.* A compound sentence has two or more subjects and two or more predicates.

And means in addition to.

But means with this exception or on the contrary.

Or introduces an alternative or another possibility.

Remember to put a **comma** before the conjunction when you form a compound sentence. If there already are commas within the parts of a compound sentence, use a **semicolon** to separate the parts.

If a compound sentence does not have a coordinating conjunction between the two parts of the sentence, use a **semicolon** to separate the two parts.

Write each pair of sentences as one compound sentence. Put commas and semicolons where they belong.

1. The snow howled outside. We were snug by the fire.
2. We could use snowshovels. We could borrow a snowblower.
3. We could build a snowman. We could have a snowball fight.
4. The snow frosted the trees. It frosted the rooftops.
5. We haven't had much snow so far. This storm made up for it.
6. Snow drifts piled high. Abandoned cars sat in the drifts.
7. I grew up in a warm climate. I love snowy days.
8. You can try to drive home. You can stay at our house.
9. We will make ice sculptures. You will build snow forts.
10. Your snow gorilla is funny. He needs a banana.
11. Would you like to ice skate? Would you rather bobsled?
12. We went sledding all day. Our clothes are soaked.

Combining Simple Sentences to Build Complex Sentences pages 298-299

A **complex sentence** is a sentence that has an independent clause and one or more subordinate clauses. An **independent clause** has one subject part and one predicate part. It expresses a complete thought and it can stand alone. A **subordinate clause** is a group of words that has a subject and predicate part, but it cannot stand alone. It does not express a complete thought. It is always combined with an independent clause.

Some subordinate clauses are **adverb clauses.** An **adverb clause** tells *where, when, why, how,* or *under what conditions.* It is made up of a subordinating conjunction, a subject, and a predicate.

Subordinating conjunctions are words that join an adverb clause to an independent clause.

Write each pair of simple sentences as a complex sentence with an adverb clause. Use a subordinating conjunction that tells *when, where, how, why,* or *under what conditions.* Use commas where needed.

1. I will cook dinner. I want to try a new recipe.
2. I must go to the supermarket. I can start the dinner.
3. I use the cookbook. I know the recipe by heart.
4. I can use the kitchen. I clean up afterward.
5. I would like a microwave oven. I have never tried one.
6. We'll put the cake in the oven. The oven is hot enough.
7. I like gleaming, modern kitchens. I like old country kitchens, too.
8. I like meat served rare. I will eat it well done, too.
9. It should simmer on the stove. The timer goes off.
10. This recipe looks complicated. It's really quite easy.
11. I always look for new dishes. I go to good restaurants.
12. I like to take cooking classes. I can fit them into my schedule.
13. The newspaper has good recipes. Sometimes things are left out.
14. I prefer to eat fish. Fish is healthier than meat.
15. I will make the sauce. The vegetables are cooking.
16. The meal was delicious. I think you burned the rice.

Avoiding Unnecessary Words pages 302-303

Remember that the adjectives *this* and *these* point out people or things that are nearby. *That* and *those* are adjectives that point out people or things that are farther away. Do not use the words *here* or *there* when using adjectives that point out.

Avoid using the word *a* where it is not needed. Remember that *these* and *those* describe plural nouns. Do not use them to describe singular nouns. Sentences that begin with *there is* (*are, was, were*) are weak sentences with unnecessary words. Also avoid extra pronouns that repeat information that is already in your sentence.

Choose the word or words in parentheses that correctly complete each sentence. Write the sentence.

1. ____ car has four-wheel drive. (That kind of, That kind of a)
2. ____ cars travel on sand dunes. (Those, Them there)
3. I want ____ sports car. (this, this here)
4. Do you see ____ motorcycle? (that, there there)
5. ____ bikes are the latest models. (Those, Them)

Avoiding Fragments and Run-ons pages 304-305

A **complete sentence** has a subject part and a predicate part and states a complete idea. A **sentence fragment** does not have both a subject part and predicate part, and does not state a complete idea. A **run-on sentence** uses the word *and* to join too many ideas. A run-on sentence also occurs when commas instead of periods are used between sentences.

Rewrite each sentence fragment to make a complete sentence.

1. The tired tourists.
2. Climbed the steps.
3. Saw a movie.
4. The New York skyline.

Rewrite this run-on sentence to make complete sentences.

5. The tourists checked their maps and they began to walk west on Forty-Second Street and they were looking for a theater where they could see a show.

RETEACHING AND ENRICHMENT

Workbook

INDEPENDENT WRITING

pages 314-315

A Narrative Paragraph in Time Order

A *narrative paragraph* tells a story about a real or imaginary incident. Detail sentences are arranged in chronological order. Logical connecting words are used to make clear the sequence of events.

Prewriting Imagine that you must tell a story for the story hour at your library. You will write a narrative paragraph in time order. Choose one of the topics below or think of one of your own. Think about the incident. Make and organize notes.

A hectic morning	*A frightening experience*
A funny experience	*A sad experience*

Writing Write a narrative paragraph in time order. Write a topic sentence that expresses the main idea of the paragraph. Your detail sentences should explain the sequence of events in time order or chronological order. Use logical connecting words.

Editing Use the editing symbols and the check questions at the top of page 315 to edit your paragraph.

INDEPENDENT WRITING

pages 318-319

An Expository Paragraph in Time Order

An *expository paragraph* explains an event, informs, or gives directions.

Prewriting Imagine that you are a traveler in a time machine. You are whisked back to Philadelphia during the 1700's. Ben Franklin asks you to write an expository paragraph on how to use one of the modern gadgets you have brought with you. Choose one of the following or think of your own. Write notes that explain the steps involved in using one of the gadgets. Organize your notes in chronological order.

calculator	*digital watch*	*flashlight*
tape recorder	*portable radio*	*electric hair dryer*

Writing Write an expository paragraph in time order explaining how to use a gadget. The topic sentence in the paragraph introduces the main idea. Detail sentences explain the sequence of events in time or chronological order. Use logical connecting words to make the sequence clear.

Editing Use the editing symbols and the check questions on page 319 to edit your paragraph.

INDEPENDENT WRITING

A Descriptive Paragraph pages 320-321

A well-written *descriptive paragraph* creates vivid word pictures for the reader. Detail sentences describe the observations of the writer.

Prewriting Imagine that you are a screen writer or a television writer. You will write a descriptive paragraph that describes one scene carefully for the set designers so that they can create their sets accurately. Write a descriptive paragraph about one of the following topics, or choose your own. Think about how things might look, feel, and sound. Make notes about vivid images to use in your paragraph.

western	*a restaurant*	*a parade*
hospital	*an airport*	*city scene*
farm scene	*a traffic jam*	*football rally*

Writing Write a descriptive paragraph about the topic you have chosen. Be sure to use vivid words.

Editing Use the editing symbols and the check questions on page 321 to edit your paragraph.

INDEPENDENT WRITING

An Expository Paragraph of Facts pages 322-323

Expository writing gives the reader accurate information based on facts about a specific subject.

Prewriting Imagine that you are a television news writer. You will write an expository paragraph of facts. Rewrite one of the following children's stories as the basis for a Nightly News item. You may add names of places, times, and other specific details if needed. You may choose another story or nursery rhyme if you wish. Use the answers to the questions *who, what, when, where, why,* and *how* to make notes of the facts about your story.

Little Red Riding Hood   Cinderella   The Boy Who Cried Wolf

Writing Write an expository paragraph of facts for the Nightly News. Write a topic sentence that expresses the main idea of the paragraph. Write your factual detail sentences putting information first.

Editing Use the editing symbols and the check questions on page 323 to edit your paragraph.

RETEACHING AND ENRICHMENT

Workbook

INDEPENDENT WRITING

A Summary Paragraph pages 324-325

A *summary paragraph* summarizes the most important facts you have identified about a subject through research in several different sources. These sources may include newspapers, magazines, encyclopedias, books, graphs, charts, or interviews.

Prewriting Imagine that a controversial issue in your community has been whether or not to save and restore the old railroad station or tear it down and build an office building on the site. Now you will write a summary paragraph for the local community paper. Read the following newspaper article and interview. Select the most important information. Make notes on the facts you have chosen.

NEWS ARTICLES

Most residents of our town support the Landmark Protection Association's effort to save the old railroad station. Last month town officials sent a list of questions to all of its 7,000 residents. Most answered the questions. Eighty percent of the people favor restoring the old station and converting it to a restaurant or shopping mall. Five percent favor building a new office building on the site in order to get more tax income for the town. Five percent don't care. Some people said the airport should be expanded.

INTERVIEW

Q. Why should the station be restored?

A. It is an outstanding example of architecture.

Q. How much will it cost to restore it?

A. Three million dollars. We can raise funds from individuals, corporations, and government.

Q. What can be done with the station if it is restored?

A. A restaurant or mall is a possibility. We could use railroad decorations such as lamps, station signs, and other railroad items.

Writing Use your notes and the information above to write a summary paragraph. Write a topic sentence that expresses the main idea. Put details in order of importance.

Editing Use the check questions on page 325 to edit your paragraph.

INDEPENDENT WRITING

A Persuasive Paragraph of Reasons

pages 326-237

The purpose of a *persuasive paragraph* is to state your personal opinion about an issue or idea and to present reasons that support your opinion. Your opinion should be based on solid reasons in order to prove to your audience that your opinion is valid.

Prewriting Imagine that you are a restaurant critic for your local paper. You have dined at a new restaurant and you must report on the quality of its food, service, and atmosphere. Decide whether each of these items is terrible, bad, fair, good, excellent, or superb. Make notes to use in your persuasive paragraph of reasons.

Writing Write a paragraph that persuades others to try (or not to try) the new restaurant. Your topic sentence should state your general opinion of the restaurant in a way that will convince people either to try it or to avoid it. State your supporting reasons in your detail sentences. Write a concluding sentence.

Editing Use the editing symbols and the check questions on page 327 to edit your paragraph.

INDEPENDENT WRITING

pages 328-329

An Expository Paragraph of Comparison

A *paragraph of comparison* presents the similarities of two or more things.

Prewriting You have been asked to participate on a panel discussion. The panel will compare the similarities between items. Choose a pair of topics. Jot down notes on the similarities between the two items. Then organize your notes.

riding a bicycle	*American pioneers*	*ballet*	*painting*
driving a car	*modern astronauts*	*sports*	*music*

Writing Write a paragraph of comparison. Your topic sentence will introduce the main idea, the two things being compared. Detail sentences will present the specific ways the things are alike. Use logical connecting words such as *resemble* and *like*.

Editing Use the editing symbols and the check questions on page 329 to edit your paragraph.

INDEPENDENT WRITING

An Expository Composition pages 344-345

An *expository composition* explains or clarifies a subject. Textbooks that explain different subjects are written in an expository style. School research reports are expository in style.

Prewriting You will write a two-paragraph expository composition. Suppose that you are an archaeologist living 1,000 years from today. You have discovered two articles that are remnants of today's civilization. You write a report for a magazine explaining what the articles are and how you think they were used. You may give the true facts about the items, or you may make up an imaginary (but logical) use for them. Choose two items from the list below or think of two of your own.

disco outfit	*food processor*	*video game*
radio-cassette player	*baseball glove*	*skateboard*
paper clip	*credit card*	*license plate*

Writing First write a thesis statement that expresses the main idea of your composition. Remember to limit your topic to a specific topic you can discuss in two paragraphs. Brainstorm for ideas and jot down and organize your notes. Next group your notes under two main headings (Roman numerals I and II). The thesis statement will be the first sentence in your opening paragraph. The second sentence will state the main idea of the first paragraph. Your detail sentences will support the main idea of the first paragraph. You may want to end the paragraph with a concluding sentence that summarizes the main idea.

Remember to relate your second paragraph to the first by using a transitional sentence. This sentence shows the reader how the ideas in the first paragraph are related to the ideas in the second. It also states the main idea of the second paragraph. End your second paragraph with a concluding sentence that summarizes the points you have made in the entire composition.

Editing Use the check questions on page 345 to edit your paragraph.

A Persuasive Composition pages 348-349

A *persuasive composition* persuades someone else to accept your point of view on a subject. Editorials in newspapers are examples of persuasive writing. Advertising messages are also examples of persuasive writing. When you write a persuasive composition, you may use *facts, examples,* or *strong reasons* to convince readers that they should accept your view on a subject.

Prewriting You will write a three-paragraph composition. Imagine that you and your family have been trying to decide where and how to spend your annual vacation. Your family decides that each person will write an advertisement for a vacation. You will submit your ads to an impartial person who will choose the most effective one.

Jot down notes on where you would like to go, what you would like to do when you get there, and why. Write down some reasons that might convince a reader to go on that vacation. Next categorize your ideas into three main topics beside Roman numerals I, II, and III. List the details that support each idea.

Writing Remember that the first sentence in the first paragraph is your thesis statement. It gives the central idea of the whole composition. The second sentence gives the main idea of the first paragraph. Detail sentences using facts, examples, or reasons support your point of view. Write a concluding sentence that summarizes the main idea or emphasizes your attitude in the paragraph. Begin the first sentence of your second paragraph with a transitional device. Continue the second paragraph with a sentence that states the main idea of the paragraph. Add detail sentences and a concluding sentence.

Begin your third paragraph with a sentence that uses a transitional device and states the main idea of the paragraph. Add detail sentences. Complete the last paragraph with a sentence that summarizes all the main ideas in the composition and emphasizes your attitude toward the subject.

Editing Use the check questions on page 349 to edit your composition.

Index